FINE MARGINS

RICHARD BUXTON

FINE MARGINS

HOW MANCHESTER CITY AND LIVERPOOL FORGED FOOTBALL'S ULTIMATE RIVALRY

First published by Pitch Publishing, 2020

Pitch Publishing
A2 Yeoman Gate
Yeoman Way
Worthing
Sussex
BN13 3QZ
www.pitchpublishing.co.uk
info@pitchpublishing.co.uk

A CIP catalogue record is available for this book
from the British Library.

ISBN 978 1 78531 669 2

Typesetting and origination by Pitch Publishing
Printed and bound in India by Replika Press Pvt. Ltd.

Contents

For Rachel and Leighton,
and the continuing love and
support they both provide

Introduction

WHEN DISENFRANCHISED cotton merchants finalised construction of the Manchester Ship Canal in January 1894, it signified the radical shift in the dynamic of England's north-west region.

The new waterway had taken six years to build at a cost of £15m, equivalent to £1.65bn in the 21st century; time and money that Mancunian industrialists felt was well spent to bypass Liverpool. Together they had created the world's first inter-city railway in 1830, which showcased Stephenson's Rocket, the pioneering steam locomotive. But the new initiative, first championed 12 years earlier by boiler manufacturer Daniel Adamson, would provide a bitter parting of ways for the two cities in a battle played out on the floors of the Houses of Parliament. Eventually, the 'Cottonopolis' plan succeeded and afforded it a direct route to the sea without the need to incur previously hefty financial costs associated with importing raw materials through the mouth of the River Mersey. Four months before the Ship Canal's completion, the seeds for this inter-city war had already been sown.

Football witnessed its ultimate culture clash on 16 September 1893, the day that Manchester City – still under the guise of Ardwick AFC – and Liverpool first faced off at Hyde Road. As with their respective cities, the two clubs had emerged from contrasting social backgrounds and reflected that disparity by becoming perennial thorns in each other's side in the modern age. They have vied for major honours and players with regularity but until, recently, the rivalry found itself marginalised by the spectacle of both sides' duels with Manchester United. Liverpool's encounters with their adversaries at Old Trafford are still widely celebrated as the most volatile rivalry in the English game after being stoked by both sides, and Sir Alex Ferguson in particular, over a quarter of a century. Yet the overspill of Red and Blue in the region, running through the M62 motorway's 35-mile stretch, has become far more compelling, long-standing and arguably more potent.

This is not a rivalry defined solely by on-field matters nor its current protagonists. Pep Guardiola and Jürgen Klopp unquestionably play significant roles but are continuers of a rich tapestry which all began with Bill Shankly and evolved over the next half-century, through a combination of managers, players and fortunes for both clubs. No fewer than 19 figures who have been directly involved in this fixture at varying times were interviewed for the book. All had a unique role to play in telling the story of the rivalry from its inception in the early 1960s through to the new millennium. My current working knowledge as a journalist covering City and Liverpool for over a decade is a comparatively minor contribution but seeks to fill in the blanks from the late 2000s to present-day.

The term 'fine margins' became synonymous with this fixture during the fiercely contested Premier League title race of 2018/19 when every inch counted, quite literally, as Klopp's challengers and Guardiola's reigning champions took their battle for supremacy down to the wire. Its origins, however, delve back even further than that. John Stones provided the seminal moment of that campaign with a sliding goal-line clearance after a first attempt had cannoned back off Ederson and looped towards an empty net. It was an act which practically helped City to reclaim their crown by a solitary point. Dave Watson, one of Stones's defensive predecessors, was not so fortunate with his own attempt at heroism in attempting to cut out a cross against Liverpool in the 1976/77 season. The men from Manchester missed out on the First Division championship by the same one-point gap that they would laud over their geographical neighbours some 42 years later.

Both moments are documented in this book alongside others which form some of the biggest bones of contention among their respective followers. Ask any fervent Liverpool fan about the on-field moment that still sticks in their throat most, and many will invariably reference Stones's now iconic clearance which prevented them from clinching their first championship since 1990. Long-suffering City supporters would hark back even further to the 1981 League Cup semi-final and referee Alf Grey's dubious officiating that denied them a place in the Wembley showpiece. Both are moments which feature in this book alongside the stories of those that were present for many of the fierce contests.

At the time of writing, the football world finds itself plunged into a rare area of uncertainty with the fall-out from the coronavirus pandemic. What the future holds remains unclear for everyone connected to the beautiful game. The only thing for certain, now that it is has been deemed safe to resume, is that Manchester City and Liverpool will continue what was begun almost 60 years ago and now assumes a rightful place on the world stage.

Richard Buxton
June 2020

Born of Frustration

EVERYTHING STARTS with Bill Shankly, both in terms of Liverpool's modern renaissance and the definitive starting point in their rivalry with Manchester City. When he pitched up at Anfield in December 1959, the Scotsman surveyed what he would later describe as 'the biggest toilet in Liverpool'. Sweeping changes were required to transform both the decrepit stadium and its team, languishing in the Second Division, to former glories.

Shankly's playing career had come to life at Preston North End, where he won the FA Cup in 1938 alongside the great Tom Finney, before embarking on a route in management which took him from Carlisle United to Huddersfield Town, via Grimsby and Workington. His arrival from Huddersfield proved to be a seminal moment in the histories of both the Reds and English football itself. An open-door policy at Leeds Road had endeared him to the Terriers' players and helped several promising youngsters make their first-team breakthrough, including Denis Law and Ray Wilson.

But Shankly feared that he had taken the Yorkshire club as far as was realistically possible due to a level of ambition that was not reciprocated within the boardroom. Efforts to sign compatriots Ian St John and Ron Yeats were rebuffed by the Huddersfield hierarchy, who claimed they could not afford even one of the pair, let alone both. His frustrations with the money men would be mirrored in the formative months of his time on Merseyside when Shankly lobbied for a reunion with Law, who had already established himself as a Scotland international. Within weeks of taking charge as manager, attempts to persuade his paymasters to relinquish the funds to lure the 19-year-old to Anfield fell on deaf ears with the club's transfer limit capped at £18,000.

On 16 March 1960, a day before the transfer deadline, Law set a new British record with a move to Manchester City. The £55,000 fee would have made him one of the first million-pound footballers in 21st-century equivalence and stood at over three-and-a-half times the figure that Liverpool had been willing to sanction. A switch to Maine Road offered the teenage forward's talents the more befitting stage of the First Division, although Law later admitted that he had expected to pitch up on the opposite side of the newly created M62 motorway.

'Well of course Bill Shankly was the manager at Huddersfield and he had just gone to Liverpool so when they were coming in, I thought that I would be going to Liverpool, really. Unfortunately, the fee was just a bit too high, so I went to Manchester City,' he told the *Blue Moon Podcast* in 2014. 'Bill Shankly was like a father to me. He looked after me for four or five years so I was a bit disappointed at the time not to go there because he was a great manager anyway and of course you know what he did to Liverpool, took them from the Second Division right through until all the honours.'

Law scored twice in his first seven appearances for City before repaying their outlay in full with 23 goals from 43 games in the following season as Les McDowall's side finished 16th in the First Division. He can legitimately claim that his figure would be far higher had an FA Cup fourth-round tie with Luton Town not been postponed after 69 minutes. The Blues had taken a 6-2 lead at Kenilworth Road, with Law scoring all six, before referee Ken Tuck called time because of treacherous conditions. When the game was replayed four days later, both he and City were on the receiving end of a 3-1 defeat.

Law, however, would not be long in Manchester's blue side and left the following summer in a £125,000 move to Torino, at a time when British players were becoming sought-after signings for Serie A clubs. On Merseyside, Shankly set aside his disappointment of missing out on the man he later claimed 'could dance on eggshells' by securing long-term targets St John and Yeats, from Motherwell and Dundee United respectively, for a combined fee of £59,500. Buoyed by the capture of players who would offer his side focal points at opposite ends of the pitch, he joked that Yeats's strong defensive presence meant his side 'could play Arthur Askey in goal'.

Within 12 months of the pair's arrivals, Liverpool had ended an eight-season hiatus from the First Division. Upon their return, they renewed acquaintances with City at a time when all seemed right for the leading cities in England's north-west. Liverpool's name resonated throughout the world thanks to The Beatles' early chart success while Manchester dominated the arts with the creation of Granada TV and its flagship programme *Coronation Street*, where Liverpool-born actors Jean Alexander and Peter Adamson were early stars of the long-running soap opera.

City's start to the new First Division campaign felt like a storyline from Weatherfield's cobbled streets as they suffered an 8-1 hammering at Wolverhampton Wanderers. McDowall's players responded in their first of two midweek encounters with Liverpool.

Home-grown winger Neil Young spared City's blushes as he cancelled out goals in either half from Ronnie Moran and Roger Hunt to hold their inter-city rivals to a 2-2 draw at Maine Road on 22 August 1962. A week later, the men from Moss Side headed to Anfield for a return fixture which City striker Glyn Pardoe, who died suddenly in May 2020, will never forget.

'It was the first time I went to Liverpool and I was talking to my mum and dad outside before I went into the dressing room,' he says. 'I went to go in and I got stopped! They said, "Who are you?" I said, "Well I'm playing," and they said, "Oh you can't be!" so I had to send for somebody to come out from the club to get me in which is funny when you think about it.'

City's side that day still contained the legendary Bert Trautmann, who had played on in the 1956 FA Cup Final despite suffering several broken vertebrae in his neck. En route to

Wembley, the German goalkeeper had played on the same ground in a fifth-round tie where Billy Liddell struck a late equaliser for Liverpool that had hit the net just after the referee blew the final whistle on a 2-1 away victory.

But Trautmann's final appearance at Anfield came in a transitional City team which married survivors from that previous trophy-winning era with a crop of upcoming local talent. Pardoe, who learned news of his first-team debut directly from the German goalkeeper, belonged to the latter category. 'When you went to Anfield, if you didn't survive for the first 20 or 25 minutes, you never got a chance,' he says. You used to go there and think, "Well, if we can survive 20–25 minutes without them scoring then we're in with a shout." When you were at the Kop end, I'll never forget it; you'd have a corner, a free kick or something like that and you'd be shouting to each other – you couldn't hear a word. It was unbelievable. That's one of the highlights of football, really; if you're playing against Liverpool at The Kop, because the noise was incredible.'

Despite falling behind to a strike from St John in the third minute, City did more than hold on against Shankly's evolving side and pulled level through Peter Dobin shortly before the half-hour. But the even score at half-time proved a false dawn as Liverpool quickly scored three times in ten minutes courtesy of a brace from Roger Hunt either side of a goal from Alan A'Court. 'That was nothing fresh at Anfield for anybody I don't think!' says Pardoe. 'They had a great side. We'd been in front a couple of times there early doors, but in the end we were very lucky if we got a point or anything like that because they were such a good team. It was very difficult scoring against Liverpool at Anfield.'

Shankly later declared the win over City to be the sign of a potential shift in the footballing landscape. With Everton taking an early lead in the First Division title race and his own team back in the top flight, he forecast that Merseyside would soon be riding the crest of a wave. 'The salad days of the north-east seem to have gone,' he said. 'Now Liverpool could be the new Soccer Mecca. I, for one, will try to make sure it is.'

His prophecy began to bear fruit at the end of a season that had been prolonged by the Big Freeze. When English football finally thawed, Liverpool had consolidated their First Division status with a respectable eighth-place finish on their maiden return while, just across Stanley Park, Harry Catterick led Everton to their sixth championship.

The picture was far bleaker in Manchester, where City's 12-season run in the First Division was finally broken as they languished second from bottom. Adding insult to injury, Manchester United, under Shankly's compatriot and friend Matt Busby, had finished one point clear of the relegation zone and won the FA Cup. Les McDowall's reign as City's longest-serving manager, a feat which is yet to be surpassed, was ended on 29 May 1963. His former assistant George Poyser was elevated to replace him in the belief that his working knowledge of the squad would give them a greater chance of securing immediate return over an external candidate. But the popular coach failed to deliver City back to the promised land by finishing sixth, 15 points adrift of the two automatic promotion spots.

They fared even worse in 1964/65 with the same shortfall but dropped down another five places. Poyser and his deputy Jimmy Meadows both resigned on 14 April, near the end of a season where the previously unthinkable idea of a merger with Manchester United had been mooted.

Put forward by vice-chairman Frank Johnson, the radical proposal would have seen City effectively absorbed into a power vacuum with Old Trafford earmarked as the more desirable home for the prospective hybrid club. Only the backlash from Maine Road devotees articulated in newspaper letter pages brought the controversial idea, which was discussed by Johnson and his Red Devils counterparts on several occasions, to a definitive end. United's march to the First Division championship seemed to confirm that Moss Side was the home to Manchester's poor relations. On and off the pitch, City were in a mess. 'We were just in a downhill spiral. We were hanging on, really,' says Glyn Pardoe, who remains the club's youngest debutant at the age of

15 years and 341 days. 'As a player, I was only a young lad, so I didn't really worry about managers and things like that. All you were worried about was playing in the first team.'

Liverpool, in contrast, never had it so good. Bill Shankly had overhauled United in the following season to earn the Reds' first league title since 1946/47 as City endured their first campaign back in the second tier. Hopes of ending a 73-year wait in lifting the FA Cup had also moved a step closer the following season after setting up a clash with Leeds United in the final, taking place just three days before a European Cup semi-final against holders Inter Milan. Ian Callaghan, who had been handed his debut by Shankly and become a mainstay of that mid-1960s side, credits the rapid turnaround in success for cementing his rapport with the Anfield crowd. 'The fans had taken to Bill Shankly like I don't know what, they really did,' he says. 'When you think about it, he came in '59; in '61/62 we came out the Second Division and then in '64 we won the First Division, and then obviously in '65 the FA Cup for the first time in our history. What he achieved in those years was just incredible.'

Shankly's body of work had drawn admirers from far and wide within English football and at least one finally appeared willing to test the strength of his bond with The Kop. In the build-up to the Reds' Wembley date, Kenneth Waite told readers of the *Daily Sketch* newspaper to 'stand by for the sensation of the season' in revealing that he had been tipped off that Manchester City were plotting an audacious move to install Shankly as Poyser's successor. 'The Maine Road bosses want a new image and are prepared to pay for it,' he wrote. Although under no illusions of the challenge that City's ambitious hierarchy faced in luring the Scot away from his adoptive home city, Waite concluded, 'It is the sort of job that appeals to Shankly, whose affection for Manchester City is something he has admitted often.'

Throughout his time at Liverpool, Shankly was routinely at odds with the club's directors. He had threatened to quit in 1962 when winger Johnny Morrissey was sold behind his back to Everton. A resignation letter had even been written before compromise was subsequently reached whereby the board agreed no future transfers would be sanctioned without the manager's approval. But Shankly became prone to making resignation threats during the summer months, when he would grow restless as the game he lived and breathed took its annual respite. Anfield chiefs, including club secretary Peter Robinson, later termed the regular occurrence as 'Bill's summer madness'.

Whether an approach from City would have turned his head is unknown. Some journalists covering Merseyside football during that period, including John Keith, who became a trusted confidant of Shankly and his coaching staff as a reporter for the *Daily Express*, have dismissed the *Sketch*'s link as a complete non-starter. Even without Shankly on board, the strength of City's ambition under chairman Albert Alexander was undeniable and eventually saw the appointment of Joe Mercer. As a player, Mercer's career had begun with his local club Ellesmere Port Town before joining an Everton team which had just clinched the 1931/32 First Division title and contained several household names in Dixie Dean, Tommy Lawton, Cliff Britton and Ted Segar. Shortly before the outbreak of the Second World War, he would win the championship in his own right in addition to captaining England during wartime internationals.

Like Shankly, he moved into management immediately after hanging up his boots and placed a similar emphasis on developing exciting young teams. His three-year spell in charge of Sheffield United had started with their relegation from the First Division. In the following season, the Blades bowed out to Shankly's Huddersfield Town in a second replay in the FA Cup's third round. In December 1958, he took charge of Aston Villa where his impact was near instant with a fresh-faced team dubbed 'Mercer's Minors' narrowly missing out on a place in the FA Cup Final in consecutive seasons. A third time proved the Villains' charm as Mercer guided them back into the First Division before delivering further success by winning the inaugural League Cup in 1961. They reached the final of the competition again two years later, where they lost to Birmingham City, and he became a firm favourite among the media to lead England at the 1966 World Cup, although he never actually applied for the vacant position. A combination of ill health and supporter unrest saw his Villa Park tenure come to an end.

Upon joining City a year later, Mercer took his health into account when deciding on the approach to take following the end to his time in the Midlands. He identified the need to work alongside a younger coach who could take a more hands-on role at Maine Road. Malcolm Allison had recently caught Mercer's eye during a session at Lilleshall, the Football Association's national training centre, after recently parting ways with Plymouth Argyle and had already attracted interest from other clubs. Raich Carter had already arranged a meeting with the former West Ham United player to discuss the possibility of joining his coaching staff at Middlesbrough when a call from Mercer brought about a sliding doors moment.

Together, he and Allison forged the perfect good cop/bad cop partnership that began to revolutionise Manchester's secondary club. 'When Joe came and Malcolm came, everything changed,' says Glyn Pardoe, who was converted into a full-back under Mercer's tutelage. 'The manner of the club, the training routines – just a completely different way of training, mindset and everything once they came.'

Allison's propensity to be outspoken worked seamlessly with the avuncular Mercer. Ian Callaghan later encountered his fellow Merseysider when they were colleagues on Littlewoods' Spot The Ball panel following the former Liverpool winger's playing retirement in 1981 and appreciates why he had been held in such high esteem at Maine Road. 'He was on Spot The Ball when I joined [Littlewoods] after I'd finished so I got to know Joe quite well,' says Callaghan. 'He'd finished managing but he had a lovely, lovely personality, he really did – and you could understand how players wanted to play for him.'

Although a 2-0 defeat to Mercer's old club Everton in the FA Cup quarter-final denied them a chance to take on Manchester United in the last four, City's rejuvenation under their new managerial double act produced an immediate return by winning the Second Division at a canter. England's triumph at the World Cup captured the feel-good mood around the country in the summer of 1966 but it was not exclusive to the international scene. Alongside City's return to the First Division, Liverpool had wrestled the title back from Manchester United after a below-par finish of seventh the season before. Not even the disappointment of a European Cup Winners' Cup final defeat to Borussia Dortmund could puncture the growing belief that Shankly's side were set to dominate the domestic game for the foreseeable future; a view that became further validated by Anfield boasting the joint-highest number of club representatives called up for Alf Ramsey's future world champions in the form of Callaghan, Gerry Byrne and Roger Hunt. Allison had attempted to make productive use of the tournament on home soil by observing the training methods of Golden Boot winner Eusébio and his Portugal team-mates at their Manchester base.

In a bid to reaffirm their top-flight standing, City spent the summer scouring for a more dependable right-back to see through the 1966/67 campaign. Allison convinced Mercer to take a chance on Tony Book, a part-time bricklayer who he had previously coached at Plymouth Argyle, for £17,000. Book's arrival at Maine Road came just weeks before his 33rd birthday; something which had initially made Mercer reluctant to sanction the move. But the player's worth, which would grow exponentially in the decades that followed, became immediately evident when Liverpool wore their now iconic all-red strip in a first visit to Moss Side on 24 August 1966. Two days earlier, on the same ground, their reserve team had emphatically run out 9-0 winners over City. Home fans feared that their returning senior players would suffer a similar experience.

First-half goals from Jimmy Murray and Geoff Strong had left the contest delicately balanced until the closing stages, when Strong teed up Hunt with a cross that caught out the home side's defence but saw the England marksman's header strike the inside of the post and bounce out, where it was smothered by goalkeeper

Harry Dowd. In the final minute Colin Bell, signed at the tail end of City's promotion-winning season, drilled past Tommy Lawrence to record their first victory back in English football's top tier.

Allison was equally buoyed by the victory and stated, 'Liverpool will provide us with our first double,' before adding, 'I am only joking, but I meant it.' Shankly's players threw that attempt at humour back in his face when City ventured to Merseyside just six days later for the return fixture. The evening kick-off was put back by several minutes owing to the visitors' team coach becoming delayed in rush hour traffic, leaving Mercer, Allison and their players to make the final stage of their journey on foot through the streets of Anfield transporting their kit skips with them. 'I think we stayed at a hotel in Lymm and [when] we set off, it was murder,' says Glyn Pardoe. 'We couldn't get there. I think we went a couple [of goals] down straight away in the first 15 minutes. We battled back a bit, but they beat us in the end. I remember it quite well. It was incredible.'

Liverpool had followed up their Maine Road ordeal with a 3-1 reversal to Everton but took an early two-goal lead against City through Hunt and Strong before Matt Gray reduced the deficit early in the second half. Allison's showmanship after his side's win the previous week did not find favour with referee Jim Finney, who gave the assistant manager a stern lecture in the dugout midway through the clash for summoning Dave Connor while Peter Thompson received treatment on a knee injury. His crime would not have been deemed heinous in the modern game but the idea of relaying instructions to players from the touchline was still considered to be something of a cardinal sin before the advent of technical areas in 1993. City's woes were further compounded by another effort from Hunt in the 80th minute, which was offset by a late Jimmy Murray consolation.

A win each provided little comfort in a season where both sides had finished empty-handed. Liverpool had relinquished the First Division title to Manchester United with a fifth-place slump that was followed by an FA Cup fifth-round exit at the hands of

Everton. They had bowed out of the European Cup's second stage in embarrassing fashion to a Johan Cruyff-inspired Ajax, who won 7-3 on aggregate. Manchester's blue side had more grounds for optimism despite being edged out by Leeds United, managed by their former striker Don Revie, in the FA Cup quarter-final. City had assembled a team which was primed to take the fight to United and the rest of the chasing pack. Key additions such as Book, Bell and Mike Summerbee had all blended perfectly into their new surroundings alongside a crop of home-grown talents. Assisted by a cocksure Allison, confidence was brewing that Joe Mercer was on the verge of taking the club back to its previous competitive heights.

Belief had swelled within both clubs' ranks when they did battle on the opening day of the 1967/68 season. Shankly spent the summer on astute signings, with goalkeeper Ray Clemence plucked from Scunthorpe United for £18,000 alongside Chelsea striker Tony Hateley, who joined for £96,000. As the Reds' new record signing, Hateley started a fiercely contested game at Maine Road where even the fans were seemingly prepared to fight it out. Police arrested 12 people following skirmishes during the opening 15 minutes of the second half between rival supporters on an afternoon when disorder had reared an ugly head at several other English grounds, including during Everton's 3-1 win over Manchester United. On the pitch, little separated the sides as Neil Young fashioned City's best chance when he struck the underside of Tommy Lawrence's crossbar. The winger proved integral again in the 75th minute when he was tripped by Tommy Smith for a penalty which Tony Book, newly installed as captain, failed to convert.

Sensing his team may have needed freshening up, Shankly had turned to one of his former allies in attempts to improve Liverpool's recruitment strategy. Geoff Twentyman had played under the Scot when he was managing Carlisle United, where he was reinvented from a left-half into a central defender. By the time Shankly left Brunton Park, Twentyman's switch had earned him a move to Anfield in 1953, where he remained until shortly after the arrival of his former boss. He would return to the club as chief scout in summer 1967, replacing the outgoing Norman Lowe. The first player that Twentyman recommended to Shankly was Francis Lee, who had left a firm impression by scoring in front of The Kop during Bolton Wanderers' 1-1 draw with Liverpool in the League Cup's second-round tie on 13 September. Also paying attention at Anfield that evening were Joe Mercer and Malcolm Allison.

Later that month, having disposed of Liverpool in the replay, Lee walked out on the Trotters citing the terms of a new contract offer as the reason for his unhappiness. But Twentyman's confidence in the 23-year-old's qualities could not wear down the Liverpool hierarchy's transfer parsimony, despite the soon-to-depart chairman Sid Reakes publicly declaring the club's wish to see at least one star name added to the squad. 'I rated Lee as fine a player as I'd seen,' Twentyman later told the national press. 'I reckoned he was being wasted at Bolton as an orthodox winger. I felt if we could let him run free … he'd be brilliant. But at that time, Liverpool were not looking for big-money players and it was obvious Lee was going to cost a fortune.'

City were also on the lookout for a talented player to strengthen their own options. Everton forward Alex Young emerged as a viable target before Mercer turned attention away from his old club and on to the signing of Lee, which was completed on 9 October for a club-record £60,000. Mercer believed that the future England international would be 'the final piece of the jigsaw' in his Maine Road masterplan.

'If Liverpool had come for me, I would have gone there straight away. There's no doubt about that,' Lee told Simon Hughes in his book *Secret Diary of a Liverpool Scout*. 'I was keen to leave and because Manchester City made the first approach, although Stoke made enquiries as well, I went there. It was as simple as that. It was quite an easy decision to make. Manchester United were linked with me too but I think City had a couple of bad results and took a gamble on me because they wanted to change things round quickly. Maybe if Liverpool had been on a bad run or something like that they would have moved quicker like City. I had no preference where I went.'

Shankly would routinely seek out Lee whenever their paths crossed to rue his mistake in not signing him. The Westhoughton-born player's second Anfield appearance that season, this time in City colours, came at a time when both teams were neck-and-neck in attempts to overhaul United. The defending champions had taken 28 points out of their first 20 league fixtures while their closest challengers were level-pegged on 27, although the Blues sat in second place ahead of the 16 December meeting due to a superior goal average. Ian Callaghan accepts that City were emerging as a formidable prospect. 'With the players they had playing for them and the management, I think we all thought they were going to be a force,' he says. Without a doubt.'

Minutes before kick-off, Liverpool's new chairman Harold Cartwright took to the stadium's PA system to announce that the game's start risked a potential delayed 'owing to unforeseen circumstances'. Traffic problems had temporarily deferred the previous season's game when City's team coach was caught up en route to Merseyside and was also the reason for the latest setback, only this time it was the home team that had been hampered. Liverpool duo Roger Hunt and Tommy Lawrence faced a similar gridlock when travelling to the match from their Warrington homes. 'They were coming from Culcheth, where they lived, and got stuck in traffic,' says Callaghan. 'When they got near the ground, they had to park the car [and walk]. We were all stripped ready and the sub, whoever it was, was going to go on but then they arrived. It was just like a quick change and then on to the pitch.'

The Football Association (FA) later hit Liverpool with a £100 fine for holding up the game's kick-off, which was put back by two-and-a-half minutes.

City's staggered pre-match arrival in the 1966/67 season may not have incurred a financial penalty but arguably contributed to them falling behind early in the game. The hold-up which was now affecting their opponents failed to dampen their own approach a second time around. 'I don't think that bothers you,' says Glyn Pardoe. 'All you're interested in is getting ready, getting out there and battling it out. It doesn't make any difference to your mindset. It might help you a little bit because they'd be rushing and they wouldn't be concentrating the same as us but I don't think it made much difference.'

Psychological warfare still played its part when the teams finally took to the field. The previous weekend, City had run out 4-1 winners over Tottenham Hotspur on a snowy Maine Road pitch in a majestic performance which was billed as the 'Ballet on Ice'. Heading into the game at Anfield, they had put together an 11-game unbeaten run. As the respective coaching outfits took their places in opposing dugouts, Bill Shankly warned Malcolm Allison. 'You're not going to tear our team apart like you have torn the others apart, you know!' the Liverpool manager roared.

His assertion rang true in an even-sided first half where Alan Oakes emerged as the game's stand-out player with Tommy Smith ranking a close second. In the 50th minute, Hunt shrugged off his previous travel sickness to drill home an opener. But Shankly's regret at not signing Lee came back to haunt him when City's new recruit seized upon a weak headed clearance by Emlyn Hughes and unleashed a ferocious drive to end the game with honours even. Liverpool, like many other clubs, learned the hard way about the forward's perennial goal threat. 'Franny was a tremendous player. He was one of the finishing touches that Malcolm and Joe bought,' says Pardoe. 'There was Mike Summerbee, Belly [Colin Bell], Franny: they bought three or four good players which was just a finishing touch because we had one or two young lads there that were coming through who turned out to be good players. But they were the finishing touch and Franny was a tremendous finisher. You couldn't give him a chance because he'd score.'

The strength of the north-west rivals' challenges did not go unnoticed. Writing in *The Guardian*, Paul Fitzpatrick surmised, 'The fairest thing that can be said of this match is that if City were majestic, Liverpool were magnificent,' adding, 'But a draw was a just result too, by far the best game I have seen this season.'

As the 1967/68 season reached a tense finale between Manchester's two clubs, Shankly's side were still in with a fighting chance of recapturing the title. City had to win a final-day trip to Newcastle United and hope that their local rivals either faltered against Sunderland or failed to rack up a superior goal average to clinch the trophy nicknamed 'The Lady', on account of the statuette which sat atop it. 'Knowing Bill Shankly, everything was possible,' says Callaghan. 'He just played to win the games and you don't worry about anybody else. His attitude was just to try and win the games. That's the way he was. He was one of those people who thought "if we win the games, well fine" and if they slipped up ... It was a tight season.'

Failure of either club to secure victory would have given Liverpool the chance to overtake their regional counterparts by a solitary point by winning their two games in hand. United's pre-eminent status as the glamour of English football saw them cast as firm favourites in the media's view. But Shankly backed Mercer's team to reach the finish line over the Red Devils. 'I regard City as favourites now,' he said. 'Any team that can do what they did at Tottenham must have a great chance.'

A brace from Neil Young, Lee's 17th goal of the season and a Mike Doyle effort ensured that City would clinch the title in a 4-3 win at St James' Park. Their triumph later became lionised in a chant set to the tune of 'Hey Jude' by The Beatles, released that summer, which is still sung by the club's supporters to this day. 'I think in that mind, all we were interested in was if we could win the games and win them well, we couldn't see us getting beat,' says Pardoe. 'But it's all about [what's] in the mind. You only get chances like that very, very rarely. We had a great set of lads who were very confident in themselves and knew we had a chance, and luckily we took them.'

United's home loss to Sunderland afforded Liverpool the chance to leapfrog Matt Busby's side into the runners-up spot with their final two games but a 2-1 defeat at Stoke City meant they finished a narrow third. Following a celebratory press conference at Maine Road the day after, Mercer returned to the family home in Chorlton to warm congratulations from his two beaten adversaries. Even in defeat, Shankly maintained his now-famous opinion, 'If you are first, you are first. If you are second, you are nothing,' and immediately telephoned Mercer to hail City's achievement. A telegram from Busby, who had played for both clubs, followed later that afternoon.

Any bonhomie became quickly forgotten at the start of the 1968/69 season. Even before the champions had stepped out at Anfield on the opening day, they were handicapped by injury to Tony Book. When City's players took a pre-match stroll around the pitch, half an hour before kick-off, they were confronted with a white-hot atmosphere as The Kop singled out Mike Summerbee for special treatment with chants of 'who the fucking hell are you?' The attempts at intimidation from English football's most famous terrace were ones which Glyn Pardoe relished. 'The fans get on your back, of course they do. That's part of it,' he says. 'That's part of the game you love because you know if their fans are getting on your back, you're doing well. If they're not getting on your back they know they're on top, they're dominating you. I used to love that. It was fantastic. That's what makes it. When you went to Liverpool and went to the Kop end, they were incredible. But it was a spur for you as well. It made you think, "Bloody hell, I'll show these." It was fantastic.'

City initially succeeded in subduing the Kopites when Neil Young broke the deadlock inside the opening ten minutes before Bobby Graham and Peter Thompson wiped out Liverpool's early deficit on an afternoon when record signing Tony Hateley had found himself dropped. It also proved a chastening encounter for the visitors. Malcolm Allison was twice reprimanded, initially by referee Kevin Howley for running on to the pitch without permission alongside trainer Johnny Hart to speak with Pardoe. His next brush with authority was slightly more severe when a policeman spoke to him about an incident near the dugout area.

'Obviously Joe [Mercer] must have thought a heck of a lot of him,' says Ian Callaghan. 'Malcolm was the one with the big cigar and the Jack the Lad type, if you like, but obviously they made a great pairing. It was like Bill Shankly and Bob Paisley.'

Pardoe reiterates the Liverpool winger's view on the close connection within the City setup, which provoked Allison's on-field encroachment. 'Malcolm was one of us [and] Joe was one of us,' he says. 'We had that little bit of respect that Malcolm was the coach and Joe was the manager. But we were very, very close as well. We were like a family. Joe was the dad, Malcolm was the son and we were just like a family.'

Mercer acknowledged after the defeat, 'We expect everyone to be gunning for us,' and The Kop had City firmly in its crosshairs at the final whistle when their travelling supporters defiantly chanted, 'We are the champions,' only to be met with a rebuttal from the home end that 'you won't be champions anymore!'

Neither would Liverpool after finishing six points behind Leeds United in the First Division, a gap which could have been reduced in their penultimate game of the season at Maine Road. Still fresh from their FA Cup Final victory over Leicester City, who had knocked the Reds out in the fifth round of the competition, Mercer's side took the spoils against the visitors courtesy of a second-half Francis Lee strike. Even Shankly's penchant for talking up his own side took a rare back seat to extolling the qualities of their regional rivals. 'City are a young side and they have so much skill,' he said. 'They can reach a standard of skill which I doubt anyone in England can equal. They are capable of thrashing any side. While some teams are content to beat you, City want to go and thrash you. They can murder a team with their skill.'

With a new decade approaching, Liverpool and City picked up in 1969/70 where they had left off in the previous season as both sides racked up four-goal hauls in their respective openers. In their first meeting of the campaign at Anfield, Ian St John had put the hosts ahead inside two minutes before an own goal from Tommy Smith, early in the second half, gave City a foothold back into the game. A quarter of an hour later, Ian Bowyer had headed the FA Cup holders into the lead, prompting The Kop to respond with a chant of 'no surrender!' With his side leading in the final ten minutes, Mike Summerbee was still on the receiving end of The Kop's heckling when preparing to take a corner. The winger responded to his tormentors by proceeding to lower his shorts, something Glyn Pardoe claims was par for the course from his City team-mate.

'That was part of the interaction with the crowd,' he says. 'It wasn't meant nastily or anything like that. The crowd in those days had a little bit of banter and they loved it. Now you can't say anything or do anything [like that].

'Mike used to go to Old Trafford and he'd go to the flag and pretend to blow his nose on it and wind them up a bit. But that was part of the game. The crowd used to wind you up. You used to go there and they'd call you a few names – "You're not winning today, you big fat sod" – that was part of the game and part of the banter. You used to love it because if they were calling you, you knew that you were doing well.'

Summerbee's show of a defiance did not come as a surprise to Ian Callaghan, his opposite number that afternoon, either. 'That was Summerbee, wasn't it really?' he says. 'He was, and still is, a larger-than-life character. He's obviously still connected with City as an ambassador so it's always a pleasure to see Mike. But I remember [after] he did that we smacked his bum!'

That act of bare-faced cheek came back to bite City as two goals in five minutes from Roger Hunt and another St John effort tipped the balance back in Liverpool's favour. The Kop were quick to sting the player nicknamed 'Buzzer' of his indiscretion by chanting, 'Show us your backside, Summerbee.'

Eight days later at Maine Road, Liverpool went in search of another two points in their duel with Everton at the league's summit and duly ran out 2-0 winners courtesy of Scottish forward Bobby Graham. Another five weeks on, the teams met again on Moss Side in the third round of the League Cup with Alun Evans cancelling out Mike Doyle's opener. But City rallied to a 3-2 win despite Graham striking back immediately after Bowyer had extended his side's cushion just ten minutes after Neil Young gave them the lead.

Chris James's verdict in the following day's *Liverpool Echo* summarised the match as 'tense, exciting and sometimes angry', but Glyn Pardoe relished the occasion which took Mercer's team a step closer to tangible success in the competition later that season. 'That was a tremendous game, what the fans want. That's what it's all about, the cups,' he says. 'The league's the hardest to win, the FA Cup's the glamour one but the League Cup is just the same. It was tremendous for Manchester City to win that. I don't understand today why they don't want to win it. I suppose it comes down to the Champions League and things like that. I suppose that's altered it but when I was playing, I would want to win everything. I'm sure the players would today [as well]. It was tremendous for us and it gives you confidence and makes you feel wanted.'

In addition to the League Cup, City claimed the European Cup Winners' Cup, a feat which elevated them alongside Manchester United and Leeds as one of the first English clubs to taste Continental success. The sky appeared to be the limit for Mercer and Allison's crack team, who set their sights on completing a 'Grand Slam' of winning every possible competition at the start of the 1969/70 season. Liverpool, meanwhile, were facing a necessary overhaul after a tilt at the First Division title became short-lived as they finished four places and 15 points behind local rivals and champions Everton.

An unexpected FA Cup quarter-final exit to Second Division strugglers Watford, though, saw Shankly hit upon a moment of realisation that his team urgently needed freshening up. Seismic changes were made, with many of the players that had delivered the club's success in the previous decade discarded. Just four of those that had featured in the League Cup exit at Maine Road retained their places for City's visit to Anfield the following season on 12 January 1971. The game, staged a month before the UK entered the age of decimalisation, ended in a goalless draw and had been rescheduled from its original 22 December date on account of Liverpool's involvement in the Inter-Cities Fairs Cup the same day.

Shankly's ruthlessness paid off handsomely with Liverpool putting together a 17-match unbeaten run at home in all competitions that was further extended against City but they still failed to find a way past Joe Corrigan, a home-grown goalkeeper who was fast gaining a reputation as a future England international. Also lining up at Anfield that evening was a player that had been on the verge of moving there several seasons earlier. Freddie Hill had joined City in May 1970 for £12,000 from Halifax Town, spending double what the Third Division club had paid Bolton Wanderers just a year earlier. The forward almost joined Liverpool's ranks in March 1964 after they agreed a £45,000 deal with the Trotters before high blood pressure saw him fail a medical. Determined to get his man, Shankly sought a second opinion only for another doctor to confirm the original diagnosis.

Bolton took Hill to see a specialist who deemed him fit to play for them against the Reds on the eve of the Grand National. 'Malcolm Allison took him to Manchester City and said he would make him the fittest player in the whole world,' Shankly later said in *My Story*, his 1976 autobiography. 'But the point was that he was not fit enough to sign for Liverpool.'

After reaching the FA Cup Final and seeking to overturn a one-goal reversal in their Fairs Cup semi-final against Leeds United, two days later, the Liverpool manager took a cautious approach when his side visited Maine Road on 26 April 1971. It was one which would cost him more than maximum points as a less than full-strength line-up were held to a 2-2 draw.

Shankly had recalled several former stalwarts, including Ron Yeats, Tommy Lawrence and Bobby Graham, who scored both of their goals. Owing to their own semi-final commitments in defending the European Cup Winners' Cup against Chelsea, City's starting XI was similarly changed but still included several mainstays in Tommy Booth, Ian Bowyer, Arthur Mann and Francis Carrodus. Both clubs faced potential inquiries from the Football League for fielding sides which devalued its flagship competition. Liverpool were later fined £7,500, the second-largest meted out to a British club at the time, after providing an unsatisfactory explanation for selecting a weakened team to the FA, who cited Shankly's stated intentions to the press before the match in their ruling.

The gamble backfired as his side suffered consecutive humiliations as they were dumped out of the Fairs Cup by Leeds and succumbed in the FA Cup Final to an Arsenal team that became the second English team to complete a league and cup double. Winds of change were blowing at both ends of the M62, but a tornado was preparing to ravage Manchester's blue half.

Maladjusted

TOGETHER, JOE Mercer and Malcolm Allison had made Manchester City seemingly untouchable. In the city where Ernest Rutherford first split the atom in 1917, the pair produced a different type of alchemy which revived the Blues' stature within English football and elevated it on the Continent. But the summer of 1971 saw the club's key coaching elements mapped on a collision course. The previous season pitted Mercer and Allison on opposing sides of a takeover war between Maine Road's old order against new pretenders. The City manager remained loyal to chairman Albert Alexander, who had first appointed him six years earlier and oversaw the club's period of unparalleled success. His assistant instead threw his support behind rival candidate Joe Smith.

Allison had instigated the battle for control midway through the 1970/71 campaign, amid a yearning for greater responsibility for the playing side and hopes of working with directors that did not bristle at his carefree lifestyle. He told City supporter and local publican Ian Niven, 'Find me a man with £100,000, and we will get control of the club.' Smith, a double glazing tycoon from nearby Oldham, emerged as the man who would make Allison's dreams come true with an offer to buy out the shares of vice-chairman Samuel Johnson, who had previously put forward the sacrilegious idea of a merger with Manchester United in 1965.

Promises to hand total control of first-team affairs over to him alongside a 20-year contract seemed too good to be true for Mercer's assistant, and so it proved. Smith's consortium included

Niven, solicitor Michael Horwich, former City director Chris Muir and Simon Cussons, a member of the Imperial Leather soap family. Johnson agreed to sell 508 of a potential 521 shares for £110.000 before reneging on the agreement due to the involvement of Muir, who had been forced from the boardroom a year earlier due to alleged illegal actions.

Once the takeover bid collapsed, Allison's public support of Smith left him at the mercy of the club's powers that be. At a board meeting, he was interrogated about his role in the planned coup and warned by Alexander that he risked being sacked. Only Mercer's insistence that 'if he goes, I go' spared him. That intervention ultimately proved the City manager's undoing and fuelled Allison's ambitions of becoming a sole authority.

Both Smith and Cussons had been invited to sit on the board in time for the start of the 1971/72 season, with Albert Alexander's son Eric installed as chairman at the end of the previous year. The pair's elevation spelled the beginning of the end for Mercer. His last outing as Maine Road's de facto manager came on 1 September against a Liverpool team whose sharp facelift and off-field continuity was in stark contrast to his own club's hierarchical feuding and perseverance with an ageing side. Bill Shankly's reinvented Reds had signed the burgeoning Kevin Keegan from Scunthorpe in the previous campaign and appeared well-placed for a long-awaited assault at the First Division title. But their new number seven was overshadowed as Ian Mellor's second-half goal helped City snatch a home win. Keegan and team-mate Alec Lindsay both ran the risk of disciplinary action after picking up a booking apiece, their third in an allotted 12-month window.

A month later, with the backing of the new regime, Allison had been installed as City's team manager with Mercer handed the newly created role of general manager. The compromise allowed the former apprentice to steadily begin making his mark as his new charges ascended to the First Division summit ahead of a 26 February trip to Anfield, where their hosts sat six points behind them.

City's unbeaten nine-game stretch in the league was decimated inside half an hour with goals from Larry Lloyd, Keegan and Bobby Graham. Any prior experience the new City boss held on Merseyside was redundant now that he had taken full charge of the dugout. After Graham's powerful strike wrapped up a home win, The Kop responded with chants of 'shut up Allison'. Shankly volunteered to do all the post-match talking as his side moved to within four points of the leaders. 'It's not for me to shout Liverpool's chances now when everybody can see them for themselves. I told you weeks ago this could happen,' he declared. 'This result has thrown the title fight wide open and now there is pressure on all of the top teams. It will be the fight to the finish all right.'

Shankly's words rang true as a four-way tussle for the championship ensued. He and Allison took their place on a pantheon of managerial heavyweights alongside Leeds United's Don Revie and Brian Clough at Derby County to provide a contest which thrilled supporters and headline writers alike.

With the title still firmly in their hands, City signed a player who embodied the Allison era while also snatching defeat from the jaws of victory. The £200,000 arrival of Rodney Marsh from Queens Park Rangers added a flamboyance that would nudge the champions-elect over the line. Signs appeared promising after a winning debut against Chelsea but a winless streak in their next three games eroded their previous four-point margin over Leeds and helped Liverpool to sneak into second place. Marsh, however, felt that Derby had been City's biggest nemesis during the run-in. 'At that time when I joined, Derby County were the team in form and I suppose Liverpool were there or thereabouts [and] were always a threat,' he says. 'But it was Derby that everybody was talking about in those days because, obviously, of the manager and everything. Liverpool were in the frame but it was Derby that we were looking at.'

As the season reached a tense climax, three of the main challengers faced off in their last two games. Derby slipped to a 2-0 loss against City but still occupied top spot thanks to a narrow victory over Liverpool in their final outing. Clough's players were on the beach as the title's destiny was being decided, having jetted out to Majorca for an end-of-season trip. With their two rivals no longer involved in games, Liverpool and Leeds had perfect opportunities to snatch the crown. Revie's FA Cup winners represented the side more likely to upstage the Rams, only needing to avoid a defeat at Wolverhampton Wanderers while a victory over Arsenal constituted Anfield's best chance.

John Toshack appeared to have clinched it for them after prodding home a late winner, only to be denied by the offside flag. That same night, Leeds were hit by a 2-1 reversal at Molineux to hand Derby the title. All three sides had finished on 57 points, one behind Clough's champions, but City's late-season downturn had seen them drop into fourth, a place below Liverpool on goal average. The repercussions of Marsh's signing became widely perceived as the reason for their capitulation. Joe Mercer could not resist referencing it in a public sideswipe at Allison, declaring, '£200,000 is a lot of money to spend to throw away the championship.' In his 2001 autobiography *Priceless*, the player himself concedes that his arrival 'cost Manchester City the 1972 league championship'.

But the breakdown of Mercer and Allison's working relationship earlier in the season was unquestionably a greater cause and effect. Marsh offers a revealing insight about the awkwardness of the new arrangement between the club's team and general managers. 'I had never experienced that before throughout my career,' he says. 'I'd joined Man City when I was 27 and I'd never experienced anything like that. I had great years at Queens Park Rangers and starting as a kid at Fulham and I'd never had a situation whereby you had a first-team coach and the manager. It didn't take me long to realise that Malcolm Allison was everything and Joe Mercer was just a token figure now. I don't know how other people saw it but that was exactly how I saw it.'

Clarity finally arrived on 12 June 1972 as Mercer walked away from the club he had rebuilt. For Allison, now handed autonomy over City's squad, the split vindicated a personal decision to turn down previous offers to coach at Juventus and Coventry City. In a twist of fate, the latter had moved quickly to install his predecessor in the Highfield Road dugout. On Merseyside, Bill Shankly was preparing to pull off a bold move in the transfer market. Liverpool had beaten Leicester City in the race for Frank Worthington's signature as Shankly brokered a £150,000 deal with Huddersfield Town, newly relegated from the First Division. Both Shankly and his Foxes counterpart Jimmy Bloomfield had travelled to London's Heathrow airport to meet Worthington on his arrival back from an England under-23 tour but the Liverpool manager had stolen an early march after being granted permission to speak to the player first by his old club.

Personal terms were agreed at a nearby hotel before the pair and chairman Eric Roberts flew back to Anfield to finalise the transfer, which would see Worthington lining up alongside Kevin Keegan in attack, on the same day that Alun Evans returned to his native Midlands to Aston Villa for £80,000. But Liverpool were forced to put their marquee transfer on hold due to an abnormally high blood pressure when the player underwent a medical, a symptom a specialist attributed to the 24-hour turnaround from flying back from representing his country in Kiev to finalising the transfer. Shankly remained unwavering in his efforts to sign the player and advised that he take a fortnight's holiday, telling the press, 'He is basically fit, he just needs a rest.'

A revitalised Worthington returned on 27 June, but his blood pressure reading again sparked concerns and caused Liverpool to break off from negotiations. Huddersfield manager Ian Greaves had once characterised the player as 'the working man's George Best'. Following in the footsteps of Manchester United's footloose and fancy-free talisman unravelled a dream move to Anfield. He had attended his brother's wedding with Carolyn Moore, the previous year's Miss Great Britain and a one-time flame of Best, before jetting out to Majorca. Even before landing on the Balearic island, Worthington had already disregarded Shankly's recuperation advice by persuading the lady sitting next to him on the plane to spend the night. His holiday hedonism extended to a threesome with two Swedish women and sleeping with a Belgian girl on the same day.

Several weeks later, Worthington joined Leicester for an initial £80,000 that would potentially rise to £100,000 as Liverpool went back to the drawing board in attempts to bolster their attacking options, with Shankly revealing that he had tried to sign two players within days of the 1971/72 season ending but refused to disclose their identities. It was speculated that the players in question were Shrewsbury Town's Alf Wood, who opted to join Millwall, and either Southampton forward Mick Channon or Brian Kidd at Manchester United. Peter Cormack eventually arrived from Nottingham Forest for £110,000 in a summer that also saw home-grown midfielder Jimmy Case sourced from South Liverpool, a team in the seventh-tier Northern Premier League, for £500.

Their challenge of going one better in the First Division met its first obstacle in an opening-day encounter with a Manchester City side already reaping the benefits of Allison's stewardship in claiming the Charity Shield. Their early strides did not go unnoticed behind enemy lines, with the *Liverpool Echo*'s pre-match preview stating, 'City are potentially the most exciting side in the country. When they hit top form not many teams know how to stop them. As team entertainers, they are the tops. Everything is there for fluent goal production. The best winger in the game in Mike Summerbee can make an ordinary player like Wyn Davies look like a King in the penalty area.'

Davies's role at Anfield became one of six-yard box villainy rather than its monarch. Liverpool had taken an early lead through Brian Hall after Steve Heighway had played a neat one-two with Kevin Keegan, before Ian Callaghan doubled the advantage in the final stages. Yet events in the 42nd minute came to define the game as Davies and Larry Lloyd were both sent off for violent conduct. An off-the-ball clash between the pair had culminated in Lloyd headbutting his City counterpart. Their collective dismissals headlined a weekend of indiscipline under English football's new rules, with five players in total given their marching orders and a further 53 cautioned.

Shankly was particularly scornful about the sensationalism of first-half events at Anfield. 'I've seen far far rougher matches than that,' he told reporters. 'None of our players committed a nasty foul and only one or two of the City players committed bad tackles. Because of the importance of the game between two teams who are both fancied for the title and because it was the opening game of the season, everybody seems to have got worked up about it. What do people expect? The players to go around kissing each other?'

Callaghan also agrees with his manager's opinion that the incident had become overblown. 'When you think about the two lads, Wyn Davies wasn't that way inclined. Larry Lloyd was a centre-half, yeah, but he wasn't what you'd call a "dirty" centre-half,' he says. 'Incidents happen in a game and players get sent off. But certainly, the two players weren't what you'd call dirty players by any means.'

The incident later set a new precedent for the game when on 9 November Lloyd became the first player to appear before the FA's newly formed independent disciplinary tribunal, after his initial appeal was turned down by the governing body's Disciplinary Committee. Television pictures of his fracas with Davies, who had since joined Manchester United, were played before the committee, and saw the defender become the first player to be cleared of wrongdoing on the strength of camera footage. A panel member attempted a face-saving exercise following the ruling, saying, 'Lloyd is not free from blame, but his sending-off is regarded as sufficient punishment and therefore his three-match suspension imposed by the FA has been quashed.'

Following the hearing, Cliff Lloyd, secretary for the PFA (Professional Footballers' Association) and a former Liverpool reserves full-back, declared the use of technology as a necessity for players seeking to exonerate themselves. 'I think it's essential,' he said. 'It would be very difficult for a player to justify his case without the use of television evidence.'

City's form following their trip to Merseyside was more akin to a video nasty. Allison's side lost five of their opening six First

Division fixtures and were 12 points off the pace by Christmas as injuries to Tony Book and Mike Summerbee, coupled with a suspension for Francis Lee, took their toll. The FA Cup proved to be their great salvation with a 3-2 win against Stoke City setting up a fourth-round date with league leaders Liverpool, who had overcome Burnley in a replay, on 3 February. Pundits believed that City had been dealt the more difficult tie in heading to Anfield. Tommy Smith proceeded to up the ante in his weekly *Liverpool Echo* column on 20 January. 'No doubt within the next fortnight, Malcolm Allison will be saying how Manchester City are going to come to Anfield and win their fourth round FA Cup tie with us,' wrote Smith. 'But Malcolm can take it from me that we fancy our chances against Man City – not because we beat them at Anfield in the first game of the season, nor because we have invariably won matches against them at Anfield. We fancy our chances because we do against any side at Anfield no matter who they are.'

Smith went on to dissect the weaknesses within Allison's side. 'I don't think their defence is good enough to stand up to the pressure we'll put on them,' he added. 'I think Malcolm knows this is where City's problems lie because he has played a number of combinations at the back as he has experimented.' Smith also predicted that his team would triumph over their Mancunian counterparts, having beaten them on the opening day of the First Division campaign, but also admitted, 'It will be a different game this time. City have improved a lot since then. They are working harder and have climbed up the table. But while their attack is scoring goals, their defence has been letting them in and for that reason they are the team that have got to do the worrying in this tie.'

Preparations were far from ideal for Shankly's players, who dropped their first home points of the season that afternoon against Derby County before succumbing to defeat at Wolverhampton Wanderers, which cut their lead in the First Division title race down to a single point. Collecting three points from City's previous two games left Allison in buoyant mood ahead of the trip to Anfield. He spent the build-up to the tie routinely talking up his side's chances of upsetting the odds and even went as far as naming an unchanged starting line-up some 48 hours ahead of schedule. Rodney Marsh remembers his manager issuing stringent instructions on their Cheadle training ground on how to frustrate Liverpool's front line.

'We had a young kid called Derek Jefferies who was 21 years old,' he says. 'Early in the week, he [Allison] said, "Derek, I want you to mark Kevin Keegan man-to-man. I don't want him to have a kick," and that's what happened. In terms of talking to me. Malcolm Allison in the years we were together must have said no more than two dozen words about the game to me. His attitude to me was, "Go and play and we'll adjust around you." I've not particularly got into this over the years when people have asked me, I think that pissed off a lot of City players that were there because I came into the club for, in those days, a massive transfer fee. It was a record at the time. And he said to me in front of many of the players, "You just play how you want to, Rodney, and the other players will adjust around you," and I think that upset a few players.'

In response to his opposite number's grandiose, Shankly chose to largely keep his counsel. Ian Callaghan saw minimal change in Liverpool's pre-match routine at their Melwood base despite the brewing sense of anticipation from their peers across the M62. 'That's the way it was with Bill Shankly and Bob Paisley as his assistant,' he says. 'It was just, "Get your head down and get on with the game." You were well prepared for the game so we just got on with it the same. For most games, or all games, that's the way it was. It didn't make any difference because it was City but at the end of the day, the top teams became great rivals. They were big games to play in and City was always a big game to play in, like it was [with] United.'

Shankly projected his indifference to the hype surrounding the tie in the media by insisting, 'It's just another game for us. When you're top of the league, every match you play is like a cup tie. This match will be nothing new to us.'

But the Liverpool manager still found time to aim a thinly veiled remark at the Maine Road dugout. 'This is always the case with FA Cup ties,' continued Shankly. 'They get blown up out of all proportion and when a little team beats a big team there is more talk for a while but it blows over and sanity reigns again. It was the same before the Burnley game with a lot of talk coming from Burnley about what was going to happen. This week it's been all Manchester City and what they are going to do. You'd hardly know there was another game in the north-west. No matter what they say, they have still got to come here and play. Barring of course they drop out and then they'll be thrown out of the competition.'

Where Shankly did not think twice about dismissing opponents within the sanctuary of the dressing room, to make sure his own players were sufficiently fired up for encounters, Allision preferred a more firebrand approach and was saving his best for last. As City were preparing to make their way to Merseyside, the *Daily Express* splashed his weekly column under the headline of 'We will bury the myth of Liverpool'. In typical fashion, he opined, 'Let's face it, Liverpool are just trial horses these days,' before denigrating Anfield's seven-year trophy drought by adding, 'When was the last time they won anything?'

In the 21st century, managers attempting to engage in mind games became commonplace but in the early 1970s, getting under Shankly's skin was an unenviable and almost impossible ask. At a time when he and Brian Clough were widely regarded as the game's great orators, always able to conjure up snappy one-liners at a moment's notice, unnerving either of the pair required near-superhuman effort.

'This might sound a little bit controversial [but] it's the truth: Malcolm Allison always thought the Scousers were thin-skinned and very easy to take the piss out of,' says Rodney Marsh. 'Coming from London, where he grew up, that was his way and that's why everybody, including Bill Shankly, took the bait. He thought the same thing about the Scots so he would try and wind up people by being outrageous and every single time they would take the bait, and Liverpool were no exception.'

On the morning of the tie, the fruits of Allison's paper talk finally drew their intended response as James Lawton, an Express journalist at the time and a doyen of British sports journalism, later relayed to his biographer David Tossell. 'At about 7am the next day I was woken up by a call from Bill Shankly,' Lawton said in *Big Mal: The High Life and Hard Times of Malcolm Allison*. 'It was like a pneumatic drill at the other end of the phone. "That fucking man is a lunatic and you are a disgrace for printing it!" He had got under Bill's skin.'

Allison was not finished with his Anfield offensive just yet. As his players surveyed their surroundings ahead of the kick-off, and with chants of 'Allison shut your mouth' reverberating, City's flamboyant manager took his pre-match showmanship to another level. 'We'd got to the ground an hour and a half early, as we did in those days, and we came out on the field and we got booed by the crowd,' says Marsh. 'We were walking around in our Man City blazers, getting a feel of the atmosphere, looking at the surface and [deciding] what kind of boots did you want to wear. The Kop was going mad; it was going crazy because we were two fantastic football teams in those days. Malcolm walks all the way down the other end of the pitch to The Kop, stood underneath the goalposts and raised his arms like he was at the Colosseum in Rome and, oh my goodness, it created an atmosphere that was toxic, really.

'I remember it vividly because I thought, "What the fuck are you doing!?" The crowd went absolutely apoplectic because he was sort of giving it "I am the big one", and it created an atmosphere where we could have played the game without the ball.'

Just like his media barbs, Allison's defiant stance in front of The Kop was hardly out of character. In December 1970, he had approached Old Trafford's Stretford End and held up four fingers to correctly predict the number of goals City would score against their local rivals that afternoon. His gladiatorial goading on Merseyside also set the tone for an FA Cup meeting that was, true to the absent Smith's assertion, a different game from their opening-day salvo. As more than 3,000 supporters were locked outside Anfield with half an hour remaining to kick-off, a heightened fervour within the stadium was only subdued by the announcement of Shankly's decision to rest Smith, which temporarily took the wind out of a 56,296-strong crowd's sails.

In the opening stages, Mike Summerbee became the visitors' main outlet and fashioned the game's first noteworthy chance after latching on to a threaded ball by Colin Bell and racing past Alec Lindsay but Larry Lloyd headed his cross clear. It would prove to be the last meaningful goalmouth action as running battles became rife, with John Toshack and Tommy Booth regularly coming to blows early on while Peter Cormack was on the receiving end of successive challenges by Tony Towers and Bell that angered the home crowd.

Those simmering tensions were finally brought to boil in the tenth minute as Kevin Keegan was floored by Derek Jefferies, Allison's designated man-marker, and immediately sought retribution on the City central defender, sparking fisticuffs between both sets of players. Play belatedly resumed on 16 minutes when Callaghan's floated free kick found Cormack but Joe Corrigan was able to save the Scotsman's header. Three minutes later, Lee appeared to have opened the scoring, but referee Pat Partridge ruled it out for Marsh's foul on Ray Clemence in the lead-up.

Fouls continued to fly thick and fast, forcing Partridge to play the role of peacemaker. Emlyn Hughes's refusal to shake hands with Lee following a stern challenge by the City forward. At the half-hour mark, the Middlesbrough official finally issued the game's first caution when Tony Book sent Heighway tumbling with a late tackle that provoked The Kop, unimpressed by the fare on show, to chant, 'We want football.' Toshack almost benefited from dubious officiating when Keegan's pass found him in a potential offside position. Despite being waved on by the linesman, the Welshman hesitated before a snatched shot was collected by Corrigan.

Football became secondary to gamesmanship in the opening 45 minutes as Lee and Hughes again flared up on two further occasions before the break, leading to the pair being pulled apart by Partridge and receiving stern lectures. Anfield's dismayed crowd let City's players know in no uncertain terms its view on the first half as a cacophony of boos and catcalls rained down on them as Allison's side headed in at the interval goalless. Their manager's pre-match shot across the bows had set a tone which was reflected in the reception when the visitors re-emerged for the second half. Rodney Marsh insists that the first-half skirmishes were nothing out of the ordinary. 'Every time that Man City played against Liverpool in those days – two very, very big teams – it was always a very sort of violent game,' he says. 'I got into it with Tommy Smith a few times and once with Larry Lloyd, not particularly in that game. It was always a very nasty game.'

Seemingly, the bad blood of the previous half had finally dissipated as the teams continued to play out a stalemate. Only an ill-timed challenge by Lloyd on Towers, which earned the Liverpool defender his fourth booking of the season and took him over the Football League's allotted 12-point limit, proved to be the worst of the latter-stage action. Even with the apparent truce, City's foul count at the final whistle stood at 37 – three times the number committed by Liverpool, prompting Allison to turn his ire on the officials. 'When you go to Anfield, you get fouls given against you which are not fouls. That is recognised throughout football,' he said post-match. 'Referees are influenced by the crowd. Three people bothered me today. I don't think they will bother me on Wednesday.'

Tony Towers appeared to share that view on the officialdom's perceived imbalance, saying, 'It's wrong for Liverpool to expect teams to go to Anfield and just lay down for them.' But referee Pat Partridge took the criticisms in good humour, saying, 'With a name like mine, you're bound to be shot at.'

The media shared in Allison's cynicism but not over any perceived home advantage. Newspapers covering the game were particularly scathing of the fourth-round clash, both locally and nationally. The *Liverpool Echo* headlined their report of the tetchy affair on the following Monday as 'The Cup-Tie That Died of

Shame'. Horace Yates, the paper's esteemed correspondent, took a dim view of the visitors' gameplan, writing, 'If this is City's normal approach it is not in the least surprising that they should remain the poor relations of Manchester.' His colleague Chris James went further and called the overall game 'a disgraceful display'.

Allison again appeared in his element ahead of the replay, which he claimed had seen 20,000 people turned away from Maine Road in the days leading up to the tie due to its sell-out status. His excitement was not universal within City's rank and file. Francis Lee used his *Daily Mirror* column to appeal to his manager's better nature by 'calling for a 48-hour truce in the propaganda battle he's been waging' around the undecided cup tie. Lee was no stranger to warring with Allison in the media, having branded him just 'a fool' three weeks prior over speculation that City were considering selling him. But the forward's latest remarks were well-intentioned, adding, 'Mal is one of Europe's best coaches. He's also a pal. But I don't believe he's helped City's cause one jot as we prepare for tomorrow's fourth round replay. This tie is hot enough already without Mal.'

'There was a not a kind of split in the dressing room, but some people were for Malcolm and others weren't particularly 100 per cent behind him,' says Rodney Marsh. 'In the "for Malcolm" were people like Mike Summerbee, Willie Donachie and players like that, and in the "against" column were people like Mike Doyle; [to them] it was like Malcolm was bigger than the team, and the team was the most important thing. Throughout my career nothing like that bothered me. I didn't give a fuck what people did or didn't say. I remember one year we played Derby County – and this is parenthetically by the bye – Brian Clough had really slaughtered me all season, saying I would go missing in games and he didn't rate Rodney Marsh because he only showed up for ten minutes of a game and blah, blah, blah, blah, blah. I just thought, "Oh, fuck it," and that was my attitude, so when Malcolm came out with it, I just thought, "Fair enough, nothing to see here."'

A home tie against either Second Division outfit Sunderland or Reading, in the Fourth Division, awaited the winners of the 7 February showdown, where City's assistant manager Ken Barnes used the match programme to air his grievances about the unfair coverage the hosts had received in the Anfield clash. 'I thought the reports were more alarmist than they should have been,' he wrote. 'There was a lot more football than we were given credit for. There were some niggly fouls particularly during the tension of the last few minutes. There were few very bad fouls. I think the nastiness was blown out of all proportion. Nor were City entirely villains of the piece.'

Beneath the floodlights in Moss Side, City ran out 2-0 winners. Their first-half opener came from a smart move between Colin Bell, Tony Towers and Willie Donachie before the latter threaded a ball through for a powerful shot by Francis Lee which Ray Clemence spilled into the path of Bell to follow up. The 'King of the Kippax' was integral in their second of the night when he headed a short Mike Summerbee free kick from the byeline for Tommy Booth to meet at the far post. Allison's combative approach in the original tie completely altered with his side's victory. Referee Pat Partridge recalled him being 'all sweetness and light' after the game.

Killing off Shankly's bid for a league and FA Cup double brought out a more punch-drunk personal from the City manager, who could not resist heaping further misery on Liverpool with a doom prophecy. 'It went just as I expected,' he gloated. 'Liverpool never looked like winning – and they won't win the league championship either. We've shown they can be beaten, and other teams will do it too.'

'When you straddle the line of genius and fool, Malcolm was on that line,' says Marsh. 'Many things that he did were genius and many of the things he did were foolish. One of the things that he did that was foolish was he was gratuitous. In other words, he would make negative comments about teams and players just for the sake of doing it. I always thought, when you're a manager, that when you went and beat an opponent at the very highest level and that was Man City-Liverpool, and it still is today, it's come back around again hasn't it? But when you beat an opponent, I always felt the best thing to do was to praise the opponent and say that they were fantastic [and] it was a very difficult game for us. Liverpool were fantastic but we were lucky to get the win – that was my attitude. Malcolm's attitude, straddling the genius-fool tightrope, was he sometimes would actually berate the team that he'd just beaten. That was Malcolm Allison.'

Shankly had hit back at his City contemporary, saying, 'The league champions will come from the top three teams at the moment, and the first of them to go out of the cup could well win the title.'

But Liverpool were still reeling from the manner of their Maine Road reversal, with Larry Lloyd claiming that Lee had 'talked the referee into booking' him for a fifth time in the season. Shankly, too, suspected that Allison's gamesmanship had helped dictate the replay's narrative. 'Malcolm Allison, by saying what he did, put even more tension into the games when there was already enough of it,' he said. 'City introduced little tricks into their game which they didn't need to. There was very little enjoyment in either of the games because there was too much niggle. City are playing for keeps. They played hard and deserved to win. But these matches were unlike all the other games we have played this season and we have now played 18 cup ties.'

The First Division leaders failed to disprove Allison's assertion with a 2-0 loss to Arsenal immediately after bowing out of the world's most famous club cup competition to be overtaken by Bertie Mee's side. Just ten days on from their FA Cup ignominy, Liverpool returned to Manchester's blue side as Shankly made a series of shake-ups as Phil Thompson and Steve Heighway came in for Brian Hall and John Toshack respectively. A different Reds side stepped out at Maine Road but found themselves on the receiving end of a near-identical goal to the ones that had dumped them out of the cup when another floated Mike Summerbee free kick allowed Tommy Booth to head home.

Memories of August's corresponding fixture also came flooding back too after Thompson pushed Booth as he attempted to meet a Summerbee corner. Marsh's attempt to take the ensuing indirect free kick quickly was met with firm opposition from a throng of Liverpool players and led to Tommy Smith's name going into referee Clive Thomas's book. With a five-man wall positioned on the goal line alongside Clemence, Marsh rolled the ball to the far post for Booth to meet but he failed to connect. City's earlier scorer made no mistake when flaring up to Thompson after the ball ran out of play, causing Smith to wade in along with Kevin Keegan. Larry Lloyd, sent off on the opening day for clashing with Wyn Davies, attempted to defuse the tensions. Smith and Booth both received lectures from Thomas, but the Liverpool defender's mouth talked him into trouble with a second yellow card for dissent, prompting the Maine Road crowd to erupt in rapture.

Smith protested his innocence as he walked towards the touchline, leaving his team with an unenviable remit of overturning the deficit in under 20 minutes with a one-man disadvantage. Within half of that time, Liverpool were level after Keegan headed a downfield free kick from Alec Lindsay into the path of Brian Hall to tee up Phil Boersma for a shot on the turn that flew into the top right-hand corner of Joe Corrigan's net. Boersma's snatching of a late point delivered his tenth goal of the season on the same ground that his professional debut had taken place less than four years earlier, in the 1969 League Cup third-round exit to City.

Rodney Marsh told reporters that he believed Liverpool had 'come through their really black period' with the result, a claim which raised eyebrows in some quarters due to their failure to win any of their previous six matches in all competitions, with the triple-header against City accounting for half of that number. 'You've got to look at football from different perspectives,' he says. 'I pretty much found that all games are not played the same way anyway and an approach in the modern game, you look at, as an example, Pep Guardiola who treats the FA Cup completely different than he treats the league that maybe Liverpool being years ahead of their time.'

Shankly had gained something of a reputation for helping his players wriggle off the disciplinary hook, having successfully defended Lloyd against his opening-day dismissal as well as one for a clash with Birmingham City striker Bob Hatton. Whether the Liverpool manager's power of persuasion could convince the FA to allow Smith to see out the remainder of their First Division title push seemed far less certain. English football's governing body had been due to hear the player's case a month later but it was postponed due to one of the linesmen involved in the Maine Road fixture being unable to offer testimony on account of being out of the country. The FA upheld Smith's three-match suspension in mid-April, only for an appeal against the ruling to an independent tribunal to delay the punishment until the same stage of the following month, by which point the defender had helped Liverpool end their seven-year silverware itch by winning the league and UEFA Cup.

City's own blueprint for success had been foiled in the FA Cup fifth round, where eventual winners Sunderland turned the tables on Allison by holding his side to a 2-2 home draw before running out winners in the replay at Roker Park. A growing disillusion with his life in Manchester was heaped on further by the enforced sale of striker Ian Mellor and a home loss at the hands of former mentor Joe Mercer's Coventry City. On 30 March, Allison tendered his resignation and immediately joined Crystal Palace. Fate brought him back to Maine Road four weeks later as the south London club bowed out of the First Division in bold fashion with a 3-2 win. In the 14 months ahead, replacing a larger-than-life character would prove to be as difficult a prospect for Liverpool as much as it was beginning to appear for City.

Ascension

MALCOLM ALLISON'S departure briefly saw Manchester City return to its roots. The appointment of Johnny Hart revived a tradition which pre-dated the 1965 arrivals of Allison and Joe Mercer. As a former player and latterly first-team trainer at Maine Road, Hart appeared well-equipped to engineer their renaissance or keep things ticking over at the very least.

His decision to re-sign Denis Law on a free transfer offered an early sign of optimism. In the 12 years since leaving Moss Side, he had risen to further prominence as part of Manchester United's star-studded forward line alongside George Best and Bobby Charlton. International recognition followed by becoming only the second British player to win the Ballon d'Or in 1964 in addition to the first European Cup win by an English club four years later under Matt Busby. But Busby's move into an executive capacity at Old Trafford saw the 'King of Old Trafford' cast out by new manager Tommy Docherty and he returned to the club where his career had first taken flight.

Similar changes were happening at boardroom level with chairman Albert Alexander, who had continued his family's three-generation link with the club by succeeding father Albert in November 1971, announcing his plans to stand down after declaring that the takeover by Joe Smith's consortium had finally been completed.

In his place, Smith installed a man who acted as peacemaker during the hierarchical change but would steer Maine Road through two decades of turbulence. Peter Swales's business career had started with a sheet-music business in Altrincham, one of Manchester's satellite towns, alongside Noel White before the pair ventured into a brief and unsuccessful stint acting as agents for pop groups. Foresight to capitalise on the boom in consumer electronics with a television rental service culminated in a £500,000 buyout by Thorn in 1968. Five years later, Swales's premiership with his boyhood club began with the target of making them 'the number one club in the country'.

Hart's attempts to lead City back to recent glories had aggravated personal health problems and, with them languishing 11th in the First Division, he was replaced by Ron Saunders.

Saunders's appointment came with the sole remit from Swales to rid Maine Road of what he perceived to be 'too much showbiz'. Ostensibly, he was tasked with overseeing what would be termed as a cultural reboot in 21st century football parlance. The City chairman took the unusual step of aligning his personal fate with that of the new man, appointed just five days after he resigned at Norwich City. 'Having seen him at work, I now know for sure that he's the right one,' Swales wrote in his programme notes. 'If he goes down, I go down with him. It's as blunt as that.'

Norwich director Geoffrey Watling echoed Swales's belief that his club's loss had become City's gain and said, 'Saunders can be a Joe Mercer and Malcolm Allison rolled into one.' The new man repaid those public votes of confidence by taking City to the League Cup Final, where they were narrowly beaten by Wolverhampton Wanderers. But his tough approach was a far cry from the glory days under Mercer and Allison's dream partnership. 'It changed completely as far as I could see,' says Glyn Pardoe. 'I was out for over 12 months [through injury] so things had changed and then things altered again, but totally different. Nothing like Malcolm and Joe. Ron was his own man. I don't think Ron would listen to anybody. He had his own opinions and would do what he wanted to do.'

Eventually, City's ongoing mid-table status snapped the soon-to-be notorious impatience of Swales, who sacked Saunders on the eve of a Good Friday visit from Liverpool. The reigning champions had largely maintained their high standards set in the previous season and had cut down Leeds United's previous runaway lead in the First Division to four points. With a further two games in hand on Don Revie's side, the prospect of Bill Shankly leading his players to back-to-back titles did not appear out of the realms of possibility.

They encountered a far more disciplined City team, now under the care of Tony Book. Swales's decision to install the veteran defender was met with derision by Saunders, who issued a stinging response to the man who had served as his assistant in telling the media, 'I wish him all that he wished me when I was in the job!'

Well-wishes were in similarly short supply from Shankly after his side were held at Maine Road by their resilient hosts. Peter Cormack had broken the deadlock with a volley in the 18th minute after Alan Oakes's header had deflected a Steve Heighway throw into his path, before Francis Lee equalised by capitalising on a miskick from Emlyn Hughes as he tried to control a Keith McRae goal kick. 'If we had played them a week ago, we could have won by four or five,' bemoaned Shankly. Four days later, on 16 April 1974, Book took his new squad to Anfield for a bruising affair under the floodlights against the FA Cup finalists as goals from Brian Hall, Phil Boersma and Kevin Keegan saw them rack up a comfortable final score inside 32 first-half minutes.

Quick-witted Kopites labelled their maligned visitors The Wombles, a reference to the popular television characters' hallmark for accumulating rubbish. Chants of 'Remember you're The Wombles', 'The Wombles of Manchester City are we' and 'Franny Lee's a Womble' all rained down from the terrace alongside a put-down for the man who almost joined their ranks before his original move to Maine Road, 'Denis Law, Denis Law, is it true what Bill Shankly says that you're really 64?'

Shankly was equally admonishing of City's beaten troops after being informed that Leeds had preserved a two-point lead over his team with a win against Sheffield United on the same evening. 'We've been the best team in England for four months now and our football tonight was sheer poetry,' he eulogised. 'It could have been 7-0 three minutes into the second half and we could have had ten by the end with the amount of [chance] creation that went on.'

Liverpool's stellar display had been helped by a pristine playing surface, which had been cut short and watered before the game, that saw Shankly revel further. 'It was just right and we took advantage of it,' he added. 'City couldn't do anything to stop us. If they don't get the ball, how can they play?'

Book's side recovered from their Anfield hammering by recording back-to-back victories in their final two fixtures and famously condemned Manchester United to relegation through Denis Law's back-heeled goal against his old club at Old Trafford. But Shankly's confidence that Liverpool would take Leeds down to the wire by winning their remaining four outings proved misplaced as they didn't pick up a single victory and finished five points behind the champions, who would have remained ahead on goal average had their title rivals maintained their 100 per cent run. Shankly's players still managed to rally to a dominant win during a third FA Cup Final appearance in eight years as they dismantled Newcastle United 3-0.

As a staunchly Catholic city, Liverpool has something of a difficult relationship with 12 July, when local branches of the Orange Lodge annually march through its streets to commemorate William of Orange's defeat of King James II at the Battle of the Boyne in 1690. That uneasy feeling extended beyond sectarian disagreements on the same date in 1974 as Shankly's resignation sent shockwaves through Merseyside and the footballing world. *Granada Reports* delegated the solemn duty of breaking the news to disbelieving pedestrians in Liverpool city centre, both young and old, to its lead reporter – and unashamed Manchester United fan – Tony Wilson. Regular threats to quit throughout his tenure had been dubbed 'Bill's summer madness', but his decision to stand down became no laughing matter. Little more than two months earlier, after defeating Newcastle at Wembley, a weary Shankly had decided to bow out; for good this time.

Successive attempts by John Smith and Peter Robinson, the club's chairman and secretary respectively, to ask him to reconsider proved in vain and prompted the question as to who the outgoing man felt should succeed him. Shankly instantly recommended the curious choice of Jack Charlton, whom he had tried to sign as a player in 1962 but baulked at Leeds's £30,000 valuation. Although he had steered Middlesbrough back to the First Division in his first season as manager, reservations about the 1966 World Cup winner's direct style of play made him an unseemly appointment for Liverpool.

So was Malcolm Allison, who could not resist trying to put one over on Shankly in retirement by claiming he had received unofficial approaches from both the Reds and Leeds, themselves coming to terms with Don Revie's departure to take charge of the England national team, to take over the vacant post. Allison's extrovert persona automatically disqualified him from stepping into the conservatism of Anfield and was further undermined by taking Crystal Palace through two divisions after leaving Manchester City shortly before the end of the 1972/73 season. Anticipating the subsequent shooting-down of the boast, he had told the press that neither job appealed to him as it would be 'too easy' maintaining the status quo with both clubs.

Other names linked with the post by the media included two of Shankly's former on-field acolytes in Coventry City's Gordon Milne and Motherwell boss Ian St John. Charlton's name appeared on Liverpool's definitive managerial shortlist alongside another unnamed candidate, thought to be Bobby Robson at Ipswich Town. Crucially, the pair were not contacted about the role as the board opted to build on the solid foundations laid by Shankly with an in-house choice.

In contrast to his shock announcement and preceding 15 years in charge, the emergence of Bob Paisley as the Scot's replacement was a low-key affair. His service to Liverpool had been unstinting ever since arriving in May 1939, fulfilling numerous roles at the club over the next 35 years. The midfielder made up for lost time from the Second World War's outbreak mere months after signing from Bishop Auckland in his native north-east by ensuring the first post-war First Division championship took up residence at Anfield. He moved into the backroom setup after retiring in 1954, with the club preparing for its first of eight years in the Second Division, in a variety of roles from physiotherapist to reserve-team coach before serving as Shankly's assistant.

Stepping into the managerial spotlight had been initially met with apprehension from Paisley, who was concerned with the public perception of him being the man to take Shankly's place and the complicated business of negotiations in both player recruitment and contract renewals. Even after receiving assurances that neither would be unresolvable issues, the self-effacing Geordie still felt a sense of unease taking the job when he addressed Liverpool's players for the first time as manager; telling them repeatedly that he had never wanted the job.

Publicly he declared the need for 'a clean break' from the Shankly regime but cutting the chord with the old regime proved an uphill challenge, particularly when his former superior made a farewell appearance by leading the side out for their Charity Shield showdown with Leeds United, where Brian Clough had begun an infamous 44-day stint as Revie's successor. The FA Cup holders won the season's traditional curtain-raiser at Wembley on penalties after the teams had drawn 1-1 in normal time, with Kevin Keegan and Billy Bremner both sent off for fighting. Both players were later handed 11-game suspensions by the FA.

Without their goalscoring talisman, Liverpool still managed to put together a six-game unbeaten start to their new First Division campaign, winning five of them, to take an early lead in the title race. Joining them in that battle for the top were Manchester City, who had encountered their own roadblocks during Tony Book's first full season in charge. The £110,000 sale of Francis Lee to Derby County at the beginning of the season would torment Maine Road mere months after his departure by his scoring a decisive goal for the visitors, made memorable by Barry Davies's iconic commentary line, 'Look at his face – just look at his face!'

Adding to Book's issues were the public pronouncements of Malcolm Allison, his one-time manager, telling reporters, 'Tony's got a fight on his hands to be his own man at Manchester City … I think he'll do well, but I'm worried if things don't go well immediately and he is pressured into doing things against his better judgement.' Allison's concerns about a poor start from his old club proved unfounded. With Rodney Marsh named as captain, City lost only one of their opening six fixtures ahead of a 14 September clash that pitted Book and Paisley, selfless men that had been thrust into the limelight at their respective clubs, against each other as kindred spirits.

City swarmed Liverpool's defence from the outset and finally reaped the rewards in the 39th minute when a lofted cross from the left allowed Colin Bell to outwit a jumping Alec Lindsay and produce a first-time delivery into Marsh at the far post to fire past Ray Clemence. Emlyn Hughes and Peter Cormack immediately beseeched referee John Yates to appeal against the award and were booked for their troubles. 'I actually handled the ball on to my chest before I scored,' says Marsh. 'The referee and the linesman didn't see it, but Emlyn did. If you play it back to the kick-off, Emlyn went ballistic for about 15 seconds at the referee. He didn't get sent off but he went absolutely ballistic because he'd recognised that I'd handled the ball. After the kick-off, I just went up to him and there was still snot coming down his nose, he was fuming and fuming at me, and I said, "Just to let you know, Emlyn, you're absolutely right – I did handball that." It didn't go down very well!'

Lindsay also took issue with Marsh's act of gamesmanship. 'Handle it? You wait until you see the smile on his face,' he told reporters afterwards. 'He took the lace out before scoring.' But Ian Callaghan takes a more considered view on the maverick striker's unsporting act. 'That was the banter between players,' he says. 'In big games between big clubs, players do that type of thing if that's in your personality, which obviously it was in Rodney's personality. I don't think it'd make much difference [to the game], just that you'd feel as though you'd been cheated.'

Any room for complaint surrounding Marsh's contentious opener were nullified just four minutes from the end of the second half as Dennis Tueart floated a ball from the right to Mike Summerbee, who drew Clemence at his near post before cutting back to Tueart to sweep home. Inflicting Liverpool's first defeat of the season still carries fond memories for Marsh, both as captain and scorer on the day. 'I've actually watched it back on YouTube a couple of times; people have sent me the links,' he says. 'Liverpool still had a fantastic team [with] Emlyn Hughes – the great Emlyn Hughes – and Phil Thompson at the back. They had Ray Clemence in goal. They had a really fantastic football team. It was 2-0 but it could have been four or five. After the game, you come back in the dressing room and you know that you've had a brilliant result.'

City's comfortable win came during a testing period for Liverpool. The defensive partnership between Hughes and Thompson was still at a developmental stage, with the latter thrust into the first-team fold by the sale of Larry Lloyd to Coventry City just days before the new season began. Paisley had been quick to shoot down his side being ranked as the bookmakers' favourites to win the First Division as 'ridiculous' before the trip to Moss Side and reaffirmed his view in the wake of the two-goal reversal.

Proof of the difficulty that the new Liverpool manager faced in attempting to expunge the stigma of Shankly was evident at Maine Road. Before the game, the stadium's announcer noted Shankly's appearance in the directors' box, which drew a warm ovation from the home crowd. His daily post-retirement exercise routine at Melwood had led to an awkwardness as players addressed their former taskmaster as 'boss' when greeted by him each morning. Shankly would jog around the training pitch with the squad, during which he would offer encouragement.

While Paisley never made any issue of Shankly's continued presence, he accepted the need for a hierarchal structure and requested that his former superior only visited Liverpool's West Derby base in the afternoon, once the players had finished their training routine and left. No ill feeling was expressed between the pair but the departed man removed any potential confusion by abandoning his visits to both Melwood and Anfield altogether. In November of that year, one Sunday newspaper misreported Shankly's self-imposed exile as an effective banishment from Liverpool. A photograph of him gleefully lighting Paisley's celebratory cigar after the latter had won the 1976 Manager of the Year award illustrated how insignificantly the story had altered their long-standing friendship but it still greatly infuriated the man now occupying the Anfield dugout.

Book was dealing with his own challenge of replacing the void left by Francis Lee's departure. Ahead of a Boxing Day trip to Anfield, the City manager signed Everton striker Joe Royle for £200,000. The towering marksman grew up in the Norris Green area of Liverpool, where his footballing allegiances have developed something of an urban myth. Royle's family were all staunch Evertonians but claims that he was a boyhood Manchester United fan are wide of the mark. His affinity with the Old Trafford club stemmed from the national mourning which followed the 1958 Munich air disaster that claimed the lives of 23 people, eight of them United players. Royle makes no secret of the fact that Bobby Charlton, one of the survivors, was his favourite player as a youngster but is adamant that his respect for the Red Devils never superseded his affection for the Toffees. 'It's a good line but it's never been totally true,' he says.

Breaking into the first team at Goodison Park, Royle became the club's youngest-ever debutant at the age of 16 and faced the onerous task of replacing fans' hero Alex Young, who had been dropped by Harry Catterick, for a game at Blackpool in January 1966. The backlash to Catterick's ruthless act had brutal consequences for the Everton manager as he was knocked to the floor when confronted by a group of between 30 and 40 of his own club's supporters in leaving Bloomfield Road.

Leading City's front line for the first time at Anfield was still a daunting prospect for Royle, who had fallen out of favour under Catterick's successor Billy Bingham despite registering 119 goals in 272 appearances. The three-hour turnaround in which his Christmas Eve move to Maine Road was sealed would seem minor compared to the breakneck speed at which most transfers are sewn up in the present day but with the registration deadline looming, time was very much of the essence for Royle and his new employers.

'They said, "Are you fit?"' he says.

'I said, "Well I'm physically fit but I haven't played in Everton's first team for a while."

'They said, "Good. We want you to meet us tomorrow in the Lord Nelson [Hotel] and we want you playing at Anfield on Saturday."'

Royle's previous experiences at Liverpool's home were something of a mixed bag; he had scored in Everton's 2-0 win in March 1970 en route to the club clinching the First Division championship, and repeated the feat to hand his side a similar lead in their next Merseyside derby eight months later, only for a 15-minute onslaught from the hosts to snatch maximum points. Any potential nerves he may have been feeling about a festive foray at Anfield were eased by his new manager's pre-match instructions. 'Tony Book gave an inspirational team talk,' he says. '[He said] "These are a great side. Everyone comes here to Liverpool and defends, and everyone loses. We're going to have a right go at them – so Dennis Tueart, you stay wide on the left. Mike Summerbee stay wide on the right and get crosses in. Don't worry too much about defending. Joe, you just stay up there and make sure we've always got a target. Colin Bell get in the box and we're going to have a right go at them." I was absolutely buzzing.'

Book's confidence had been helped by the dismal recent form of Paisley's side, who produced just one win from their previous eight league games and dropped to fourth place behind City, who were in a three-way fight with Everton and leaders Ipswich Town for top spot. The Liverpool manager accepted that the early hype claiming his team would romp to the championship by a ten-point margin had taken a psychological toll on them and added, 'We have no divine right to be at the top. But the title is there for the taking.'

When Book's players stepped out at Anfield, their aim of ending a winless run at the ground that had stretched back to 1953 fell away inside a 19-minute spell. Brian Hall struck first after John Toshack and Ian Callaghan combined in the build-up. Two minutes later, Toshack extended the lead with a stooping header from Steve Heighway's free kick. A self-inflicted wound compounded City's misery when Colin Bell gifted the architect of Liverpool's second goal with one of his own. The realisation that an already tough debut was becoming insurmountably more difficult had started to dawn on Royle.

'We came off at half-time and I'd touched the ball three times – all [for] kick-offs,' he says. 'That was my sort of introduction to Man City. It was a funny time. There were a lot of top players in the side. Asa Hartford, obviously, Mike Summerbee was still around, Colin Bell was awesome. Big Tommy Booth, Mike Doyle, all these players. You look at the side, it was the base of the side that nearly won the league a couple of seasons later. It wasn't an easy start and it certainly took me a while to settle down. I didn't score for a while because I'd been fit but not match fit. But certainly, Anfield was a raw baptism for someone, particularly [as] an ex-Everton player, coming into a game [there] was always going to be hard.'

City fared little better after half-time as Joe Corrigan spared their blushes with acrobatic saves from Phil Neil and Hall, who completed a comfortable home win in the 72nd minute. An impressive lobbed finish by Bell, deceptively dipping under Ray Clemence's crossbar, became an afterthought as Book's side trudged out of Anfield's floodlit glare.

Liverpool's return to winning ways restored their position atop the First Division for the first time in six weeks while City dropped down to sixth in the table with only a point still separating the teams. Paisley shook off the early problems of Shankly's legacy by ending his debut season as runners-up, two points behind champions Derby. Book's full managerial bow at Maine Road had yielded a credible eighth place but crucially five points off their north-west counterparts.

With solid starts under their respective belts, Merseyside and Manchester's ascended men returned for the following campaign with success firmly in their sights. City let the veteran Mike Summerbee join Burnley for £25,000 and reinvested the proceeds in the £200,000 signing of Sunderland defender Dave Watson. Fellow England international Alan Ball was expected to join him, with speculation that either Rodney Marsh or Dennis Tueart would be sacrificed to facilitate the World Cup winner's arrival.

Much like Ball's proposed move from Arsenal, City's title challenge also petered out fairly quickly as a promoted Manchester United assumed the role of keeping pace with Liverpool in the battle for the First Division. Their local rivals sat in seventh place when they prepared to take on the league leaders on 27 December, just 24 hours after an 18-game unbeaten stretch in all competitions had been ended by Leeds United on home soil. That impressive run of form had been put together during another spell of transition, with captain Marsh joining Tampa Bay Rowdies in the growing North American Soccer League (NASL). But Colin Bell's knee injury at the end of the previous season threatened to hit City the hardest. 'He was irreplaceable really,' says Joe Royle. 'Whoever we signed, we thought it was going to be a hard one [to overcome].' Steering the club through the precarious period won Book the distinction of November's Manager of the Month award.

Paul Power was under no illusions of the task ahead in his first Anfield appearance. The Openshaw-born midfielder had grown up idolising City's holy trinity of Bell, Francis Lee and Mike Summerbee over the previous decade but been something of a late developer professionally; earning a law degree at Leeds Polytechnic before signing full-time with his boyhood heroes. Earlier in the season he had made his senior debut as a substitute against Leicester City before making a full bow in a defeat to Aston Villa the following weekend.

'You always knew that you were in for a tough time when you visited Anfield in particular. You were in for a tough time when we played them at Maine Road as well because they had fantastic players,' he says. 'They always had good strikers who made a good partnership and then they'd have other players like Steve Heighway who'd create chances for them. When these players drifted away, they always seemed to be able to buy top players from [across] the divisions, experienced players. When you played against Liverpool, you knew you were playing against men: experienced footballers like Tommy Smith, and Jimmy Case to a lesser extent.'

Taking the place of the injured Peter Barnes, Power encountered a Liverpool midfield containing polar opposites. At 33, Ian Callaghan was showing little signs of slowing down and foiled his opposite number's attempts to fire in a cross after beating three players in succession with the score still goalless early in the second half.

Going toe-to-toe with a player 11 years the winger's junior proved a more Herculean task to negotiate. 'Ian was honest, a little bit like Steve Coppell at Man United,' he says. 'If you went past him, you knew that he was going to chase you because he had that great sort of attitude. You just didn't get past Jimmy Case because if the ball went past him you didn't go past, or if I went past him the ball didn't go past. Never the two went past together. The word that I would describe playing at Anfield was intimidating, but not just the players. Originally it was Tommy Smith but then it was Phil Neal and Jimmy Case so it didn't matter who you came up against, the players were quite intimidating on my side of the pitch. Some players would experience the word "fear" but I'd definitely say that the atmosphere was intimidating – but not just the players, the crowd as well.'

Book was full of admiration for Callaghan and Kevin Keegan after Peter Cormack's first goal of the season on the hour handed Liverpool a timely festive gift by pouncing on his side's failed attempts to clear their lines before sliding the ball past Joe Corrigan. The City manager praised the pair as 'world-class' players following their respective performances against his side, whose already dim hopes of an outside shot at the First Division title were effectively killed off.

Solace came in the form of a second League Cup Final in the space of three years on 28 February 1976. Goals from Peter Barnes and a Dennis Tueart bicycle kick helped City to a 2-1 win over Newcastle United that saw Book become the first person to win the trophy as a player and manager. Both inside Wembley and at the subsequent homecoming, supporters of Manchester's blue half marked their first piece of silverware in six years by breaking into full-throated renditions of 'You'll Never Walk Alone'. Given Liverpool's synonymy with the song created by Rodgers and Hammerstein, and made famous by Gerry Marsden, the sight of City fans performing it may be a puzzling sight to modern-day observers. But the terrace anthem was as much a staple among the Maine Road faithful in the 1970s as it had become with The Kop's swaying masses and remained part of their matchday repertoire until the midway point of the following decade.

City's post-Wembley form became the definition of 'after the Lord Mayor's show', with just three wins from their next league outings before taking on a Liverpool team whose assault on the championship had led to just two defeats from 16 games since the turn of the year. Bob Paisley's side were also fighting on dual fronts after booking their place in the UEFA Cup Final with a 2-1 aggregate win over Barcelona. An Easter Monday meeting on Moss Side still became a must-win affair for the visitors with Queens Park Rangers level-pegging them heading into their final games of the First Division season. Mike Doyle, City's newly installed captain, faced a difficult afternoon up against David Fairclough and on one occasion practically lifted the shirt off his back late in the first half trying to contain him. The teenager would play a crucial role in the eventual 73rd-minute breakthrough after sprinting past Peter Barnes down the right-hand side. The recently crowned PFA Young Player of the Year was further tormented by Fairclough, who turned him twice in addition to team-mate Alan Oakes before angling a cross for Steve Heighway to sweep home the opener.

Provider turned poacher in the game's closing moments as Fairclough continued to run rings around Doyle in a prelude to a left-footed shot which beat Joe Corrigan with the help of a slight deflection. A minute later, he doubled that tally from a Kevin Keegan tee-up to angle a 14-yard shot with his right foot into the net. The Cantril Farm-born youngster was already beginning to gain recognition as an impactful player, often from the substitutes' bench. His place in Anfield history was secured the following season when he scored a decisive third goal just ten minutes after coming on in the latter stages of Liverpool's European Cup quarter-final encounter with Saint-Etienne. A surging run and finish in front of The Kop helped his side through to the last four of Europe's elite club competition and was christened by ITV commentator Gerald Sinstadt with the immortal words, 'Supersub, once again!'

Fairclough's relentless drive was picked up in Book's post-match assessment as he lamented the perils of teams taking their foot off the pedal against the champions-elect. 'You can never let up against Liverpool,' he said. 'They play for 90 minutes.'

Paisley's side would need every fibre of their being to clinch the title in their final game of the season at Wolverhampton Wanderers. QPR's narrow lead carried wide-ranging permutations for Liverpool's trip to Molineux, where anything other than a defeat or a 2-2 draw would be enough to take what Bill Shankly once described as 'the bread and butter' back to Merseyside. Steve Kindon's first-half opener had boosted the Hoops' bid for their first crown, but a late 13-minute onslaught saw the Anfield club home and dry en route to further success in the UEFA Cup Final against Club Brugge. Broadened horizons had eradicated doubts about Paisley's suitability to management, including his own, while myopia was beginning to reign supreme in Manchester.

Dizzy Heights

AS LIVERPOOL'S league and European double drew admiring glances from far and wide, Peter Swales continued to navel gaze. Manchester City's eighth-place finish, 17 points adrift of the new champions, could not dim the optimism swirling around following their League Cup success. But instead of looking westbound on the M62, their chairman remained fixated on what was happening in the same direction of the A56.

Swales's devotion to his City was intertwined with a desperation to eclipse Manchester United. Repeated vows to make them 'the number one club in the country' were underpinned by a personal mission to put one over on 'the rags', a pejorative term still actively used by some supporters in reference to their counterparts at Old Trafford. Tony Book attempted to fulfil his superior's bold ambitions by drafting in one-time United hero Brian Kidd from Arsenal for £100,000 during the summer. Double that figure was spent at Anfield for another frontman formerly behind enemy lines as David Johnson arrived from Ipswich Town. From an early age, the England international had been a devout Liverpool fan but slipped through the club's net and was enlisted by Everton. Bill Shankly attempted to right that wrong with regular attempts to lure Johnson across Stanley Park. Four years spent at Portman Road saw him help usher in a new age for strikers as Bobby Robson paired him with Trevor Whymark in an upwardly mobile attack.

Johnson's recent employers would form half of Liverpool's sternest opposition in their quest to reclaim the First Division.

The other came from a familiar foe, as City put together a six-game unbeaten opening to the 1976/77 season alongside a 1-0 win in the opening leg of their UEFA Cup first round tie with Juventus. A League Cup exit to former manager Ron Saunders's Aston Villa provided the sole blemish in that promising early run. Liverpool's own impressive start to their title defence had been the only barrier to City occupying the summit in the opening weeks of the campaign. But on an afternoon when Paisley's charges lost at Newcastle United, their closest challengers also were hit by a 3-1 defeat at home to United, allowing their local rivals to level-peg them on nine points. Briefly, Manchester's two clubs could claim domestic superiority as they fought it out for pole position before the Old Trafford side found itself playing second fiddle to Book's side, who usurped them with a midweek draw away to Everton.

Paisley's side went one better against their local neighbours by running out 3-1 winners on the same afternoon that City endured a second stalemate, this time at home to Queens Park Rangers. Both clubs were forced to take a rare backseat in the coming weeks as a late equaliser by Leeds United knocked Liverpool out of top spot while City fell to seventh with a 1-0 reversal against fellow title rivals Ipswich.

Maine Road still had plenty to shout about after going nine matches undefeated in the build-up to a 29 December visit from the Reds, whose return to the top was only interrupted by back-to-back defeats earlier in the month. Home fans were already dreaming of equalling the leaders' points tally. Some hoped City might go one better by racking up a 3-0 scoreline that would edge them ahead of their north-west neighbours. Inclement weather had laid siege to not only those plans but also the English football calendar for the first time since the Big Freeze of 1962/63, postponing no fewer than 19 matches and threatening to claim the top-of-the-table clash. Playing on a snow-laden pitch became the least of the visitors' worries as Kevin Keegan was ruled out with a shoulder injury after colliding with Peter Shilton in a 4-0 win over Stoke City two days prior.

The treacherous surface, combined with high winds, commanded unique approaches from themselves and Manchester City. Joe Royle led the line in a pair of white trainers not dissimilar to the footwear worn by ex-Everton team-mate Alan Ball and was well-versed on the perils of playing in two of the most-feared weather conditions.

Liverpool's forward-thinking approach on the pitch had been concocted by Paisley and his cohorts in the club's Boot Room, a pokey broom cupboard in a corridor of Anfield's Main Stand that doubled up as its fabled nerve centre, and guaranteed their preparedness for every eventuality, as Callaghan remembers fondly. 'We had special boots to play on frosty pitches and even when you got transferred, you couldn't take the boots – you had to leave them at Anfield!', he says. 'Somebody else would get into them so they were always at Anfield. You didn't take them if you got transferred somewhere.'

Bespoke footwear choices did little to stop both sets of players struggling to handle the slush underfoot, with many unable to stay upright while maintaining the core movements associated with competitive football. Royle's decision to sport trainers had initially favoured City as they took a 35th minute lead when the striker prodded home the ball after Dennis Tueart's cross had been headed back across the penalty area by Phil Thompson and wreaked havoc in the Liverpool defence. A game of limited chances appeared to be falling in City's favour and with it the chance to make inroads on a first title since the 1967/68 season.

In the final minute, however, a moment of tragicomedy gave Liverpool an unlikely lifeline in avoiding a fourth straight away defeat. Callaghan's attempt to float the ball into the penalty area for a lurking David Fairclough was mishit but still produced its desired effect. City's sturdy rearguard of Dave Watson and Joe Corrigan found themselves caught in the crossfire; the goalkeeper rushed 15 yards off his line to intercept the delivery, only to see his defensive ally meet it first and head the ball into a gaping net. A moment of pure chance had kept Paisley's side in the box seat for the title. 'I suppose with frost-bound pitches and two good teams, anything can happen,' says Callaghan. 'Thank god we got the goal.' Royle is still unsure about the sequence of events that saw City surrendering their narrow lead in the closing seconds. 'Dave Watson [is] still one of the best English centre-halves I've seen and Joe certainly improved so much from a young keeper to be an England keeper. They'd both been magnificent,' he says. 'I don't know whether Joe shouted or what he shouted but Dave Watson back-headed it with Joe coming out further than he should be and it was 1-1.'

Whatever the reasons for the miscommunication, Peter Swales later pinpointed Watson's own goal as the single moment which had cost City the championship – something that midfielder Paul Power admits was far from out of character with the club's overbearing chairman. 'It doesn't surprise me that Peter Swales had said that because he was Man City through and through and he was very critical,' he says. 'I can imagine if Peter Swales had been my father, he'd have given me a right bollocking for bringing home a poor homework or something like that. He was always critical, never encouraging nearly enough.

'I was captain at City for about ten years when he was the chairman. He only spoke to me about three times and all those were bollockings! But when you know the dressing room – and Peter Swales rarely came into the dressing room – and the type of player that Dave Watson was, it was only going to be an honest mistake. He was a top, top professional and sometimes you make mistakes. Sometimes you get away with them and other times the consequences are more severe. It just so happened that he paid the penalty for that one.'

Watson would redeem his last-gasp misfortune shortly before City's corresponding fixture, four months later, by scoring the winning goal against Ipswich. After that game, Bobby Robson told Tony Book, 'If we don't win it, I hope you do.' His own side had prospered from Liverpool's involvement in the European Cup semi-final by nudging ahead of them on goal difference in midweek having played a game more. But City were far from out of contention with only three points separating them from the summit. Before the trip to Merseyside, Book admitted that a Liverpool team fast becoming both feared and admired also represented a blueprint for his own charges. 'They're a machine. They have a pattern of play which is outstanding,' he said. 'This is what I'm trying to build here, I promise you. Liverpool are a model for any team.' In their second of three games over the Easter weekend, and boosted by a 2-1 win over Leeds the day before, City ventured to Anfield with visions of stating their title credentials.

Hundreds of would-be matchgoers had seen the turnstile doors shut ten minutes before the start of a genuine four-pointer. Those privileged enough to be inside the stadium were treated to a close-run affair as Brian Kidd and Tommy Smith were both reprimanded for exchanging pleasantries in the early stages while Liverpool enjoyed the lion's share of chances. Only smart defending from Book's side frustrated them as Corrigan had to tip the ball over The Kop's crossbar with his right hand after Jimmy Case had driven at goal in the opening minutes. City would also be thankful for Tommy Booth's interception to thwart a long-range effort from Emlyn Hughes. Two minutes from half-time, Liverpool turned the screw as the visitors attempted to avert the danger of Steve Heighway's corner. Case hooked the ball at the byline into Hughes's path for a flick-on to Kevin Keegan, who outjumped Watson to power his header beyond Corrigan's outstretched hand.

The visitors' challenge heading into the break was worsened by Royle picking up an ankle strain which saw him replaced by Peter Barnes in the 50th minute. A fightback ensued when Ged Keegan won a corner with a deflected right-footed shot. Barnes's outswinging set piece from the left-hand side was headed clear by Smith but only as far as Ged Keegan, who turned his opponent and threaded the ball back out wide to the winger for a cross into Booth. City's captain found himself sandwiched between Ray Kennedy, Bill Shankly's final signing, and Joey Jones as the ball broke for Asa Hartford, who flashed a shot goalwards. Hughes succeeded in blocking the initial effort on the line but could not stop Brian Kidd from following up to snatch an equaliser.

In the Anfield Road End, an unmistakable sound of Maine Road started to chime. Helen Turner had become a part of City folklore for her distinctive beehive hairstyle and handing Corrigan a sprig of lucky heather before each game. The previous year, she had been invited on to the Wembley pitch to celebrate with their triumphant squad after the League Cup Final. Her trademark, though, was a large brass bell which was rung during matches whenever the Blues needed a lift. More than musical encouragement would be required in the following minute when Liverpool retook the lead. At the restart, Steve Heighway rolled the ball to Kevin Keegan, who sent it out wide for Case. His pass to Terry McDermott was intercepted but the midfielder was able to win it back before crashing a 20-yard shot against the crossbar. Watson attempted to hook clear Case's rebounded effort as far as Heighway to control the ball and drill it into Corrigan's top right-hand corner.

'They wouldn't probably have expected us to get the equaliser but the reaction to conceding was a great one,' says Paul Power. 'I always remember when we used to play Nottingham Forest and if they'd scored against us, when we kicked off the only thing that Brian Clough always used to shout [was], "Get the ball back!" because he never wanted teams to switch off when they'd conceded a goal. I don't know whether the Liverpool staff encouraged the players to do that or whether they just took it upon themselves but it doesn't surprise me at all.'

Joe Royle, now watching from the sidelines, felt that the 60-second turnaround had ended his team's chance for the title. 'It was a seminal moment,' he says. 'The 1-1 would've seen us [finish] as champions. I said then that it cost us the championship only drawing but there was plenty of time afterwards if we're being realistic about it.'

Beaten yet still unbowed, City went on to win their next three games to maintain a touching distance with Liverpool. As domestic and European glory beckoned for the reigning champions, who had the chance to clinch an unprecedented treble after booking their place in the finals of both the European Cup and FA Cup, the latter coming in successive semi-final clashes with Everton at Maine Road. Two points kept the sides apart heading into April's final weekend, when the Reds and Ipswich went head-to-head as the league's top two sides. Only goal difference would separate them and City if both teams won.

A 4-0 reversal at Derby swung the pendulum away from the underdogs but with a game in hand still to play, Tony Book was unwilling to give up the ghost. 'There's no way I am going to concede that the First Division championship is lost,' he said. 'We've made it very hard for ourselves following that heavy defeat at Derby, but until it is proved mathematically impossible to catch Liverpool, I refuse to give up the chase.'

A week later, City's 1-1 draw with Aston Villa kept them in contention for the championship. Manchester United did their neighbour's domestic aspirations little favour by faltering to a one-goal loss at Anfield.

Three points from the final four matches would now be enough for Bob Paisley to claim successive crowns. A draw with QPR kept the gap with City down to two heading into a crucial midweek round of fixtures. The leaders took on relegation strugglers Coventry while their title rivals entertained Everton, where anything other than a win would see their title bid falter. But Hughes, Liverpool's captain and the newly crowned Football Writers' Association (FWA) Footballer of the Year, was not fixating on what might happen with their local adversaries' trip to Moss Side. 'We don't care what happens at Maine Road,' he told the press beforehand. 'We aim to win the title by our own efforts. We've got where we are on our own and will finish the season the same way.'

A carnival atmosphere greeted City's penultimate match of the season as their players kicked plastic footballs into the home crowd in recognition of the part they had played throughout the title chase. Festivities were taken up a notch when Kidd slotted home from Royle's cross. News of Liverpool's stalemate at Highfield Road gave them hope of taking the domestic duel down to the wire, only for Mick Lyons's 77th minute equaliser to see them evaporate. Even a perennially optimistic Book had to finally concede defeat, saying, 'I must confess that the championship seems over now.'

Another goalless draw at home to West Ham United delivered the first in a potential hat-trick of trophies to Anfield before a defeat on the final day at Bristol City saw Book's side finish one point behind the champions. Liverpool's eased-up end to the campaign may have been a different prospect had Colin Bell's injury lay-off not befallen Maine Road just 12 months earlier. Paul Power feels their dearth of quality in the absence of 'Nijinsky' became evident against a Liverpool squad that was brimming with it. 'I think Liverpool had a stronger squad than us probably. Maybe that's the reason that they ended up winning the league by one point,' he says.

'They had a more complete squad so if they did get any injuries, I think they always had good subs to bring on or good people in the squad who could make a little bit of a difference. Maybe we didn't have the depth of squad that we needed if we got injuries to key players. But when you think of the sort of experience that Liverpool had, if it was Ray Kennedy, Terry McDermott and players like that, they were unbelievable. Whatever department, Liverpool were always strong, and they were all men. There were no timid players in the Liverpool side. There was no psychological weakness. They were all mentally tough. All team players as well. We had one or two individuals in our team, which wouldn't make us as strong a unit as them, but they all worked hard for each other – as they do now. It must be a Liverpool trait.'

A winning habit had again started to form on Merseyside, but it did come with the occasional setback. The FA Cup Final was one of those instances as Liverpool's treble bid was downgraded as Manchester United took a 2-1 lead in a breathless four-minute period at Wembley where all three of the game's goals had been scored. Heading to Rome for the European Cup Final against Borussia Mönchengladbach, Paisley had a member of the City clan sitting alongside. Stuart Hall, a lifelong fan and BBC broadcaster, had struck up a healthy rapport with Anfield backroom dating back to Bill Shankly's time. When plans to film a behind-the-scenes documentary on the club's biggest game to date were kyboshed by authorities in the Eternal City, Paisley hatched an elaborate plan to smuggle Hall into the Stadio Olimpico's dressing room. Each member of the squad carried a piece of his equipment with them into the stadium while the raconteur was handed a number 14 shirt which allowed him to sit on the coaching benches as Liverpool's 13-year wait to conquer the zenith of European club football was finally ended.

Finishing behind the new kings of the Continent in the league saw City refuse to diminish their own accomplishment during the summer of the Silver Jubilee. 'Pride in battle' became a long-standing motto on the club's reimagined crest during the mid-1990s but the mantra first came to be 20 years earlier with the inclusion of 'First Division Runners-Up 1976/77' on their shirts for the new campaign. Peter Swales also sought to capitalise on their narrow shortfall by enlisting John Stapleton, another BBC broadcaster and dyed-in-the-wool City supporter, to chart the club's highs and lows for a feature on the current affairs programme *Nationwide* titled 'Saturday's Heroes'. The access offered the wider public a detailed understanding about life at Maine Road, with staff at all levels interviewed during the filming process. A promotional photo captured the club's entire workforce standing outside the stadium's main entrance in a variety of poses and Swales front and centre. Mick Channon's £300,000 arrival from Southampton was another sign of an ambitious new era.

Liverpool had set about replacing like-for-like even before their European Cup triumph in with the signing of Partick Thistle defender Alan Hansen for £100,000 signifying a changing of the guard as a long-term successor to Tommy Smith, who had scored in the 3-1 win over Gladbach. Kevin Keegan's plans to seek pastures new had been outlined to the Anfield hierarchy at the start of that 1976/77 season and he sealed a £500,000 switch to Hamburg just nine days after the glory of Rome. Birmingham City striker Trevor Francis was touted as the man to take his place, having been a regular target since the start of the decade.

But the new England international's questionable fitness record had deterred Bill Shankly from taking the plunge and similarly saw Paisley waver on signing him.

Keegan's heir to the number seven shirt was another player on the Reds' long-term radar in Kenny Dalglish. The Celtic forward had first been touted when the club's now departed talisman was preparing to make a break with Merseyside just 12 months prior and he moved for a British transfer record of £440,000. After drawing a blank in the Charity Shield against Manchester United, Dalglish went on to score six times in his next seven matches as The Kop's new messiah filled the void of his predecessor.

But Paisley's target of a third First Division title in as many seasons had miscalculated the threat posed by Nottingham Forest, who had emerged as early favourites for the title. A 2-0 defeat at Old Trafford saw Brian Clough's side briefly usurped by City on a superior goal difference. Four weeks later, Liverpool had moved back up to second place as they aimed to close the gap with a trip to Maine Road, whose hosts had suffered a 2-1 reversal to the new champions-elect. On 29 October, the two members of the chasing pack met with Paisley in a quietly confident mood. 'We've had some good results at Maine Road in the past few years,' he told reporters. 'I hope for another one tomorrow.' Those hopes came to fruition shortly before the half-hour mark when Dalglish threaded a pass that beat Mike Doyle and City's offside trap to allow David Fairclough to squeeze a shot underneath Joe Corrigan.

The *Daily Mirror*'s Frank McGhee later reported that Book had delivered a half-time rocket to his players which 'blistered the paint off the dressing room walls' as they were warned about the dire consequences of a likely fourth defeat in five league matches – a claim which Joe Royle contests. 'Tony's a nice fella [and] a good guy, I think that's indisputable,' he says. 'He was never really an angry man. He would sometimes be angry in training. You would know on Monday morning if he joined in training that he had a stare about him at times, but I can't remember him every being a cup thrower or a vicious swearer, or anything like that. He'd have his word, he'd get his point over but you could see he was angry rather than him showing he was angry. Ian MacFarlane and Bill Taylor [his assistants] were certainly more vocal at half-time.'

McGhee also alleged that Paisley had remarked from the dugout, 'The only thing that can save City is if the floodlights don't work.'

Those purported words came back to haunt him in the 60th minute when Channon's flick-on from a Peter Barnes corner evaded Joey Jones's clutches, allowing Brian Kidd to follow up with a shot on the turn at the far post. Dalglish's prolific early-season form had tailed off and led to a run of one goal in his previous eight games. He spurned a chance to break both his barren record and the stalemate when Jimmy Case nutmegged Barnes and played a ball into Fairclough, who let it run through for Dalglish. His effort beat Corrigan but clattered against the post before Dave Watson cleared his lines to deny Fairclough any chance of converting the follow-up. City's grip tightened just ten minutes after equalising when Watson shook off a challenge by Dalglish before turning Case and floating a ball over the top for Channon. Emlyn Hughes could not stop the striker, who also warded off Jones's run to narrow the angle and beat Ray Clemence at his near post with a shot across goal.

Hughes would play a further part in Liverpool's downfall when his venturing higher up the pitch exposed their defensive line, allowing Barnes to dart forward. An interception from Hansen took the ball out of the winger's path but was hoovered up by Royle to shoot on the edge of the D after checking inside Jones. The striker's last goal in City colours was celebrated with a Christ the Redeemer pose before being mobbed by team-mates Power, Gary Owen and Kenny Clements.

The humiliation was almost laced with farce in the final minutes as Doyle's lung-busting run was curtailed by Clemence some 30 yards from his line. On the ground, the defender had managed to nudge the ball towards an empty goalmouth. Maine Road held its collective breath before the ambitious effort trickled half an inch wide of the target. 'If that had gone in, they'd be showing it on TV all season,' Doyle grumbled to the press afterwards.

Personal frustrations aside, his goal that never was would ultimately have contributed little to City's points tally, with their position in fourth already consolidated, although it may have moved them into joint-third in the First Division's list of highest-scoring teams. The win over Liverpool had taken the goal return for Book's side to 24 while the second-placed visitors had the lowest outlay of the top six sides with 16. City's manager, though, still viewed the fallen champions as the benchmark. 'If we had gone down as we looked like doing, Liverpool would have been five points in front of us,' he said. 'And you don't pull back five points on the Liverpools of this world.' Clawing back Forest was proving just as difficult at Anfield, where a six-point shortfall and a resurgent Everton occupying second place confronted their side when the calendar year ended.

Bill Shankly had once declared, 'If you've got three Scots in your side, you've got a chance of winning something,' and the man who replaced him started to come around to that way of thinking. On 10 January 1978, Paisley made Graeme Souness the most expensive player to be transferred between two English clubs when he joined from Middlesbrough. The £352,000 fee broke the previous record set by Joe Jordan's move from Leeds to Manchester United a week earlier, for £2,000 less.

Liverpool's strong Highland connection dated back to the club's formation in the late 19th century and had continued through the decades. Shankly himself included no fewer than three of his compatriots in each squad for all except one of 15 seasons spent at the helm. With Hansen, Dalglish and now Souness all signed in the space of eight months, Liverpool had not only preserved its Scottish links but also recruited players who would go on to form the team's spine for the best part of a decade. The trio were still powerless to prevent a League Cup Final defeat by Forest and the club languishing in the First Division's also-ran positions by mid-March, two places below City.

A month earlier, the previous season's runners-up appeared to be the only team capable of challenging Clough's unassailable dominance after moving into second and within four points of the leaders with a 1-0 win over Everton courtesy of a Brian Kidd goal. Book's accomplishment had again come in trying times as Dennis Tueart followed in Rodney Marsh's footsteps with a move to the NASL, turning out for the New York Cosmos alongside Franz Beckenbauer, Johan Neeskens and Carlos Alberto.

City's momentum did not last long and saw them slip into fifth at the end of April. On 1 May, they came up against a Liverpool side that had booked a second European Cup Final appearance and nudged ahead of Everton in the league's best of the rest standings. Paisley's players started limbering up for their Wembley meeting with Club Brugge as David Fairclough took advantage of the ball rebounding off Dave Watson to float a cross at the byeline in for Dalglish to head home. The one-goal deficit at half-time was only made possible by Joe Corrigan saving an effort from Jimmy Case.

Liverpool's ascendancy grew after the interval when they were gifted a penalty after Watson's short pass back to Corrigan allowed Fairclough to steal in before being brought down by the goalkeeper. Phil Neal dispatched from 12 yards before Dalglish's second of the evening arrived barely a minute later. A slick attacking move saw Terry McDermott chip the ball over Willie Donachie for Case to bound towards and cut back for Kevin Keegan's successor, who trapped the ball with his right foot before drilling the ball with his left just inside the penalty area into Corrigan's top-left corner. Two minutes from time, Dalglish claimed only his first of two league hat-tricks as he converted a narrow-angled pass from Fairclough. The previous summer's marquee signing took the headlines but Souness's influence on proceedings at Anfield was already becoming obvious.

The following month, during Scotland's failed World Cup campaign, the combative midfielder would be denigrated by international team-mate Archie Gemmill as a 'chocolate soldier', as in 'if he was made of chocolate, he would eat himself'. But

City midfielder Paul Power, who would be commissioned by the PFA in later life to produce a landmark report on youth development within the English game, saw Souness as a perfect hybrid of enforcer and architect. 'When I did some work on this report with Dave Sexton, he used to have a term for players: they were either soldiers or artists,' he says. 'I think I was just a soldier [because] I'd get the ball and I'd give it to Trevor Francis, who was the artist and would score the goals for us. There aren't that many players who were both a soldier and an artist, but I think Graeme Souness was one. He was certainly able to stop things happening and could make things happen as well. He was as much a thorn in our side as Fairclough.'

Further proof of Souness's handiwork was on show just nine days after the rout of City when, at Wembley, his exquisite control of a Brugge clearance saw Dalglish score the European Cup Final's decisive goal. A year after missing out on a multiple trophy haul, retaining their Continental crown marked a treble of sorts for Liverpool, with the Charity Shield and UEFA Super Cup, won against Keegan's Hamburg, added to the collection.

Success did little to alter Paisley's plans to replenish his ranks, with the remaining pillars of Shankly's first great team finally moving on. Tommy Smith and Ian Callaghan linked up with former team-mate John Toshack, now player-manager of Swansea City, in the early months of the 1978/79 season while Joey Jones returned to Wrexham, having not played for the previous nine months. Replacing the Welshman at left-back was Alan Kennedy, who had arrived from Newcastle United in a £330,000 deal. The defender's start to life on Merseyside was hardly ideal with a below-par display during the First Division opener with QPR typified by knocking off a policeman's helmet with a miskick. A quick introduction to Paisley's dry wit was administered to Liverpool's summer recruit at half-time when his manager reflected on the 45-minute display with the words, 'I think they shot the wrong Kennedy.'

City's only quantifiable success in the previous season was ending the Reds' five-year grip on the Central League, a competition consisting of reserve teams from clubs in the north of England and the Midlands, but they were also laying down a marker to move beyond a bygone era after finishing fourth in the previous First Division campaign. Mike Doyle, one of only three players still at the club from Joe Mercer's early years, joined Stoke for £50,000 with defender Paul Futcher arriving in his place on a £350,000 price tag and equally weighty expectations.

The Chester native was already a fledgling England under-21 international and widely expected to become the new Bobby Moore when he arrived from Luton Town. He hailed from a distinctly footballing family with brother Ron, a striker, joining him in trading Kenilworth Road for Moss Side while elder sibling Graham had a brief stint with their hometown club. The dynasty extended into the next three decades with Paul's son enjoying a 13-year spell with teams across the Football League's pyramid while nephew Danny Murphy became a regular fixture in Liverpool's midfield in the early 2000s.

Attempts to sell ex-Liverpool striker Keegan on a return to the north-west failed to materialise, as did a pursuit of QPR midfielder Gerry Francis. One high-profile player eventually arrived in the form of the £100,000 capture of Colin Viljoen, who had helped Ipswich reach the previous season's FA Cup Final. The South Africa-born midfielder did not feature in the Wembley showpiece and similarly missed City's start to the new league season with an ankle injury. Tony Book's side drew their opening two matches before a visit of Liverpool. Although reigning European champions and the First Division's early table toppers, they had not won on Moss Side since May 1976. Travelling supporters had confessed that it was among their club's more difficult away fixtures to BBC commentator Barry Davies, who added, 'They also asked me, incidentally, where the European Cup Final is to be held this year.'

'Going to Manchester City and particularly Maine Road was a difficult place to get any result,' says Kennedy. 'It was a big pitch, a very patriotic crowd. They were very much behind the team and City had some decent players. I remember watching them in the early to mid '70s with Franny Lee, Mike Summerbee and people like that, and I always thought they were a particularly good team. They were a good team to watch. They might be a little bit flamboyant, but I always felt as though you were going to get a game. If you caught City on a good day, they could turn anybody over. But I have to say whenever I went there as a Liverpool player, we always felt confident about getting a result.'

Fuelling the visitors' belief of ending a two-year hoodoo was the disruption caused to Futcher's acclimatisation of his big-money switch to Maine Road. His first two appearances had been helped by the presence of Dave Watson alongside, but a stomach muscle problem ruled out the England international against the Reds. Even with the experienced Tommy Booth partnering him in defence, the fair-haired defender faced a potential baptism of fire against the visitors' attack spearheaded by Kenny Dalglish. Early in the first half, both he and City surpassed expectations by creating a series of chances through midfielder Gary Owen, who was notably denied his own sight at goal by Kennedy's well-timed interception.

Barely quarter of an hour in, Terry McDermott launched a cross-field ball that allowed Dalglish to pick off Booth and let Souness run through the vacant space to beat Kenny Clements and side-foot a half-volley past Joe Corrigan. City's efforts to match Liverpool finally told in the 23rd minute through a well-worked move from Paul Power, who exchanged passes with Mick Channon to beat the offside trap before drawing Ray Clemence and squaring to Brian Kidd to slide the ball home after his initial touch had taken the ball away from goal.

'I was a sort of midfield player that would make runs from deep and Liverpool were a different class at holding the line,' says Power. 'If a player had time on the ball, then they would drop so that there wasn't as much space in behind them. If our player was under pressure from one of their players, they'd hold the line and invariably players that made runs from deep would run offside. They had it off to a fine art, condensing the game and working together as a back four but occasionally there'd maybe be somebody who'd come along and break the system down. It was probably as much as a good through-ball and then when I got through, I just had a little look inside and Kiddo was there on his own. In fact when I crossed it, I just expected him to slot it in with his left foot. But he took a touch and it looked as if he'd lost the opportunity to score but he's a top goalscorer, Kiddo, so he slotted it in.'

Levelling up lasted all of 12 minutes as Liverpool continued to step up the pace and retook the lead when Steve Heighway sent McDermott clear with a pass from the halfway line. The midfielder's touch played the ball inside to Ray Kennedy for a first-time finish. From then on, City became their own worst enemy with Asa Hartford and Kidd both wasting a succession of chances.

A coming together between Owen and Alan Kennedy led to the City player coming off worse but saw the free kick awarded Liverpool's way. Emlyn Hughes's ensuing set piece shifted play down the hosts' right-hand side, culminating in Dalglish helping on a McDermott cross into the path of Souness to record a brace with a left-footed shot past an advancing Corrigan. 'I'll tell you what, on this form they wouldn't be a bad bet for the Grand National,' chirped Davies from the Maine Road gantry. Kennedy was again involved in Liverpool's fourth when he skewed a received pass from Souness. Unlike his mishap against QPR, the ball broke kindly for Dalglish to run on to before skipping past Corrigan and slotting home – an act that the full-back attributes to his team-mate's ingenuity rather than a slice of fortune.

'I think if you look at Dalglish and other players like that, they're watching the ball all the time and they're watching players and they're looking at opportunities to get into a position where the player can't mark him,' he says. 'He's always between two players if you know what I mean. You look at the way City were lined up and you think yes, on paper they were a good team and had good players and established players. But Dalglish was just a master of finding a way of sort of like getting beyond them and scoring goals. I have to say City in terms of how they played against us, it was only in '81 when they beat us at Anfield that they showed what they were capable of against us. The other times they never seemed to have enough about them. I wasn't disappointed because I was playing for Liverpool. I was quite happy that my job had been done and was to keep the winger, whoever was playing on the right-hand side, to keep him quiet.'

Barry Davies remained in fine form as he summarised events of the five-goal affair at the final whistle, saying of Liverpool, 'To call them a machine, really, is an insult – unless you're talking about a Rolls Royce.' The BBC commentator credited their below-strength hosts for 'doing well to stay in there … They weren't disgraced. I can't think of any other team who would have held Liverpool on this sort of form.' Her Majesty's press were far less charitable as *The Guardian*'s John Roberts signed off his match report by suggesting that sadism might have seen Liverpool send on David Fairclough to punish City further but argued that *Coronation Street* star Len Fairclough, portrayed by the Liverpool-born Peter Adamson, 'may have proved equally devastating'. Tony Book took no shame in describing the performance from Bob Paisley's side as 'out of this world'.

Relations were far less cordial when the City manager took his troops to Anfield on 18 November for a clash which was as ill-tempered as the rain which battered the stadium. Both sets of players were involved in niggardly incidents with Tommy Booth booked for flinging mud at Jimmy Case while Ray Kennedy also received a caution for charging over to referee Ken Walmsley, almost flooring him, for giving a free kick against him for a foul on Peter Barnes. The Blackpool official was forced to intervene in a flare-up between Souness and Kidd, which Phil Thompson followed by jokingly sizing up an unimpressed Barnes. Alan Kennedy also failed to find favour with Walmsley, who waved away a penalty appeal for a trip from Kenny Clements which was adjudged to be a dive. Although the marauding left-back accepted the decision, he bristles at accusations that he engaged in simulation.

'It's one of them – it could have been [given] but it wasn't given so you immediately brush it out of your mind straight away,' he says. 'If the referee hasn't given it, it may or may not have been a penalty. What I was concerned about was the fact that City were struggling to cope with Liverpool and I was just itching to get into forward positions and I wanted not to ram it down their throat but I wanted to get beyond them and give them problems. They didn't know much about me because I was a left full-back. Left full-backs don't normally venture as forward as I used to. I wanted to give anybody, whether it was Ray Ranson or someone else, I just wanted to create havoc in their box and City were sometimes at sixes and sevens, who was marking who and who was doing what. Sometimes on occasions they went a little bit to sleep and you can take advantage. That's what Liverpool were good at. I'm not saying whether it was a penalty or not a penalty, but I never, ever dived to get an advantage which some players might do in the modern era.'

Four minutes from time, Liverpool were eventually awarded a penalty through Kennedy's midfield namesake for a push from Dave Watson, who earned a yellow card for dissent in the aftermath. Phil Neal duly converted from the spot. At the final whistle, Book ran on to the pitch to lead his aggrieved team away while goalkeeper Joe Corrigan was clearly in no mood for pleasantries as he rejected Clemence's offer of a handshake as they headed towards the players' tunnel.

Covering the game for *The Guardian*, Patrick Barclay reported that City's entire travelling party, from Book, his players and coaching staff right through to chairman Peter Swales, had shown 'various expressions of bitterness and pathos, vituperation and ire' after the defeat. 'A reasonable man might have been excused for thinking they were the victims of some massive moral outrage,' he observed. 'It was not so.'

The self-righteous indignation was more attuned to Malcolm Allison's brief yet incendiary spell as City manager than the four-and-a-half years of progress that Book had overseen. Less than two months after that Anfield appearance, history was about to repeat itself.

Bigmouth Strikes Again

SIX YEARS in the wilderness had changed Malcolm Allison, and not necessarily for the better. He returned to Manchester City on 5 January 1979 following managerial stints with Crystal Palace, Galatasaray and Plymouth Argyle. But any hopes that Allison's time away might have led to a more enlightened man breezing through the doors at Maine Road again would prove to be unfounded.

At Selhurst Park, and fuelled by the bright lights of his spiritual London home, an alter ego had been born: Big Mal. Gone were the fitted suits and white-collared shirts matched with Slazenger jumpers; replaced by oversized sheepskin coats and fedora hats accessorised with a Cuban cigar. It was an appearance more akin to a 1920s American mobster than a football manager yet Allison's influence in Croydon arguably merited such attire. Months after his departure from City near the end of the 1972/73 season, he had changed Palace's home kit to mimic FC Barcelona's colours. The club's original nickname of the Glaziers was altered to Eagles in a nod to Benfica, who also provided the inspiration for the club's modern-day crest.

Off the pitch, too, Allison was making waves by inviting the soft-porn actress Fiona Richmond to join his players in the communal bath after training for a photo opportunity captured for the *News of the World*. The publicity stunt saw him charged with bringing the game into disrepute by the FA and sacked by Palace. That constant ability to generate headlines, however, chimed with Peter Swales and the City chairman's relentless obsession with overtaking Manchester United.

Allison's homecoming under the title of 'coaching overlord' coincided with the Winter of Discontent, when one and a half million public sector workers went on strike across the UK. Tony Book, the man who had been his long-term successor on Moss Side, told the press that his former mentor returning 'could be the answer' to City's winless run of 11 First Division matches. Approval for the new arrangement was not as widespread as Book and the club's supporters, reared on the dream ticket of Allison and Joe Mercer in the late 1960s, would convey.

Assistant manager Bill Taylor, a well-respected coach both at Maine Road and with the England national side, resigned from his post after four days. Book, similarly, had relinquished power to the man who had first taken him to Maine Road with Allison transfer-listing Mick Channon just 18 months after his arrival from Southampton.

The UEFA Cup allowed City some rare escapism from their underwhelming mid-table fortunes in the First Division, where Liverpool had already taken a commanding four-point lead despite surrendering their European Cup crown to Nottingham Forest.

Bob Paisley tried to offer Allison some helpful pointers ahead of his side's decisive quarter-final second leg with Borussia Mönchengladbach on 7 March 1979. Five previous meetings with the West German champions, most recently in the previous year's European Cup semi-final, had allowed Paisley to gain an extensive knowledge of how to combat them and he felt that City could benefit from that first-hand insight. He highlighted the hosts' dangermen in a team still graced by the mercurial presence of Allan Simonsen as well as 1974 World Cup winner Berti Vogts, while also recommending that Dave Watson and Tommy Booth be utilised for their aerial prowess; a tactic which had allowed Tommy Smith to flourish in the 1977 European Cup Final against the same opponents.

But Allison disregarded that sage advice and on the same night that the Reds solidified their domestic dominance against Wolverhampton Wanderers, City bowed out in a 3-1 defeat at a stadium locally known as 'The Gravel Pit'. His gamble on untested youth backfired spectacularly. Teenager Nicky Reid, who had made his debut in the first leg, made only his second outing at Borussia Park while midfielder Tony Henry was handed a starting berth despite only featuring in two league games prior. Like Channon, Brian Kidd was another that fell afoul of Allison's new regime and threw his shirt in protest at the de facto manager when they fell two goals behind.

Kidd was moved on to Everton later that month as Gary Owen, Peter Barnes and Asa Hartford also found themselves dispensed with at the end of the 1978/79 season. Watson departed of his own volition, having informed Swales that he would leave if Allison stayed on, and joined Werder Bremen.

City's First Division campaign ended in an unflattering 15th, their worst position for over five seasons, and they were 29 points behind runaway champions Liverpool. Paisley's side had redefined the top flight's standards with an eight-point advantage over Forest, who would replace them as European Cup holders, in addition to an impressive return of 85 goals and just 16 conceded, with four of the latter coming at home and two of them being own goals overall. In spite of the all-conquering nature of the team he had assembled, their manager's tendency to misremember the names of opponents during tactical briefings had led to Paisley being nicknamed 'Duggie Doins' by his players. Another moniker festooned on him was 'The Rat', which not only recognised his Second World War military service in General Montgomery's Eighth Army – better known as the Desert Rats – but also a nous which had served him immensely throughout his time at Anfield.

Such canniness brought the close-season arrivals of midfielder Ronnie Whelan, a future first-team regular who joined from the Dublin-based Home Farm on a free transfer, and Maccabi Tel Aviv defender Avi Cohen, already an established Israel international, for £200,000. In contrast, Allison had subscribed to Viv Nicholson's philosophy of spend, spend, spend. City had confirmed his total control over first-team matters, with Book repositioned into Joe Mercer's one-time role of general manager, and splashed the cash freely. Steve McKenzie became the costliest teenager in history when he joined for £250,000 from Crystal Palace despite failing to make a senior appearance for Allison's former club. Preston North End striker Michael Robinson, a boyhood Liverpool fan, was next through the door at a more eye-watering £750,000 fee before Yugoslavia international defender Dragoslav Stepanovic and Wrexham forward Bobby Shinton completed the free-spending quartet for a combined £890,000.

In the season's opening weeks, Allison set another transfer record with Wolves midfielder Steve Daley becoming the most expensive British footballer for £1.45m on the same day that Stockport County forward Stuart Lee also joined for £80,000, although Daley maintained that Peter Swales had hiked up the fee from his original £650,000 valuation.

Including Barry Silkman's capture for £60,000 earlier in the year, City's outlay during Allison's formative months back at the helm totalled £3.7m – over 18 times Liverpool's own financial undertakings. Paul Power had been named as the club's new captain ahead of the 1979/80 campaign and feels such largesse was a sign of his manager's flawed judgement. 'Mal brought players in that weren't good enough standard to even give Liverpool a good game,' he says. 'People like Paul Sugrue, who he saw playing for Nuneaton; Barry Silkman, who was at Crystal Palace, and Bobby Shinton, who he brought from Wrexham. Liverpool bought players like Graeme Souness from Middlesbrough, who was [already] an international, playing in the First Division and setting the world alight. That's the sort of player that they went for.

'Mal seemed to go for players that if they were successful, they'd make a name for him as the scout of a good player. But we just had a lot of ordinary players by that time. He loved Kazi Deyna but didn't play him. He brought players in that were good athletes so the likes of Tommy Booth, who'd been a good servant, who was good in the air and great at defending crosses, corners and set pieces, was left out for the likes of Tommy Caton, Nicky Reid [and] Ray Ranson.'

Buyer's remorse became a hallmark of Allison's post-football life, particularly whenever the subject of Daley's transfer was broached, but a sense of regret dawned on him far sooner as City hovered just outside the relegation places with an abject return of three points from their opening five league matches. Compounding their plight had been Colin Bell's decision to announce his retirement at the start of the season due to ongoing injury problems. The new 'King of the Kippax' was afforded a fond farewell as seven of Liverpool's established players turned out at Maine Road on 11 September in a combined all-Merseyside team which took on their Manchester counterparts for his rearranged testimonial, a game that had originally been due to take place on 20 December of the previous year. Readers of the two cities' flagship newspapers, the *Manchester Evening News* and *Liverpool Echo*, had determined the identity of both line-ups and saw former fans' favourite Francis Lee joining members of the Blues' current contingent alongside their Manchester United adversaries. Goals from Lee and Tommy Caton, a boyhood Liverpool fan hailing from the city's housing overspill town of Kirkby, sealed a 2-1 win with David Johnson racking up a consolation.

The defending champions' complete ensemble returned to Moss Side over a month and a half later as the Reds sought to place themselves back in contention for the league title race alongside pace-setters United and Nottingham Forest. City's upturn in form had propelled them into the table's top half, aided by wins over Leeds United, Forest and Norwich City. Allison's young guns had also drawn level with Liverpool, in fifth, on 13 points, although had played a game more, which left Paisley to acknowledge the need for his own side to be adequately prepared. 'They've had some good results against good teams recently,' he said. 'We usually do well at Maine Road and we're looking forward to what should be a cracker. Our task is to get our game together … then we should be all right.'

Across the M62, Book retained the mindset of his previous managerial position despite the new job title, saying, 'It is always important to win at home but doubly important to beat a team like Liverpool.'

A promising opening from the hosts wilted in the 12th minute as Kenny Dalglish punished sloppy defensive play from McKenzie and Paul Futcher to set up Johnson for the opener. On the half-hour, Liverpool's talisman found himself among the goals with a sweeping left-footed finish before adding another early in the second half through a half-volley after Ray Kennedy had flicked on a free kick from Phil Neal. In the closing stages, Kennedy added a fourth as Allison was left to mull over how to counteract what he believed as 'the best system of play in the world' and argued that England would enjoy greater success in the following year's European Championships by following Anfield's directive. 'They are so difficult to combat,' he said. 'They are constantly pushing up on you, not letting you make attacking runs. They defend in your half. It is a method that makes them almost impossible to plan against.'

In typical Big Mal fashion, sipping champagne from a tulip glass, he continued to outline his vision for the future and, like Book, saw transferable aspects to his own team. 'I look forward to the day when we will be able to do to teams what Liverpool did to us today. They pressured us all the time and turned every situation to their advantage. I could have protected our young players by playing negatively and getting a more respectable result, but what would have they learned? We gave Liverpool a little bit more room than us and because their passing is so quick and accurate, they punished us, but our players will be better for the experience.'

Liverpool had preoccupied Allison in his brief first spell as City manager, but begrudging respect now took the place of the antagonism which had existed in the early years of the decade. 'He probably hated Liverpool because he'd be jealous of them and what they'd achieved,' says Paul Power. 'He was an incredible thinker about the game. If we'd have been playing Liverpool, he would have been thinking from the Monday of that week how to break them down, what's the best way to do it.'

The Maine Road trouncing had laid the groundwork for Paisley's side to produce an 11-match winning streak in the First

Division that helped restore them to its top spot. City, conversely, struggled to clamber up the table and hit freefall when the new decade rang in. A 4-1 defeat to Brighton & Hove Albion in late December was followed up with an FA Cup third-round humiliation against fourth-tier outfit Halifax Town.

Like their precarious league position, confidence was nearing rock-bottom when they travelled to Anfield on 11 March 1980. A dour first half had forced one elderly Liverpool supporter stationed close to the Main Stand's press box to hang his head and complain, 'We always do this against bad sides.'

An own goal from Tommy Caton, turning an angled shot from Johnson into his own net, before Graeme Souness's drilled effort from the edge of the penalty area after a cutback from Terry McDermott wrapped up maximum points. Habitually a man of few words in public, Paisley's post-match verdict summed up the evening's events when he said, 'It was one of those matches when you could have gone for a kip.'

Minutes before the end of the game, a teenage City fan had been left fighting for his life while leaving Anfield. Neil Jackson's lung was punctured while another deeper wound missed his heart by an inch. A bottle was also smashed over the 17-year-old's legs and arms in the attack after he had been dragged into Arkles Lane by his assailants. Police believed the pottery worker from Crossheath in Ashton-under-Lyme was a victim of mistaken identity due to wearing a red scarf belonging to his second team, Stoke City. He was taken to Walton Hospital, where his condition steadily improved, but the incident marked the growing prevalence of hooliganism within the English game at the time.

***

Five days before reclaiming the First Division title, Liverpool again started to build for the future and finally avenged City's 1967 signing of Francis Lee. Alan Oakes and Cliff Sear, two of the striker's former Maine Road team-mates, had taken the reins at Chester City and given notice to their old club about a rising star in Ian Rush. Allison and Book visited Sealand Road to run the rule over the teenager, who scored the second goal in the Third Division side's FA Cup fourth-round win against Millwall. Oakes later confirmed that discussions had already been opened with City over a potential transfer, although the Seals had pledged to keep fellow suitors Liverpool abreast of developments on Rush's future.

Still only 18 years old, the marksman had hit 12 goals in 17 outings for Chester that season and was a matter of weeks away from making a senior international bow with Wales. But the Blues passed up the chance to sign him, clearing the way for Rush to join the ranks at Anfield on 1 May. Liverpool's chief scout Geoff Twentyman later admitted that the move was payback for City's snaring of Lee, his first recommendation on Merseyside, 13 years earlier.

Conflicting accounts have been offered as to City's reasons for failing to land a player who would stand at the vanguard of elite-level football for over 15 years. Allison insisted that Peter Swales had been dissuaded by Chester's asking price. 'I'd agreed to sign Ian Rush from Chester for £340,000 when he was a kid,' he told the *Sunday People* in 1993. 'I knew he'd be a world-beater, but Swales didn't fancy Rushie and blocked the deal. Liverpool got him a few weeks later.'

But Oakes maintained that it was the manager, rather than his chairman, who had kyboshed the transfer. 'Tony was keen but Malcolm didn't rate him for some reason and it all collapsed,' he later told author Gary James in *Manchester: The City Years*. 'He went to Liverpool and the rest is history, but I wanted him to go to Maine Road and I wish the deal had occurred. Of course, you never know how these things would have worked out.'

With the deal discounted, City completed the £1.25m signing of Kevin Reeves from Norwich.

Reeves was not the sole late-season arrival at Maine Road as Dennis Tueart returned in a £175,000 deal following a two-season spell with the New York Cosmos. But the pair could not prevent City from sinking to new depths in the top flight with a 17th-place finish as Allison's wholesale changes obliterated the feelgood factor generated by his return less than 18 months earlier.

Even from a distance, it was becoming obvious that his second Maine Road honeymoon was doomed to fail. 'Malcolm was a straightforward manager [but] he was flamboyant,' says Alan Kennedy. 'You saw not [only] the type of hats or coats he wore but he said things sometimes to get the best of his team, and sometimes maybe have words with the other managers. He called a spade a spade. I don't know whether he'd been invited into the Boot Room because every manager as far as I was aware was invited into the Boot Room after the game at Anfield.

'But Manchester City was made for him with those types of players and that type of skill. It was made for Malcolm Allison to get the best out of the players, but I just always felt sometimes that City didn't quite have it throughout the 42 games. They on occasion could turn it on as they did in the '76 [League] Cup Final but over 42 league games it was asking a bit much of them and they couldn't quite do it.'

Bob Paisley had attempted to offer some backing to the beleaguered City boss earlier in the season by saying, 'Critics can crucify as much as they like, but he is one of the few positive coaches in the game. At least he is looking in the right direction at Maine Road. Malcolm is constructive in his outlook when too many are not.'

Offloading Michael Robinson and Barry Silkman within 12 months after their arrivals was hardly a ringing endorsement for the Liverpool manager's public support. Swales's desire for fresh media exposure did not help Allison's attempts to steady the club away from perilous terrain. Three years since he had last allowed television crews to prowl through Maine Road's inner sanctum, the City chairman negotiated a deal to hand Granada TV unprecedented access to all levels of club business in negotiations with the regional network's head of sport Paul Doherty, whose father Peter had played in the Blues team that achieved the rare feat of winning the 1936/37 title and being relegated the following season. The result was a fly-on-the-wall documentary titled *City! A Club in Crisis*, with the opening scene charting Liverpool's visit to Maine Road on 4 October.

In the days preceding the clash, a public stand-off between Swales and Allison had ensued with City languishing in the First Division's relegation zone, who challenged his superior to either sack him or allow him to continue. It culminated in an awkward joint appearance of the chairman and manager on Granada's *Kick Off* preview show. Away from Maine Road's battle lines, Allison had enjoyed a watching brief of Liverpool's 10-1 slaying of Finnish outfit Oulun Palloseura in the first round of the European Cup. He took in the double-figured win from the Anfield directors' box alongside Tony Book as the hosts set up a meeting with Scottish champions Aberdeen, then managed by Alex Ferguson, in a clash that was predictably hyped as the Battle of Britain. It was Allison's opinion that Liverpool were 'the best-equipped team in the land to triumph in Europe'. As kick-off approached and with the cameras rolling, high praise for the visitors gave way to the alter ego of Big Mal. Standing topless in the dressing room, he set out City's basic instructions. 'I want you to get at 'em right from the off,' he said. 'Just imagine you're one down and play that way.'

Paisley's reigning champions travelled to Moss Side intent on securing their first away win of the season. In the 38th minute, they set about achieving that aim when Avi Cohen found Kenny Dalglish, who twisted and turned past Tommy Caton before angling a shot from the edge of the penalty area which squeezed past Joe Corrigan. Trailing at the break, Allison used half-time to keep City's subdued players on their feet in the stadium's gym as he barked further orders at them.

Paul Power felt that the presence of Granada's cameras during the interval had negated any efforts to provoke a fightback from their first-half deficit. 'I would imagine that the club would've been offered a fair amount of money to allow the cameras into the dressing room, but it was definitely unsettling,' he says. 'Players do have a go at each other when things go wrong. Half-time is a pretty volatile atmosphere when you've got senior pros who are prepared to speak up for each other and against each other as well. We had players like Dennis Tueart, who would speak his mind if he didn't think that he was getting the service he should have got. But with the cameras there, it became a little bit muted and it might've had an adverse effect on us. Mal wanted to be star of the show, I'm sure. The cameras would've focused on him a lot more than they would've focused on the players.'

Matters worsened in the second half when, on 53 minutes, Graeme Souness met Terry McDermott's floated cross to head a bobbled effort beyond Corrigan. Paisley handed a senior bow to winger Howard Gayle in the final third of the game before Sammy Lee piled on City's misery from a five-man break just seven minutes from the end. The 3-0 win helped Liverpool to lead the First Division's chasing pack behind Ipswich Town while City languished in 21st, only spared rock-bottom spot by Allison's old club Crystal Palace.

The Guardian later claimed that an unidentified member of the home side had accused his team-mates of betraying their creed inside the dressing room immediately after the defeat, something which Power's recollections fail to corroborate. 'I don't remember it to be fair but in any dressing room, there'd be a player who was trying to steal the limelight,' he says. 'I don't remember who it would've been, who it might've been. It should've been me really because I was the captain of the team so it should've been down to me to sort out. But I would normally support the players. I tried not to lambast players unless I felt that they hadn't given 100 per cent effort and they were capable of giving more.'

Allison was particularly dismissive of Dalglish's well-worked opener when conducting a post-match autopsy with two journalists in his office over a glass of wine and a trademark Havana cigar; all recorded for posterity by a Granada cameraman.

'It's a bad goal! It's going into the net at about 2mph,' he told them. 'How can that be a good goal, from 20-odd yards?'

'I take your point, but we're looking at it from the other point of view,' one replied.

'If you're looking at it, you're dreaming up miracles. You're saying "he did this, he did that" – he turned, and he turned, he made a little chance and had a shot, and it's gone in the net. If it had been anybody else, you wouldn't even mention it.'

'I don't know many players who can do that.'

'What, make the ball bounce?'

Pensively, he conceded, 'The third goal was a good goal – that is a good goal, the third goal.'

Sensing his audience, the City manager then broke the fourth wall by looking directly at the camera and shaking his head while muttering, 'A good goal, fuck me.'

Once the television crews departed, Allison unleashed fury on the written press. 'I don't understand you people. All you're after is headlines,' he blasted. 'The goal was a disgrace and we need locking up for it.' He went further by arguing that a schoolboy and even himself could have dived across the goal and headed it clear. 'It was a crap goal.'

City's under-fire manager was not the only one playing up for the cameras. Peter Swales appeared in his element during a post-match meeting in the Maine Road boardroom in which he suggested that the answer lay in bringing back 'the fella we let go' in Asa Hartford, prompting Allison to fire back, 'Do me a favour!' while drawing back on another of his trademark Cubans as his chairman cackled mischievously. The fall-out from the loss continued on the pitches of their new Platt Lane base in the days that followed when Allison took Steve Daley to task for failing to pick up Graeme Souness, who had 'caused all of the problems', in a fiery exchange.

Six days after Liverpool's visit, Allison finally received his marching orders as his former assistant Tony Book and chief scout Ken Barnes took charge of first-team affairs for a 3-1 loss to West Bromwich Albion. City's appointment of John Bond as Allison's eventual successor indicated a change in direction but not conduct.

City were accused of being overly physical and intimidating towards First Division newcomers Norwich City on the opening day of the 1975/76 season, a claim which Book had openly contested. Yet Bond's continual ire towards Merseyside's two clubs was more distinguishing, with the contrary nature in which he had turned down the chance to become Everton's assistant manager in summer 1972 a possible root cause. Harry Catterick's heart attack a year earlier had forced the Goodison Park board to consider emulating City's approach with Allison and Joe Mercer by drafting in a younger man to aid him. Bond announced that he had been offered an annual salary of £8,000 to serve as Catterick's deputy and held talks with the dour disciplinarian at the club's Bellefield training base.

Newspapers later reported that he had turned down the offer but claims he had even been approached were publicly shot down by both Everton and Catterick himself. He was tipped as the forerunner to succeed Catterick, who had moved into an executive role, in the following year only for former Toffees player Billy Bingham to be handed the post.

Neither Merseyside club were spared from Bond's barbs whenever they took on his Norwich side throughout the 1970s, but Liverpool drew the most stinging criticisms. He had previously feuded with Paisley after a bad-tempered game in March 1976 saw Carrow Road's hosts suffer a 1-0 loss and scorched the Anfield side's defensive tactics on the road. 'It would be the worst thing to happen to football if Liverpool won the title,' he said. 'Their negative thinking sickens me. They haven't the courage to admit it.'

Paisley hit back in typical fashion, saying, 'One way to get more entertainment in football would be if the goals were as big as John's mouth!'

Bond's job interview with the City hierarchy and tough-talking introduction to the club's players were all featured in Granada's upcoming documentary. The latter became parodied almost word for word by Tim Healy in the late 1990s on the comedy drama *Bostock's Cup*, which centred on a fictional Third Division team that won the 1974 FA Cup against all odds.

Bond followed his predecessor's lead by immediately drafting in Coventry duo Bobby McDonald and Tommy Hutchison, tenacious Bristol City midfielder Gerry Gow and Southampton's Phil Boyer at a cumulative cost of £717,000. The Blues' early relegation fears subsequently became a distant memory by the end of 1980 as they moved into 13th, four points clear of the bottom three, while Liverpool saw out Christmas at the top of the First Division tree once more. Bond's instantaneous success saw him win successive Manager of the Month awards for November and December.

Additional progress in the League Cup helped set up a semi-final meeting with the current leaders, with the new City manager talking up his side's chances in the build-up and insisting, 'There is no way we can be classed as underdogs,' before adding, 'We have to play Liverpool at their own game. Down the years they have earned a reputation of being a big team who adopt cat-and-mouse tactics and the number of times they come up on the post to win matches is tremendous. But at the same time, we have proved recently our own ability to strike back to win points in games.'

Paisley attempted to sound a note of caution to his opposite number, saying, 'The onus is on the home side to go for a lead – although I don't think City are equipped for anything but going forward.'

Ineligibility prevented City from utilising their full complement of recent signings, with only Boyer permitted to play, leading the Liverpool manager to consider the circumstances in which his own side had lost the 1978 final against Nottingham Forest. 'They were missing a number of new signing who were cup-tied just like with City and we still lost,' he conceded. 'We'll treat City like a foreign side.'

Liverpool's declining fortunes in the battle for the First Division title added to their sense of trepidation having slipped to third with a six-point shortfall to make up on Ipswich Town and Aston Villa at the summit.

City's hopes of taking an early lead in the tie were dashed by referee Alf Grey, who disallowed a third-minute header from Kevin Reeves for what he perceived as 'illegal jumping' on Alan Kennedy as the striker vied with his Liverpool counterpart and Ray Clemence in an aerial duel. Paul Power remembers the scenes of disarray as play continued while he and his team-mates had rushed over to congratulate the striker. 'You could tell by the reaction of all the players,' he says. 'It was a ball that was crossed in and Kevin Reeves just got up and challenged Ray Clemence. The keeper was expecting it to come into his hands but Reevesie scored the goal. We were all running to the corner to congratulate him. The referee disallowed the goal but allowed Liverpool to take a quick free kick and they were attacking down the other side of the pitch to where we were all in a huddle. It was really bad refereeing. Whether he'd made a mistake or not, to allow what happened afterwards to carry on was pretty amateurish to be fair.'

Supporters of the Maine Road club would continue to take Grey's name in vain in the decades that followed. One of them, Eddie Large, found himself in the company of Bill Shankly in the stadium's executive lounges at half-time. Paisley's predecessor proceeded to wax lyrical to the comedian of Little and Large fame about Tommy Hutchison from the hosts' ineligible trio situated nearby.

'See that man over there, son? The greatest signing of all time,' said Shankly.

'You've made some great signings,' replied Large.

'Aye, but not like that. The greatest signing ever.'

Ray Kennedy settled the closely contested first leg in the 81st minute with a cool finish from a threaded ball by Terry McDermott; something which the midfielder's Liverpool team-mate Alan Kennedy points to as a sign of the team's collective strength. 'For me, the one thing Liverpool had was goalscorers from every position apart from the centre-backs,' he says. 'The centre-backs were there to do their role of defending and that was Phil Thompson and Alan Hansen. Phil Neal scored a few goals, I was chipping in with two or three a season, Ray Kennedy was coming in with maybe 10 or 11; Graeme Souness with maybe eight or nine, Jimmy Case and Terry McDermott would have 20-odd between them.

'Everybody was capable of scoring. It didn't matter who scored and we said that after each and every game, we all get the plaudits. Ronnie Moran and Joe Fagan knew how good that team was.

They knew what the best qualities were from that team, but we always felt for some reason confident against City. We always felt as though they would give us a game, and they did give us games, but they were always susceptible to a counter-attack or a mistake in the team. We always felt as though they were just not quite what Liverpool were. They were just lacking a little bit, not in skill, but lacking a little in thinking about the game or something. You've got to cover your mates and I just felt as though they were always susceptible to the attack and giving something away.'

Bond sought out Grey after the final whistle for an explanation on his reason for disallowing Reeves's early effort and later complained to the press, 'The referee must have been the only man in the ground who didn't think it was a goal ... We were crucified by that decision. Liverpool got away with a little bit of murder.'

The burning sense of injustice inside the City dressing room was also directed at the Great Yarmouth official. 'We knew we had the second leg to come even though it was going to be tough to go away to Anfield, trying to defend a 1-0 loss. But we'd have been well confident that we could do that,' says Power. 'Up to Mal losing his job, we couldn't win a bloody game. I think we were second-bottom of the league [at the time]. After that, we won the majority of the games and didn't lose many. We also got to the FA Cup Final that year, where we got beaten by Ricky Villa's goal, [and] got to the semi-final of the League Cup as well so we'd had a fantastic season so there wouldn't have been any animosity in the dressing room, not against the players. It would've been directed at the referee I'm sure.'

Graeme Souness and Phil Thompson rubbed further salt into City's wounds by admitting in their post-match interviews that Liverpool had resignedly traipsed back to the centre circle preparing for the restart before the referee's crucial intervention. But Paisley remained guarded about his side's prospects of reaching the League Cup Final and warned, 'There's still another game to go yet. It's nice to be one-up at half-time but there's no way we are going to take anything for granted.'

Grey had been stood down by the time the sides contested the return fixture on 10 February 1981. The night before the Anfield tie, Granada aired its *City!* documentary which provided an access-all-areas glimpse of Maine Road's inner workings and contained more than its fair share of toe-curling moments. In the game itself, Reeves eventually scored a goal in his own right but his 50th-minute effort was nullified by Kenny Dalglish breaking the deadlock early in the first half against an under-strength City side which acquitted itself well against their Wembley-bound opponents.

Bond conceded that Liverpool's 'name was on the cup' following their 2-1 aggregate scoreline while Paisley admitted, 'It was a battle. We are just grateful to get through.' The terminology used by Liverpool's victorious manager reflected the scenes outside the stadium after the game as violence flared between the two sets of rival supporters. A total of five stabbings were reported and had seen a 20-year-old from Harrogate and a 17-year-old from Halewood both being admitted to hospital for treatment on knife-inflicted wounds. Coaches carrying away supporters were also attacked with stones as they travelled down Walton Hall Avenue and the East Lancashire Road respectively, while police recovered an arsenal of metal chains, iron bars, hockey sticks and baseball bats from one gang of youths.

Separately, a total of 30 people were arrested for offences in connection with the Public Order Act, ranging from drunkenness to possession of offensive weapons and led John Carroll, Merseyside Police's chief superintendent at the time, to admit, 'We expected trouble and we got it. There were very ugly scenes indeed. Both Manchester City and Liverpool followers were as bad as each other and knives were in evidence for attacks.'

Their next midweek meeting at Anfield on 19 May was played against a wholly different backdrop as both clubs had endured forgettable campaigns in the First Division, with Liverpool finishing in fifth and City sitting in an inconsequential 12th. Bond's side had taken a Ricky Villa-inspired Tottenham Hotspur down to the wire in the FA Cup Final before narrowly losing the replay 3-2 while the Reds had won their first League Cup, beating West Ham in a replay, and were targeting a third European Cup against Real Madrid, the indomitable powerhouse of Continental football, in Paris.

Attention had visibly shifted to the showpiece in the City of Lights with a crowd of 24,462 constituting the dethroned league champions' lowest attendance of the season. The *Liverpool Echo* theorised that the below-par turnout was attributable to either a diminished appetite for football in the local area, which had hit crippling economic hardship inflicted by Margaret Thatcher's Conservative government, or a sign of how the club's domestic campaign had 'long ago died a death'. A third and more simplified hypothesis was that thousands of supporters who had failed to obtain tickets for the European Cup Final simply chose to vote with their feet.

Ray Kennedy's slotted finish proved decisive on an evening of minimal chances for both teams, with City deploying Alex Williams in goal rather than Joe Corrigan. Liverpool's precursor for Paris saw Alan Kennedy returning from a broken wrist sustained against Bayern Munich in the semi-final and to road test a technique which would serve him well in the French capital.

'I'd gone on the run and had beaten a couple of their defenders and, typical of me, I don't see anybody else,' he says. 'I only see the whites of Alex's eyes and I'm thinking, "Oh, bloody hell!" He's a big lad but I hit the ball and I'm not sure whether it hit the post or grazed the post, but it was a good effort. Yes, you can say it was a dress rehearsal [for the Real Madrid match] but I was always capable when I got in those positions of scoring goals. I just saw glory and thought, "Right, I'm going to give it a go and if it goes in fine, if it doesn't then the keeper might save it, Dalglish might be waiting to pounce, something like that. It wasn't the dress rehearsal for Paris because I didn't know whether I was going to play in Paris until three hours before the kick-off.'

Six days later at the Parc des Princes, BBC commentator Barry Davies inimitably hailed Kennedy as 'the unlikely man again' when he breached Real's defence to score the goal that delivered Liverpool's third European Cup. Greater shocks were to come when Paisley's side had returned from the FIFA Club World Championship, where they had suffered a 3-0 defeat to Flamengo in the final, near the end of that year. In late September, Bill Shankly passed away at the city's Broadgreen Hospital. The 68-year-old had been a picture of health, never drinking or smoking and exercising daily, yet suffered two heart attacks in three days with the latter proving fatal. The city was united in grief for a man whose achievements in a 15-year spell at Anfield had helped cement their status as a cultural epicentre which was home to more than just the birthplace of The Beatles.

Shankly's death had arrived during an uncharacteristic run of form by the team that in life he had taken pride in building into 'a bastion of invincibility'. Liverpool failed to excel beyond seventh place in the First Division in the first half of a season where transition had been the order of business. Paisley had sanctioned the departures of Ray Clemence to Tottenham and used Jimmy Case as a makeweight in a £900,000 deal for Brighton & Hove Albion's versatile defender Mark Lawrenson. Steve Nicol, another defender, also joined the ranks alongside Clemence's direct successor Bruce Grobbelaar. At Maine Road, Bond had also strengthened considerably during the summer months. Trevor Francis, Britain's first million-pound footballer, arrived and was reunited with one-time Nottingham Forest team-mate Martin O'Neill, who had been sourced from the City manager's former club Norwich. Kevin Bond continued a family tradition of playing under his father at three different clubs after moving from Seattle Sounders. Such lavish signings were incompatible with the growing deprivation both Liverpool and Manchester endured in the first wave of Thatcherism.

Football, however, was still not far removed from its societal roots. A common sense approach by the game's authorities ensured that clubs only made short trips to their regional rivals during the Christmas period, a move which became distinguishable from the lengthy journeys and antisocial kick-off times that supporters face in the Premier League era to satisfy the demands of television coverage. City's visit to Anfield on Boxing Day 1981 was a prime example. On an ice-specked pitch, Liverpool approached their first domestic test since flying home from Japan and received a rude awakening. Asa Hartford fired an initial warning shot after Steve Kinsey's cross at the byeline found him for a looping header which had Grobbelaar well beaten in front of The Kop but was chalked off for a push by Tommy Hutchison on Sammy Lee. Hartford later avenged his disallowed goal by scoring an indisputable opener after stealing possession from Phil Thompson in the six-yard box and firing a shot on the turn which squeezed past Grobbelaar at his near left-hand post.

The Kop's goalmouth would become a focal point of action early in the second half when Joe Corrigan was struck on the head by a glass bottle thrown from the home terrace, causing him to lie prostrate on the turf. Supporters responded to the unprovoked attack with shouts of 'throw the bastard out!' and attempted to point police officers in the general direction of the culprit but to little avail. After the City goalkeeper rose to his feet, chants of 'Corrigan for England' reverberated alongside warm applause. Although the stopper bore no ill feeling towards the home crowd for the mindless act, the FA launched an investigation which later saw Liverpool cleared of any wrongdoing with sworn statements from 'responsible witnesses' claiming that the bottle which had struck Corrigan had been found in the goal net some time before the incident occurred.

At the other end, Thompson suffered a calamity of errors; first with an awkward header from a downfield kick from City's number one that forced Alan Hansen to handle the aerial threat of Kevin Reeves before it again broke for the Liverpool defender. His scuffed attempt at a clearance sent the ball back into the danger zone, where Grobbelaar rushed off his line to unsuccessfully challenge Reeves. Thompson completing his hat-trick of misfortune by tipping Kinsey's ensuing half-volley over the crossbar with his hand to concede a penalty.

Kevin Bond had yet to score since joining City and could not have asked for a better chance to open his account with a well-struck spot kick which nestled in the corner of Grobbelaar's goal before running over to a small enclave of travelling fans housed in the far right-hand side of the Anfield Road End with two clenched fists raised aloft.

Moments earlier, Paisley had sent on Alan Kennedy with the nondescript instruction, 'Go out there and do your best.' Within ten minutes the full-back had helped reduce the deficit with a long diagonal to Lee, who headed inside to Graeme Souness. His effort was deflected by Tommy Caton but only as far as Ronnie Whelan to strike a bobbling shot for his first league goal of the campaign. Fading hopes of a spirited comeback completely evaporated in the final two minutes as Hutchison's cross-field ball allowed Ray Ranson to release Kinsey down Liverpool's right-hand side before playing a cross into Reeves at the near post for a back-flick that was palmed on to the post by Grobbelaar only for a rebound off the Zimbabwean goalkeeper's chest. City had scored just once and conceded 24 goals in their previous seven meetings with Liverpool yet ended a 28-year hoodoo at Anfield in comprehensive fashion.

For the hosts, a third home league defeat from their previous four hammered home the realisation of how far standards had slipped in just a matter of months. Kennedy recalls the wildly different scenes in the home dressing room to the ones he had experienced in Paris seven months earlier. 'Mayhem. Mayhem,' he says, frankly. 'It was ridiculous, it really was. Everybody was shouting. Everybody wasn't listening [as] the manager's going round. Ronnie Moran, particularly, was going around shouting, "You fucking" whatever, "you've gone you lot, you've gone!" They didn't look you in the face, they didn't shout names out, they just said it for the whole team to listen to. Bruce Grobbelaar had one of his games that he'd probably like to forget. He mishandled Kevin Reeves's shot and that was a killer; the third goal to go in in the last few minutes of the game.'

Possibly damned with faint praise, John Bond declared that he had seen 'a lot of the old Liverpool' in City's deserved victory, although Hartford was more forensic in his analysis, saying, 'They knocked more long balls than any Liverpool side I can remember.

The front men did not seem to be blending and I think they have problems because they have no width up there.'

Paisley's own post-match assessment was a conciliatory one which suggested the onus rested on the players. 'We never deployed ourselves properly,' he said. 'You can say inexperience cost us the game, but it was our experienced men who made vital mistakes … The score is a little bit flattering, but you can't concede goals as easily as that.'

Kennedy believes the 3-1 reversal became a watershed moment for Liverpool's tactical deployment. 'I think the writing was on the wall for the system that we played,' he says. 'Lawrenson must have had words with the manager and said, "Listen, I'm not playing left-back again. I don't like it, I'm not a left-back. I need to play centre-back," so Phil Thompson or Alan Hansen had to move to accommodate Lawrenson and it was Phil unfortunately. City were very, very, very good on the day, and we never put anything together. I think it was mainly because we were playing a different system but also the fact that City were up for it and they sensed for me that Liverpool were there for the taking. We hadn't had a good run before that. We were still struggling and all of a sudden, we find ourselves out of the top four or five in the First Division.'

Joe Fagan, Liverpool's assistant manager and a former City player, had sifted through the wreckage with his colleagues in the Boot Room and added a withering assessment in his personal diary. 'Dismal,' he wrote. 'Not up to the standard we require. I would say two blokes in our team are playing to their ability. But the rest? No.'

Paisley's right-hand man was not alone in weighing up the potential rebuilding task ahead of the European champions. After recording his side's first victory in the red half of Merseyside since 1953, Bond confidently told his hosts during a customary post-match drink that their chances of winning the First Division had disappeared into the winter night's air. 'Just you wait and see. There's half a season to go yet,' first-team coach Ronnie Moran reminded City's gloating manager. 'We'll see who's top in May.'

Fagan and Moran were both left seething as their visitors made their way home. In a year which had seen racial tensions spark rioting in both Merseyside and Moss Side, City were handed a fresh reminder of that lingering hostility as they departed Anfield. A hail of missiles rained down on their team coach when it pulled out of the Main Stand's car park. Bond ordered his players to lie down on the vehicle's floor to avoid injury in a shellacking which would have historical parallels little under three decades later.

Critics refused to spare Liverpool's fallen troops in the aftermath of City's surprise victory. The *Daily Mirror* splashed a banner headline of 'The Empire is Crumbling' while doom prophets were hardly in short supply on home soil either. Contributors to the *Liverpool Echo*'s letters page argued that Paisley was sleepwalking the reigning European champions into decline. Their subsequent transformation following that fifth loss of the domestic campaign has gone down in Anfield folklore as the ultimate comeback, but they still had two games in hand owing to participation in the Club World Championship. Nevertheless, it prompted Fagan to take matters into his own hands. On 28 December, when Liverpool's senior players reported back for duty, he advised Paisley to travel on ahead to the club's Melwood training ground. 'I'm going to have the lads,' he said. His superior offered zero resistance with the words 'say what you want' as he vacated the dressing room.

What followed was an evisceration which spared no one within Liverpool's inner sanctum as Fagan delivered some uncomfortable home truths to the club's mid-table malingerers. 'You think you're running midfield?' he asked Graeme Souness. 'You haven't won a tackle for a month. You're nowhere near anything.' Next in the firing line was Kenny Dalglish: 'How many goals have you got so far this season? You should have twice as many by now.' Bruce Grobbelaar did not get off lightly either in the aftermath of his blundering display against City: 'You look more like a ballerina. Come and collect the ball like you're supposed to.'

Individual criticisms evolved into a strict order that the players' debrief meetings that had become a common occurrence after matches would no longer take place. The only reprieve from the ear-bashing came when Fagan issued Liverpool's players with a call to arms. 'At the end of the day, we're getting out of this,' he said. 'You're all playing like individuals: start playing as a team. I'm not having another meeting from now till the end of the season.' The fiery outburst was at odds with Fagan's usually placid demeanour and a sign of how drastically Liverpool's title defence had deteriorated in the first half of the new campaign.

Hours later, Paisley followed up his lieutenant's rollocking at the start of a post-training meeting in Anfield's lounges by holding up a copy of the First Division table from one of the day's newspapers. 'In case any of you haven't realised, it says here we're 12th – and you know these things, they don't lie. Bloody Swansea top of the league,' he said. 'When I see the likes of Brighton and Southampton above this club, it tells me something's wrong here.'

The Welsh club, now managed by former Kop hero John Toshack, had started the day as First Division leaders but did not see it out as City reclaimed top spot for the first time since October 1977 courtesy of a 2-1 win over Wolverhampton Wanderers. John Bond's side surpassed the Swans, who lost 3-1 to Toshack's former sparring partner Kevin Keegan and Southampton, to become champions-elect at the midway stage. Paisley showed immediate ruthlessness as Graeme Souness was installed as Liverpool's captain in place of Thompson, who had lifted the European Cup for his boyhood club just seven months earlier.

Aided by the three-points-for-a-win system that had been introduced at the start of the 1981/82 campaign, Liverpool began to again climb the First Division table as the old standards were both revived and maintained. Where they had conceded 19 goals in their opening 17 league fixtures, culminating in City's Boxing Day win, just seven were shipped in their next 15 while also retaining the League Cup before a trip to Maine Road on 10 April which would determine whether their surge to the top was capable of lasting the distance. Sammy Lee set the visitors on their way in the opening ten minutes with a 30-yard piledriver which was followed up by a Phil Neal penalty after Caton was penalised for a last-ditch tackle on Ian Rush. The City defender met his match in the striker for Liverpool's third as Rush evaded his sliding challenge to meet a David Johnson flick-on into the box before squaring to Craig Johnston to round off a fluid move and prompt the travelling supporters to chant 'we're gonna win the league' with gusto.

Less than a minute later, Kennedy scored an impressive yet unexpected goal from the narrowest of angles. 'Nicky Reid was playing and I somehow get the better of him on the byeline and I'm looking and it's on my right foot,' he says. 'I'm thinking, "Well I'll curl it," and the wind's blowing a little bit so just hit the far post. Then I hit it; I actually curled it so well that whether Joe Corrigan mistimed or whatever, it went in at the far post. I went, "Fucking hell – that was incredible!" It meant a lot to me [because] even though it was 3-0 at the time; you're on the score-sheet and you've completed the rout of Man City.

'I was really happy that I'd scored against Man City. It was only when Joe became the goalkeeping coach at Liverpool did he give me a thump on my arm and say, "You didn't mean that, did you?" and he was reacting to that cross-cum-shot that I'd scored against him. I'd been around the training ground and Joe said, "That's for scoring the goal against me," and then he made a joke of it. "I had to retire after that!"'

Wearing a brown moleskin coat and matching flat cap, Bob Paisley resembled a racehorse trainer far more than the mastermind of the football season's most remarkable comeback story. His keen interest in thoroughbreds was evident by Rush's collected finish in the 73rd minute. The Wales international's early Anfield career had been beset by an inability to regularly find the target. Developing a near-telepathic understanding with Kenny Dalglish went some way to disproving those doubts and also culminated in Liverpool's fifth of the afternoon as the Celtic duo beat an offside trap to see Rush hold his nerve and place the ball over Corrigan and into the bottom left-hand corner of the net. City's refusal to sign the 20-year-old a year earlier had returned to haunt them with a prolific 27th goal of the season from 39 appearances in all competitions.

John Bond's back-handed compliment four months prior was replaced with the more familiar and long-standing disdain after the visitors moved five points clear of nearest challengers Ipswich Town. 'I felt that it looks very much in many ways, and all the football people will understand this, as they [Liverpool] just do what they want to do, when they want to do it,' he told BBC's *Match of the Day*. 'When you're not able to change it about too often, you just have to live with it and that's sickening really.'

The City manager's nausea was a common complaint among his First Division peers as Paisley's side steamrolled to the title with 20 wins from their final 25 league matches, registering 56 goals and conceding just 13 in the process, ensuring a four-point advantage over runners-up Ipswich. 'We were flying. Not so much in the other competitions but in the league, we couldn't wait to play teams,' says Kennedy. 'Coming to Maine Road on that occasion, you're not exactly looking at their team because you just think "he's not bad, this is how you deal with him", or whatever. On that occasion, I scored one of the flukiest goals I've ever scored in my life. But if we had a shot at goal, it seemed to go in. We might have only had five shots at goal but the five of them went in and we ended up playing sublime football.'

City's own title challenge had been lost around the same time that they had tasted a long-awaited Anfield victory. A season-ending Achilles tendon injury to Dennis Tueart robbed Bond's team of the blossoming partnership with Trevor Francis and led to their season tailing off with only five victories from their 22 fixtures following their successful Merseyside outing. A tenth-place finish, just inside the First Division's top half, was offset by edging ahead of the soon-to-be crowned European champions Aston Villa, who took over Liverpool's mantle just eight days after the domestic campaign ended.

Chairman Peter Swales had spent the previous eight years attempting to elevate City to the top club in the country, with seemingly no expense spared, but was now scrambling around for quick fixes. John Sainty, one of Bond's trusted assistants, was released in a penny-pinching exercise which extended to trimming the club's squad down to 24 senior players and nine apprentices. Swales also struck City's first shirt sponsorship deal in a two-year arrangement with Swedish car manufacturer Saab worth £400,000, a figure designed to satisfy the bank manager far more than Maine Road's coffers. Francis's £900,000 sale to Sampdoria signalled a further sign of the times as West Ham United striker David Cross was tasked with the unenviable duty of replacing the club's leading scorer in the previous season at a sixth of the price.

The good times continued to roll at Anfield, where Paisley informed his players ahead of the new campaign that it would be his last as manager. A seven-year contract signed in Christmas 1976 was set to run until the following summer and the incumbent was happy to bow out once it expired. Unlike with Shankly's resignation nine years earlier, there was no cause for consternation as Paisley pressed ahead with evolving the reigning league champions' squad as stalwarts Terry McDermott and David Johnson both departed with the Kirkby-born midfielder rejoining Newcastle United, the club where his career had begun, while Johnson also headed back to his roots with Everton. Early success arrived in the Charity Shield against Tottenham but designs on taking a similarly premature grip on the First Division were denied by City putting together a 100 per cent record in their opening three games and the early resurgence of Manchester United. After a 3-1 win over Brighton in late October, Liverpool refused to look back. A five-point lead over Nottingham Forest at Christmas had brought a resigned acceptance that the title was already heading back to Anfield.

City's first brush of the season with the champions-elect on 27 December 1982 came amid unabashed festive cheer as Anfield witnessed its biggest gate of the season, although not all of the 44,664 crowd had been present for the start of the early-morning encounter due to prolonged queues outside The Kop's turnstiles before kick-off. Some fans only managed to enter the ground after the first half-hour of play, by which point Liverpool had raced into a commanding three-goal lead through Phil Neal's 30-yard strike and a Kenny Dalglish brace. Cross reduced the deficit by lobbing Bruce Grobbelaar but his next act would be one of infamy after an off-the-ball exchange with Graeme Souness left the Liverpool captain upended on the turf holding his face. The City striker later made Ronnie Whelan his designated target, eventually leading to the midfielder limping off with an ankle injury. Away from the running battles, which produced three bookings, Ian Rush and Dalglish had extended the hosts' lead before Tommy Caton scored a late consolation.

'I always felt as though City were slightly vulnerable and once you get at them, you know if you keep them quiet, you're going to win the game,' says Alan Kennedy. 'Because they sometimes allow you half a chance and sometimes that's all that Dalglish needed. I remember the five goals that we scored, and it didn't matter about them getting the two, although we were disappointed that we'd conceded. We didn't ask any questions about the defence. It was just about how many we scored [because] we knew we'd score more than what they did.'

Worse was still to come for City as a humiliating 4-0 defeat to Brighton in the FA Cup fourth round lead to a departure for John Bond, something he would later claim was extorted by threats at boardroom level to leak details of his complicated private life to the press. His assistant John Benson took charge and, if nothing else, boasted a prerequisite of being a former City player. Fans half-joked that Swales had chosen to promote from within as it meant the initials on the manager's tracksuit would not need to be changed.

Prior to Bond's departure, the club had consolidated a mid-table position of tenth but suffered a sharp downturn under his replacement with six defeats from the next ten matches that plummeted them down to 17th, just seven points clear of relegation having played at least two games more than the teams below them. Amid the dismal run, City had offloaded evergreen goalkeeper Joe Corrigan to join Seattle Sounders for £30,000. His successor Alex Williams played only three times before Liverpool headed to Moss Side on Easter Monday with the title already in touching distance.

No club had been able to displace Paisley's players since their late-September ascent as they collected a third consecutive League Cup, defeating Manchester United at Wembley for good measure. City spurned the chance to take an improbable lead when Grobbelaar flapped at a cross, but Kevin Reeves steered his headed attempt off target. Graeme Souness punished the hosts' early profligacy by dispossessing Graham Baker and struck a 25-yard effort. Just before half-time, Sammy Lee drew a throng of defenders and teed up David Fairclough to double the lead. A short-lived fightback ensued in the second half when Asa Hartford blasted an effort from the edge of the area which Grobbelaar misjudged and saw the ball ricochet off his body and loop just over the crossbar. Alan Kennedy added Liverpool's third of the afternoon as he beat Williams with an angled shot before Fairclough, deputising for an injured Ian Rush, completed a personal brace as he fired beyond the City goalkeeper after Kevin Bond failed to connect with a Grobbelaar clearance.

The win preserved Liverpool's 16-point lead at the top and heralded a complete break from Bill Shankly. Ray Kennedy's move to Swansea shortly after the season's midway point constituted the final cutting of ties after his arrival from Arsenal on the same day in 1974 as the Scot announced his retirement. Paisley converted the brooding out-and-out striker into a proficient midfielder.

But Alan Kennedy argues the departure of his namesake alongside Jimmy Case and Terry McDermott that season caused an overdue evolution within the ranks at Anfield. 'We'd lost several players in Ray Kennedy and Jimmy Case. McDermott had left as well so we'd had the midfield decimated in less than six months,' he says. 'But the players that came in were just as good and people might say maybe even it was a different Liverpool; a more fluent Liverpool, a quicker Liverpool because there's no doubt about it that we did like keeping the ball and we weren't a fantastically quick team. We were a bit slower than other teams but the introduction of [Ronnie] Whelan and Rush in the team, and then [Craig] Johnston, moved it into the 21st century.'

Any hopes that City would rediscover their previous form under Benson were ambitious at best with Paul Power, a lifelong fan and now club captain, admitting that John Bond's habits continued to die hard under the man who had previously worked with him at two different clubs. 'There was absolutely no change,' he says. 'They had worked together from being at Bournemouth, they went to Norwich together and then they came to City so they were of the same opinion of how to play the game. John Bond liked to go direct, he liked to play the ball into Kevin Reeves, who was as good as Dalglish holding the ball up, but just didn't score as many goals. Then we'd have Phil Boyer who worked his socks off playing alongside Reevesie.

'There were three Johns, actually, and the [other] coach was John Sainty. I think probably what had happened then was the chairman would've been under pressure to make a change. He couldn't get in the man that he wanted, that ended up being Billy McNeill. He wouldn't have been able to get him at that particular time so he handed the reins over to John Benson just hoping really that he'd be able to prevent the slide. But I think the writing was on the wall then.'

The latest edition of *Shoot!* magazine on 7 May highlighted the contrasting fortunes with an image of Craig Johnston and Power jostling for possession in the Maine Road encounter with their eyes closed accompanied by the headline 'Man City in turmoil'. On the following weekend, the Blues faced a do-or-die home encounter against fellow relegation battlers Luton Town. A draw would have been enough to keep the hosts up, but Radomir Antic settled a previously scoreless encounter with four minutes remaining. As David Pleat performed a celebratory jig across the Maine Road turf in his brown suit, City bowed out of the top tier of English football for the first time since 1966/67.

Benson fell on his sword three weeks later with a firm warning to the next man planning to take the reins, saying, 'Whoever comes in will need time, a minimum of three years. Even if it were

Bob Paisley, he would need that time.' Time was something which Paisley had in abundance after winning his eighth and final First Division title. Liverpool's easing up in their final seven games of the season, suffering five defeats and two draws, still could not overshadow the feat of finishing as comfortable champions with second-placed Watford some 11 points behind. Paisley's signing off on his Anfield tenure eclipsed the imposing legacy that he had inherited nine years previous. His expertise was already being sought by clubs from across England and overseas. On 17 June, Ian Hargreaves reported in the *Liverpool Echo* that 'an alleged managerial offer' had been lodged from Maine Road to Paisley while also carrying quotes from the outgoing Reds manager where he said, 'I have been a one-club man, and I could not bring myself to work in opposition to Liverpool.'

An interest in David Fairclough was more concrete. The striker had been the scourge of Moss Side after scoring there five times in the previous seven years, although the tally could conceivably have been higher had he not spent the 1981/82 season on loan with Toronto Blizzard in the NASL, where he shared the stage with former adversaries George Best, Peter Lorimer and Kazimierz Deyna, formerly of Maine Road. City took their place among a chasing pack that included Watford and FC Twente in the race for Fairclough's signature before he joined Swiss outfit Lucerne. Two years later, aged 28, the man known as 'Super Sub' would find himself at City but it came to pass after just one month and without making a senior appearance.

Warriors of the Wasteland

FRESH CHALLENGES awaited Liverpool and Manchester City in the summer of 1983 as much as the UK itself. Margaret Thatcher's landslide victory at the General Election on 9 June strengthened her grip on a nation which had been firmly split between the haves and have-nots. North-west England continued to find itself among the hardest hit by ultra-conservatism.

Liverpool's succession plan for a life after Bob Paisley led them to temporarily gravitate to an external appointment. In March 1982, with his Swansea City team leading the First Division, John Toshack had been approached by the Anfield board about replacing Paisley on the assumption that his former manager was preparing to retire once that season had concluded. But with the title clinched from a position of adversity, Paisley stayed for the entire course of his seven-year contract and ended the Welshman's hopes of a hero's return.

A year later Liverpool again chose to promote from within, only this time without the initial signs of apprehension that had accompanied their previous appointment. Like Paisley, Joe Fagan had answered the call of duty as a long-serving member of the Anfield ranks since joining as a coach in 1958. Before that, the Walton-born defender had been part of the Manchester City side that won promotion back to the top flight in 1946/47 and made 158 appearances in a five-season spell, scoring twice. On Merseyside, he proved an integral cog in the brains trust that was the Boot Room and served Bill Shankly and Paisley during their respective periods at the helm. Now, at 62, it was his turn to step up to the plate.

Replacing a man widely believed to be a reluctant genius held little fear for Fagan. After all, it was his verbal rocket in the aftermath of the club's Boxing Day defeat to City in 1981 that had been the catalyst for their title triumph later that season. His nickname of 'Smokin' Joe' may have suggested otherwise but Fagan proved he was far more than a chain-smoking caricature. In a first season at the helm, and helped by the £250,000 signing of ex-City striker Michael Robinson, he led Liverpool to an historic treble of the League Cup, clinched at Maine Road courtesy of a replay against Everton, the First Division and European Cup. Bettering that accomplishment appeared likely in the 1984/85 season but Everton's emerging side under Howard Kendall ended that ambition by finishing 13 points clear of their neighbours in the league while Manchester United put paid to a first FA Cup Final appearance since 1977 in a semi-final replay on Fagan's second visit to his former stomping ground. Retaining the European Cup became immaterial following the Heysel tragedy, where 39 predominantly Juventus supporters were crushed to death when a wall collapsed as a result of fighting between both sets of fans. Fagan had already announced his intention to stand down after the final but the unfolding horror in Brussels' crumbling stadium beforehand left him a broken man; evidenced by his distraught journey across the tarmac at Liverpool's Speke airport the following day.

City's life in the Second Division had started in difficult circumstances. Peter Swales occasionally referred to himself as The Cincinnati Kid, a nod to his favourite film, where Steve McQueen overplays his hand in a game of high-stakes poker and is told by rival Edward G. Robinson, 'You're good, kid, but as long as I'm around, you're second best. You might as well learn to live with it.'

Swales could not accept being secondary to Manchester United and the cumulative effect of that fixation finally came home to roost. To paraphrase a line from another box office smash, the chairman's ego was writing cheques that City could not cash. Malcolm Allison and John Bond had both been armed to the teeth in the transfer market but like McQueen's character Eric 'The Kid' Stoner, Swales simply did not know when to stop and the interest payments alone were costing the club £1,000 daily. The only way to limit the bloodletting was by reining in future spending, something which took new manager Billy McNeill by surprise.

John Benson's successor had been convinced to leave Celtic, where he had won a major trophy in each of his five seasons at the helm, including three Scottish League titles, for a club which had fallen on hard times. McNeill only realised the extent of City's financial dire straits when he consulted chief scout Ken Barnes about the situation only to be informed, 'You've picked the wrong day to come to me for sympathy, Bill – I've had my fucking phone cut off this morning.'

Swales's own blueprint for success, which ranged from a new purpose-built training ground in Cheadle to the installation of executive boxes at Maine Road, also had to be shelved in the cost-cutting measures. City's transfer spending did not break into six-figure sums until the December arrival of Mick McCarthy from Barnsley for £200,000, a fee which was offset by Tommy Caton's £450,000 sale to Arsenal earlier in the month.

But the centre-back could not prevent a failure to secure promotion back to the First Division at the first time of asking in a season when ex-Liverpool striker David Johnson, drafted in from Everton, scored once in six appearances as the Blues finished in fourth, ten points off the final promotion place. Just 12 months later, McNeill's side sealed their return to the top flight with a 5-1 home win over Charlton Athletic on the same afternoon that news filtered through of the tragic loss of life at Valley Parade, where 56 people had perished after an inferno tore through the main stand of Bradford City's ground. An already dark day became further blighted by hooliganism as a teenager was killed during fighting between Leeds United and Birmingham City supporters at St Andrew's. Manchester City's return to the top flight had arrived in the midst of a truly bleak period for the domestic game.

Later that month, events at Heysel led to UEFA banning English clubs from its competitions indefinitely, ultimately reduced to a five-year period, while a stand-off with television executives raged on the home front. Football League clubs had unanimously rejected a joint proposal from existing rights holders BBC and ITV, worth £19m over four seasons, due to a strong-held belief that the figure should be closer to £90m. City and Liverpool had previously found rare common ground in the 1974 battle to preserve the game's growing link with TV. Football League clubs had originally rejected another BBC/ITV offer worth £2m over the next three years, prompting the north-west rivals to join forces with Leeds and Chelsea in a four-club coalition to back the bid to retain broadcast rights. Teams later voted in favour of the financial package, when it was revealed that some faced potential advertising losses of up to £60,000 without the exposure provided by the country's flagship channels.

In Britain's battle-hardened environment of 1985, such moments of clarity were conspicuous by their absence. No competitive football was shown in the first half of the following season, after which a compromise was finally reached to screen six First Division fixtures at a cut-price fee of £1.3m. Armchair viewers impacted by the blackout were denied the sight of Manchester United taking a nine-point lead in the campaign's early weeks, with an end to a 19-year wait to win the First Division appearing a formality. The *Daily Mirror* even went as far as imploring that Ron Atkinson's side were handed the title forthwith with the headline 'Now United Will Be Champs'. At Christmas, the gap had been shortened to four points. Under Kenny Dalglish, Liverpool were still very much a side in transition; shaken by not only the harrowing experience of Heysel but also Graeme Souness's departure for Sampdoria some 18 months earlier. Yet they remained well placed to take advantage of any potential slip-ups by their counterparts from across the East Lancs Road.

A trip to Maine Road on 26 December could conceivably have halved the deficit with United taking on Everton at the same time. Their impressive record against City, winning in all six of their previous visits to Moss Side, augured well for putting the 16th-placed hosts to the sword. City assistant manager Jimmy Frizzell attempted to put the club's unflattering league position into perspective, saying, 'The team has been playing well for most of the season but not getting goals … If we had taken 30 per cent of our chances created, we would be close behind Liverpool in the league now.'

On Boxing Day, the visitors' dominance saw them win ten corners to their hosts' one, but left-back Clive Wilson scored the game's only goal with a follow-up after Gordon Davies's initial shot had rebounded back off Bruce Grobbelaar. Dalglish's introduction from the substitutes' bench moments before the opener led to a hatful of chances in retaliation, the most notable coming from Steve McMahon hitting the crossbar with a chipped effort. Exactly four years since last tasting victory over Liverpool, City also had a first win on home soil since 1977 to match.

'We definitely wouldn't have been expected to win that game but there was pride in the dressing room,' says Paul Power. 'Whatever dressing room I've played in, players don't get to the First Division without having pride in their own performance. Some of them are selfish and don't play for the team, some of them like Trevor Francis for instance, was a selfish player, didn't work his socks off when the opposition had the ball or anything like that but he'd win the game for you because he was that good of a finisher. It takes all different types to make a dressing room.

'Liverpool, at the moment, have got players who are both artists and soldiers. The front three run their socks off when the opposition have got the ball, but they can be fantastic when they've got the ball as well. City are exactly the same. David Silva and Bernardo Silva, for me, are like artists and soldiers combined. They're able to make things happen and stop things from happening. I think that is a sign of a successful team. If you've got more of those players in your squad, you're more likely to win than you are to lose. Liverpool had loads of them.'

Two months later, the Anfield club had fallen eight points off the pace after a 2-0 defeat to Everton. The reigning champions had built on their initial success by replacing Andy Gray with Leicester City striker Gary Lineker and were on course to ensure the title remained on Merseyside for a fourth straight year. Dalglish still refused to concede defeat to his side's old enemy and responded by stringing together an impressive run which saw the Reds snapping at their neighbours' heels by winning four of their next five league games. A chance to leapfrog the Toffees presented itself in the form of a Manchester City side that had lost 5-4 to Chelsea in the inaugural final of the Full Members' Cup, a supplementary competition created in the aftermath of Heysel for teams in the Football League's top two tiers, just eight days earlier. The 31 March meeting came on an afternoon where plummeting temperatures had seen snow falling in some parts of Merseyside.

City captain Paul Power remained the sole survivor from their most recent visit to Anfield four years earlier, a 5-2 reversal. Ahead of the game, McNeill had drafted in Ellesmere Port-born goalkeeper Barry Siddall on loan from Stoke for his debut, with Eric Nixon unfancied and Alex Williams recovering from a back injury. The debutant had his work cut out in a first half where Liverpool peppered his goal and finally yielded a breakthrough on 33 minutes after Mick McCarthy headed away Craig Johnston's corner but only as far as Jan Mølby, whose flick-on was met with an attempted overhead kick from Ian Rush that caused confusion in the visitors' defence before Steve McMahon ran on to the loose ball and drilled it into Siddall's top right-hand corner for his ninth goal of the season.

'He was a typical Liverpool player; he was another Jimmy Case; he was another Graeme Souness,' says Power. 'He had aggression, but he had creativity as well. I don't know who went to watch players when they signed for Liverpool but I bet that they'd delve right into the character of the player as much as the ability. Sometimes the ability's obvious but you need players in the dressing room and I've got to say from the reports I've heard about Pep Guardiola, he wants players in the dressing room that are going to play for each other – not themselves. I think that is a massive thing about the Liverpool dressing room of that era.'

Early in the second half, City almost equalised against the run of play when McCarthy pressured Jim Beglin into making a poor back-pass which Steve Kinsey intercepted and squeezed goalwards after drawing Bruce Grobbelaar, only for Gary Gillespie to hook it clear on the line. Alan Hansen's new centre-back partner had been reintegrated into the Liverpool line-up following a four-month spell on the sidelines with a knee injury picked up in a pre-season fixture at Brighton but Mark Lawrenson's own absence with an ankle problem saw the versatile defender step up. Beglin would again be indebted to Gillespie later on in the half when McCarthy again forced him into overrunning the ball for Clive Wilson to cut out and beat the offside trap with a floated ball for Kinsey, prompting Grobbelaar to rush 25 yards from goal in an effort to stave off the threat but was skipped past. As three City players waited in the penalty area, Gillespie met the centre with an instinctive block.

Power believes Gillespie's penalty area heroics were typical of a team which continued to show signs of its collective qualities even in a disadvantageous position. 'That was the thing about Liverpool. They were always strong as a unit,' he says. 'I can't remember a Liverpool team where they had individuals who would stand out, certainly not in the era that I played in. Clive would've played on the left and Jim Beglin was left-back wasn't he so I'm surprised Clive came into contact with him unless Jim maybe played on the right side of that game. That might be a reason why he was a little less comfortable on the wrong side of the pitch but I don't know, I'm just guessing. It didn't matter where Liverpool players played, they always played well – certainly at Anfield.'

The hosts continued to imprint themselves on the game before City's second breakaway as a flowing move between Dalglish, Mølby and Johnston allowed McMahon to stab the ball into the roof of The Kop's net from close range.

McMahon's career had started out at Everton, a club he had supported and served as a ballboy in his younger years, before a £175,000 move to Aston Villa in May 1983. At that time,

Liverpool had attempted to coax him across Stanley Park but the midfielder opted against a double-your-money switch out of respect to his erstwhile employers. A strong-tackling ruthlessness saw McMahon become the first signing of Dalglish's tenure little more than two years later.

'Macca was probably a bit of an underrated player at the time,' says Gillespie. 'He probably didn't get the recognition that he deserved. He was an all-round midfield player who could defend, tackle and obviously could score goals. I think in that team he was given a bit of license to get forward more than maybe he had done in the past. It was a great time to be playing in that side, it was just so confident – not just Macca but everybody else involved in the middle of the park. It was one of these great sides to play in, albeit Alan Hansen said it was the worst Liverpool team he'd ever seen!'

Hansen's now infamous remark had been made to Dalglish over a meal on the evening of the 22 February home loss to Everton. 'This team is going to win nothing,' the club captain told his team-mate and now boss. Barely a month later, Liverpool had surpassed their local rivals in the First Division table on goal difference with a win over City where the player-manager made only his fourth league start of the calendar year. City manager Billy McNeill was full of praise for the impact that Dalglish, a one-time team-mate at Celtic and the man who later replaced him as skipper at Parkhead, had on the Reds. 'They are still the best passing team in the country. Their composure on the ball is better than any of their rivals,' he said. 'Dalglish gives them that composure when he's playing. His greatest asset is not his own incredible ability, but the way he can make the people around him respond … I wonder sometimes why he leaves himself out, but that is up to him.'

Gillespie also believes that Dalglish's return to the spotlight sparked an upturn in their fortunes which culminated in a league and FA Cup double, both secured at Everton's expense. 'I think it's one of these things that, having seen Kenny and been about the club before he became manager, it's something that you just forget about and don't understand or appreciate,' he says. 'I always remember playing a testimonial game years after we'd all finished [playing] and Kenny came on as sub, and he still had it. He still had that little bit that separated him from every other player. Looking back in hindsight, him coming back into the side at that moment in time was the impetus we needed. He was such an influential player, such a great player, not just an individual but really embodies the spirit and camaraderie that Liverpool had at that time. I never thought about it at the time, but I suppose when you do look back it was a massive boost for us.'

As Liverpool hit the midway point of what would become a 12-game unbeaten streak, drawing just once, City were in the middle of their own, inauspicious dozen. They consolidated First Division status at the end of 1985/86 with a four-point safety net from the relegation zone but failed to win any of their remaining fixtures, taking three points from a possible 36.

In the bowels of Anfield, cracks were starting to appear as Jimmy Frizzell hijacked the invitation of a customary post-match drink in the Boot Room to air personal grievances about McNeill's team selections. The Blues' assistant manager had been brought in by his compatriot in 1983, just a year after being sacked from a decade-long spell in charge of Oldham Athletic, but now felt it necessary to speak out of turn. Attempts to garner either advice or sympathy from his Liverpool counterparts, though, was met with stern opposition. 'Hey, don't be telling us mate – be telling your manager!' retorted Ronnie Moran. 'It's easy to criticise.'

One figure in the City side that afternoon who was immune from criticism was Steve Redmond, an 18-year-old who would captain the club to FA Youth Cup glory two months on. Coached by two Maine Road greats in Tony Book and Glyn Pardoe, the Liverpool-born defender was part of a team which later produced six future first-team players.

Redmond also formed part of a three-man ensemble which heavily shackled Ian Rush in a Bank Holiday Monday stalemate at the start of the following season at Anfield. Barely 48 hours after plundering a brace against Newcastle United, the striker found little joy against a combination of the Netherley native,

McCarthy and Kenny Clements. Earlier in the summer, Liverpool had agreed a £3.2m transfer with Juventus but retained Rush on a season-long loan due to Michel Platini and Michael Laudrup already occupying the Serie A club's two allotted slots for overseas players.

Referee Ken Walmsley's refusal to award a penalty when substitute Kevin Macdonald's shot had struck the arm of Clements led to Rush confronting the Blackpool official at the final whistle and being retrospectively sent off for using 'foul and abusive language'. An automatic two-game suspension risked Liverpool being without any experienced strikers for their upcoming fixtures as well as a player that had never finished on a losing side of any Reds' games in which he scored.

Under the existing guidelines, the FA later confirmed that Rush could have only been booked for the incident with his misconduct reported. The moment of madness still came as a surprise as the talisman of the First Division's best-behaved club in the previous season. 'Rushie was never that way inclined to be honest with you,' says Gary Gillespie. 'It must have taken something for him to be upset because he definitely wasn't that kind of player. Whether he had a bee in his bonnet or not, I'm not 100 per cent sure. He'd got a couple of goals in the first game [against Newcastle] so I don't know if he'd had a bad game or not and he maybe had a little bit with the referee but [it was] totally out of character and unlike him.'

Disorder was a common theme in the August encounter as a City fan became the first person to be prosecuted under the Sporting Events Act, introduced the previous year, for running on to the pitch during the game and gesturing towards the home crowd. The 22-year-old, who also swore at police officers when arrested, pleaded guilty to a charge of public drunkenness at Liverpool Magistrates Court and was ordered to pay £10 in costs.

If the City supporter in question thought that things could not get any worse after a brush with the law, worse was set to follow. In mid-September, chairman Peter Swales led a campaign to restore the First Division's intake to 22 teams from the previously agreed reduction of 20. The move gained backing from a swathe of top-flight clubs including Liverpool, where Swales's former business partner Noel White had recently been appointed a director. The initial plans to streamline the league only won support from Anfield's corridors of power on the understanding that it would lead to the creation of the British Cup, with teams from England, Scotland and Northern Ireland all involved. Fears that UEFA would exploit the new competition by deeming its winners to be sole entrants to the European Cup Winners' Cup, at a time when four teams from the collective were still involved even with the post-Heysel ban imposed on English sides, had rendered the idea a virtual non-starter.

Swales's powers of persuasion among his peers did not have the same impact closer to home as Billy McNeill resigned as City manager just seven games into the season, with the club 15th in the First Division, to join an Aston Villa side rooted to the foot of the table. Frustrations over the club's perilous financial situation led to a bewildering departure as he disembarked the team coach at its final pick-up point in Cheshire's Bucklow Hill ahead of a League Cup tie at Southend United. Months after attempting to call the shots in Anfield's Boot Room, Frizzell was promoted to the hot seat but oversaw City's descent to below Villa in the league's bottom three by Christmas.

Liverpool's title defence fared little better with Arsenal leading them in the table by eight points, a gulf which had extended further by the turn of 1987. Everton had assumed the role of key challengers to George Graham's side and sat just one point behind before a trip to Maine Road left the Reds requiring a statement of intent against a team that had climbed back to safety in 16th, having taken seven points from a possible 12 in their previous four matches. Boosting the hosts' chances ahead of the 17 January meeting was the return of Peter Barnes following an eight-year absence. The former City winger, and son of chief scout Ken, moved across town from Manchester United in a £300,000 deal which saw him receive a rapturous reception ahead of kick-off.

Shades of Barnes's previously dazzling displays in a sky blue shirt were still obvious on his homecoming bow but the end product left a lot to be desired. In the tenth minute, he beat two Liverpool defenders with skill before wildly overhitting a cross, much to the relief of Liverpool's defence. 'Barnesy used to play on the left wing so I probably came up against him,' says Gary Gillespie. 'I'd played against Manchester City a few times for Coventry as well so I can remember the first time he was there, probably back in '77, '78, '79, round about that time. But he certainly wasn't the same player coming back into the City side than what he was before he went away. I think he'd lost a little bit of his pace. He certainly still had the skill and the ability on the ball and everything like that but I think his game was about taking on people and running past people, and I'm not quite sure he managed to do that as effectively when he came back for the second time around.'

Barnes's lack of finesse hampered the hosts' ability to engineer an opening against a Liverpool team hardly at the peak of its powers despite fashioning regular chances. Their most incisive arrived on 73 minutes when a run by McMahon allowed Lawrenson to overlap and send a cross into the far post, where Rush prodded home his 24th goal of the season.

Gillespie's display at both ends of the pitch in the game, defending resolutely while also inspiring an otherwise languid attack, had earned him the *Liverpool Echo*'s man of the match award with a run early in the second half that saw his shot fly narrowly wide singled out for particular credit. 'We were given our heads to go and do that,' he says. 'One thing we were always told as defenders was that if you start the move and you get involved in the move, see the move through. Whether it be [from] in your own 18-yard box or the opposition's box, we always had that license to go ahead and do that. Other players would automatically just fill in for you. It was just part and parcel of the way that we wanted to play. We were capable and saw the opportunity to go forward and get ourselves into good positions. We certainly had the confidence and understanding from the coaching staff and the manager to go and do that. It was drummed into us, not just to give the ball easily and knock off – if you saw an opportunity to go and move forward, well why not go and do it?'

Dalglish's absence through an ankle injury still provoked questions about his status as player-manager, having missed 15 of the previous 17 matches, as the champions' attempts to reascend were still falling short. Leeds United legend John Giles wrote in the *Sunday Tribune* that the man in the dugout would 'be considered a failure' if he could not follow up on the impressive double success that had commemorated his debut season in charge. Giles also said that Frizzell 'might as well be given the Freedom of Manchester if he keeps his team in the top flight'.

A small slice of retribution for their First Division loss arrived just three days later for City when they faced Liverpool's reserves with Barnes featuring in the Maine Road encounter against a second string that contained midfielder John Wark and future Anfield first-teamer Gary Ablett, whose back-pass helped complete a 5-0 hammering for the home side.

By mid-March, Liverpool had returned to the First Division summit with a nine-point lead but three straight losses saw Everton, now shorn of 1986 World Cup top scorer Gary Lineker, supersede them and eventually be crowned champions by the same margin. A League Cup Final defeat to Arsenal earlier in the season had ended Rush's talismanic streak and ensured that they finished empty-handed for the second time in three seasons. The Wales international's imminent departure to Juventus had seen Oxford United striker John Aldridge joining his boyhood club as a replacement. Over the summer, Dalglish had further strengthened his attacking options with Watford's John Barnes and Peter Beardsley at Newcastle United arriving for a combined £2.8m.

On Moss Side, Swales was facing a genuine uprising as City bowed out of the First Division once more, joined by McNeill's Aston Villa. Opposition to the suddenly spendthrift chairman had been minor during their last demotion in 1983 but had returned with a vengeance as supporters launched a visible protest movement. His attempted solution saw a return to a model which had previously seen former and current City managers sharing the stage on two separate occasions. Frizzell became general manager, a position previously occupied by Joe Mercer and Tony Book, to facilitate the arrival of Norwich City's assistant coach Mel Machin as team manager. The new double act led to confusion as to who was the real power behind the throne, with the pair alternating both media duties and programme notes throughout the 1987/88 season.

Frizzell's role in developmental matters appeared to extend to transfers as he confirmed that inquiries had been made for Liverpool midfielder John Wark among a host of players in the opening month of the campaign. Some of those leaving Maine Road at the same time were drawing interest from the opposite direction as the First Division runners-up emerged as part of a chasing pack for Mick McCarthy, with Celtic eventually winning the race for the centre-back with a £500,000 fee.

Graduates from City's 1986 FA Youth Cup-winning side were commanding even greater attention in the less glamorous surroundings of the Second Division. A 10-1 demolition of Huddersfield Town on 7 November 1987 saw Andy Hinchcliffe, Steve Redmond, Paul Lake, Ian Brightwell and David White all feature in the club's biggest scoreline for over 94 years, with White racking up a hat-trick alongside trebles from Paul Stewart and Tony Adcock. A similarly emphatic 6-2 win over Plymouth Argyle arrived three days later in the Full Members' Cup as Hinchcliffe opened the scoring under the keen eye of Kenny Dalglish, who saw the left-back as a potential Liverpool signing. Dalglish's own side were in equally impressive form and had pulled clear of their competitors in the First Division with a 15-point hold over Alex Ferguson's Manchester United by the time an FA Cup quarter-final meeting pitted them against City's burgeoning home-grown crop.

Bookmakers priced City as 66/1 outsiders to progress against Liverpool's 11/8 odds but supporters headed into the clash on 13

March with genuine relish, having triumphed on the previous two occasions that the clubs had met in the world's most famous club competition, in 1956 and 1973. Frizzell considered his side's recent form with their Merseyside counterparts as a sign for optimism, saying, 'We have quite a good recent record against Liverpool. We defeated them 1-0 at Maine Road three years ago and last season we held them to a draw at Anfield and went down to a solitary goal at home. It would be foolish to make predictions, but we will give them a good game.'

Dalglish, however, dismissed the prospect that recent results would have any bearing on the outcome. 'Our record against Manchester City is history and counts for nothing at all,' he insisted.

But as Gary Gillespie admits, Liverpool's players still felt buoyed heading into their latest trip to Moss Side due to the extensive preparations undertaken before every game ensuring they were best prepared for every eventuality. 'In the eight years I was there, we never finished outside of the top two, so I think that gives you confidence in any game that you're going to play,' he says. 'Certainly, going to a club like Man City, who we had a decent record against and the big open pitch at Maine Road, suited us well. I think confidence was always part and parcel of the way we approached any game. We believed that we could get a result against any team. Kenny looked at teams to worry about us as opposed to us worrying about them and we knew that if we played to our capability and capacity then that should, more often than not, be good enough to get a result. That's why it was always drummed into us about our attitude, effort and commitment – if you got these three things right then your technical ability should shine above everybody else and obviously for us that's the way it was for a long spell.'

A prospective giant-killing attracted the attention of ITV's *The Big Match*, which screened the game live despite the more enticing prospect of a tie between George Graham's Arsenal and Nottingham Forest, still led by the venerable Brian Clough, on the same weekend.

Undeterred, a crowd of 44,047 turned out to produce a cacophony of noise and colour as blue and white balloons were interspersed with reams of toilet roll ahead of a showdown with English football's most exhilarating side.

John Bond, the former City manager and previously a scathing critic of Liverpool, admitted in a pitchside interview with Elton Welsby before the game that even he had been converted by Dalglish's upwardly mobile team. 'I wasn't always a great fan of theirs, but I am now,' he confessed in a eulogy which extolled the visitors' individual and collective qualities. The gods seemed to also be smiling on Liverpool with a torrential downpour softening the pitch to provide optimum playing conditions for the First Division's champions-elect.

'I think if you asked any Liverpool player at the time, what we hated was a pitch that had long grass, a little bit maybe bobbly and a little bit uneven underneath,' says Gillespie. 'We liked it to be greasy on top and nice and nippy with the ball so we could knock the ball about. That was our skill: forward-thinking, quick thinking, passing it quickly, moving it quickly. That's ideal conditions when it's like that. When it's rainy and wet and slippy on top, that did suit us down to the ground to be fair.'

City were able to weather the storm for the best part of half an hour, when Peter Beardsley's pass sent John Barnes to the byeline. The winger skinned John Gidman before delivering a cross for Ray Houghton, a mid-season arrival from Oxford, to volley past Mike Stowell. The home fans were incensed that Barnes had seemingly handled the ball in the build-up despite television pictures suggesting he had instead chested it down. Maine Road's sense of injustice simmered after the interval as a mis-headed clearance by Steve Redmond allowed auxiliary striker Craig Johnston to go on a mazy run and round Stowell but Paul Lake pushed the Australian to the ground in the direct aftermath. From the penalty spot, Beardsley doubled Liverpool's lead with a shot squeezed past the Everton loanee at his right-hand post.

Seconds after the restart, an irate home fan ran on to the pitch to confront referee Allan Gunn with several finger-wagging and

V-sign gestures before being led away by a steward who found himself on the receiving end of a right-handed punch from the invader as police officers moved in to escort him off the turf. Tensions continued to boil over in the stands, where rival supporters traded both insults, blows and occasionally saliva. Snippets of the disorder were later used in crowd shots from the game for a segment on the BBC's *Panorama* programme which explored the problem of hooliganism in English football in the run-up to Euro '88. City's chairman Peter Swales, in his role as an FA board member, attempted to make a case for clubs to be reinstated into UEFA competitions following the current three-year expulsion incurred by the Heysel tragedy.

The only notable chance for City arrived when Neil McNab twisted and turned through three Liverpool defenders before spraying the ball out to Imre Varadi on the left for a first-time cross which Paul Stewart met with a leaping header that produced an acrobatic save from Bruce Grobbelaar. But the visitors ramped up their dominance in the 77th minute as Johnston again skipped past Stowell to slot home a third of the afternoon. Five minutes from the end, the combination of Beardsley and Barnes rounded off the win as the latter ran on to a through ball and rolled it past the City goalkeeper and into an empty net. The tenth occasion on which Liverpool had scored four times in a game received a standing ovation from most of the Maine Road faithful at full time.

That appreciation was not reciprocated when the two teams headed towards the dressing rooms. As ITV's Martin Tyler approached a mud-splattered Johnston for a post-match interview, teatime viewers were treated to an off-camera exchange as City's general manager Frizzell confronted referee Gunn over his decision to award the penalty for Lake's shove on the Liverpool forward.

'Fucking grow up!' shouted Frizzell.

'Hey, you wanna fucking grow up,' replied Gunn.

'That was horrendous.'

'They were marvellous. They deserved to win today.'

John Giles echoed Gunn's assertion in his piece for the *Evening Herald*, saying, 'Once Ray Houghton scored the first goal, everyone might as well have gone home, as City were never going to come back.' He added, 'Liverpool were at their aristocratic best and they exposed City for what they were.'

Frizzell still continued to wage war over the circumstances which led to the visitors' opening two goals by telling the press the following week that Barnes's alleged handball could have been given against him and bizarrely referred to Lake's handled challenge on Johnston as 'a good one'. Johnston, for his part, credited City's resilience in attempting to back the tide. 'To be part of that atmosphere was great,' he said. 'The lads did terrific. City are a good young side, they just kept going and kept going. It's as good a battle as we've had this year.'

Liverpool's awe-inspiring display led Bond to opine that Dalglish's side could go through the remainder of the First Division season unbeaten. 'I would be surprised if anybody in this country beat them,' he said. 'I don't think there's anybody good enough to beat them.' The former Blues boss pointed to the following weekend's Merseyside derby as only the 'biggest danger' facing the runaway leaders' record. His prophecy rang true with Everton ending a 29-game streak, which had drawn level with Leeds United's feat of 1973/74. Another defeat to Nottingham Forest, their FA Cup semi-final opponents, still failed to stop Liverpool from finishing nine points clear of Manchester United.

Plaudits were plentiful in supply for a team which Tom Finney claimed was better than Brazil, but their bid for a second double in three seasons was scuppered by Wimbledon's 'Crazy Gang' in the FA Cup Final. Ian Rush's £2.8m return from Juventus that summer reinforced their firepower ahead of a 1988/89 season where they went toe-to-toe with Arsenal in the hunt for the title throughout.

Football, however, paled into insignificance following the Hillsborough disaster. The unlawful killing of 96 men, women and children at an abandoned FA Cup semi-final against Forest took an immeasurable toll on Liverpool, both as a club and a city, with emotional scars that are unlikely to ever be healed. Dalglish and his players spent the next three weeks attending funerals of those who had lost their lives in Sheffield and comforting bereaved relatives.

Their return to action saw a punishing schedule of eight matches played across 24 days, including a symbolic FA Cup Final win over Everton and a First Division finale where Arsenal snatched the title by one point at Anfield with Michael Thomas's late goal made famous by ITV commentator Brian Moore declaring, 'It's up for grabs now!'

On the eve of the rescheduled 7 May semi-final at Old Trafford, Dalglish ventured to Maine Road as Manchester City attempted to cinch automatic promotion from the Second Division in their penultimate game of the season against Bournemouth. Mel Machin's players had been promised an end-of-season trip to Australia if they secured a runners-up spot to Chelsea with one fixture to spare and were on course to achieve that aim by racing to a three-goal lead before half-time. Under the Liverpool manager's watchful eye was a player who would later endear himself to his new City team-mates by helping to put paid to their plans of a premature getaway Down Under.

Bournemouth midfielder Ian Bishop had grown up on the sink housing estate of Cantril Farm, a short distance from Liverpool's Melwood training ground, and regularly watched games from The Kop as a youngster despite his allegiances belonging to Arsenal. Ahead of the Moss Side encounter, he was aware of the prospect of moving to either of the season's First Division title contenders. 'I obviously knew by then something was afoot about me getting a move to a top club,' he says. 'There was actually talk of Liverpool and Arsenal, and I know for that Bournemouth-Man City game that Kenny Dalglish was there and there was talk about whether he was watching me or Paul Lake. There were whispers going around at that time which for me: Liverpool, a team I used to go and see at Anfield growing up, or Arsenal, a team I'd supported. I had no inclination that City were interested to be honest.'

With his team coasting to certain victory, Machin delegated the half-time briefing to comedian and lifelong City supporter Eddie Large, a familiar presence within the dressing room in recent years. Dressed in a shiny grey suit with the sleeves rolled up, he doled out tactical instructions through the medium of celebrity impressions. Lake was ordered to keep it tight in defence by Deputy Dawg; Frank Carson implored Neil McNab to utilise David White's pace and width in attack; Cliff Richard demanded that Trevor Morley shot on sight; Ian Brightwell found himself advised to keep it simple by the former British prime minister Harold Wilson, while Paul Williams, deputising for the injured Andy Dibble, was told to stay alert by Benny from *Crossroads*. Whether the City goalkeeper was confused by the orders or the sheer litany of impressions that Large worked through at the break is unclear, but he could not prevent the hosts from conceding three times in a six-goal thriller, with Bishop pulling the strings in midfield for the Cherries. A return to the top flight was eventually secured in a 1-1 draw at Bradford City the following weekend.

Some 85 days after Bishop's favourite club had snared the First Division crown at Anfield, he stepped out as part of a City team seeking to make up for lost time. Returning to the ground for a first time as a player on 19 August 1989 conjured up a maelstrom of emotions. 'What I remember most is the feeling when you walked up as a supporter through the gap in the stairs and you got your first glimpse of the pitch,' he says. 'Once you'd seen the pitch, a different feeling came over you. Even as a kid going to watch games, once you saw that green and as soon as they start singing 'You'll Never Walk Alone', it was something that stuck with me. Going there as an adult, in a Man City shirt, I remember before kick-off when they did start singing, the lads were warming up around me and I was just standing there. I was lost. I was standing there staring at The Kop and I was somewhere else because of that feeling.'

Also making his City debut that afternoon was a player who appeared to signal an end to Peter Swales's penny-pinching phase. Clive Allen had moved to Maine Road as City's first £1m-plus signing since Trevor Francis in 1981, following an unsettled season with French side Bordeaux. On Merseyside, the former Tottenham Hotspur striker was treated to sun-drenched climes similar to the ones he had enjoyed on the banks of the Garonne river. Referee David Phillips was also benefitting from the new season's surroundings, with match officials' fees raised from £60 per match to £100 at the start of the campaign. The FA Cup holders' record in winning each of their opening home league games since rejoining the First Division in 1962 and an eight-year unbeaten streak against the Blues on Merseyside suggested their opponents stood little to no chance of pulling off a surprise result.

Bishop's immediate task in sky blue colours was to negotiate a moral maze when tasked with inflicting a reducer on Liverpool's midfield duo of Ronnie Whelan and Steve McMahon, whose boots he had cleaned as an apprentice coming through the ranks at Everton. 'I played alongside Neil McNab and he obviously knew I'd been down the divisions and this was sort of my first time back up,' he says. 'He said to me, "First thing you do, just go and kick one of them."'

'I knew Stevie from when I was an apprentice at Everton so I didn't know how he would react to me now being on the same pitch as him and against him. I ended up going in late on Ronnie and sort of chopping him down. He jumped up, got in my face, "First game is it, sonny?" I went, "Yeah, it is – and you're gonna know about it." He then said, "D'you wanna come home and see my medals?"'

'To be fair, after the game I did see him in the players' lounge and say, "I really would like to come and see your medals!"'

Andy Dibble repelled a Liverpool onslaught in the first half's early stages and impressively beat away an Ian Rush effort with his left hand. But his heroics were undone when a Peter Beardsley shot struck Brian Gayle's arm in the seventh minute, allowing John Barnes to fire a low penalty past Dibble. The First Division returnees continued to create openings, with Nigel Gleghorn's curling shot that Bruce Grobbelaar beat away being the highlight, before Bishop faced an unavoidable collision with his former

Goodison Park superior just outside The Kop's penalty area. 'I saw Stevie coming in and I'm thinking, "Ohhhh fuck!"' he says. 'He's coming in and I thought there's no way he's going higher than me, so I went for him above knee-height. I caught him just above the knee, but he comes in with an elbow and smashes me in the face! I knew he was coming. It was unavoidable and I thought I've got to protect myself, just in that split second. We both went down, and he's really smashed me in the jaw. I got straight up and he's sort of faked it a little bit because he knew he'd caught me. He stayed down a little bit longer.'

The ensuing free kick from Andy Hinchcliffe ricocheted between Barnes and Barry Venison, both positioned at the end of a five-man wall, to wrong-foot Grobbelaar and bobble into the net. City's impetus grew after the equaliser as Allen started a move from deep in his own half before squaring to David Oldfield for a deflected shot which the Liverpool goalkeeper had to pull off an agile stop to beat. The closing seconds of the first half saw Trevor Morley have the beating of Alan Hansen as he bore down on goal, only for the referee's whistle to bring proceedings to an end.

Liverpool's stalled plans for a flying start drew a frustrated response from Dalglish in the home dressing room with Glenn Hysen, a Swedish international defender newly signed from Fiorentina, later admitting his manager had been 'a little bit angry with us'. Bishop argues that City's 23rd-minute level-pegging set them up for an eventual fall. 'I think that was the worst thing we could have done,' he says. 'Because they then just stepped up another two gears and they were fantastic. You never go out thinking you're gonna lose but it was one of those teams that you'd be saying to yourself, "How the friggin' hell are we going to get a result here?"'

Liverpool responded after the interval with a renewed drive which helped them retake the lead on the hour as Steve Redmond, a boyhood fan of the hosts, stabbed the ball towards his own goal while trying to cut out a cross from Steve Nicol. Dibble produced an instinctive reflex stop but it simply delayed the inevitable as Beardsley pounced to score an unstoppable follow-up. Another almost followed when Gayle attempted to cut out a cross from defender David Burrows which fell for Rush, who attempted to steer it past Dibble. Only Gayle's headed clearance on the goal line spared City's blushes as well as his own.

In stoppage time, Beardsley found Barnes on the left-hand side. The winger performed a mazy dribble into the penalty area which evaded challenges from Paul Lake and an advancing Dibble before squaring to Nicol to strike a decisive third goal which raised the Kop's decibel levels to raucous levels.

A piece of City history was created in the immediate aftermath of their 3-1 humbling. Supporters leaving the Anfield Road End after being held back for half an hour on police advice, a move which had become commonplace whenever Liverpool and Manchester clubs met, broke out into a spontaneous rendition of 'Blue Moon'. Created by lyricist Lorenz Hart and composer Richard Rodgers, one half of the Rodgers and Hammerstein partnership which spawned the Liverpool – and one-time Maine Road – anthem 'You'll Never Walk Alone', the song had become a number one hit worldwide with American doo-wop group The Marcels in 1961 and had been previously covered by a number of artists including Elvis Presley and Billie Holliday.

Earlier in the decade, Crewe Alexandra fans sang their own variation of the ballad but the melancholic strands that began in the stadium and carried on into the streets set in motion a new tradition which would grace the terraces on Moss Side and further afield over the next three decades. Fans had little to sing about with City winning just one of their next six games before a memorable 5-1 demolition of Manchester United that reduced Alex Ferguson to lying on the bed of his Wilmslow home with a pillow over his head.

Ferguson's exasperation would continue in the months ahead but City's problems were far from over as Machin recorded another four wins in their next 12 matches, with half of them coming in the League Cup, that left the club rooted to the foot of the First Division. His dismissal ahead of the impending clash with Liverpool carried an explanation from chairman Peter Swales that 'he had no repartee with the fans'. John Deehan, a player-coach previously signed from Machin's old club Norwich, and club stalwart Tony Book were placed in temporary charge as Swales documented his failed pursuit of Joe Royle in a series of television appearances.

The first came on Granada's *Kick Off* show on 1 December and was followed by a lunchtime grilling on *Saint & Greavsie*, where he confirmed that City's approach for their former striker had been turned down by Oldham Athletic just hours before Liverpool's visit. Royle's decision to hang fire with the Second Division side paid off in a season when they would finish as runners-up in the League Cup Final and reach the FA Cup semi-final, something he admits had a key bearing when approached about returning to his old club.

'It was all about Oldham. It was nothing to do with City,' he says. 'I'd spoken to Peter Swales and I'd made it very clear that I was happy at Oldham, but it was an offer that I had to consider. The only problem was Oldham were having their season of all seasons. We were going for promotion, still in the League Cup, still in the FA Cup and I didn't want to turn around and be seen as the one who ran away and left them when we were on the verge of our biggest-ever season. So, it was all about Oldham and not about City. If City had waited until the end of the season, or at the start of the season, there wouldn't have been a problem. It was just the timing was wrong.'

Book and Deehan's brief joint venture saw Mark Seagraves handed a maiden outing of the season that pitted him against Liverpool for a first time since making a £100,000 switch in September 1987. The Bootle-born defender had been a peripheral figure in the club's double-winning side of 1985/86, making two appearances in the early rounds of the League Cup and FA Cup. Success at City had been more fortuitous with 48 appearances in the next season and a half before a back injury at the midway stage of their promotion-winning campaign limited his first-team prospects. Seagraves's first test against the Reds was to ward off a goal threat from Jan Mølby after he had been sent clear by an

Ian Rush pass. The Denmark international had the beating of his one-time team-mate but not Andy Dibble, who rushed off his line and spilled the ball directly into Rush's path as Seagraves was left watching helplessly as the ball trickled into the gaping net.

Already shorn of John Barnes, Alan Hansen and Steve Nicol through injury, Liverpool's depleted squad had to contend with another setback in the 17th minute as Gary Gillespie was withdrawn with a hamstring problem. Nick Tanner, a £20,000 signing from Bristol Rovers the previous year, was handed an impromptu first-team debut and deputised at right-back despite being naturally left-footed. City almost atoned from a similar move to the one which saw them fall behind after Bishop cut out Ray Houghton's pass intended for Ronnie Whelan in the 25th minute. The Scouser made inroads before threading a ball through for Paul Lake, who evaded a sliding tackle from Steve McMahon with only Bruce Grobbelaar to beat but rolled his shot wide.

The hosts still created another chance as David White, operating in an unfamiliar role on the left wing, drew a sprawling save from Grobbelaar with a long-range effort. At the other end, a well-worked move involving Mølby, Peter Beardsley and Ray Houghton saw the latter draw a stop from Dibble before defender Steve Staunton's cross-cum-shot tested the reflexes of City's goalkeeper, who also denied Beardsley later on. A one-goal deficit at half-time appeared to be damage limitation for the hosts but Bishop admits that Lake's missed opportunity earlier in the half was one which may have altered the match's trajectory. 'I always feel like it would've been a different game,' he says. 'But they stepped it up [again] in the second half.'

True to Bishop's recollection, Liverpool moved through the gears and went further ahead just three minutes after the restart when Beardsley received a Grobbelaar dropkick on the halfway line and embarked on a solo run through City's half during which he nutmegged Colin Hendry, signed a month earlier from Blackburn Rovers, before shaking off Steve Redmond and slotting under an advancing Dibble. McMahon almost caught out the

City goalkeeper with a looping header on the edge of the area from Houghton's corner that forced him to tip over the crossbar. Soon enough the midfielder was on the scoresheet as he raced past Bishop, his one-time Everton colleague, to beat the offside trap and bear down on Dibble. A shimmying run left the onrushing keeper second-guessing where McMahon would send the ball, with Rush now on his inside in support, before placing it into the bottom-right corner.

Immediately from the kick-off, Clive Allen sent a floated ball for Trevor Morley to latch on to but he barely made contact before being floored by Grobbelaar for a penalty. His strike partner comfortably dispatched the spot kick, sending his opposite number completely the wrong way with an effort into the top left-hand corner of the net. Reducing the deficit spurred City on with Bishop almost pulling back another goal when substitute David Oldfield's low cross eluded Liverpool's back line but was kept out by an instinctive stop from Grobbelaar. Allen later fired a half-volley straight at the Liverpool number one after White had done the legwork.

Dalglish's side continued to put their hosts under pressure and put the game beyond reach two minutes from the end when McMahon surged downfield before laying the ball off to Rush, who chipped Dibble to complete the rout. A forgettable afternoon for City was only lightened by Liverpool's travelling fans echoing chants from the Kippax of 'Swales out' in protest at the shambolic events presided over by the club's polarising chairman.

Parts of the thrilling contest were later immortalised in film for the Channel 4 drama *Shooting Stars*, which followed the story of a City player kidnapped by the jealous partner of a girl that won a date with him on a radio competition. Lead actor Gary McDonald, a former apprentice with Wimbledon, stepped out of the Maine Road tunnel alongside City's players wearing the number ten shirt. Months before he appeared alongside John Barnes and New Order for England's 1990 World Cup anthem 'World In Motion', Keith Allen played the role of a club chairman whose arrogance made Swales appear borderline saintly. Artistic license was used for a scene filmed mid-game inside the Main Stand when Allen relayed 'It's 3-1!' over the phone after his namesake slotted home the conciliatory penalty. There was little inauthentic about Book and Dalglish's respective post-match comments. 'Liverpool is a quality side and whenever they broke they looked as if they were going to hurt us,' said City's caretaker, while his opposite number surmised, 'You cannot fault City for effort but it is a tremendous achievement [for us] to score four goals away from home.'

Just months into Howard Kendall's tenure, which arrived four days after the defeat to Liverpool, City midfielder Gary Megson found himself in the company of fellow ex-Everton players with Peter Reid, Adrian Heath, Alan Harper, Wayne Clarke and Neil Pointon all moving to Maine Road alongside former apprentice Mark Ward. Getting the old Goodison Park gang back together let to a series of part-exchange deals, with Bishop and Morley sacrificed to West Ham for Ward, Andy Hinchcliffe moving to Everton for Pointon's signing and David Oldfield traded as collateral in the transfer of Clarke from Leicester City.

Kendall's reunion with key components from his class of 1985 caused Manchester's own Blues to be dubbed 'Everton reserves' on account of the sheer volume of his former lieutenants in the first team squad. The move still had merits in the short term as City climbed to 14th, only beaten to a place above by Manchester United on goal difference. United continued to laud it over their local rivals in winning the FA Cup, an act which saved Alex Ferguson from a near-certain sacking and was a catalyst for their eventual upturn.

Higher up the table, Liverpool saw off a challenge from Aston Villa to win their 18th championship with nine points' breathing space. The title had left Merseyside just twice in the previous 12 seasons but would subsequently elude it for the next three decades as both the Reds and Everton failed to recapture past glories.

Kendall did not stick around to see the full fruits of his Maine Road labour and left a fifth-placed City on 5 November 1990 to return to Goodison for the second time. He further twisted the knife into his former club by declaring the previous 12 months of marked progress to be 'a love affair, but with Everton it's more like a marriage.' Scorned supporters who had embraced a man formerly the youngest player to appear in an FA Cup Final later chanted 'Judas' at him during their future meetings with the Toffees. Unlike his previous managerial decisions, chairman Peter Swales bowed to fans' requests by installing Peter Reid, who had arrived as a player-coach from Queens Park Rangers in the previous year, as Kendall's successor.

Kendall had actively coerced the veteran midfielder into following him back to his hometown club before abandoning Moss Side, only to be told by Reid that he was staying put. A week to the day since he had been handed the reins, the Huyton-born player did eventually return to Merseyside as City went in search of a first away win of the season against Liverpool, again occupying the First Division's top spot. Reid had grown up as a boyhood Reds fan but shifted allegiances to Everton during a seven-year spell which began with the club literally breaking the bank for him by switching its finances from Midland Bank to TSB in order to secure his £60,000 signing from Bolton Wanderers. The new City manager selected himself as one of five former Everton players stepping out behind former enemy lines.

That degree of familiarity is something Liverpool defender Gary Gillespie believes had the potential to stand his own side in good stead before the game kicked off.

'That's what made it so interesting being on Merseyside at the time,' he says. 'They were all good players in their own right. City weren't a powerhouse like they are at this moment in time so it was always a game that you went into, regardless of the personnel that you were playing against, thinking that you were going to get the three points and win the game. I think any time you've got a settled squad and players, that's going to help you. There wasn't so much analysis of opposition done back then than maybe what it is these days. So it was all about us and how we approached the game. We didn't really look at the opposition too much at all. I think it helps sometimes if you know and you've played against these players on a regular basis. As an individual, you kind of know what to expect, where their strengths and weaknesses are; for instance, if he was a left-footed player or a right-footed player, if he liked to run in behind you or he liked to go short. All these little things, if you have played against them on a regular basis, I think that does help you and maybe that gave us a slight advantage, I'm not 100 per cent sure. You'd have to ask them that.'

Dalglish resisted the temptation to draft captain Alan Hansen back into his side and instead persisted with the defensive partnership of Gillespie and Glenn Hysen that dealt with City's heavy pressing in the opening stages and continued during a cagey opening 45 minutes. Shortly after the hour, the visitors finally made a breakthrough when Heath slipped the ball to David White for cross which Niall Quinn met with a bullet header that Bruce Grobbelaar kept out. From Megson's recovery, Ward was brought down by Ronnie Whelan in the penalty area. The right-winger converted the penalty as he drilled past Grobbelaar for only the second time that the goalkeeper had been beaten in a First Division home match that season. Liverpool's flawless record at Anfield in the league was now firmly under siege.

'I think you're always conscious of it but just because you're behind in games, the onus is still the same,' says Gillespie, who went off injured less than ten minutes earlier. 'The onus is on you obviously to get back in the game, but I don't think you do too much differently because you're behind. I just think you go and you still play your game and still play the way that you want to play and just believe that you can get something out of the game. When you've got the players of the calibre that we had, we always felt even if we went behind that we still had the ability and capability to get back into games.

'I don't think it really came into mind so much that if you lost a game, you lost the record. Records weren't really a big thing back in the day for us. The only thing we were concerned about was winning football matches and winning league titles. If records came along on the way that was fantastic, but it wasn't the be-all and end-all. I think very much the way Jürgen Klopp talks about it today, he's not really interested in records. He wants to win titles and Champions Leagues and things like that. It didn't really play on our minds too much to be quite honest with you. It's nice to have that recognition but it's not a big deal really. I think most of the players that certainly played in our time would probably say the same thing.'

Liverpool later pulled level from a Peter Beardsley corner on 82 minutes as Hysen headed the ball into John Barnes's path to trap on the bounce and control before a shot on the turn was helped home by Ian Rush. Within four minutes, Dalglish's side had finally taken the lead. Ian Brightwell's attempted interception of a Gary Ablett header sent the ball goalwards for Ronnie Rosenthal to pounce on and draw Andy Dibble before dinking his shot into the net. Grobbelaar still proved the busier of the two keepers in the final stages as he had to beat away a free kick by Ward. But the Zimbabwean could do little about City's injury-time equaliser when Quinn challenged Hysen from a Ward corner and headed past both Grobbelaar and Ray Houghton at the near post to snatch a valuable point for the visitors with the added distinction of being only the third team in 1990 to take something away from Anfield.

As one of Kendall's final City signings, Quinn's £800,000 move from Arsenal offered an element of surprise to their attacks on account of his physical stature. Gillespie had previously encountered him while playing for Coventry City but was forced to watch on from the sidelines as his team-mates struggled to deal with the Republic of Ireland international's presence. 'He was six foot four and back in the day that was a little bit unusual. You didn't come up against players like that,' he says. 'I think it's common practice these days but certainly back in the day there wasn't too many of the physique and stature of Quinny so it was always a problem. You always felt you were going to have a fight and a challenge in the air, which he was very good in the air, but he was also a good player. He had a decent touch as well.'

Quinn's last-gasp equaliser had sparked scenes of elation in the away section of the Anfield Road End and given Reid reasons to be positive. 'We haven't won but I'm sure if we continue to play like that it will come,' he told reporters. 'If you come to Anfield and get a point you are usually happy but I'm disappointed not to have got three.' Dalglish was similarly praising of City's efforts in earning a draw but warned of sterner challenges ahead for his fellow player-manager. 'City competed well but the season does not finish with two games against Liverpool,' he said. 'They have got to play like this every week. If they played like that every week, they wouldn't be so far adrift.'

Burdened by the psychological trauma of Hillsborough, the Liverpool manager did not oversee the corresponding fixture on Moss Side just four months later and resigned two days after a chaotic 4-4 draw with Kendall's Everton in the FA Cup in February 1991. Dalglish's bombshell announcement, like Bill Shankly's own just 17 years earlier, rocked Anfield to its very core.

'We certainly, even with all the players within the football club, didn't see the fact that Kenny was going to leave,' says Gillespie. 'We were just rolling along like we would normally roll along; approaching each game as it comes, the next game's the most important and all these old adages that were taught to us. The onus if you had lost was always to win the next game, not dwell on the past and look forward to the future. We were experienced enough that you can go through a season and obviously you're going to lose games and be disappointed after certain games. But it wasn't an indication that the standards or the mentality was slipping. It was just one of these things that can happen in football. Certainly, from a player's point of view, I didn't see any drop in standards or attitudes. It was just a case of you roll along and see where it takes us.'

Boot Room stalwart Ronnie Moran assumed caretaker duties during the search for Dalglish's successor and was an even-money favourite among the bookmakers to take the job permanently on a shortlist that included a retiring Hansen and a host of former Reds players in John Toshack, Graeme Souness, Phil Thompson and Phil Neal. As reserve-team coach, Thompson had stepped up to assist Moran and Roy Evans to steady the ship. Successive defeats to Luton Town and Arsenal allowed the latter to overtake the defending champions in the First Division table before Moran took his new charges to Manchester City, now sitting in eighth, on 9 March. Before reacquainting with his old business partner Peter Swales, Liverpool chairman Noel White announced that the 56-year-old would remain in post until the end of the 1990/91 season. Moran continued to exercise caution over the trip to Moss Side despite the extended tenure, saying, 'I know Peter Reid and how he performed at Everton. He will use his spirit and experience to make sure it's not easy for us.'

Reid, similarly, stuck to his guns by refusing to take Liverpool's hat-trick of defeats, coupled with injuries to Ronnie Whelan and Steve McMahon, for granted. 'The critics have been going on about a sinking ship,' he said. 'I saw them against Everton and then Arsenal … We could face the backlash of those defeats, but I'm looking forward to the challenge. I always enjoy games against them because they are one of the best, if not *the* best.'

Nine of City's starting line-up that had taken a point at Anfield earlier in the season were retained for the latest meeting. Reid's own inclusion took the contingent of Scousers in City's matchday squad to quadruple the number in Liverpool's, with Gary Ablett the sole standard-bearer. Geography became irrelevant in the closing minutes of the first half, when a lofted Steve Nicol ball was headed back towards City's goal by Colin Hendry and allowed Peter Beardsley to take a touch before being scythed down by Tony Coton.

The goalkeeper, signed from Watford at the start of the season, accused the Liverpool forward of diving in a heated exchange between the pair and was subsequently booked by referee George Courtney. Coton's misery was further heaped on by Jan Mølby wrong-footing him from the penalty spot for the visitors' first goal in almost five hours of play.

Minutes later, Hendry spurned a golden opportunity to equalise when he fired a Niall Quinn flick-on tamely at Grobbelaar. Controversy reigned again before the first half was out when Ray Houghton threaded a pass for Ian Rush, who took the ball past Coton but was upended for a penalty which sent Maine Road into uproar. Again, Mølby sent City's number one the wrong way. Coton had little complaints about his end to the afternoon when, on 86 minutes, Houghton stole possession off Neil Pointon before setting John Barnes away down the left before executing a low finish to complete the comfortable win.

Newspapers credited Courtney's decision to award Liverpool two first-half penalties as the driving force behind their maiden victory under Moran in a view which appeared to resonate with Reid after the final whistle. Ken Rogers wrote in the following Monday's *Liverpool Echo* that the former Everton midfielder had made his 'quickest run of the afternoon' in heading to the referee's room to question why Ablett had avoided a second yellow card after taking down Clive Allen when the game was still deadlocked.

The win ensured the visitors were only separated by goal difference from Arsenal at the summit but had drifted five points behind their title rivals when Moran stepped aside for Graeme Souness, Dalglish's eventual successor, in mid-April to end 1990/91 as runners-up, seven points off the Londoners. City secured a fifth-place finish, again ahead of United, but were still overshadowed by their local rivals clinching the European Cup Winners' Cup. Unbeknown to themselves and the rest of football's populous, Anfield was already entering a terminal decline at the worst possible moment, just as the dawn of a new era lurked on the horizon.

This Is How It Feels

A BRAVE new world beckoned English football in 1991. BBC Radio 5 Live's *606* phone-in show afforded supporters across the country a nationwide platform to share their views of the game. Those in influential positions were similarly making themselves stand out from the crowd as radical proposals to sever a 103-year-old link with the Football League were finally put in motion.

The concept had first gained traction in late 1990 when chairmen of the top flight's 'Big Five' clubs – Liverpool, Everton, Arsenal, Tottenham Hotspur and Manchester United – met with London Weekend Television's managing director Greg Dyke to gain his backing for a new breakaway league. In May of the following year, formal discussions were taking place at the FA's headquarters in Lancaster Gate about the creation of a division independent of the old order. On 28 June 1991, 15 top flight clubs unanimously agreed to resign from the Football League as part of the movement which would pave the way for the formation of the Premier League.

Both Manchester City and Liverpool were notable absentees from the meeting at the FA's Lancaster Gate headquarters, although Peter Swales declared the outcome to be 'very positive'. Swales's Anfield counterpart and former business ally Noel White dismissed concerns about his own club's commitment to the planned new league by saying, 'We will follow the same course.'

Graeme Souness was also not one for turning in attempts to imprint his inimitable style on Liverpool as a manager, just seven years after departing as a player. The former midfielder's five-year spell in charge of Glasgow Rangers had produced seven major honours as well as receiving partial credit for helping them win a second consecutive Scottish Premier Division title, with his ex-assistant Walter Smith seeing the Ibrox club over the line once his predecessor left in mid-April.

At Anfield, Souness's willingness to ring the changes as he had done north of the border was met with resistance from established first-team figures who had been reared on the Boot Room's staple of success. Four of the players that had been part of Liverpool's First Division triumph just 12 months earlier were moved on before the start of the 1991/92 season; Peter Beardsley crossed Stanley Park to join Everton, Steve Staunton moved to Aston Villa and Gary Gillespie was offloaded to boyhood heroes Celtic. In their place came defender Mark Wright, a member of England's 1990 World Cup squad, and Dean Saunders, whose father Roy had lined up for Liverpool in the pre-Bill Shankly era, alongside Souness's old Ibrox lieutenant Mark Walters for a cumulative price of £6.35m.

Equally proactive changes were taking place at Maine Road, where Peter Reid offset Mark Ward and Alan Harper reuniting with Howard Kendall at Everton by signing Wimbledon centre-back Keith Curle for £2.5m. City's new arrival was immediately appointed captain in place of Paul Lake, who had suffered a cruciate knee ligament injury which would blight the remaining years of his playing career. Curle's first home outing with the armband came on 21 August against a Liverpool side depleted by injury but now in possession of Steve McManaman's precocious talent. In the 29th minute, the defender's downfield clearance was helped on by Niall Quinn into the path of an on-running David White, who had stolen a march on Gary Ablett and fired past Bruce Grobbelaar. A point-blank stop from Tony Coton then prevented Saunders from recording an assist after he had teed up Ray Houghton for a close-range finish.

The key protagonists for City's opener were again involved in their second as Quinn flicked on a Coton goal kick for White to again best Ablett and drill the ball beyond Grobbelaar to strike the underside of the crossbar. Referee Paul Vanes belatedly awarded the goal, which bore striking similarities to England's third in the 1966 World Cup Final against West Germany; a reference Clive Tyldesley quickly reminded viewers of Granada's *Soccer Night* in saying, 'Well it's Geoff Hurst all over again, isn't it?' The Urmston native later attempted to catch out the Liverpool stopper with a lobbed effort that was tipped over the upright.

McManaman's ubiquity in the City penalty area finally paid dividends in the final quarter as he met a cross from fellow Anfield youth graduate Mike Marsh with a flying header to reduce the deficit. With fewer than eight minutes remaining, the winger turned provider with a threaded pass for Saunders, who was caught by Andy Hill with a sliding challenge to win a penalty. The Wales international's previous visit to Moss Side with Derby County, just four months earlier, had been a forgettable one as he saw a first-half penalty saved by fellow striker Quinn, deputising in goal for a sent-off Coton. His effort beat City's first-choice stopper but not the crossbar as it cannoned back into play as the hosts recorded a 100 per cent start to the new league season.

Claims that White's brace should not have stood, owing to a possible offside ahead of his first and the contentious nature of the crossbar-assisted effort, were backed by Liverpool midfielder Steve McMahon, who insisted post-match, 'I think the referee was wrong to award goals on both occasions.' City player-manager Reid chose to offer up a defence of Vanes. 'The referee made his decisions and there's no changing that,' he insisted. 'I might disagree with some referees' decisions, but I don't moan after them.'

Souness refused to discuss the goals his side had conceded but still took issue with the Midlands official as Mark Wright and John Barnes joined Liverpool's growing casualty list during the Maine Road encounter. A recurrence of an Achilles injury was diagnosed as the cause of Barnes's issue while Wright sustained a dead leg mid-game. 'What I will comment on – and which distresses me – is the referee not being strong enough in the first half,' said Souness. 'I've got two players with bad knocks. John

Barnes got a kick in the first couple of minutes which caused him to leave the pitch early on. We came to play football and in the early part of the game we were looking for a bit more protection.'

Any perceived unfairness that Souness felt still failed to mask the fact that Manchester was no longer likely to be the happy hunting ground it had once proved for the Reds, with the *Liverpool Echo*'s Ric George acknowledging, 'The visit to Maine Road used to be ringed with relish on the Liverpool calendar. Not anymore.'

A potential power shift also appeared in the offing as City and Manchester United occupied the First Division's leading positions. Some newspapers were already hailing the Old Trafford club as the season's de facto champions, conveniently ignoring their previously premature claims in the opening months of the 1985/86 campaign. Those declaring victory for Alex Ferguson's side were momentarily left with egg on their faces when the Blues overtook the Red Devils at the top the table four days later, but had fallen behind their local rivals and Liverpool before August was out.

When the two north-west clubs met again at Anfield on 21 December, both had slipped to just inside the league's top five with Liverpool only ahead on goal difference and having played a game fewer. Souness's continuing evolution led to fringe players David Speedie and Jimmy Carter departing while promising Crewe Alexandra right-back Rob Jones was drafted in alongside Arsenal midfielder Michael Thomas, the club's title nemesis in 1989. The latter's arrival paved the way for McMahon's exit after over five years with his hometown team.

Reid had reportedly identified Thomas as a potential arrival at Maine Road but cooled his interest once it had become public. Attention shifted to McMahon, four years the player-manager's junior, to succeed him in central midfield. City's tabled bids of £750,000 and £850,000 for the 30-year-old were rebuffed ahead of their trip to Merseyside as Souness continued to hold out for a £1m valuation. Reid's negotiating headache was worsened by the threat of newly appointed Blackburn Rovers manager Kenny

Dalglish potentially snaring his one-time player with a £12m war chest. At Anfield, McMahon was serenaded by the home crowd before kick-off as he lined up for his third farewell appearance in a red shirt against the club that he would finally join three days later for £900,000. His current employers enjoyed a flying start when Houghton teed up Saunders for a 25-yard strike which Coton fumbled into his own net on nine minutes. But memories of City's August win became fresh in the mind at the beginning of the second half as David White struck twice in the space of seven minutes, again with near-identical finishes.

A long ball by Tony Coton was back-headed by Niall Quinn into the striker's path to lob a stranded Bruce Grobbelaar with a looping effort that generated hearty renditions of 'Blue Moon' from the City fans occupying the left-hand corner of the Anfield Road End. White inflicted further misery on his hosts in the 55th minute, this time after Ian Brightwell's downfield ball saw Nick Tanner and Quinn both lose out in an aerial duel, allowing the latter's strike partner to steal in at the byeline and hook the ball beyond Grobbelaar. White's outpouring of emotion after recording another brace against Liverpool saw him punch the air in celebration and shouting 'fuck off!' – an act which was misinterpreted by home supporters as a show of defiance rather than genuine and unbridled joy. For the remainder of the game, he was the target of catcalls and vitriol, with chants of 'you Manc bastard' still ringing in his ears in the hours after the final whistle. Eight minutes from time, City's efforts to end a decade-long wait for a win in the red half of Merseyside unravelled as Marsh pulled a cross in behind the visitors' defence for Steve Nicol to drill home an equaliser with his first goal for nine months.

Souness raged at his players in the aftermath of the four-goal affair. The Liverpool manager's disappointment was shared by City's St Helens-born attacker Mike Sheron, who had been eager to shine on a debut outing at the stadium where he previously enjoyed fond memories as a boyhood Reds supporter. 'It was my first time playing at Anfield and I don't think I played particularly well. I think I was overawed on the day to be fair,' he says. 'I wanted to impress all my mates who were definitely watching the game. It was good to get a draw from the team's point of view but personally I don't think I did particularly well.'

Sheron had risen through the ranks at Maine Road after joining the club as a schoolboy but still managed to split his time between a budding professional career and his lifelong obsession. He stood among The Kop's masses on the night that Arsenal snatched the First Division title in May 1989, when McMahon ill-advisedly raised his index finger to remind Liverpool players that they only need to see out the game's remaining minute to clinch the championship.

Even in the twilight of McMahon's time at the top, Sheron admits that the Halewood-born enforcer's qualities were still evident when he arrived on Moss Side. 'Steve was obviously coming to the end of his career when he signed for us, but you could tell he had quality,' he says. 'I could make runs and he'd find passes to try and provide a bit of quality at times. Peter Reid was a fantastic footballer [but] obviously he's more of a ratter. But Steve had a bit more passing range and I particularly enjoyed playing with him to be fair.'

McMahon's influence stretched beyond City's senior ranks as upcoming midfielder Jim Whitley later discovered when lining up alongside one of his childhood heroes for a reserve-team fixture in 1993. 'I'd watched him growing up in the glory years of Liverpool and he is probably the only player and the player I can say that guided me through a game,' he says. 'I've never been guided or talked to by a senior professional as I was with Steve McMahon, and I haven't since. He just played my game for me; taught me everything to do. He was a fantastic role model because I'd always seen him as this hard-tackling, scary kind of man. He was unbelievable and he was the best professional I'd played with in centre-mid that guided me through the game.'

Liverpool's inconsistency in the months after McMahon's departure reduced them to a role of casual observers as Manchester United and Leeds United fought it out for First Division supremacy. City's own role in trouncing the Yorkshire club on 4

April saw them roundly booed by the Maine Road crowd amid fears that their arch-rivals had just been helped a step closer to their first title in a quarter of a century.

The following day, Souness's side took on Portsmouth in an FA Cup semi-final which forced Sheron to reassess his divided loyalties between Manchester and Merseyside. 'We beat Leeds 4-0 on the Saturday and I remember going to watch Liverpool play Portsmouth at Highbury in the semi-final,' he says. 'But I swore I'd never do that again because on the Tuesday night Leeds and Man United were going for the title and I had to play at Old Trafford in the derby. I had a really good game against Leeds on the Saturday when we won 4-0 but I think I was probably a bit too tired to perform again. I swore that I had to become more professional than just being a fan so that taught me a lesson to be honest.'

For Souness, the Highbury encounter would have life-altering consequences as he was rushed to hospital a matter of hours after the game to undergo emergency triple heart bypass surgery. The Scot conducted an interview with Mike Ellis, with whom he had enjoyed a good working relationship despite Ellis being *The Sun*'s Merseyside football correspondent, about his health scare. On 13 April, a photographer from the newspaper approached him for a picture which would appear the following day alongside coverage of Liverpool's semi-final replay at Villa Park; a request which Souness only granted if his side reached the final. A place in English football's showpiece was eventually clinched after extra time and a penalty shoot-out, by which point the celebratory photograph had missed the copy deadline for the following day's paper. Instead, *The Sun* splashed the image across its front page on 15 April, the third anniversary of the Hillsborough disaster. Anger towards the red-top tabloid had been strong on Merseyside ever since its publication of spurious claims about Liverpool fans in the days following the tragedy led to a sustained region-wide boycott. To this day, Souness's legacy at Anfield remains indelibly tainted by the episode.

A 2-0 win over Sunderland at Wembley delivered Souness's first trophy at the helm and arrived a fortnight after Liverpool had killed off United's First Division hopes with an identical scoreline at Anfield allowing Leeds to claim their first title since 1973/74. City's own role in extending the gulf saw them holding Old Trafford's hosts to a 1-1 draw just three days after they had stunned Howard Wilkinson's side at Maine Road. Reid's side may have finished eight points shy of United but strengthened Manchester's superiority over its M62 counterparts by finishing one place and six points clear of the Reds, who languished in sixth.

Months earlier, the hard-fought battle to create the Premier League had finally been won. Ratification arrived from the FA following a High Court battle and threat of a players' strike over the plans. But it was not long before Liverpool and City were again at loggerheads, off the pitch as much as on it.

In the summer of 1986, just months into his spell managing Rangers, Souness had enlisted the services of Liverpool's former chief scout Geoff Twentyman, who had left the club after close to two decades' service. Among the players who had caught his eye was one located a short distance from his former Merseyside parish. On 18 October of that year, Twentyman took in Blackpool's 3-1 win over Notts County in the Third Division and had noted Paul Stewart's performance for the hosts. 'Plenty of movement with good pace,' his report read. 'I feel he would do well in a good team.' Stewart finished 1986/87 as the Tangerines' leading scorer with 21 goals despite leaving for Manchester City in a £200,000 switch barely two months before the season had ended. He finished the following campaign as his new club's leading scorer as well, with 28 goals from 52 matches in all competitions before joining Tottenham Hotspur that summer for £1.7m.

Twentyman's recommendation clearly stuck with Souness when he pursued the three-time England international some six years later. Stewart's return to the north-west appeared inevitable with his family moving back to Blackpool towards the end of his time in north London. City appeared to have an upper hand in the race for Stewart's signature courtesy of Peter Reid's assistant Sam Ellis, who had managed the converted midfielder at Bloomfield Road prior to his Maine Road switch. But it was Liverpool, armed with the £900,000 proceeds from Ray Houghton's sale to Aston Villa, who saw off their rivals to clinch a £2.3m transfer on 29 July 1992.

Returning to familiar surroundings failed to elevate Stewart's performances as he appeared just 42 times for Liverpool over an 18-month period, scoring three times. Attempts to restore him to the striker role which had sealed his rise to prominence also failed before his remaining two years at Anfield were spent on loan with Crystal Palace, Wolverhampton Wanderers, Burnley and Sunderland.

'When I signed him from Tottenham, I thought I was getting an aggressive, strong holding midfielder, but it just didn't happen for him at Liverpool,' Souness reflected in his 2017 memoir *Football: My Life, My Passion*. 'It didn't turn out the way I planned although now I can see that he had been through things that must have had a terrible toll on him.'

Like several English professional footballers at the time, Stewart was harbouring a dark secret. He later revealed that he had been subjected to a harrowing four-year ordeal of sexual abuse by junior football coach Frank Roper. His one-time City team-mate David White endured that same traumatic experience at amateur club Whitehill FC by the predatory paedophile Barry Bennell, who was branded 'sheer evil' after being jailed for 30 years in February 2018 over historic sex offences. Stewart's attempts to block out flashbacks of the abuse suffered as a child led him down a path of crippling addiction, habitually consuming alcohol and cocaine to get him through a torment which lasted over four decades.

***

Within months of the Premier League's inception, the clubs that had joined forces to create it were already at each other's throats over its commercial direction. Eight teams vetoed plans for Bass Breweries to sponsor the new competition on 9 September 1992, with Liverpool joining Arsenal, Everton, Manchester United, Aston Villa, Nottingham Forest and Queens Park Rangers in rejecting the £13m proposal. Sam Hammam, Wimbledon's eccentric owner, demanded that the FA took disciplinary action against the insurgents through points deductions and potentially automatic relegation.

Separately the group had been key players in a £3m deal with stadium perimeter advertising company Dorna, which prompted Peter Swales to rally against the perceived cabal, which no longer contained the backing of his former cohort Noel White at Anfield. 'What concerns me is that a group of clubs have clandestine meetings,' said the City supremo. 'It's a dangerous precedent which could lead to a league within a league. They fought pretty dirty.'

Accusations that the modern English top flight immediately forsook its predating history were heightened by City and Liverpool's decisions to do away with several of their own time-honoured hallmarks ahead of the 1992/93 season. Souness's bid to win over a dubious Anfield faithful, scarred by his underwhelming first full season in charge and recent dalliance with *The Sun*, was further undermined by reports that he had personally seen to the death of the Boot Room; in reality it was demolished to make way for modernised press facilities which would later form part of the country's successful bid to host Euro '96. At Maine Road, long-serving physio Roy Bailey and esteemed former player turned youth coach Glyn Pardoe were both moved on while chief scout Ken Barnes retired.

City forward Mike Sheron learned the hard way about how habits had changed when a pre-season bonding session in Italy saw him incur the wrath of Peter Reid. 'Steve McMahon was playing for us and we had a sing-song one night,' he says. 'We all had to stand up and sing a song. Steve sang 'Poor Scouser Tommy' and I actually stood up and started singing from the top of my lungs, as such, and all the lads were loving it. The next morning, I got a rollocking from Peter, "Don't you ever do that to me again." I thought he was joking. "I'm serious," he says. I'm thinking, "What!?" so he gave me a bit of a rollocking for my true colours coming out.'

Reid's aversion to his former Everton nemeses did not extend to McMahon's signing from Liverpool at the end of the previous year, nor seemingly a reported interest in his ex-team-mate Jan Mølby as a potential replacement when the midfielder suffered a toe injury during the season's early weeks. Following the £2.5m signing of Manchester-born defender Terry Phelan from Wimbledon, Swales imposed a limit on City's future spending which led Reid to fear that three of the club's current assets would be sacrificed to their Premier League peers, with the Reds credited as potential suitors for captain Keith Curle. Financial disparity was the only thing separating the two clubs when they faced off at Anfield on 28 December with both languishing in mid-table.

Nine days after a 5-1 hammering by Coventry City, their heaviest defeat in over 16 years, Liverpool faced the prospect of another sky blue humiliation when Manchester City travelled to Merseyside. The visitors regularly peppered Mike Hooper's goal and saw an opener ruled out for offside after Flitcroft and White dovetailed before the latter strolled the ball into an empty net. Fewer than 15 minutes later, a long ball from Tony Coton allowed Niall Quinn to hold off Steve Nicol and play the ball to the right flank for Sheron, who raced past Bjørnebye but was stopped in his tracks by Nicol. Four City players waited for Ian Brightwell's follow-up cross into the penalty area which was headed home by Quinn.

Liverpool drew level four minutes after the interval when a lofted ball by Bjørnebye was headed clear by Andy Hill before Rob Jones beat Flitcroft and set Steve McManaman away down the right to send a deflected cross into the penalty area for Rush. Anfield's record goalscorer struck a powerful volley over the head of Hill and into the net in front of City's travelling supporters. 'It was a great volley to be honest,' says Sheron. 'Rushie took it from 18 yards out. You feel a bit sick but then you appreciate the greatness of the guy to be honest. You just want to try and keep pushing up the table as high as you can. The big thing at City at the time was trying to get into Europe but obviously we didn't quite do it. But I'm proud of the fact that in the first three years

I played in the Premier League, we finished in the top ten which was great. At times we questioned our football because people said we didn't play great football, especially with Quinny up front, but we had some good players and a good team ethic.'

Quinn's ability to prove a handful for opposing defenders had seen Souness credited by newspapers with a potential £3m move for the striker to add goalscoring substance to Liverpool's attack. The former midfielder's routine deployment of a target-man figure during his success-laden spell with Rangers had reportedly led him to believe the Republic of Ireland international may offer a solution and was said to have earmarked Rush and Paul Stewart as potential makeweights, while the uncertain long-term futures of Nicol, John Barnes and Ronny Rosenthal meant they might also be in the mix.

Souness's alleged interest failed to amount to anything tangible but he was given food for thought at the other end of the pitch at Maine Road on 12 April 1993. Newly signed goalkeeper David James offered an early glimpse of what would follow over his next six years at Anfield as he came out and flapped at a City corner, which was converted by Flitcroft with a free header. England manager Graham Taylor found few positives on his latest visit to Moss Side as national team hopefuls Mike Sheron and David White both had to be withdrawn before the interval with injuries, while John Barnes failed to impress for the visitors. The winger's sole contribution was to hook a David Burrows throw back into his team-mate's path for a surging run and low cross which was prodded home by Rush at the far post.

Neither side benefited from the stalemate but City's failure to secure maximum points practically ended their already dimming bid to achieve European qualification and was typified by Peter Reid's frank post-match reaction. 'Fair result. It wasn't a classic,' he admitted. 'I don't think there's much more I can say about it.'

With fewer than three weeks of the season remaining, the prospect of Liverpool finishing outside the league's top ten for the first time in half a century remained a genuine one as the pressure on Souness intensified. Speculation surrounding his likely successor threw up myriad names including Anfield great John Toshack and Queens Park Rangers manager Gerry Francis. But Reid's surprise inclusion as a forerunner for the job with his boyhood heroes on 25 April drew an angry response from Swales. 'These rumours are a complete nonsense,' he insisted. 'He is our manager and he is staying here.' City's chairman was facing fresh opposition from supporters increasingly disillusioned at the standards he had continually failed to uphold.

On Merseyside, boardroom unrest was also rife. Tensions over Souness's failed second coming had been brought to a head. His absence from a 6-2 trouncing of Tottenham Hotspur on the final day of the 1992/93 campaign had prompted scenes of widespread delirium across Anfield. The *Liverpool Echo* revealed that 67 per cent of supporters polled by telephone wanted their former captain to depart the dugout after a campaign when they had finished sixth but 25 points behind champions Manchester United. George 'Tony' Ensor, a boardroom opponent, appeared to have persuaded his fellow board members to enact Souness's sacking. Just 24 hours later, chairman David Moores publicly affirmed the club's support for the beleaguered Scot to see out the remaining three years of his contract, adding 'and I hope he will remain for much longer than that'. Roy Evans's elevation to the position of assistant manager following a lengthy apprenticeship in the Boot Room's ranks was also confirmed but neither move was welcomed with unanimity.

Ensor tended his resignation in protest, citing his 'strongly held views' as being out of step with the decision to grant a stay of execution. Over the previous eight years, he had been a highly respected figure within Liverpool's corridors of power as club solicitor and had provided expertise in the aftermath of the 1985 Heysel tragedy. He had also witnessed the unfolding horror at Hillsborough in 1989, a subject inflamed by Souness's direct dealings with *The Sun* ahead of the disaster's third anniversary. Ensor's place on the board was taken by Tom Saunders, Liverpool's former youth development officer and a key player in the old Boot Room setup.

Souness declared himself both 'relieved and delighted' at the board's declaration but made no secret of his displeasure at the decision to promote Evans. When questioned at a press conference whether he had advocated the Bootle-born coach's instalment, he replied bluntly, 'No – it was the board.'

Souness's relief was offset by a multitude of regrets within the Anfield hierarchy as Moores publicly apologised to the media for the club's lack of cooperation during negotiations over their manager's future. Chief executive Peter Robinson, who had served Liverpool since arriving as club secretary in 1965, was particularly mournful at the departure of Ensor, his former colleague and personal friend, who had 'made a tremendous contribution to the club, particularly following the two tragedies'.

The summer of 1993 became Swales's personal hell. Manchester United had just ended a 26-year domestic drought by winning the inaugural Premier League while supporter backlash saw him pelted with eggs as City ended 1992/93 with a 5-2 humiliation at the hands of Everton. He responded by briefing that the club would spend £6m on reinforcements over the summer. Like many of the claims made during his two decades as chairman, it lacked any genuine substance.

City's overdraft stood at £3m and saw several potential new arrivals vetoed, including the eyebrow-raising prospect of John Barnes trading Merseyside for Manchester in a £1.5m transfer. Reid continued to harbour ambitions of luring Paul Stewart back to Maine Road in a £2m deal but Swales had other ideas, having sanctioned the arrival of Ajax midfielder Alfons Groenendijk for a quarter of the fee as the club's sole summer signing. A story later appeared in the *Manchester Evening News* written by Paul Hince, the paper's chief sports reporter and formerly a City player, claiming that Reid planned to resign if the move for Stewart fell through. It prompted Swales to suffer a rare fit of the vapours as he called both Reid and Hince into his office, warning the managerial incumbent, 'If you ever pull a trick like that again, I will fucking sack you.'

Sensing that control was ebbing away from him on multiple levels at Maine Road, Swales appointed an external figure to oversee the day-to-day running of the club. John Maddock had enjoyed a stratospheric rise in print journalism after joining the expanding northern operations at the *Daily Express* in 1960 as an 18-year-old before switching to the *Sunday People*, where he was promoted to the paper's northern deputy and sports editor. Robert Maxwell's 1984 takeover of Mirror Group Newspapers led to Maddock being transferred to London, where he acted as an advisor to the larger-than-life media mogul. Away from the industry, he had been a commercial consultant in Liverpool's ground-breaking 1979 shirt sponsorship deal with Japanese electronics firm Hitachi and served as deputy director of Manchester's bid to host the 1996 Olympics. Steeped personal connections in north-west football saw him utilised by City in their 1989 appointment of Howard Kendall.

Where Swales, for all his faults, had remained largely hands-off when it came to the brass tacks of first-team matters, the man to whom he had delegated responsibility took a more sledgehammer approach and publicly insisted that he had 'the power to hire and fire'. Four games into the 1992/93 season, Maddock's new role had claimed its first victim as Reid was sacked with City sitting in the Premier League's relegation places. Fans already smarting from the shock departure were roused into protests outside Maine Road after news that his replacement would be Oxford United manager Brian Horton emerged during a 1-1 home draw with Coventry City. As a player, Horton had been the first person to greet David Pleat when he jaunted across the Moss Side turf after Luton Town avoided demotion from the First Division at the Blues' expense in May 1983. Cynical supporters believed that his appointment as Reid's successor stemmed from a close friendship with Maddock.

'I knew John Maddock through my days at Port Vale when he was very friendly with Rory Sproson and a guy called Reg Burks, who was assistant manager, so I knew John but not as a personal friend or anything like that,' says Horton. 'He'd recommended Mark Lawrenson for the job at Oxford United and obviously when Mark left he recommended me to the Maxwells also. Then he obviously got the job at Man City and put my name forward for the [manager's] job there. I went through the process after Peter Reid got the sack – I never spoke to City before that and I would never speak to another club while a manager was [still] in charge. I first spoke to Freddie Pye, who was the vice-chairman, and John Maddock and went through that process, and then met Peter Swales and discussed the terms and who I could bring with me, i.e. David Moss, who's now working for Liverpool on their academy scouting. Me and Mossy came and took over and that was the only fact about John Maddock and me at that time.'

A largely promising start saw Horton record just one defeat from his opening eight matches in all competitions yet failed to mask the growing disapproval that Swales was facing from The Kippax, whose former hero Francis Lee had made known his plans to launch a takeover of the club. Swales's role in selling the striker to Derby County in 1974 finally came back to haunt him.

So, too, did his treatment of Paul Stewart. On the eve of Liverpool's visit to Moss Side on 23 October, the player added his voice to the 'Forward with Franny' movement in a newspaper interview. 'I don't have a soft spot for the club, not a bit, especially after some of the things the chairman has said over the last few months,' said Stewart. 'Maybe I will if he goes, but not until. I'm just amazed the man is still there hanging on. He's made a mockery of the club. The only people I have a soft spot for at City are the fans. They want the man out and I think he's let them down a few times. It's well noted that he hires and fires people and yet he has the cheek to accuse players like myself of not giving the club 100 per cent when all the fans know I did.'

Stewart's outspoken comments led to him being docked a week's wage, around £5,000, while Liverpool chairman David Moores offered a full and frank apology to his opposite number which prompted Swales to declare, 'It's all wrong for a player to slag off the chairman of another club. I'd like to say a few things, but you keep your mouth shut.'

The Maine Road crowd did all the talking for him as Stewart was serenaded with chants of 'hello, City reject' throughout the latest outing at his former stomping ground, including while he lay prostrate on the turf after a fifth-minute challenge by Garry Flitcroft. Derision was still plentiful in supply as those backing 'Forward with Franny' leafleted outside the stadium while a plane flew overhead with a banner bearing the campaign's slogan. Flitcroft later played a through ball for David White to slot past Bruce Grobbelaar in the 66th minute, by which point Swales had ducked out of the match to attend a wedding. Within five minutes City almost doubled their lead as White turned provider, sending a ball into Niall Quinn at the far post which Grobbelaar kept out.

Souness brought Stewart's unhappy homecoming to an end on 73 minutes as he made way for Don Hutchison before Ian Rush struck in the penultimate minute of normal time after pouncing on a poor back-pass by Fitzroy Simpson and laying the ball off to Rob Jones. The right-back's shot was half-saved by Tony Coton and then cleared off the line by Alan Kernaghan only as far as the Welshman, who prodded home. A further 13 minutes' injury time failed to separate the sides, after which Horton found himself seeking inspiration from other sports. While watching a Nick Faldo putt in his unsuccessful defence of the World Match Play Championship from the Maine Road press room, the City manager mused about the golfer's winning mentality. 'Maybe I was doing that to throw them [the press] off!' he says. 'I'm still watching things like him win The Open the other day because they're showing all the old stuff. He was just an eternal winner and that's what you want your players to have. That mindset, it's an unbelievable mindset and they're the people that sportsmen look up to.'

City's form in the weeks that followed was more akin to Scott Hoch, who threw away the 1989 Masters on the play-off holes against Faldo, than British golf's poster boy. They won just one of their next 12 Premier League games and hovered just above the drop zone before a trip to Liverpool on 22 January 1994. A fortnight earlier, Graeme Souness had masterminded his side's first away league win for over six months at Ipswich Town to move up to seventh.

Their next encounter at Anfield coincided with the first top-flight games played since the death of Sir Matt Busby, who represented both clubs as a player and later served as Manchester United manager. A minute's silence before kick-off was interrupted by the continued chanting of City fans, who were booed by The Kop in efforts to shame them. Anfield's unsavoury pre-match scenes were replicated at several other Premier League grounds across the country. Leeds United fans at Ewood Park disrupted the silence by chanting 'there's only one Don Revie' in protest at the lack of recognition afforded to Busby's former adversary by the FA following his own passing five years prior. Chelsea's support also hijacked the period of reflection to mark Andy Townsend's return to Stamford Bridge with chants of 'Judas' and 'traitor' before their meeting with Aston Villa, while a Steel City derby at Hillsborough saw fans of both Sheffield United and Wednesday trading abuse.

In keeping with their previous two visits, City took a surprise lead through Carl Griffiths. The 22-year-old striker had become Horton's first signing at Maine Road in October 1993 from Shrewsbury Town for £450,000. His impressive return of 38 goals in 56 previous outings for the Third Division outfit had evoked memories for the City boss of one-time Liverpool striker Dean Saunders, who excelled under him at Oxford. The Welshman's fourth-minute opener came after a Tony Coton goal kick was headed on by Flitcroft, allowing his team-mate to steal a march on Neil Ruddock and lob Grobbelaar.

Souness's side struck back when Nigel Clough threaded a pass through for Jamie Redknapp, who drew a good save from Tony Coton but Ian Rush followed up at the far post. An even-sided affair exploded into life in the final minute as Julian Dicks's two-footed challenge on Kare Ingebrigtsen went unpunished by Roger Milford, only for the referee to give a free kick against City for Michel Vonk's late tackle on Clough. The son of Old Big 'Ead threw the ball forward for Dicks to take a quick set-piece which found Rob Jones, who exchanged passes with Steve McManaman before sending a cross into the far post that Rush met with a downward header.

So incensed was Horton by the X-rated nature of the events leading up to Liverpool's late winner that he had to be restrained by City assistant manager David Moss at the final whistle when attempting to remonstrate with the officials over Milford's apparent double standards. 'When you're competing and having played against a lot of top players, Souness, Dalglish, Case and all those kind of people, you go to Anfield and have to deal with that kind of stuff. They're tough players some of those midfield players,' he says. 'It must have been a bad tackle [by Dicks]. I can't remember it to tell you the truth but for me to react like that, it must have been bad. Because I was that type of player that liked a tackle and liked competition, liked a battle during the game with the likes of Graeme Souness, Peter Reid and players of that ilk, who were competitive people. I relished playing against that type of player because I felt I was, not saying I was good as those, but I liked a battle. I was never shy to have a battle with anybody.'

Accusations of refereeing bias remain a staple for opponents trudging away from Anfield empty-handed, but Horton insists that the perception of Liverpool was no different to that of his own side. 'You can say that, but Man City were classed as one of the bigger clubs – no disrespect to the smaller sides that were the Premier League back then,' he says. 'Oldham were in in the Premier League back then; would they think that [about] coming to Maine Road? Probably, yeah. I never thought about things like that. Decisions go against you at some of the bigger clubs – we know that. I don't think that'll ever change. That's human nature sometimes, but the staff at Liverpool, whoever you managed against, were always top-class and fair. You'd get praise where it was due. They were just a different quality of people that were in charge at Liverpool.'

Liverpool's manager had a rare chance to revel in the victory as he admitted, 'I enjoyed that, I enjoyed it very much.' That savouring lasted all of six days as Souness was sacked following a humiliating FA Cup third-round replay exit to Bristol City. Anfield's kingmakers again chose to promote from within as Evans became the final pillar of the Boot Room to step to the fore, fulfilling the prophecy of former Liverpool chairman John Smith who said in August 1974, 'One day, Roy Evans will be our manager.' Among the 45-year-old's immediate tasks in the hot seat was to field an approach from Manchester City for Rush. Francis Lee's £3m takeover of his former club had just brought an end to two decades of frustration under Peter Swales and set about realising the ex-striker's aim of transforming Maine Road into 'the happiest club in the land'.

Successive enquiries were lodged for Rush, now in his final 18 months on Merseyside, over two days ahead of a potential £2m offer. But the talks came to nothing with Evans announcing on 19 February that the player had no intentions of moving to the team that had first passed up a chance to sign him in 1980. 'There's always interest in players like him, a prolific goalscorer with pace about him and everything really,' says Horton. 'We were always interested. It might have been the time when Niall [Quinn] did his cruciate. I can't remember the date on that one, but I was short of strikers. That's when I got Uwe Rösler in, but Uwe came for next to nothing basically. Rushie would've been probably a lot money in terms of their valuation than what we would probably be able to pay.'

Rösler's arrival a month later from Nurnberg came on an initial three-month loan which was made permanent for £500,000 in the summer alongside the signing of Paul Walsh, a member of Liverpool's 1986 double-winning side, from Portsmouth for £750,000 and Everton winger Peter Beagrie, who also joined for £1.1m. As a result, City won their battle for Premier League survival with a 16th place finish by finishing one point ahead of Beagrie's old club, who pulled off a 'Great Escape' on the final day of 1993/94 by winning 3-2 against Wimbledon.

Liverpool's eighth-place standing, 32 points behind back-to-back champions Manchester United, encapsulated the bitter end of Graeme Souness's tenure and the transition under his replacement. The muted finale saw a last outing for The Kop in its original guise, with terraced stands at all top-flight stadiums converted into all-seater structures as recommended by Lord

Justice Taylor's report that was commissioned to investigate the Hillsborough disaster.

Evans demonstrated his willingness to adapt to English football's evolving new landscape on 22 October 1994 by appointing former City stalwart Joe Corrigan as the club's first dedicated goalkeeping coach, a role previously fulfilled by a combination of Boot Room members. Prior to his permanency, Corrigan was already working at Melwood as a consultant while liaising with clubs further down the Football League pyramid as well as Aberdeen in Scotland. 'I was surprised that such an institute as Liverpool, which has won trophies by doing the same things year in, year out, didn't have anyone coaching the keepers,' he told the press. 'But I think the club was big enough to think about the future. You have to progress. It's up to me to try and get the best I can out of the lads.'

Evans also enacted proactive changes within the Reds' disjointed squad, releasing half of the club's six remaining survivors from its 1990 title win in addition to offloading Julian Dicks and Don Hutchison, both to West Ham United for £1.8m, while Torben Piechnik, a member of Denmark's triumphant Euro '92 squad, was allowed to return to his homeland after barely flattering to deceive in the previous two years. Supplementing the prodigious talents of Steve McManaman, Robbie Fowler and Jamie Redknapp were defensive duo John Scales and Phil Babb, sourced for a combined £7.1m from Wimbledon and Coventry City respectively. But the upgrades failed to catapult Liverpool into the reckoning for the Premier League title, with United and Blackburn Rovers already slugging it out in the middle distance by the midway point of 1994/95.

Horton's own rebuilding task at Maine Road led to a familiar name returning to their ranks in the form of Nicky Summerbee. The winger followed in his father Mike's 1960s footsteps by joining from Swindon Town for £1.5m and helped City move into sixth at the start of December only for a downturn in form to demote them to just inside the league's top half. Heading to Anfield on 28 December, they had a chance to climb up to those previously dizzying heights while the hosts set their sights on moving into third, closing the gap between themselves and United to just six points ahead of a potential left-field challenge for top spot. McManaman routinely caused City problems in the first half before a series of late tackles from Steve Lomas attempted to limit his impact, with the midfielder walking a disciplinary tightrope after ten minutes. A moment of misfortune befell City in the second half when McManaman again tormented them in feeding Babb for a cross on the left which sailed over the head of Alan Kernaghan and was intercepted by Terry Phelan, who headed the ball past a sprawling Andy Dibble and into the newly seated Kop's net.

Dibble later reprised a dual role of sinner and saint in the 80th minute after fouling Rush in the penalty area before saving Fowler's spot kick. But City's goalkeeper, covering for an injured Tony Coton, was powerless to the striker's follow-up as Fowler unleashed a left-footed shot from 25 yards which took him beyond the previous benchmark of 18 goals recorded in his breakthrough season at Anfield.

City arguably may have fared better in the game using a more defensive approach, but Horton is adamant that abandoning his tactical principles never entered into the equation. 'I didn't change really very much,' he says. 'That was probably my strongest attacking line-up with those two [Lomas and Garry Flitcroft] in midfield and then that front four or five when Quinny [Niall Quinn] was back were, for me, as good as anything. I wasn't necessarily going to Liverpool to put up shop and just defend. That's the way I wanted to be. I'd had two top managers in Alan Mullery and David Pleat who had always wanted us to play that way so I never in my managerial career went defensive. Obviously if I had the players which I thought I had at Man City, to go to Anfield and just defend [didn't appeal].'

The next meeting between the teams was mired by a brief yet bitter public feud over plans for the Maine Road fixture to take place on 15 April, the sixth anniversary of Hillsborough. Liverpool and City lobbied the Premier League for the match to be brought forward a day but were told that the original date would stand. Anfield chiefs requested that their Manchester counterparts considered moving the Saturday kick-off time to 11.30am in order for players, officials and fans to attend a memorial service at their stadium later in the day. City refused the request due to it inconveniencing their own match-going fans but chose to delay the game's start until 3.15pm. 'We have a lot of supporters travelling the length of the country and the early time would have been too disruptive,' said club secretary Bernard Halford. 'The feedback was that we should kick off at 3.15 pm. Obviously six minutes past three is not the time to be playing football against Liverpool. We believe we have given due respect to the anniversary of the tragedy.' City's efforts to strike a balance between the needs of both parties was met with justifiable anger on Merseyside, with travelling fans planning to boycott the fixture if it went ahead on the afternoon of 15 April.

Liverpool chief executive Peter Robinson described the decision as 'unfortunate' and added, 'We are hoping that they will still have a change of heart.' The Merseyside branch of the club's International Supporters' Club went further by slamming the decision as 'disrespectful to all the 96 who died', while spokesperson Peter Millea responded to Halford's claims by stating, 'Surely it's more important to honour the memory of those who died than to worry about inconveniencing supporters.'

Francis Lee attempted to extinguish the furore by laying blame for the logistical issues at the feet of the footballing authorities rather than City itself. 'We are prepared to look at anything rather than have all this friction,' he said. 'There would have been no problem if the authorities had taken our advice in November and changed the date. We have bent over backwards to save causing any offence, and it is unbelievable that we have been made out to be villains.'

Belatedly, the Premier League accepted Liverpool and City's renewed request for the match to be staged 24 hours earlier while retaining its 3.15pm start time. Halford disclosed that City would incur an additional £25,000 in policing costs for the rescheduled game but insisted, 'We were anxious to help out in this unique situation.'

When the teams took to the field on that Good Friday, City struck first against the new League Cup winners when Maurizio Gaudino intercepted a short pass by Redknapp and played a one-two with Summerbee before the winger side-footed home for his first league goal of the season. 'Nicky was a fantastic player and ironically came from Swindon the same [as his dad],' says Horton. 'Quinny, I think, said to someone or was quoted that Nicky Summerbee was the best crosser he'd ever played with. He'd played at Sunderland with him as well. Nicky played right wing-back when he was at Swindon, played right-winger, could have played right-back – he had that ability. He had a good engine, a great crosser of the ball, very quiet unassuming lad. When I threw it in that I wanted to buy him, Blackburn and Kenny Dalglish were in and we were competing with them. I think we got it for £1.5m. A good player, Nicky, and very unassuming. Mike obviously was a different person. He was just a character, wasn't he? He knocked about with Bestie and was more flamboyant if you like.'

But McManaman haunted City again just five minutes later after receiving a pass from new recruit Mark Kennedy and working the ball between himself and Fowler before hooking an effort from just inside the penalty area which beat a stranded Tony Coton. In the second half, Flitcroft succeeded where Steve Lomas had failed in their previous meeting with a strong tackle that forced him off just one minute before his side fell behind again. The partnership which had opened the scoring for City also contributed to its winner as Summerbee fed Uwe Rösler down the right before his cross into the box was powered in by Gaudino with a diving header. Gaudino's heroics in the final quarter moved City up six places to 11th and left them only requiring four points from the remaining five games to retain their Premier League status by Horton's estimation. A shock win over champions-elect Blackburn three days later and successive draws with Newcastle United and Aston Villa proved enough before losing to Nottingham Forest and Queen's Park Rangers. 'It wasn't bad, was it?' he says. 'We'd beaten Liverpool, beaten Blackburn and drawn at Newcastle. Seven points out of nine out of those three teams, if you're in a relegation battle and you're looking at that, those three games thinking, "What can we pick up out of those?" We won at Blackburn, which was a shock to everyone, but we played so well that night and then to beat Liverpool on the Good Friday, putting back-to-back wins out of three in that little sequence is unbelievable.'

Adding to City's joy at the end of 1994/95 was the failure of Manchester United to clinch a consecutive league and cup double, having surrendered the title to Blackburn by drawing with West Ham on the final day, despite Kenny Dalglish's side themselves losing at Anfield, and being beaten by Everton in the FA Cup Final the following weekend.

Horton witnessed the Red Devils' complete downfall but did so no longer as manager of their local rivals, with his tenure ended just two days after the end of the Premier League campaign on 16 May. Speculation over his successor saw a flurry of names linked but Francis Lee followed in Peter Swales's footsteps by again turning to Merseyside in efforts to revive City's standing. Attempts to lure Alan Hansen, the former Liverpool captain who had become a renowned pundit on BBC's *Match of the Day*, ended as quickly as they had begun. 'Francis Lee, who was chairman at the time, phoned me up and said he thought I would have fancied it,' said Hansen. 'But while I told him I was flattered, I just said I wasn't interested in managing a football club. When I left Liverpool in 1991 I was in the frame for the job at Anfield but if I wasn't going to take the Liverpool job, I wasn't going to take any job.'

Next in line was Ron Atkinson, United's former manager who was born in the Old Swan district of Liverpool, but Lee was again denied by the recently appointed Coventry City boss. Brian Kidd, a home-grown former City player, appeared a genuine forerunner but Alex Ferguson's assistant at Old Trafford had no intentions of stepping into frontline management at that time.

Alan Ball's eventual appointment failed to convince supporters that the future remained bright. The flame-haired former midfielder had been a decorated player with Arsenal and Everton as well as the youngest member of England's 1966 World Cup-winning side. But not even the inclusion of one-time City favourite Asa Hartford as his assistant could deflect from the fact that Ball had been an underwhelming candidate, having led Portsmouth to a short-lived spell in the First Division in 1987/88 and steered Southampton to a top-ten finish in the most recent Premier League campaign.

Liverpool's own fourth-place achievement and League Cup success was followed up by breaking the British transfer record, with Stan Collymore's £8.5m signing from Nottingham Forest expected to supplement the shortfall left by Ian Rush's impending departure at the end of 1995/96. By late October, they had cemented a regular place in the top five ahead of a League Cup third-round meeting with City. History suggested that whichever team had won their third meeting in the competition would conceivably go on to win it outright, a rare point of positivity for the visitors, who were rooted to the foot of the league table with just two points from ten games.

Ball's side were handed a boost in their efforts to sign Liverpool outcast Nigel Clough immediately ahead of the trip to Merseyside, with the versatile attacker imploring Roy Evans to lower his asking price from £2m due to City's inability to meet the valuation. 'I think everybody has to be sensible,' he said. 'It's very difficult playing reserve-team football, so maybe moving on is the best thing. I've given it a good year or two and things haven't worked out. Hopefully, if someone is interested, we can work things out.'

That would be as good as things got for the visitors at Anfield, where Eike Immel evoked comparisons with the last German to stand in between the sticks for the Blues, Bert Trautmann, by repelling an early assault from Ian Rush and Robbie Fowler. But the Reds took the lead on nine minutes when Redknapp's free kick into Rush was cleared by Kit Symons, his international team-mate with Wales, and broke to John Scales for a half-volley which evaded Immel's best efforts.

City fashioned three noteworthy first-half opportunities in front of goal. The first arrived from a long diagonal by John Foster that allowed Quinn to best Scales with a flick-on to Uwe Rösler. The German lifted the ball over Mark Wright and took it on to his stronger right foot but dragged his effort past the post. Another long ball, this time from Richard Edghill, appeared to have produced an equaliser when it bounced fortuitously for Quinn to rifle a half-volley which nestled in David James's bottom-right corner but the offside flag had already been raised. Rösler's low cross later in the first half beat Mark Wright and led to a poor attempted clearance by Phil Babb, who missed the ball completely and allowed it to run through to Quinn. The Republic of Ireland international raced ahead of Steve Harkness to meet it at the far post but fluffed his lines. Liverpool's record of conceding just twice in their opening six home games further undermined City's already uphill task.

Yet it was the home fans that grew increasingly fraught after half-time as their team continued to dominate possession and chances without affirming their dominance. With 16 minutes remaining, Rush and Fowler combined as the latter rushed past Symons to double Liverpool's lead as he fired past Immel, who misjudged the shot and tried to save it with his feet. 'You know how dangerous they can be so you certainly don't underestimate them. That's the biggest sort of fear in football, if you underestimate an opponent,' he says. 'But certainly when it's Ian Rush, there's not much chance I was going to underestimate him! I had played with him for Wales but anyone who knows anything about football knows what a great, incredible player Rushie was. I played against him in the FA Cup semi-final with Portsmouth [in 1992]. He played in the first one at Highbury when we drew 1-1 so I'd played against Rushie before at club level and sort of done alright. As much as I knew obviously he was a world-class striker, I also knew I could play against him and do well because I'd done it previously. But him and Robbie Fowler were flipping unplayable that day.'

Rush hit the target on 79 minutes with a header from a Redknapp delivery to see him close in on Geoff Hurst's League Cup record of 49 goals. As resigned City supporters streamed for the exits in the final ten minutes, Harkness secured his side's safe passage into the next round with a drilled effort after his initial shot had been blocked and rebounded back into the left-back's path. Ball reflected on the late onslaught and how it would be packaged by Granada's *Soccer Night* programme, which asked for his thoughts after the game. 'This might be daft, because you'll have edited it wonderful, and you saw some fabulous goals scored, but I think it flattered them a little bit,' he said. 'We were in it for a long period after half-time. Goals change games and, as I say, the way you'll have edited it, it will look very, very one-sided but Liverpool know that it wasn't.'

His self-belief led to a renewed confidence when City returned to Merseyside three days later. 'I think that's what gave us confidence turning up at Anfield on the Saturday – misplaced confidence, granted!' says Symons. 'We were sort of reasonably pleased and that was Bally's team talk before the game on the Saturday, basically saying, "We came here in midweek, we played well, you should have got something out of it – make sure you get something out of it today." But we came into a Liverpool team that was bang on form on the Saturday.'

City had drafted in Barcelona striker Thomas Christiansen on loan in a move which came about as a favour to Ball from his personal friend Johan Cruyff, with the option to make the move permanent for £500,000 included. The ethereal Dutch coach also tried to include Gheorge Hagi, already an eminent force in European football, but an inability to meet his reported £12,000-per-week wages saw the offer passed up. Christiansen returned to the Camp Nou within days of his arrival and most of his prospective new team-mates probably wished they were joining him after suffering fresh humiliation at Anfield. Within five minutes, City had already fallen two goals behind, first after Fowler crossed to Jason McAteer, a £4.5m signing from Bolton Wanderers a month earlier, to hit a low shot which Immel spilled into Rush's path. Redknapp further punished the lacklustre visitors with a free kick which was deflected past Immel. Shortly after half-time, Wright brought the ball out of defence and teed up Fowler, who turned both Ian Brightwell and Symons before skimming a shot past Immel – a move which Francis Lee stood applauding in the directors' box.

An outswinging corner from Redknapp produced a powerful header from Neil Ruddock, who replaced an injured John Barnes. Liverpool's stand-out strike came on the hour mark as Scales released McAteer down the wing for a cross which Rush helped on, allowing Fowler to loom behind Symons. The Toxteth marksman impressively recalibrated his positioning for a left-footed shot on the turn. The hammering was rounded off four minutes later as Redknapp drove a shot at Immel, who again parried the ball into Rush's path.

Already long resigned to another hefty defeat, City's travelling support began to invoke gallows humour in the Anfield Road End. Their team's first corner was greeted with a level of delirium usually reserved for goals before chants of 'Alan Ball's a football genius' and 'we're shit – and we're getting worse' rang out. More imaginatively, they channelled the spirit of Dame Vera Lynn with a rendition of 'we'll score again, don't know where, don't know when'.

Uwe Rösler's attempt to atone to supporters at the final whistle, amid growing speculation over his immediate future, were not particularly well received. 'I sort of sensed the atmosphere walking off,' admits Symons. 'You clap the fans obviously and thank them for coming but you don't push it too much if they're not in the mood for it. There was a lot of talk about Uwe leaving at that time and so it was almost like a farewell thing as a gesture, but it wasn't necessarily taken in the right way and the boots got thrown back!'

If Rösler's rejected gesture was a sign of the frustration brewing in the ranks at Maine Road after their failure to score in over nine hours of play, Ball's lack of nuance saw him admit to deriving genuine pleasure from sitting back and watching his team's thrashing. 'You could pick up that it was a strange time and there were some weird things happening,' says Symons. 'You almost weren't surprised by anything really during that season.'

Francis Lee had continued to put on a brace face, even when Liverpool rallied into an early lead, but that sunny disposition gradually fell away as the afternoon progressed. Former playing adversary Tommy Smith exchanged views with the City chairman across the divide between Anfield's press box and directors' seats during the game. But even the old pals' act did not spare Lee from a brutal assessment of his club's fortunes by Smith in the *Liverpool Echo* just 48 hours later. 'Quite frankly, they are not just like a ship going down,' he said. 'They are like the *Titanic* – already on the bottom of the ocean with little or no chance of a salvage job.' City belatedly moved off the foot of the Premier League table but not out of the relegation zone ahead of the 1995/96 season's final day.

Maine Road's date with destiny on 5 May came against a Liverpool team that had booked its place in the FA Cup Final, against mutual foes Manchester United, but had still failed to win on their domestic travels since February. 'We fancied it [because] Maine Road was going to have a real good atmosphere,' says Symons. 'There was definitely a lot of nerves about but an element of confidence as well going into it that we could get a result in that game and then it would be enough to keep us up because it was going to better either Southampton or Coventry's result. We felt confident going into it. You don't necessarily want to be in a relegation battle, but you play for the big games and the pressure, the atmosphere and things like that.

'We knew Liverpool were a great side, and a good team, but we knew they weren't sort of unbeatable during that season. Although we'd got obviously a tonking in the league game earlier on, we genuinely believed we had a chance of getting a result.'

The week leading up to the showdown was dominated by figures on both sides sizing up City's task. Mark Wright, hoping to stake a claim for the Wembley showpiece after returning from injury, admitted, 'Manchester City are going to be fighting for everything. If you don't look after yourself in a match like this, you don't come out with any credit, and could come out getting hurt. Unless you're on your game, you'll get found out.' The England international fired a warning to former team-mate Nigel Clough, who had eventually moved to Maine Road for £1.5m in January, that their cordial relations would be on hold for the next 90 minutes. 'Nigel is a friend of mine, but he knows there is no sentiment in this match,' he added. 'If my brother was on the opposing side I would always try to beat him, so Nigel knows what to expect. It is unfortunate we should meet up again in these circumstances. But, really, City's future is out of their hands already. They could still go down even if they beat us.' Fellow Reds defender John Scales shared Wright's view of the pressure on the hosts in their scrap for survival. 'City will be fighting for their lives,' he said. 'The tension in their crowd will be unbelievable because they have to get a win.'

Ball conceded that he was 'expecting no favours' in the form of a Liverpool let-up to save his side's skin, while Niall Quinn issued a rallying cry in his *Sunday World* column, declaring 'Manchester City cannot afford to go crashing down … it is up to us to get ourselves out of trouble by beating Liverpool at Maine Road. And yes, I know that we could do that and still go down, that would be the ultimate football cruelty.'

City needed to better the results of Southampton and Coventry, the two teams directly above them in the table, to avoid relegation. In a nod to future events, Quinn insisted that he and his team-mates must not become preoccupied by events elsewhere: 'The crowd will let us know how our fellow relegation strugglers are doing anyway.'

What would become a highly bizarre afternoon began on a quite literal difficult footing after a series of homecoming gigs by Oasis at the stadium in the previous week had left the playing surface in a far from pristine condition for the crucial fixture. In the match programme, beneath the headline of 'We'll Win The Fight', Lee insisted that his manager's position would not come under fire in the aftermath of the do-or-die match. 'Alan Ball's job will not be affected,' he wrote. 'By nature, he is a winner.'

Before kick-off, local compere Vince Miller, a City fan who became a regular fixture in Old Trafford's corporate lounges for the best part of three decades, attempted to rouse the home supporters with renditions of club anthem 'Blue Moon' before misguidedly following it up with 'Land of Hope and Glory', which was drowned out by the Kippax. Both teams were still greeted by a raucous reception when they took to the pitch and observed an impeccable minute's silence in memory of ex-City chairman Peter Swales following his sudden passing three days earlier.

Swales had ceded his control of the club to Lee in 1994 following a 21-year spell where he sacked 11 different managers and became a figure of growing resentment among the Maine Road faithful, something which deterred him from ever returning once the takeover battle finally ended. The *Daily Mirror* carried the alleged words of the 63-year-old's final wish: 'Tell them the last thing I want is for City to go down.' Swales's worst fears would become realised in a game which carried the same hallmarks of chaos, confusion and disappointment that accompanied large parts of his premiership.

Liverpool drew first blood from a Redknapp corner which eluded Wright's head but broke inside the penalty area for McManaman to float a cross through Keith Curle's legs and into the danger zone, where Steve Lomas catastrophically turned the ball into his own net. Controversially, City were denied a penalty after Georgi Kinkladze put Nicky Summerbee through on goal with a neat chipped pass before he was tripped by Neil Ruddock. Appeals from both Maine Road's fans and players fell on deaf ears with referee Stephen Lodge, who had taken charge of the League Cup encounter earlier in the season, as he ruled that the foul had occurred on the edge of the area. Liverpool packed the box for the ensuing free kick, which Kinkladze wasted.

The visitors moved further into the lead shortly before the interval as McManaman used blistering pace to beat Symons on the counter-attack and played a cross-field pass for Rush on the edge of the box. A well-struck effort from the veteran striker from 22 yards took a deflection off Curle as it rocketed into Eike Immel's net for only his seventh goal of the season and, more pertinently, the last of 346 strikes in a Liverpool shirt. A cacophony of boos greeted the half-time whistle as the previously unthinkable was writ large.

'Things in the first half didn't go our way and Liverpool were far the better team,' says Symons. 'Lomey had scored an own goal so you sort of get the feeling things are going against you. I think we struggled to get going and we were up against it a little bit but the half-time sort of gave us a bit of an opportunity. We had gone in there and if it stayed as it was, we were definitely done – that was us relegated. So it's almost like, "We've got nothing to lose now. Come on, let's have a right go at this." Bally sort of got stuck in a little bit and everyone thought, "Let's just go for it – we've literally got nothing to lose. We've got to give everything in this second half and try to salvage something out of this game."'

Ball still waited until the hour before ringing the changes, with Martin Phillips replacing Quinn to widespread jeers before Mikhail Kavelashvili, Kinkladze's fellow Georgian, came on in place of Clough. McManaman should have put Liverpool further ahead with two efforts in the space of a minute before City received an unlikely lifeline when a quickly taken throw-in by Lomas allowed Kinkladze to perform a skilful dribble before he was bundled over by Ruddock. Lodge immediately pointed to the penalty spot, from where Rösler struck the ball straight down the middle to beat David James for his 13th goal of the campaign.

Seven minutes later, a cross from Phillips avoided McAteer's reach and found Rösler, whose back-header fell for Symons at the far post to half-volley an equaliser. With less than a quarter of an hour remaining, Ball's side were still in with a shout of survival. 'Straight away just scoring the equaliser, it's like we've now got a chance,' says the goalscoring defender. 'If we had lost, we were done. But suddenly coming level, you get all sorts of things going through your mind. For a split second, I'm thinking this could be the goal that keeps us up, which would have been huge.'

What followed thereafter was the epitome of 'typical City', a default idiom whenever the club's serial under-performance never came as a surprise. News filtered through to Francis Lee that Southampton were losing against Wimbledon. City's chairman relayed the message to reserve goalkeeper Martyn Margetson near the home dugout. Ball beckoned Lomas over and urged him to run down the clock. 'We're up. Kill this game off,' the World Cup winner told his mop-haired midfielder. 'Just do whatever you can.'

On 84 minutes, Summerbee laid the ball off to Lomas, who followed Ball's instructions to the letter by keeping possession in the corner area despite challenges by Mark Kennedy and Robbie Fowler. From the ensuing throw-in, Lomas played a one-two with Summerbee before continuing to play for time as the Liverpool duo actively battled to win the ball back from him. 'It was all a bit murky to be honest,' says Symons. 'I can remember seeing Steve sort of putting his foot on the ball in the corner wasting time, just trying to get throw-ins to delay things and literally just time-waste. It was sort of quite obvious what the message was that had been given to him and so we all picked up on that. With me in defence, if it was coming to me, I was just going to kick it as far as I could anyway to get it away from our goal. It wasn't going to change my attitude on the game too much anyway. But it was clear what message Steve had got and made us think a draw's enough.'

Two minutes later, and contrary to his Kippax 'disco pants' chant, Quinn frantically charged down the touchline in beige slacks while simultaneously telling his team-mates that they had been given false information as well as hope regarding Southampton's result. 'Quinny comes running down the stairs and saying, "No, it's not enough – we've got to win!" so there's all mixed messages on the pitch,' says Symons. 'No one quite knew what was happening and it was all very bizarre. Even then at the final whistle we ended up with a draw, I think the Coventry game was a delayed kick-off so we're waiting in the tunnel still not knowing our fate until we know the other result.'

By the time sense finally prevailed, City could launch only two attacks with Kavelashvili's potential match-winning header punched clear by James in the game's dying embers. When the final whistle all but confirmed Maine Road's fate, Lomas launched the ball into the home crowd in frustration.

City's players lingered in the tunnel area awaiting news from The Dell before heading back to the home dressing room to contemplate a life in English football's second tier for the following season. 'Everyone's individual in how they deal with things. I literally got in there and just shut down,' reveals Symons. 'It's a horrible feeling but this is football. The good times, the promotions and things like that are fantastic but then the feeling that you get as a player being relegated is horrible. It's really, really horrible and I can just remember staring blankly into space and not speaking to anyone or saying anything for ages. I vaguely remember there was a bit of an inquiry into "how did this information come about?" or whatever but still to this day I've got no idea what actually happened with that.'

Recriminations extended to Liverpool as Evans was forced to deny suggestions that his side had gone through the motions in their final domestic fixture due to having one eye on Wembley. 'We only had fitness and pride to play for,' he said. 'City were fighting for their lives and they had a right good go. I thought we coped with them well for an hour and then, as is our wont, we relaxed a bit. We fought right to the end. We can hold our heads up and say we didn't let anybody down … If we weren't at our most committed, we would have got battered. City had quite a few chances and our goalkeeper was fantastic again. There were always going to be times when City threw balls under our bar, but we dealt with them reasonably well.'

The sombre mood later turned to anger as it was alleged that a coach carrying travelling Liverpool supporters found itself attacked with stones by disgruntled City fans as it attempted to leave Maine Road.

One mischievous Manchester United fan later rang BBC Radio 5 Live's *606* phone-in, claiming to mourn his local rivals' demise. 'I'm really sad they've gone down,' he said. 'Well it's six points, isn't it?' Feelings were not spared on City's relegation on Merseyside either as the following morning's *Liverpool Echo* revelled in their misfortune with a handful of quintessential 1990s tabloid puns. The headline on their double-page spread screamed 'You're My Blunder Ball' while, under the sub-heading 'What's the story? Mourning glory', Ric George considered Maine Road's penchant for playing Oasis songs before matches as 'a sign of desperation' and claimed their hosts' demotion was vindicated because 'no team deserves to stay up if it cannot defeat a disinterested Reds side which offered minimum resistance'. He agreed that Summerbee's first-half penalty claim had been cruelly denied but added 'they would probably have missed that too'.

George's colleague Phil McNulty was far more scathing in delivering his view 'Manchester City are the kings of footballing high farce – and it doesn't come much funnier than the fare on offer as the relegation trap-door creaked open.' He added, 'You've heard the one about the teams who were too good to go down. City were the team who were too bad to stay up.'

Ball's presence in the home dugout was considered 'an accident waiting to happen' and McNulty asked, 'How can this greatly talented world-class player turn into such a managerial dud?' – a question which would be repeated on numerous occasions in the ensuing decades as similarly decorated stars unsuccessfully tried their hand at elite-level coaching. His sign-off conceded that City would be missed but only on the grounds that 'laughs are in pretty short supply in the Premier League these days'.

Gloating was in far shorter supply a week later as Liverpool suffered a late FA Cup Final defeat to United in a muted end to Ian Rush's long and illustrious 15-year spell with the club. City prepared for their First Division existence by making a third and final attempt to coax the marksman, now 35 and available on a free transfer, to Moss Side. Leeds United and Sunderland, now led by ex-Blues manager Peter Reid, also joined the hunt for Rush, who eventually chose Elland Road as the next destination in his career swansong. The trials and tribulations of Maine Road's long road to redemption were only just beginning.

Seven

BY THE time he joined Manchester City, Georgi Kinkladze had gained something of a reputation for being in the right place at the wrong time. Wherever the playmaker went, his face never seemed to fit.

His career began in earnest with Dinamo Tblisi, who previously held the distinction of eliminating the Anfield club from the European Cup in 1979/80. Georgia's capital was no longer hidden behind the Iron Curtain when Kinkladze became a fully fledged professional with his hometown club but it remained beset by political turmoil. A rancorous civil war between the newly independent country's first prime minister, Zviad Gamsakhurdia, and his successor, Eduard Shevardnadze, raged for well over two years. The man who had served as Mikhail Gorbachev's foreign secretary prior to the collapse of the Soviet Union replaced Gamsakhurdia in office after he had been overthrown in a coup d'etat.

Shevardnadze won the battle of wills over Gamsakhurdia when the nationalist dissident was found with a gunshot wound to his head in Khibula, a village situated in the west Georgian province of Samegrelo, on New Year's Eve 1993. Before the conflict ended, Dinamo president Merab Jordania sought to extricate the club's most promising assets by facilitating their departures either on permanent or loan deals. The latter became Kinkladze's designated path for the beginning of a truly nomadic journey.

A brief stint with FC Saarbrucken in the German second division offered a chastening introduction to European football that spanned just 11 games, produced no goals and registered a sending off in their 3-1 defeat to Hertha Berlin as his only meaningful contribution. Kinkladze subsequently went on trial with Atlético Madrid, who were offered the chance to sign him for a modest fee of £200,000, but they expressed reservations about both his fitness and tactical disciplines. Local rivals Real were similarly dissuaded when the player trained with the club's reserve team. But the short time spent in Madrid led to a surprise switch to Boca Juniors, whose resident scout in the Spanish capital recommended that Kinkladze be taken on a month's loan. During his time in Argentina, he met his idol Diego Maradona, now a shadow of his former self and readying himself for a short-lived international comeback at the 1994 World Cup. That proved to be as good as it got at La Bombonera before Kinkladze returned to Tblisi, having made just three appearances in Argentina's Primera Division, with the Boca dressing room's obsession about securing moves to Europe ringing in his ears.

Moves to the Continent's elite leagues appeared inevitable during his final season at Dinamo. Several Serie A clubs monitored Kinkladze's performances following a stellar display for Georgia in their Euro '96 qualifier with Moldova on 7 September 1994. The Italian press even went as far as to declare him the Black Sea's answer to AC Milan legend Gianni Rivera. Yet it was a starring role in his country's double header with Wales, racking up a 5-0 home win and scoring a 20-yard lob over Neville Southall in the return fixture in Cardiff, that convinced City they were witnessing a potential legend in the making. Francis Lee and Colin Bell, two thirds of the club's fabled 'Holy Trinity', were among those at Maine Road who ran the rule over Kinkladze prior to his £2m transfer on 15 July 1995. The decision to hand him the number seven shirt previously worn by club icons such as Mike Summerbee, Neil Young and Lee himself reaffirmed the view that their new signing was destined for greatness. Even the player's new nickname of 'Kinky' had a distinct feel of his new surroundings.

On 19 August, in the same week that the 'Battle of Britpop' had taken place, Kinkladze made his City debut in a 1-1 draw with Tottenham Hotspur. Sitting in the Maine Road directors' box on that afternoon, Oasis lead guitarist Noel Gallagher took time out from his band's north v south duelling with Blur in the UK singles chart to ponder whether he was witnessing the birth of a new era at his boyhood club or just another false dawn. 'I watched Kinky for the first time and it was like, "Jesús, this is either the most frightening thing I've ever seen or it's the best thing I've ever seen." I couldn't decide which one it was!' he said. 'You'd only get that at City.' A 1-1 draw was followed up the next day by Blur's 'Country House' beating Oasis's 'Roll With It' by 58,000 copies.

Gallagher's uncertainty of what to expect from the Kippax's new poster boy was reflected by the Georgian's new team-mates. Kit Symons, a fellow summer recruit signed from Alan Ball's former club Portsmouth, remembers the pros and cons of Kinkladze's three-year spell on Moss Side. 'Georgi was easy to find. He always wanted the ball so he would come into areas that he could easily collect the ball but that's not necessarily always what we wanted because generally he's quite a long way from goal,' he says. 'It wasn't always necessarily the areas of the pitch where he could hurt the opposition so there was an element of that certainly. But he was a talent.

'He's still obviously a massive hero at City with the fans because of his ability, dribbling, running with the ball. He wasn't always easy to play with because the type of team we were, we were struggling a little bit and he was what you could almost deem as a luxury player. Now, we weren't a good enough team to carry a luxury player, which was a bit of a problem! He scored Goal of the Month against Southampton at Maine Road that year, which was a phenomenal goal. We could've done with a bigger return of goals and assists but he was a mercurial talent without any shadow of a doubt.'

Symons's description of Kinkladze's strike against the Saints on 16 March 1996 does not undervalue its significance. That 14-second spell of individual brilliance only earned City a rare win in their battle for Premier League survival and saw Kinkladze awarded the BBC *Match of the Day* Goal of the Month prize. His effort was crowned runner-up in the Goal of the Season contest, won that year by Leeds United's Tony Yeboah. After shrugging off Simon Charlton, ghosting past Ken Monkou and deceiving a sliding challenge from Neil Heaney, Kinkladze deftly chipped Dave Beasant off his line. Kinkladze's brief acquaintance with Maradona may have flown largely under the radar at the time but Ball was quick to compare the solo effort to the Argentine's second goal against England in the 1986 World Cup quarter-final, before adding the unnecessary disclaimer, 'Not the one with his hand, the one where he did everyone and put it away.'

Not everyone within the Maine Road dressing room was equally enamoured with their diminutive talisman as Ball. Paul Walsh would later claim that Kinkladze had been 'the catalyst for City's problems' due to their manager's persistent indulgence of the player. Symons, who joined in a £1.5m part-exchange deal from Portsmouth, had been handed his senior debut by Ball during his final game as manager at Fratton Park in January 1989. When Ball returned to the South Coast five years later, he was quick to redefine Matt Le Tissier's role in a Southampton side heading towards near-certain relegation. His new focal point returned the favour with six goals during Ball's first four games in charge. By the end of that 1993/94 season, he had scored 15 times in 16 outings.

When it came to City and Kinkladze, though, the blueprint proved non-transferable. 'Bally loved a talented footballer,' says Symons. 'Obviously he had Le Tissier at Southampton and Georgi at Man City. We had Stevie Lomas and Garry Flitcroft, both really, really good players, but a little bit of their job was to get the ball and give it to Georgi, which for me wasn't quite right because they were both very good players in their own right.'

Less than ten days after scoring his wonder goal against the Saints, City chairman Lee was forced to dismiss speculation linking Kinkladze with European heavyweights Barcelona and Inter Milan as 'total rubbish'. But it was clear that the vultures were circling. Some had been alerted to the player's qualities far sooner than his late-season flourish. When City were trounced 4-0 by Liverpool in the League Cup third round on 28 October 1995, no visiting player stood out greater than the one wearing the number seven shirt. Kinkladze was routinely at the heart of counter-attack moves with a series of incisive runs which led to the Anfield crowd growing fraught at defending a one-goal lead up until the 74th minute. His best opening came just moments before Robbie Fowler doubled the hosts' slender advantage, when an interception from Symons allowed him to surge downfield and have the beating of Phil Babb twice in quick succession before skewing his long-range effort wide of goal. In his post-match analysis on Granada's *Soccer Night*, former Anfield hero Jim Beglin highlighted the Georgian's inconsistency before adding the caveat, 'I think if you stuck him in that Liverpool side, he'd be a hell of a lot better.'

When City headed back to the red half of Merseyside just three days later in the Premier League, any hopes that Kinkladze would produce a repeat performance ended in the 41st minute, when he stumbled on the ball in an attempt to control it and had to be stretchered off. That freak injury, coupled with a meagre return of just four goals in 37 appearances, did little to extinguish the admiration for Kinkladze's abilities by the time City's Premier League status had been downgraded from perilous to condemned at the end of the 1995/96 campaign. With the club's £26m debt proving unsustainable outside the English top flight, player sales became a necessary evil. Garry Flitcroft had already joined defending champions Blackburn Rovers for £3.5m, while Keith Curle was stripped of the club's captaincy and sold to Wolverhampton Wanderers, one of City's new rivals in the First Division, for £650,000 during the summer. Kinkladze, their reigning Player of the Year, appeared next.

Supporters' worst fears were confirmed on 19 September when newspaper reports claimed that Lee was preparing to listen to offers in the region of £5m. Later that month, Kinkladze went public about his own exit strategy and identified Liverpool as a preferred destination. 'They don't want to let me go, although

I openly informed Francis Lee that I'm not going to remain in the First Division,' he told reporters. 'I said I wouldn't stay with Manchester City even if I started the season playing for them. The best club for me is Liverpool. Their style appeals to me most and I have friends there. Yes, playing for Liverpool I would feel like a fish swimming in deep water.'

While Kinkladze openly yearned for Anfield, some of his future City team-mates were receiving a first-hand experience. As an upcoming midfielder in the club's ranks, Jim Whitley's place in a reserve-team fixture against Liverpool helped fulfil a personal ambition held since relocating to North Wales from his native Zambia at the age of ten. 'I didn't know anything about football so when I moved to Wrexham I just wanted to fit in,' he says. 'A load of lads would come up to me and ask, "Who do you support?" I didn't know what they were talking about and the first thing they said is, "Do you support Liverpool? Don't tell me you support Everton," and so I supported Liverpool from ten right through to 15/16 when I moved to Manchester City! At that age, everyone wanted to be John Barnes so I watched the era of Liverpool that was just incredible. I mean, I was trying to watch any player I could to try and better my career but John Barnes was the main man. So I watched Liverpool and I only changed allegiance when I signed for Manchester City.'

Whitley had a ringside seat on the substitutes' bench as City's reserves suffered a hefty defeat on Merseyside, having been caught unawares by another precocious talent who was on his way to setting the footballing world alight. 'We came in at half-time and I've never seen a dressing room in total disarray of what to do with a striker,' he says. 'The striker was Michael Owen and there was arguments in the dressing room. If they went tight, he'd turn and run behind. He was too quick. If they left him, he'd turn and run at you. I'm not sure if we lost 3-0 or 4-0 but Michael Owen was the catalyst. I'd played in many games and you don't remember names, but I remember that name. He was talked about for many weeks after until he made his debut and you went, "Okay – that's Michael Owen," and so I remember that vividly because he was just tearing them apart – and it was first-teamers as well! The whole back four was more or less the lads that had played in the first team as well so it wasn't kids. He was phenomenal, absolutely phenomenal, and went on to have a great career.'

Owen's senior breakthrough proved to be a rare positive at a time when capitulation had started to become as commonplace at Anfield as much as it had consumed Maine Road. Roy Evans's side threw away a chance to assume the Premier League's top spot with six games remaining and saw their title hopes effectively killed off less than a fortnight later by a 3-1 home defeat to Manchester United, who had both a five-point lead and a game in hand. Owen then announced himself to the footballing world with a consolatory strike in a 2-1 defeat to Wimbledon.

Liverpool still headed into the final day of the 1996/97 season in second place and on course to make a long-awaited return to the Champions League in its newly expanded format. But a failure to win their game at Sheffield Wednesday allowed Newcastle United to sneak into the runners-up position by the sole virtue of a superior goal difference. Stan Boardman's jibe about United's mid-1980s shortcomings now applied to his beloved club after they finished fourth in a two-horse race.

Four was not the magic number at Maine Road either after a season where a quartet of managers guided City to a disappointing 14th place in the First Division, the worst finish in their history at that stage. Ex-Liverpool captain Phil Neal had briefly assumed the hot seat for a month-long spell following Steve Coppell's resignation. The Merseyside native and one-time United winger lasted just 32 days before the pressure told. A failure to reach the play-off positions saw the threat of Kinkladze, who had won the club's Player of the Year award in consecutive seasons after producing his best return of 12 goals from 39 league appearances, leaving for a higher standard than English football's second tier revived. Those fears were only briefly allayed by a new three-year contract that was signed just under a fortnight after he had been taken into the Maine Road centre circle following a final day win over Reading. Kinkladze played no part in City's resurrection from a two-goal deficit due to injury but became the post-match focal point while surrounded by Georgian flags and numerous signs written in his mother tongue pleading for him to stay at the club.

Liverpool's interest in Kinkladze resurfaced with Barcelona seemingly preparing to lure Steve McManaman. The Spanish giants had courted the Kirkdale-born player 12 months earlier with a tentative approach which was firmly rebuffed by Anfield's powerbrokers. But with McManaman reluctant to agree a new long-term contract, the danger of losing him for free under the Bosman ruling when his existing deal expired in summer 1999 prompted the Reds to strike a £12m deal. When the move fell through, a bitter public fall-out ensued with the winger and the Barça hierarchy pointing the finger of blame at each other for its collapse. Joan Gaspart, the Catalan club's vice-president, accused the player of making excessive wage demands while McManaman himself believed that the Camp Nou's hierarchy had used him as a pawn in their eventual £16m capture of Brazilian playmaker Rivaldo from Deportivo La Coruña.

As a result of McManaman's failed transfer, Liverpool subsequently put plans to lodge a £7m bid for Kinkladze on hold. Evans had checked on the 24-year-old in person during City's defeat to Blackpool in the opening leg of their League Cup first-round tie, while Ron Yeats, the club's chief scout, observed him during an opening day First Division draw with Portsmouth. 'I can remember there being links and his name mentioned with Liverpool,' says Kit Symons. 'We couldn't afford a luxury player like Georgi, with all his ability, in the team we were in. Could he have gone and played for Liverpool? He would've done some brilliant things there, without a doubt. Whether he would have fitted into the actual team's framework or not, I don't know. I remember there was talk of it and he was linked and stuff like that. But I don't think the players thought too much of it really if I'm perfectly honest.'

Dressing room apathy was not universal within the Maine Road chain of command. Following a 3-1 win over Nottingham

Forest, assistant manager Alan Hill reacted angrily to the persistent talk surrounding Kinkladze. 'There seems to be some kind of plot to continually unsettle the lad,' he claimed. 'We're all fed up with this nonsense and we want to reassure the fans that Georgi is going nowhere. I'm sick of hearing about all this Kinkladze speculation. Enough is enough.' Questions about Kinkladze may have pushed the club's coaching staff to their limits but worse was yet to come when his taste for fast cars finally backfired.

An unhealthy habit of picking up parking fines at the start of his time in Manchester was replaced by something more severe on 28 October when his Ferrari Testarossa crashed en route to training with team-mate Nicky Summerbee and friend Paul Ashbee, the man credited with helping put Oasis together, driving alongside. Kinkladze lost control of the £150,000 vehicle as it made its way along Manchester's Princess Parkway and was thrown through the car's sunroof when it hit the wall of an underpass, leaving him requiring 30 stitches in his back. He missed two games before returning in a 3-2 home defeat to Port Vale. But there was a growing sense that his abilities were not long for the blue side of Manchester.

Jim Whitley became one of Kinkladze's newest team-mates at City after breaking into the first team in January 1998. 'The problem was he was that good,' he says. 'In my opinion, he should be spoken about in the same way Cristiano Ronaldo and Lionel Messi are – he was that good. He was incredible at the beginning, but because he was that good he only had to take on one man in the game and he was man of the match. He just became lazier and lazier. I don't want to say it's the fans' fault because they loved him but he just didn't work anywhere near what he should have. He could have probably thought, "I'm playing with some footballers who aren't at my level." We'd do sprints and he'd just pull out of them. He'd just say, "No, not today," and he'd walk off! It got to the stage where we were playing with ten men unless he wanted to turn it on.'

At the opposite end of the East Lancs Road, Liverpool were still wrestling with the thorny issue of Steve McManaman's unresolved future. Attempts to tie him down to a new long-term deal had proved unsuccessful, while Barcelona reignited their pursuit of the player, only for premature claims of a £12m deal – the same figure agreed between the clubs in the previous summer – to be scotched by their Premier League counterparts. Tommy Smith, similarly, poured scorn on the notion of Kinkladze making the leap from Maine Road to Merseyside.

In his *Liverpool Echo* column on 26 January, underneath the headline of 'Genius or liability?' Smith acknowledged that the player 'would move heaven and earth to sign for Liverpool', but added, 'Down the years, I've seen many players like Kinkladze. They look a bit special at certain moments and the fans adore them. But more often than not, they shine in defeat,' a reference to Kinkladze being hand-picked by Kevin Keegan as ITV's Man of the Match in his side's recent FA Cup fourth-round defeat to West Ham United.

Smith concluded that Steve McManaman was 'the nearest thing you will get to Kinkladze in terms of skill and having the ability to go past people' before questioning, 'But could Liverpool operate with both of them in the same side? Would they want to? I don't think so. If McManaman moved on, the scenario might be different.'

Four days later, on the eve of City's First Division trip to Tranmere Rovers, Kinkladze's close friend and personal adviser Roberto Ferraro responded to Smith in the same newspaper. 'I'm sure Roy Evans would agree that with McManaman on the right and Georgi on the left, Robbie Fowler and Michael Owen would be fed more chances,' he insisted. 'They could bombard opposing defences. Georgi once told me that Fowler is tailor-made to feed off his approach play. He could guarantee him 30 goals a season.

'He rates Roy Evans highly. I'm sure Georgi would consider a move to Anfield, although he is not as desperate to join the club as some people have made out. What is certain is he loves Liverpool people and admires Liverpool FC … If it ever happened, I am certain that Merseyside fans would see some of the most effective and attractive football in the world with Georgi in the side.'

Addressing Smith's recent comments, Ferraro, a self-confessed Liverpool fan, said, 'I wouldn't be surprised if Georgi and Tommy became good friends in the end. Like the "Anfield Iron", Georgi plays football with his heart.'

When the subject of Kinladze was broached again in the *Echo*'s pages on 18 April, Smith was recovering from a car accident. But another member of Anfield's old guard remained similarly unconvinced by the player's suitability. Jan Mølby, filling in for Smith, responded to a reader's letter that suggested Liverpool should consider cashing in on McManaman at the end of the season for £10m and use half of the profits to sign City's own want-away star. 'I am in favour of the 4-4-2 system and there is no room for Kinkladze in that,' he insisted. 'If you bought him, you would have to change the system. I don't think they should … Let's just wish Georgi all the best with Ajax!'

Deliberately name-checking Ajax was not borne from intimate connections that Mølby still had with his old club but confirmation of what had now become European football's worst-kept secret.

Kinkladze had reaffirmed his desire to join Liverpool just a month earlier despite being tracked by a host of European clubs, with Inter Milan and Real Madrid credited among those interested. 'Liverpool have always been a team very close to my heart and I am a fan of the way they play,' he admitted. 'They have many great players.' But his next destination would be the Dutch capital in a £5m transfer, just months after City were relegated from the First Division. His time at the Amsterdam Arena was similarly frustrating after being signed as a successor to Jari Litmanen, whose plan to move to Barcelona was put on hold for an additional 12 months and scuppered Ajax's succession plan in the process. Kinkladze cut an isolated figure among his new team-mates despite having the reassuring presence of lifelong friend and compatriot Shota Arveladze alongside him in the ranks. The reigning Eredivisie champions recorded a sixth-place finish – their worst since 1964/65, when a young Johan Cruyff had forced his way into their first-team reckoning.

The following season, Kinkladze was back in the Premier League with Derby County on an initial loan deal. But the outcome of returning to his second home proved no different than the first time around; within three years, the Rams had been condemned to the First Division with Kinkladze in their ranks, just as City had six years prior. Spells with Cypriot side Anorthosis Famagusta, managed by his former international team-mate and one-time Newcastle United midfielder Temuri Ketsbaia, and Rubin Kazan followed before retiring in 2007. Over two decades since he left, Kinkladze's links with his former Manchester roots remain strong; his son Saba still lives in nearby Cheshire, while he returned to the city in 2019 to promote a new import-export venture promoting Georgian wine and brandy.

City fans continue to adore Kinkladze for persevering with them through the bad times. Joe Royle, who had the unenviable task of overseeing his departure as the club's manager in 1998, remembers a player whose promise did not meet up to its overall expectations. 'He was an awesome talent that didn't always display that awesome talent,' he says.' He had a talent that at times was almost like [Lionel] Messi. His close dribbling and finishing when he did get there were awesome. What he didn't have was either Messi's consistency or the willingness to work for the team. We knew that when we went down, the division below was going to be far from what Georgi needed.

'Put it this way, he'd been player of the year two seasons running when we got relegated. It's like being kissed by a bloody vampire but it was a strange situation. He himself was never a problem. He was a very quiet, introvert boy. We had a couple of other boys like [Kakhaber] Tskhadadze and [Murtaz] Shelia who all played with him in the national side and they were more involved in the squad and the spirit of it. It might've been a language thing because I don't think he was an outgoing boy. He came back to Derby County, don't forget, later on after not having quite got there with Ajax and it didn't work for him at Derby either. This is not damned with faint praise, don't get me wrong. I think Georgi was the right player at the wrong time and had he come into the current Man City setup, who knows?'

In many ways, Kinkladze's time at Maine Road is perfectly aligned to Britpop's rise and fall. City fans had saluted his penchant for winding runs in a chant set to the tune of 'Wonderwall' by Oasis that finished with the misjudged crescendo of, 'Maybe, you're gonna be the one that saves me. And after all, you're my Alan Ball.' By the time their team was sleepwalking towards the Second Division, both Kinkladze and the genre were both in rapid decline. *Be Here Now*, Oasis's bloated follow-up album to the heavily acclaimed *(What's the Story) Morning Glory?* from which 'Wonderwall' had been plucked, became a fitting soundtrack for the pair's simultaneous spirals. Noel Gallagher had written the album that he would later disown while holidaying on Mick Jagger's private island alongside Kate Moss and Johnny Depp in May 1996, the same month that City's seven-season spell in the top flight ended. Gallagher later admitted that he believed Kinkladze would either take the club into the Champions League or the fourth tier of English football.

At the dawn of a new millennium and five years after his Maine Road bow, the guitarist explained why the player had become so revered in such troubling times. 'All City fans are arsed about is the pitch looking good on a Saturday and turning up to see the one player who's better than anyone at Man Utd,' he said. 'For three or four years, it didn't matter that we weren't in the same league or that United were winning everything and qualifying for Europe because we had the best player in Manchester, bar Roy Keane. Kinky was amazing. It was widely accepted that we had the best player in the country, plus he looked good in the kit. In the end he had to go because he was frustrated. Why did he score all those great goals, where he took on eight players? Because he had no City player to pass to. They were all shit.'

Chasing Yesterday

DECADES OF dominance had allowed Liverpool's 1990s generation to rest on its laurels. Though undoubtedly talented, many players were happy to enjoy the trappings of the club's Boot Room culture without maintaining the winning habits of its previous era. Success and partying went hand in hand as Anfield swept all before it but in the years immediately following their last league title triumph in 1989/90, a new strand was beginning to mutate.

As Manchester United's Class of '92 became the poster boys for the Premier League, the prospects nurtured at the Reds' own centre of excellence were being held up as examples of everything that was wrong with football. Public perception dictated that Alex Ferguson's home-grown players were serial winners because of a clean-living lifestyle and unquestionable commitment to the cause. Their north-west counterparts, meanwhile, were hard-drinking, loutish and lacked the necessary discipline to regularly challenge for major silverware. A cursory glance at the two clubs' honour rolls from the advent of the modern English top flight in the summer of 1992 through to the end of the previous millennium does little to disprove that assertion. United had lifted the Champions League, five titles and three FA Cups. The only trophy that had eluded Old Trafford in that seven-year period was the League Cup, Liverpool's sole tangible success.

Graeme Souness was no stranger to his former club's off-field methods, having been one of its main beneficiaries as a player, but sensed that the diligent approach to conditioning he had experienced at Sampdoria would be more appropriate for the imminent game-changer that would become the Premier League. Large parts of his doomed three-year spell as manager were spent vainly attempting to move away from players consuming fish and chips with lager on the team coach after away games. At Glasgow Rangers, Souness was able to convince an impressionable young squad but the efforts to break from tradition were met with stern opposition by Liverpool's long-serving players, some of whom he had played alongside in the previous decade. His replacement, Roy Evans, restored to the time-honoured traditions but inadvertently allowed some players to take advantage of it.

Unsubstantiated claims that a £1 coin would be passed between players during matches, with the unfortunate recipient at the final whistle picking up the team's bar tab that evening, have moved into infamy. Neil Ruddock later dined out on stories of how he had personally gamed the system by refusing to put in the hard yards. While working his way back to fitness at Melwood, the defender was left to his own devices by Ronnie Moran and proceeded to take a load off by sitting down with a cup of tea and a bacon sandwich. Once alerted to the coach's returning presence, he would pour water over his head to simulate sweat, jump back on the treadmill and begin panting excessively to give the impression that he had been running the entire time. Moran unwittingly hailed Ruddock as an example for his team-mates to follow if Liverpool were to return to English football's pantheon.

Most players refused to play so openly fast and loose as the stocky centre-back, yet there was no escaping the fact that Anfield's young guns were gaining an unwanted reputation for their active social lives rather than the brand of free-flowing football they would routinely produce. Gary Neville, the former United defender and a Class of '92 graduate, highlighted the gulf in regimen between Anfield and Old Trafford. 'Neil Ruddock, Phil Babb, Jason McAteer, [Robbie] Fowler, John Scales; all those lads, they loved a pint. And a pint of beer will cost you the league, if you drink ten a night, three times a week,' he told Newstalk's *Off The Ball* show in 2019. 'The fact of the matter is, if you've got a team that's drinking six [or] seven pints three times a week or twice a week and you've got a team that are not – forget talent, forget professionalism. The difference is enormous.'

Liverpool's crop of talent at that time was arguably as strong as United's, but the goalscoring feats of Robbie Fowler, Jamie Redknapp's midfield qualities and Steve McManaman's wing wizardry became consumed by an off-field lifestyle which had attracted the media's glare. David James's catwalk appearances for Armani became a source of intrigue and derision, as did Jason McAteer's endorsement of shampoo brand Wash & Go in a television advert. Redknapp dated pop star Louise Nurding, once of the girl group Eternal, while Rob Jones's friendship with Robbie Williams saw the soon-to-be-former Take That member sitting on the team coach before and after an away defeat to Aston Villa, taking a pre-match stroll on the pitch for good measure. Fowler's chance meeting with Emma Bunton at the Brit Awards led to the *Daily Mail* nicknaming the group 'the Spice Boys', a term which would later encompass Anfield's era of underachievement.

The nadir came ahead of a 1996 FA Cup Final defeat to Ferguson's fledglings as Liverpool's players stepped out in garish cream-coloured suits matched with sky blue shirts and candy-striped red ties that resembled something the Man from Del Monte would pull out of his wardrobe. James's connection with Armani had paved the way for the bold sartorial choices, although the goalkeeper maintains that his involvement extended solely to passing on a contact number for the designer brand to club officials. Evans's side headed to Wembley in a bus sponsored by Emporium, a Soho nightclub hired by the squad for its after-match festivities irrespective of the result. Eric Cantona's late strike ensured Liverpool would be drowning their sorrows as United clinched a league and cup double. An awkward open-top bus tour around the city still went ahead the following day, leading to bemused expressions on the faces of players and crowds alike.

In 1998, the Reds broke new ground as part of efforts to instil some much-needed resolve in a prodigious yet flawed team by appointing joint managers, with John Toshack identified as their preferred choice. The former striker appeared a perfect fit as someone who possessed both a working knowledge of the club's values from his time as a player and a proven track record in Europe, having won a La Liga title with Real Madrid in 1990. But an approach from Anfield officials came at the end of a debut season with Besiktas which had culminated in lifting the Turkish Cup, while a 14-year spell managing on the continent meant Toshack passed up the opportunity. The bruising experience Souness had received in his own return to Merseyside earlier in the decade may have also dissuaded the Welshman from a reunion. Four days after France had won the World Cup, Gérard Houllier was finally unveiled as Evans's new partner in crime.

The incoming 50-year-old's stock was particularly high after overseeing the rise of the new world champions in his role as the country's technical director. He had previously been manager at Lens and Paris Saint-Germain (PSG) before taking charge of Les Bleus in a spell which lasted just a year and became pockmarked by a dispute with winger David Ginola that saw them fail to qualify for the 1994 World Cup finals. Weeks earlier, Houllier had been on the verge of joining Sheffield Wednesday only for contractual disagreements to derail the move. His links with Liverpool were far more steeped than the appointment initially suggested, having served as a teaching assistant at Alsop High School, located on the route between Anfield and Melwood, in the late 1960s and stood on The Kop. But the bold experiment lasted little under four months before Evans decided to sever his own 35-year personal connection in the club's best interests.

Houllier began his first summer in sole charge by spending just shy of £25m moulding Liverpool's squad with a series of astute additions predominantly from the Continent. Bringing them up to speed with their new surroundings led to a slight change in the club's traditional pre-season schedule, with several First Division teams earmarked for games, culminating in a trip to Manchester City. 'From day one when I came in at Liverpool, they were trying to get me as soon as possible the experience of Premier League football,' says Sander Westerveld, a £4m arrival from Vitesse Arnhem. 'Obviously I already had a certain level of quality, or talent, but it's a special style to play as a goalkeeper in the Premier League, especially with strikers that can challenge you. As goalkeepers, the referees don't protect you as much as they do in Europe. One of the few things I remember about that game is that they wanted, not only for me, to play games against a Championship team because they played a typical English game with long balls. So it was a sort of test for me.'

Maine Road's ascent from the doldrums of English football's third tier had restored both overdue pride to their long-suffering supporters and righted the wrongs of its previous era. Returning to his old club in February 1998, Joe Royle had been confronted by the remnants of Francis Lee's ill-fated ownership with the first team's swelled ranks spread across three full-sized changing rooms at their Platt Lane base. 'It was unbelievable, but it became the norm,' says City midfielder Jim Whitley. 'You'd get the first team [in one], another dressing room of reserves and then another dressing room of the ones that think they should be in the first team – that was a bitter, bitter dressing room and it could come into the reserve squad. You'd get players in [from there] and then it was nasty. There's that many players that you can't keep everyone happy because only 11 players can play in the first team at the end of the day. This bitterness was almost like a cancer in the dressing room and it would spread like wildfire. It's only when you come out of it and realise what was happening, you look back and say, "Wow." But there was a lot of bitterness and it needed a fresh start.'

Royle failed to prevent City from tumbling into the Second Division at the end of the 1997/98 season but bounced back emphatically a year later by securing immediate promotion through a play-off final win over Gillingham that remains widely perceived as the catalyst for their modern renaissance. As attention turned to the new campaign, Maine Road's optimism was evident as a crowd of 20,178 supporters flocked to see their side take on Liverpool in a friendly on 3 August 1999. Four of the visitors' seven summer signings were handed starts against their hosts, whose own new recruit Mark Kennedy lined up against his old club for a second time in three months, having faced them in his last Wimbledon appearance on the final day of the previous Premier League season. Westerveld remembers a challenging experience as the hosts peppered his goal in the opening stages. 'Some people criticised me for coming off my line or not enough. In Holland I was famous for that. I think I came off my line quite a bit,' he says. 'But it's difficult with corners and with those long throws, and that's what we got in the friendly game against Man City. They threw a lot of balls into the box and if they had free kicks on the halfway line, they put the balls into the box. I came for all of those and I just tried to do my part.'

Although David Thompson handed the visitors a late first-half lead, Kennedy proved a perennial thorn to his former employers. 'Mark was a great talent but we needed him to settle down his lifestyle,' says Royle. 'I knew of his lifestyle at Liverpool, which wasn't really what you would expect from a professional, but Mark did great for us. He came on and he had that great season with us when we did get promoted. I'll never forget him running up the touchline at Blackburn Rovers that night when we got promoted back to the Premier League – and his talent was Premier League. I think he went into coaching after he finished. I'm not sure what he does now. A good guy and an outstanding talent but, like a lot of talented players, lacked consistency.'

The Republic of Ireland international's wing play eventually produced an equaliser as his cross shortly before the hour mark led to a penalty being awarded in City's favour after Westerveld fumbled Terry Cooke's header from the delivery and saw Rigobert Song handle the ball.

Kevin Horlock dispatched the ensuing spot kick to draw the hosts level before City prospered from another ball into the box in the 88th minute, this time from Danny Granville, for Shaun Goater to convert. Westerveld's crash course in English football at Maine Road had provided a valuable learning experience. 'I remember it was not an eye-opener [necessarily] because I was known as an English goalkeeper in Holland,' he says. 'They used to call me an English goalkeeper because I came off my line a lot, which is a bit ironic because they criticised me for [doing] that in England, for not coming too many times for crosses. It was a real test, especially for the foreigners, to get used to the English style of football.'

The Dutchman was not the only one experiencing a difficult evening as Chris Bascombe, the *Liverpool Echo*'s Anfield correspondent, was forcibly removed from the press room ahead of City's post-match briefing. That extreme reaction had been caused by an ongoing acrimony over the paper's editorial coverage of Royle's time in charge at Everton, where chairman Peter Johnson had put the stoppers on a trio of transfer deadline day signings in 1997, although the discord never extended to its on-the-ground reporter Dave Prentice. 'They seemed to be waiting for us to have a bad spell,' says Royle. 'I always said that I gave them a silver service but unfortunately they used one of the knives to knife me in the back.'

Erroneous and disparaging stories run by other pillars of the Merseyside press pack saw the Norris Green native give written journalists in general a wide berth on his subsequent return visits to both Anfield and Goodison Park.

His first since guiding City back to the Premier League came on 9 September 2000 as they took on a Liverpool team again looking to challenge for major honours, including the trophy which had eluded them in the previous decade. Ten minutes in, a long throw from Song saw Emile Heskey hold off Paul Ritchie and feed Michael Owen, who shot past Nicky Weaver to break the deadlock on his 100th Premier League appearance. Liverpool's front two had first linked up together for England at the European Under-18 Championships in 1996 but were now developing an innate understanding since being reunited at club level earlier in the year. 'We obviously tried things in training and stuff like that, and then you just pick up an understanding,' says Heskey. 'You pick a good relationship with someone because you have that understanding between you. It just clicked for us both.'

Heskey doubled up on duties as City attempted to lay siege to Westerveld's goal when he cleared a bicycle kick from Alf Inge Haaland off the line. The England international was in the thick of the action again when Nick Barmby threaded a ball for him to chase and won a free kick from a foul by the advancing Weaver. Liverpool stepped up the offensive when Steve Howey headed Song's long diagonal into the path of Dietmar Hamann to chest the ball on the edge of the penalty area and volley into the top-right corner of City's net. But tempers frayed when Heskey went on a surging run, turning several opposing defenders, before being cut short by Howey's interception. As play contined, Ritchie and Spencer Prior became involved in scuffles with the striker, who received a booking for shoving Ritchie in the face two-handed. Mark Kennedy's latest outing at his former stomping ground was curbed on 57 minutes as Royle sent on new signing George Weah in efforts to claw back the deficit.

The Liberian's arrival in Manchester had been something of a coup after turning down a £1m offer to stay at AC Milan for another 12 months. Now 34, Weah's quality became evident as he opened his account within ten minutes of introduction by taking on Song and Stephane Henchoz before a firing past Westerveld in The Kop's goal.

Weah would cause further problems for the hosts when Haaland played a one-two with him to draw Djimi Traore out of position before the left-back hauled down the 1995 Ballon d'Or winner in the penalty area. From 12 yards, Horlock sent Westerveld the wrong way to level the game.

A week on from throwing away a three-goal lead at Southampton, history appeared to be repeating itself for Liverpool, but their response was swift and emphatic, coming a minute later, as a throw-in from Christian Ziege was flicked on by Heskey into the path of Hamann to rifle home his second and secure maximum points for Houllier's side. City's frustrations came to the boil in the final minutes as Dickov, Howey and Paulo Wanchope were all booked by referee Graham Barber, who was put in the post-match firing line.

Afterwards, Royle told TV reporters that the PFA needed to 'name and shame divers' in an apparent reference to events which preceded Heskey's second-half flare-up with Prior and Ritchie. 'It's always been a bugbear of mine,' says Royle. 'I don't see why anyone should dive. I went through a career without diving and then it started creeping in, really, I think started with the influx of foreign players and then was readily accepted and taken on by English players well and that's still the case.' Houllier slammed his opposite number's comments as 'out of order' and implored, 'If you look at the incident again you will see he clearly tried to continue his run before he fell over.'

By his own admission, Heskey's start to life at Liverpool had been consumed with feelings of doubt and despair. Homesickness left him soul-searching as to whether the £11m move from Leicester City had been the right one and routinely lying on the floor in tears.

Royle's remarks, however, did not unnerve the striker as he neared the end of that rocky six-month spell. 'To be honest with you, I never really listened to what people said about that sort of stuff,' he says. 'It didn't really bother me as much. I was just concentrating more on myself and performing than anyone else having their say on whether I went to ground too easily or not. I think as a player, you can't take anything too seriously because you've got the next week to think about and get your head around playing. I didn't read too much into it. I didn't think he was having a real go at me or anything like that. I know the media might have read into that a little bit differently but for myself, I didn't really read into it too much.'

City's early-season fortunes had descended into a relegation dogfight when the new calendar year began, with a 1-1 draw away to Coventry putting them back in the Premier League's bottom places. An FA Cup run provided the sole positive and set up a fifth-round clash at Anfield. Before that, they would welcome Houllier's trophy-chasing side for their second league meeting on 31 January 2001 in a scrappy affair which was notable for the inclusion of Andrei Kanchelskis, who had arrived on loan. Royle had convinced his one-time Everton talisman to join him from Glasgow Rangers in a short-term move. The Russian had to wait until the second half before his first involvement, by which point Liverpool had taken the lead through Vladimir Smicer's cross into the box which Heskey beat City captain Andy Morrison in the air to head home his 17th goal of the campaign. Morrison's return to the side came after a loan spell with Crystal Palace, where he regained fitness following a lengthy knee injury lay-off. The defender admits that the running battle with Heskey in the first half was one he savoured. 'That was my kind of game. Somebody who's big and strong and wants to back in and be physical,' he says. 'I felt I dominated him on the night and had a really good game. We just seemed to come up against each other throughout the game.'

Kanchelskis's introduction in place of Morrison after the interval produced a swift return as he set up Danny Tiatto for City's equaliser, with the Australian full-back drilling the ball home from inside the penalty area, within three minutes of coming on. The strike was Liverpool's first goal conceded in over 420 minutes of play and arrived on a Maine Road pitch which had seen far better days and was described by Royle as 'disintegrating'.

The Blues' failure to win for an eighth successive league game since hitting fellow strugglers Everton for five in December still offered belief that they could beat the drop while Houllier's hopes that the League Cup finalists would challenge Manchester United for the title next season had been dealt a setback. 'I can remember a lot of frustration from the Liverpool players after the game,' says Morrison. 'I asked Steve Gerrard for his shirt and Gerrard said to me, "Heskey should be asking for your fucking shirt tonight." He was flaming in his eyes because I had actually dominated him in the game and put in a really good performance. It was a great point [to earn].'

Heskey offers an alternative take on the City defender's version of events from his visit to the away dressing room. 'I don't remember that,' he says. 'You're best off asking Stevie and he might be able to tell you a bit more about that one. People can make up and see a story however they want to say a story and in their mind it's true. I don't know if Stevie said it, but he never said it to me.'

Something all parties were able to agree upon was the emerging force of Steven Gerrard. The natural midfield player had operated at left-back in the game and produced a competent display which led Royle to forecast that he would be 'a future England captain one day'. Morrison remembers his manager's admiration for the Huyton native leading to similar musings by City's elder statesmen. 'The one stand-out thing that everybody spoke about after the game was Gerrard,' he says. 'He was just the supreme athlete [even] then. He was just a specimen. Manchester City always speak about Colin Bell, how he glided over the pitch and the qualities that he had. I can remember one of the older directors saying that Gerrard reminded him of Colin Bell at his best. That's something that stuck with me. He said that the last time he saw anybody that glided and got around the pitch and carried themselves that way was when Colin Bell played at Maine Road.'

Ahead of the FA Cup meeting, Liverpool made strides towards another trophy by overcoming AS Roma in the first leg of their UEFA Cup fourth-round tie. Returning from the Eternal City, Houllier warned his players, 'Manchester City will be under no pressure. They will play with more freedom and easier in their minds. We have to be ready for that.'

But Heskey insists that Anfield's charges were never going to take a place in the quarter-final as a foregone conclusion. 'At the end of the day, you're Liverpool so whenever you go into a game, regardless of what game it is, you're expected to win,' he says. 'There's a high expectancy there and the pressure comes with it. Even when you look at Liverpool now and they play what is classed as a weakened side, whether it be young players or players that are sitting on the bench and get their time to play in the cup, you're still Liverpool. You're still expected to win. You're still expected to go out there and perform.'

The Frenchman's pre-match comments also failed to cut through City's own preparations. 'When I think back to that period, I don't know if you were that aware of what other people were saying,' says Morrison. 'I know now with social media and the coverage that football has on so many different platforms that you can't help but hear what a manager or somebody has said, and you would try to use that to galvanise your own team. But back then it didn't seem to be that way. We just knew we were going to Liverpool, it was going to be really tough and the expectations for me were low. We weren't going there as the favourites. We were the severe underdogs.'

News of Houllier's attempts to bolster his goalkeeping ranks had broken ahead of the game. After efforts to sign Chris Kirkland hit a stumbling block by his penning of a new five-and-a-half-year contract with Coventry, Nicky Weaver was identified as a possible alternative before his second Anfield appearance. Royle disregarded the reported pre-match interest in his player but Sander Westerveld believes the emergence of a link with Liverpool was not designed to distract the player and his team-mates in the build-up to the tie. 'Sometimes politics come in and I understand that sometimes people release statements, or they let agents talk to the press before important games about players that are transfer targets,' he says. 'I'm not sure if Liverpool did it on purpose or Liverpool did it in the first place, but it wouldn't have affected me anyway so I don't think it would have affected Weaver.'

Kirkland's eventual arrival alongside fellow goalkeeper Jerzy Dudek saw Westerveld leave Liverpool later in the year but he remains unsure whether Weaver would have entertained the idea of trading a first-choice role at Maine Road for a different prospect on Merseyside.

'If you play for City as their number one, even for a big club like Liverpool, you don't go there to just sit on the bench,' he says. 'Although a manager can never tell you, "Okay, you are my number one," because everybody has to fight for their place, I don't think they were getting a new reserve goalkeeper. They were trying to bring at least another goalkeeper in and let them fight for the number-one spot. But I don't think Weaver would have come to Liverpool if they would have said that he was going to be in the number-two position. I understood that my job was not on the line, but it was more like, "Okay, we need two goalkeepers and it's all about me. I have to show to everybody that I'm the number one here, and I will do that." That was my confidence, but I never had the chance to prove my point.'

Weaver's potential audition started off on a poor note when, in the seventh minute, Smicer raced into the penalty area to meet a Jari Litmanen pass and won a dubious penalty after going to ground when the City goalkeeper had attempted stop him. 'I didn't think it was a penalty at all,' insists Morrison. 'I think it was just the pressure of Anfield and the referee crumbling under a shout or a scream and took the easy option.'

Royle echoes his captain's belief that referee Graham Poll had acceded to the will of The Kop. 'I think that anyone that goes to Anfield over the years would feel that,' he says. 'I did complain about a penalty that was not given and then eventually given when the referee realised that the tackle was so bad that it had to be a penalty. I think you'll find that that's a common complaint at Anfield over the years, not just from Manchester City's side or my sides even. I'm branded a Blue by the Reds so there's no problem in me saying that I thought there was some soft penalties – and there are still some soft decisions there – but they would say that there are some at the Etihad and at Old Trafford too, so what the hell. I wouldn't make a big play of it.'

Litmanen, one of four unforced changes that Houllier made from his team's Roman conquest, converted from the spot before teeing up Liverpool's second goal just seven minutes later with a weighted pass for Heskey to fire an angled drive from the edge of the penalty area.

The early scoreline still failed to reflect the hosts' level of dominance and handed City a route back into the game just before the half-hour, when Kanchelskis unleashed a 22-yard effort into The Kop's net. Royle's side continued to fight back as an archetypal blood-and-thunder clash played out between the teams for the remaining 25 minutes.

Their pluck unravelled after the interval when Weaver again fell foul of Smicer's bursting run into his area, with the Czech Republic international stepping up to convert the penalty. Six minutes later, Morrison's afternoon was up as he was substituted for Tony Grant, another of Royle's former Everton players, and bowed out with a literal splash. As chants of 'you fat bastard!' rang across Anfield, the Scottish-born player sat down in the dugout and squeezed a bottle of water over his shoulder, soaking six Liverpool supporters in the process. 'There's always banter between players and fans,' he says. 'I don't know if it's changed there now but where we were actually sat, the fans were all around you. One was within touching distance of you. You could hear the comments and there were a few chucked my way. I just took a bottle of water and spurted it back, which was the wrong thing to do because that can be quite explosive. There was a bit of a melee and I think a few police officers came up that way. I had taken as much as I was giving [out] and it just petered away to nothing really.'

Markus Babbel inflicted further misery on Morrison's City team-mates when he glanced a Ziege free kick past Weaver five minutes from time, before Shaun Goater reduced the score by converting Darren Huckerby's cross.

Morrison did not escape the long arm of the law for long at Anfield. After the final whistle, a Merseyside Police officer tasked with a box-ticking exercise in the tunnel area explained that no further action would be taken despite adding a quip about how he 'should have thrown them a bar of soap too, the dirty Scouse bastards' when asked for his version of events. 'I'm sure you would be in all sorts of trouble if you fired a bottle of water towards a load of howling fans now,' he admits. 'But not back then, just a quick word and that's it.'

Royle was also in no mood for decorum as he described Smicer's first-half penalty as 'fiction' and 'a ridiculous decision' which had disrupted the game's initial fine balance. Liverpool's victory fuelled an already burning desire to sweep all before them, which they duly achieved by clinching an impressive treble of the League Cup, FA Cup and UEFA Cup. 'We had so much confidence to think, "Okay, this is the moment, the season when we can really win something,"' says Westerveld. 'The FA Cup was another step closer to a trophy and that was, at that moment, I think the most important one. For us foreigners, I thought the European cups were bigger until very early in the tournament told me that the FA Cup was for them [more important].

'The Champions League is maybe more important but not the UEFA Cup. As foreigners, we knew what the importance was in the FA Cup and when we beat City, after the Roma game, I think that really kicked things off. It gave us so much confidence and belief that we had a strong side. We changed the team a bit and even though we changed the team every match, all the different teams were performing and winning. That gave us a confidence that maybe this could be our year to win a trophy.'

An 18th-place finish at the end of the 2000/01 campaign sealed City's second Premier League demotion inside five years and drew criticism from BBC commentator Stuart Hall, who described Maine Road as 'the Theatre of Base Comedy. A sense of humour is essential. It's a rollercoaster ride.'

Upon their eventual return, City would have the last laugh by capturing the flag from Anfield.

Kick and Complain

ALL ROADS led back to the Premier League in Nicolas Anelka's quest for redemption. England's shores had provided the striker with a home away from home when Arsenal prised him away from PSG in February 1997. His arrival in north London proved to be as contentious as the exit which would follow less than two and a half years later.

Arsène Wenger had successfully exploited a loophole in French law whereby young players were required to sign their first professional contracts with the club they had represented at junior level. Unfortunately for Les Parisiens, overseas sides fell outside of that jurisdiction, which allowed the Gunners to snare the 17-year-old talent for just £500,000. 'He didn't leave in any special way, he just left like every single player who changed clubs,' says Sylvain Distin, who had played alongside Anelka in PSG's youth ranks. 'It was a bit of a blow in the way that you want to retain your best assets and he was definitely one of them. It was more like a disappointment because you wish that players like that would remain in your club but not a shock because he's an amazing talent. A lot of people could see and recognise that.'

Wenger's cunning was rewarded almost instantly as Anelka helped his new club clinch a Premier League and FA Cup double in 1997/98 after taking the place of an injured Ian Wright. He scored the Gunners' second goal in their FA Cup Final win over Newcastle United and excelled in the follow-up campaign with 17 goals from 35 Premier League appearances, a haul which saw him crowned the PFA Young Player of the Year.

But off the pitch, trouble was looming. Throughout that banner season, Anelka had regularly slammed Marc Overmars, labelling his team-mate 'selfish' and accused the Netherlands international of costing him a place in France's triumphant World Cup squad by deliberately passing to compatriot Dennis Bergkamp instead of him. Speculation of being unsettled in London may have led to a series of candid admissions but Anelka's social life had improved by the time the PFA held its annual gala dinner. Instead of accepting his Young Player of the Year award at the Grosvenor Hotel, he was seen partying in the swanky Mayfair Club a short distance away at the same time the ceremony was taking place.

By the end of 1998/99, it had become increasingly clear that Anelka was not prepared to stay the course at Highbury, not least when Marseille claimed that the player had been continually calling them and pleading for a move back to France. He laid fault for the desire to return to his homeland at the feet of the English media, claiming they had caused him 'enormous problems on a personal level', and adding, 'As they aren't going to stop, that marks out my road for me.'

Arsène Wenger dismissed the player's claims and insisted that he had been treated 'relatively well' by the press but tabloid newspapers did not hold back as the nickname 'Le Sulk' was born. A protracted summer transfer saga saw Lazio and Real Madrid both vying for his affections until the Serie A club broke off discussions with the Arsenal hierarchy, clearing the way for Anelka to move to the Bernabéu for a British transfer record of £23m, a deal Real president Lorenzo Sanz described as 'an act of beautiful madness'. But Anelka had still failed to master the art of winning friends and influencing people in the Spanish capital.

Familiar gripes about team-mates were raised early into his time in the Spanish capital, with the *Evening Standard* publishing an interview in which he singled out Fernando Morientes and Raul as 'players who always give each other the ball' – echoing the criticism of Overmars and Bergkamp at the start of the previous season. Although Anelka denied saying it, he did not dispute speaking with the newspaper. After ending a five-month goal drought by opening the scoring against a Spanish league XI in a match for an anti-drug charity, his Real career finally took flight with three goals in their opening two games at the FIFA Club World Championship. Upon returning from Brazil, Anelka also struck in a comfortable win over Los Blancos' arch-rivals Barcelona but that accounted for half of his disappointing La Liga tally.

Worse was still to come when he claimed the club had treated him 'like a dog' as a three-day absence from training led to a 45-day suspension without pay. A 90-second press conference a fortnight later allowed a contrite Anelka to return to the fold in time to take Real past Manchester United in the Champions League quarter-final. In the last-four meeting with Bayern Munich, he scored twice but his reducer in the return leg at the Olympiastadion tipped the balance in Los Blancos' favour to set up a return to his former Paris stomping ground. He again led the line as Real comfortably saw off domestic rivals Valencia to clinch 'La Octava' – their eighth European Cup – at the Stade de France. But the club were already preparing to offload him. Lorenzo Sanz and Florentino Perez both stood on platforms for the upcoming presidential elections which pledged to recoup a substantial portion of Anelka's original outlay in efforts to reduce debts of close to £75m.

Real's prayers were answered when PSG sanctioned a £22m return of their prodigal son; a deal which was predominantly funded by the club's backers. Canal Plus, the French cable television broadcaster, had the controlling share in the Ligue 1 side at that time and financed the player's homecoming, while kit manufacturers Nike subsidised the bulk of his post-tax wages, amounting to between £30,000 and £35,000 per week. 'That's the type of player that you want to see around you so it was great,' says Distin, who had rejoined his former club in the same summer. 'PSG, at the time, had a project to try and sign players from Paris or the outskirts of Paris, young players, and have a lot of senior pros around them. They wanted to build a project and

Nicolas fitted perfectly for this project.' Anelka was supposed to spearhead a home-grown resurgence at the Parc des Princes but became the architect of its downfall within a matter of months of returning.

Problems first started manifesting in mid-January of the following year when he became involved in a fracas with Sebastien Tarrago, a journalist for the French sports newspaper *L'Équipe*. The incident stemmed from Anelka ignoring Tarrago after he accosted him while leaving PSG's Camp des Loges training complex. When pressed on why he did not want to speak to Tarrago, he replied, 'I don't like your face,' which led to the reporter to repeatedly call him an 'asshole'. Anelka hit back at his tormenter physically as well as verbally by slapping Tarrago, who lodged an assault claim with the Parisian police force. That Friday afternoon flare-up would later be avenged by Tarrago's employers during France's mutinous 2010 World Cup campaign. *L'Équipe* reported that Anelka had launched an expletive-laden tirade at national team coach Raymond Domenech during the interval of their Group A match with Mexico, which was goalless at the time. It ended in a 2-0 defeat.

Following the publication of Anelka's dressing-room outburst, splashed across the newspaper's front page, the French Football Federation immediately sent him home from the tournament in disgrace. Later, it would add an 18-game suspension to the punishment, which was ridiculed publicly by Anelka after already announcing his international retirement. He attempted to sue *L'Équipe* for libel over its coverage of his verbal assault on Domenech, claiming that his words had been taken out of context, but a judge ruled in the publication's favour when the case went to court. 'I think that's the media; they target players, some positively and give them a really good press, and some negatively,' says Distin. 'Unfortunately for him, Nicolas was one of the players that was not really appreciated by the press or targeted by the press. I don't know the reason and I still don't understand the reason to this day but it happened. It happened to a lot of players and unfortunately it happened to him.'

Compounding Anelka's woes in his second spell with PSG was the departure of manager Philippe Bergeroo shortly before the midway point in the 2000/01 season. He had enjoyed a productive spell under the former goalkeeper, a member of France's 1984 European Championship-winning side. But poor results saw Luis Fernandez returning to the club he had previously guided to success as both a player and coach. A total of eight additions were made in the following season with more than half going on to become household names in the form of Mauricio Pochettino, Gabriel Heinze, Mikel Arteta, Jay-Jay Okocha and Ronaldinho. Those wholesale changes led to several established first-team players, including Sylvain Distin, Laurent Robert and Ali Benarbia, being moved on to the Premier League.

Anelka was widely expected to be the next earmarked for departure. Where he had scored 13 goals in all competitions in the 2000/01 campaign, his follow-up produced a stagnant tally of just five with only two coming in Ligue 1 appearances. Speculation of a rift between himself and Fernandez grew during a four-game absence due to a toe injury. When Anelka was substituted in the second leg of PSG's UEFA Cup third-round clash with Glasgow Rangers, his own supporters jeered him for missing a late chance to snatch victory from the two-legged stalemate. The Scottish side won their first European penalty shoot-out in the Parc des Princes after the teams could not be settled by extra time.

Just two months earlier, Anelka's hope for a return to his former life appeared trivial compared to Gérard Houllier's fight for his own. Delivering an historic cup treble had heightened expectations that the French coach would be the man to finally end Liverpool's long-standing domestic drought. But Houllier's best-laid plans suffered an early-season setback in 2001/02 as successive defeats to Bolton Wanderers and Aston Villa left them trailing Leeds United by five points. When the Premier League's champions-elect arrived on Merseyside, that slump had been arrested and replaced with a three-game winning streak.

As the age-old adversaries clashed in a midday showdown, however, Liverpool's bold ambitions were about to be thrown into fresh turmoil. David O'Leary's promising side appeared well placed to extend their current advantage over the Reds, who found themselves trailing at half-time to Harry Kewell's fifth goal in as many games. Houllier's attempts to coax his players at the interval were interrupted by chest pains. He sought medical advice from Mark Waller, Liverpool's club doctor, while he was treating Emile Heskey for a slight calf injury. As both teams re-emerged for the second half, Waller was accompanying Houllier in an ambulance as he was rushed from Anfield to the Royal Liverpool University Hospital.

What had transpired in the home dressing room brought Bill Shankly's famous quip about football's importance superseding 'a matter of life and death' into focus. On 10 September 1985, nearly four years since his own passing from a heart attack, Shankly's great friend Jock Stein also suffered a fatal cardiac arrest at the end of Scotland's vital World Cup qualifying draw with Wales. A late Davie Cooper penalty had given the visitors a priceless point that would seal their place at the following summer's finals in Mexico. Fatefully, they would be heading to the land of the Aztecs without the man who had made it all possible. As players and supporters of the Tartan Army celebrated at the final whistle inside Cardiff's Ninian Park, television cameras captured an ashen yet still conscious Stein being rushed into the stadium's medical room. Graeme Souness, who would endure his own heart problems while managing Liverpool in the early 1990s, kept vigil outside. Half an hour later, one of British football's most iconic coaches had died. He was 62.

Like Stein's untimely death in the Welsh capital, the majority of the 44,352 people inside Anfield on 13 October 2001 were oblivious to Houllier's health scare. Only keen observers and those seated around the dugout area would have sensed that something was amiss as the frantic Premier League contest continued apace without the Liverpool manager's presence. Danny Murphy clawed back an equaliser for the hosts after Robbie Fowler's long-range effort had cannoned back off the crossbar. But the result was immaterial once news of Houllier's condition became public knowledge. Tests ruled out a heart attack as the possible cause of his chest pains but revealed that he had suffered an aortic dissection, a tear to the heart's main artery, which required a surgical procedure that would last 11 hours. Prophetically he had joked to his Leeds counterpart David O'Leary before kick-off, 'This job is not good for your health.'

Later that year, Houllier would reveal that he had suspected 'something was wrong' physically in the weeks leading up to the game but refused to show any signs of weakness in his players' presence. Liverpool expected him to spend several weeks in recovery before returning to full-time management. Doctors recommended that he forewent up to a year away from the cut and thrust of the touchline. He returned after five months. Convalescence prevented Houllier from fulfilling some of his regular duties yet he was still able to carry out a number of monumental decisions that altered the face of Liverpool's squad. The biggest came in the form of Fowler's departure to Leeds. At 26, the Toxteth-born striker had not yet reached the traditional peak of a footballer's career, but the writing appeared to be on the wall for him at the club he had first joined as a trainee in 1992.

Fowler had been dropped from the squad for the Charity Shield victory over Manchester United following a training ground bust-up with Phil Thompson. Liverpool's 1981 European Cup-winning captain accused the striker of almost hitting him while taking part in shooting practice. Houllier had not been present during the incident but ordered Fowler to apologise for being 'rude' to his assistant manager.

The player's presence in the Anfield directors' box six days later, as Liverpool edged out West Ham United on the Premier League's opening weekend, did not go unnoticed. The Kop routinely broke out into chants for their exiled hero while Fowler's attempt to make a discreet exit was stalled by several autograph hunters, which drew further adulation for him from the stands. The following day, Houllier brokered a peace summit between the club's de facto captain and Thompson. Despite Melwood's recent transformation from basic amenities in a converted cricket pavilion that had stood since Bill Shankly's time into a 21st-century facility, he elected to speak with the pair on the training pitches. The incident was captured by a photographer lurking over the training ground's concrete fence and splashed in the following day's newspapers. Little more than three months after the flashpoint, Fowler moved to Elland Road in a £12m transfer.

'I think the press blew up the Phil Thompson argument too much because it was just something that happened in training,' says Sander Westerveld, one of Fowler's Liverpool team-mates at the time. 'It happened before with another player after the Southampton game as well in the dressing room. Phil Thompson is just a very emotional man, like everybody knows, and if he doesn't like stuff, he starts shouting – that's the way he is. I never had a problem with that and I don't think Robbie had a problem with that.

'If you shout to somebody, sometimes they shout back, but I think if you walk off the pitch, everything is okay. I don't think that was the reason he had to leave. Everybody knew how big Rob was and how important he was, especially in training. He was the best finisher in the box I've ever seen, together with Michael Owen. He was very confident. If you trained with him in finishing, you had a feeling you couldn't touch any balls so we knew how important he was.

'We obviously wanted him [back] but we never had, especially me and the foreigners, the power or courage to step up as a team and say, "Hey, boss." It happened very quick and he was gone very quick. We didn't have the feeling that we could change anything. It's the football world as well so sometimes you have to think about yourself and I didn't have the feeling that if I would've said something that it would have made a difference. It wasn't the bust-up with Phil, it was more about what Houllier thought he could bring. I think it was the same with me. It's just the way the manager thinks and afterwards you can say it's wrong or right, but at that that moment it just happened. As players, and I think we said it in the press as well, we wanted him to stay but it's the manager that makes the decisions.'

Prior to Fowler's exit, Liverpool had racked up a 3-1 win over Manchester United on an afternoon when Houllier assumed centre-stage in absentia. A pre-match display of solidarity from The Kop saw the recovering manager's initials featured in a crowd mosaic against a backdrop of the French tricolour. Houllier himself was already exploring that Gallic connection in his efforts to source a replacement for the outgoing 'Toxteth Terror'. No fewer than five French players emerged as potential targets. Euro 2000 winner David Trezeguet appeared unwilling to sacrifice a regular first-team spot at Juventus while the agent for Djibril Cisse and Olivier Kapo insisted the pair had no plans of leaving Auxerre before their contracts expired in summer 2003. West Ham also discounted the prospect of allowing Frederic Kanoute to join a Premier League rival, although the player himself admitted he 'would have thinking to do' if Liverpool's reported interest had become concrete. Even after becoming a peripheral figure at PSG, Nicolas Anelka intimated that he had zero appetite to join the ranks at Anfield. That feeling appeared to be mutual on Merseyside with misgivings about his aptitude still firmly rooted in English football's stream of consciousness over two years since leaving Arsenal under a cloud. But with Fowler departed, Michael Owen's hamstring problems recurring and Emile Heskey unable to supplement the recent Ballon d'Or winner's goalscoring shortfall, they were forced to reconsider.

Houllier had previous form with Anelka. A year after resigning as France coach, following their failure to qualify for the 1994 World Cup finals, the former PSG manager had returned to the national setup to take charge of Les Bleus' under-18 side that would go on to win their third European Championship in 1996. Alongside Trezeguet and Thierry Henry, Anelka had starred in the tournament that ended in a 1-0 victory over Spain. Both master and apprentice moved up to the under-20 side but the circumstances of their quarter-final exit at the FIFA Youth Championships would be weaponised by Anelka at the height of his Arsenal endgame. The striker had missed the decisive penalty in the sudden death shoot-out against Uruguay but felt that his manager was responsible and pointedly asked in June 1999, 'Since things aren't working out at Liverpool, is he going to say it's Owen's fault? Sooner or later, the truth will come out.'

Anelka also claimed Houllier had tried to blame him for France's opening loss at the tournament in Malaysia, where they shipped three goals against Brazil, and dismissed his compatriot's subsequent public endorsements. 'He only does that today. He should have done it before,' he sniped. 'Now it's too late and too easy.'

Simplicity was in short supply when Liverpool stepped up their efforts to sign Anelka. A host of Premier League clubs had already been offered the chance to take him on loan, including Manchester United, Tottenham Hotspur and Chelsea. Their own attempts through an emissary with links to both Anfield and PSG were met with strong apprehension from the player, who was wary of accepting an olive branch from the manager that had neglected his international career. Houllier summoned his former protégé for face-to-face talks in Corsica, where he was continuing his return to full health, in the hope of convincing him to revive his fortunes at Anfield.

On the island south-east of France's mainland, the pair's new honeymoon period began. Anelka was unveiled as a Liverpool player just days before Christmas. His late arrival had prevented a swift reunion with Arsenal in his new club's upcoming fixture but Houllier hailed the move, which would be made permanent for £15m if the player excelled, as 'a fantastic deal' and downplayed concerns about his well-documented fall-outs elsewhere, including at Highbury. 'I've taken him because I believe in him,' he said. 'If there are any risks, they are worth taking.'

Concerns over Anelka's reputation were still proving difficult to shake, especially when PSG president Laurent Perpére announced that the player had sparked a row with the club just eight days before securing a return to England. But Chris Kirkland remembers Anelka's consummate professionalism shining through at Liverpool. The goalkeeper had joined his boyhood club earlier that season on the same day that Jerzy

Dudek arrived from Feyenoord in a £10.85m double deal. 'I know obviously when he came in, there was a lot of talk about his personality and his trouble on and off the pitch,' he says. 'But I can honestly say that there wasn't an incident where he caused any trouble with us. There's no doubt he was a top player. A lot of people said he drifted in and out of games a bit but when he was at Liverpool, I think his performances in general were of a pretty good standard. You could tell in training he had class. He always trained and played the same way.

'He had this way about him; some would say he just looked too easy but he wasn't. His work rate was up there with everyone and, as I say, he was never any problem at all. He was a top player, there's no doubt about it. You don't do what he's done in his career, play for the teams he has done and had the moves that he has without being an exceptional player.'

Anelka's impact on the Liverpool attack was more profound than his five strikes in 22 competitive outings may suggest. All except two of Emile Heskey's nine goals were amassed in 18 games playing alongside the Frenchman. Michael Owen, too, prospered from the loanee's presence with more than half of his 12-goal haul in the second half of the season arriving in a three-pronged attack. The magnitude of Anelka's direct contributions to Houllier's side were similarly positive. He had spared their blushes in a Merseyside derby against Everton with a second-half equaliser before taking on a starring role in a 3-0 demolition of Newcastle, when he faced former PSG team-mate Sylvain Distin, despite failing to find the target. 'I thought he was a great addition for us; a fantastic player,' says Heskey. 'He was very quiet, but he made his football do all his talking. He didn't need to be loud and brash or flash. He was a quiet player, but [when] he went out on that pitch, his ability shone. You look at what he's achieved and what he won, it shows why.'

A familiar complaint among Liverpool supporters in the years when they were beaten to the punch for the Premier League was that their best challenges all arrived in seasons when the bar of standards had been incrementally raised; 2001/02 was a shining example. Gérard Houllier returned to the touchline to see his side emulate the 80-point haul which had taken Manchester United to the title just a year earlier. But their best was not quite good enough as they finished runners-up, seven points adrift of Arsenal. Bragging rights over reigning champions United, ten points behind in third, felt almost hollow after playing second fiddle to a team that Arsène Wenger was in the midst of fashioning into one that would become familiar to millions as 'The Invincibles' just two seasons later. Anelka's permanent return was expected to strengthen Liverpool's resolve for a renewed tilt at the elusive league title.

Everything had aligned in Anfield's favour as Houllier was able to lean on his friendship with PSG president Laurent Perpére to bargain the club down from their original £15m valuation to a more agreeable figure of £12m. A five-year contract was also struck with Anelka's representatives for just over half of the player's previous wage demand of £60,000 per week. But on 20 May, Liverpool announced that they would not be taking up the option to sign Anelka, insisting in an official statement, 'This was a difficult decision but the manager has always had to do what he thinks is best for the club and the development of the team.' Houllier had informed the player of his decision in a telephone call earlier that day, which provoked a sour grapes public response from Anelka. 'I wanted to stay and I thought we had an agreement,' he said. 'I feel as though Liverpool have let me down. They haven't explained to me why they didn't want to keep me.'

Phil Thompson would later claim that the seminal moment arrived towards the end of the previous season when Arsène Wenger had contacted Houllier to relay that Anelka's brothers had tried to sell him back to Arsenal while still on loan at Anfield. Long-held suspicions that Claude and Didier Anelka were the real power behind the throne prompted Houllier to banish the pair from both Anfield and Melwood before negotiations commenced. Even so, Liverpool's volte-face still came as a surprise to all of the relevant parties. PSG's vice-president Alain Cayzac described his personal conversation with Houllier as 'short and cold' while the manager himself attempted to reassure The Kop's disheartened masses by insisting, 'We are looking and we will find the right player. You can trust me on this.' Djibril Cisse, who would eventually move to Anfield for £14m as the Frenchman's parting gift in summer 2004, and Freddie Kanoute again became viable targets.

But with Auxerre and West Ham United both unwilling to sell, Liverpool sanctioned the £10m signing of Rennes striker El-Hadji Diouf, who had just been named man of the match as Senegal stunned France in the opening game of the 2002 World Cup, just weeks after Anelka had been deemed surplus to requirements by the defending world champions. The bleach-haired forward went on to produce a pitiful return of three goals from 55 appearances during a three-year stay which was laden with as much controversy as Anelka's lengthy career if not more.

When Heskey reported back for pre-season training the circumstances behind the striker's failed move remained shrouded in mystery. 'I don't know what happened in between,' he says. 'I don't know the full ins and outs but from what I understood he was actually coming back [beforehand]. Going from there, to going on holiday, and then coming back to training and he wasn't there was interesting. It was just weird for me, but we moved on.'

Anelka himself moved on and far closer to his recent domicile than many expected as Manchester City sought to make Liverpool's loss their gain. Anfield legend Kevin Keegan had taken over the Maine Road hot seat following Joe Royle's departure at the end of the 2000/01 season and sealed an immediate return to the Premier League as First Division champions. Efforts to consolidate the club's top-flight status led to a series of astute additions and Keegan enlisting the services of Blues midfielder Ali Benarbia as a go-between in their efforts to sign Anelka. 'I think he convinced me more than Kevin,' Anelka told the *Blue Moon Podcast* in 2019. 'But because Kevin was there also, I know he was a striker – a very good striker, one of the best – and I wanted to work with him. So the combination of Kevin and Ali made me sign.'

Sylvain Distin, another of Benarbia's former PSG team-mates, arrived just four days before the striker's £13m move was completed. 'It rarely makes sense,' he says. 'A player's transfer is just like, "Does the two clubs agree?" and, "Does the player agree?" so it's difficult to anticipate. Possibly he [Anelka] might have been influenced by the project, like me, or maybe he just wanted to stay in England and decided that was the best opportunity; I've got no idea. That's something you need to ask him.'

The shock about his move to Moss Side was not reflected within his former ranks at Anfield. 'I don't think anything surprises you in football these days,' says Chris Kirkland. 'I think he lived in the Manchester area and obviously he was promised he'd be the main man at City, who'd just come up. I don't think there was too much surprise within us. We know these things happen with football. There's been far more surprising moves and there always will be.'

Anelka would later describe Liverpool's decision to pass up on signing him as the reason why he 'ended up joining a club against my will'. That lack of diplomacy was already becoming notorious as he used an inaugural address as City's record signing to put across his side about the scrapping of a permanent switch to Merseyside. 'Why didn't I stay at Liverpool after having achieved what I wanted to do: to play, score and of course to relaunch my career?' he asked rhetorically. 'I cannot answer that. It is better to put the question to Gérard Houllier because I really wanted to stay. I did well, and they played the game that I had been looking for and the atmosphere was good. For me there was no question. But obviously that did not suit Mr Houllier.'

Throughout the summer, he continued to publicly lay the blame for the failed switch to Anfield squarely at Houllier's door, claiming that the refusal to sign him permanently stemmed from a problem with having 'someone around who could stand up to him' before later offering the more considered hypothesis that his former manager was 'imagining future problems, and he imagined the worst'.

Ahead of Liverpool facing Anelka for the first time since he had joined City, in September 2002, Houllier reignited the disagreement by telling reporters, 'I don't want to expose the reasons why I didn't want to sign him, but I think he knows why and it has nothing to do with football. Whatever has happened, people should not forget we relaunched his career. He should be grateful to this club.' Keegan countered his opposite number's claims by extolling Anelka's model professionalism and insisted that the marquee signing 'has found the right club'. Any hopes that Anelka would punish his former side faltered on that first outing in City colours as he was upstaged by Michael Owen. The reigning Ballon d'Or holder had not scored from open play in seven Premier League games but atoned with a hat-trick in a comfortable away win at Maine Road.

'He was just incredible,' says Kirkland. 'Obviously we all know about the injury problems he had, because he was so explosive, with his hamstrings and back then there wasn't as much sport science in it as there is now. I'm sure Michael, if he was playing now with the sports science, probably wouldn't have been injured as much. But he was frightening. I mean, he could beat anyone. Defenders playing against him when he was in his pomp must have thought, "Jeez, we're in for a long afternoon here." That afternoon he scored a hat-trick and I bet the defenders couldn't wait to get off the pitch!'

Sylvain Distin can attest to enduring a difficult outing as he and City's defence were run ragged by the Liverpool talisman. 'You don't win the Ballon d'Or for no reason,' he says. 'I think like every striker, sometimes he went through a dry period when you don't score goals. It's for you to get out of this period as fast as you can because if you start doubting, as a striker, things get a bit difficult. It happened to a lot of strikers, possibly all the strikers at some point in their careers, and that was the time for him. But that doesn't change the fact that he had good qualities.'

Liverpool would make one more return to Maine Road in its final season when they were pitted against City in the FA Cup's third round. Pressure was starting to mount on Gérard

Houllier after his side's failure to win any of their previous ten Premier League matches – their worst run for 80 years – and sat seventh in the table, just three points ahead of their hosts in tenth. Cup competitions had stolen focus for the Anfield club, who had reached the League Cup semi-final and the last 16 of the UEFA Cup. Adding to their woes was the return of Owen's malaise in front of goal, having failed to score in his previous five outings, although the England international sat out the trip to Manchester with a hamstring problem.

Attention invariably shifted back to Anelka, not least because of the player himself. He used a newspaper interview ahead of the game to freshly air his grievances with Houllier, speaking of his resentment at being 'left in limbo' and alleging that the presence of his brothers, Claude and Didier, had been at the heart of Liverpool's final decision before adding, 'I don't give a damn what happens to Gérard Houllier.' City team-mate Shaun Wright-Phillips was similarly bewildered by the Reds' approach as he hailed Anelka's contribution to his new club. 'No disrespect to Liverpool,' he told journalists. 'But any team who had the chance to sign Nicolas or keep him and didn't do so made an error in my opinion'.

Keegan also found himself preoccupied with Anelka ahead of the showdown with his one-time employers. Until his 82nd-minute withdrawal in a draw with Everton on New Year's Day, Anelka had played every minute of City's 2002/03 campaign and shunned persistent attempts to offer him some respite. Keegan revealed his recuperation plan for the club's star man, saying, 'We will not train him at all. We will just put him out against Liverpool and let him get on with it.' Bookmakers offered slim odds on City clinching a fifth FA Cup in their history with their chances of going all the way to Cardiff's Millennium Stadium priced at 50/1. But with no fewer than five all-Premier League ties in the third round, Keegan was confident of making significant progress if City could pull off what he described as 'a giantkilling'. Houllier attempted to offer a more amiable view on Anelka's move across the M62 despite lamenting his recent decision to reject a call-up to the France squad for their friendly against Yugoslavia. He believed that his former striker had flourished at City because, 'The spotlight isn't on him like it was at Liverpool or Arsenal and he has been allowed to develop his game again in the shadows.' He added, 'That doesn't mean I have regrets about not signing him.'

City's preparations for the tie were hampered by their backline suffering two key absences with Steve Howey failing to shake an Achilles injury and Richard Dunne suffering from a virus. In the absence of Owen, Houllier handed Neil Mellor a second senior start against the club he had supported as a boy and where his father Ian's own footballing career had began. If the 20-year-old was feeling potential nerves about running out at Maine Road, it did not show in a first half where Liverpool had taken a firm grip of the tie. Vladimir Smicer let fly with a 25-yard volley which cleared a swarm of players before Peter Schmeichel pulled off a similarly spectacular save. City's goalkeeper proved the busier of the two on the afternoon as his defence struggled with the visitors' ascendancy and were caught napping when Sami Hyypiä was allowed a free header from a corner which he flashed just wide. Anelka toiled against his old club and failed to meet a defence-splitting pass by Niclas Jensen in the 20th minute.

For a second time in the season, Liverpool's central striker had put their former one in the shade as Mellor forced two saves from Schmeichel in the space of a minute. An enforced change allowed City to regain a foothold with Lucien Mettomo's replacement Eyal Berkovic immediately drawing a low save from Chris Kirkland minutes before half-time. But the hosts' best effort would be undone barely a minute into the second half as referee Uriah Rennie was inundated with a succession of penalty appeals. The first was waved away when El-Hadji Diouf fell to the ground after turning Sun Jihai but the Sheffield official pointed to the spot when Smicer's cross struck the raised arm of Marc-Vivien Foé. Danny Murphy brought back memories of previous cup injustices for long-suffering City fans as he rolled the ensuing spot-kick past Schmeichel.

It prompted a spirited fightback as City fashioned a series of attempts that saw Kirkland become the busier of the two goalkeepers. 'I think I made a couple of saves with my feet,' he says. 'I remember that because I think I had my cap on for that game. But I don't remember being overly busy. It was quite a tight game, but I remember making a couple of saves, I think, in front of our fans in the second half.'

Foé, Berkovic, Kevin Horlock and Shaun Goater all had chances to equalise but were let down by their finesse. At the other end, Diouf nearly embarrassed Schmeichel as he tried to catch out the former Manchester United hero with a 45-yard volley after he had rushed off his line to head a clearance into the Senegalese forward's path.

Keegan's post-match verdict on City's FA Cup exit doubled up as a character assassination. 'I never talk about Uriah Rennie, except to say that I don't like him as a referee. Never have, never will,' he said in the press room. 'He is a law unto himself. Ask his agent if you can have an interview with Mr Rennie.' The former Kop idol acknowledged that the penalty decision was 'technically' correct but added, 'It was a horrible way to settle a cup tie. It's like as if someone has been chopped down in the box.'

Keegan would incur a greater wrath than the one he had administered to the Sheffield official when City completed the £7m signing of Robbie Fowler from Leeds United on 13 February. Fowler had originally opted out of the deal earlier in the month after passing a medical, despite reservations from chairman David Bernstein about his injury record, but was swayed by a personal visit from the man whose mantle he had previously assumed in Liverpool's front line. 'I risked getting my tyres nicked and my wheels gone to talk to Robbie and his wife,' Keegan joked at the player's unveiling. That attempt at humour was not well-received in his former Merseyside parish. A host of local celebrities, including Stan Boardman, condemned Keegan while the phone lines of Radio City were flooded with callers irate at the faux pas. One warned the former Liverpool forward, 'After what he said he'd better wear a tin helmet when City play at Anfield in May.

His joke may raise a laugh in Manchester, but he's going to get some stick from Liverpool fans.'

That meeting on 3 May carried further significance as Liverpool attempted to secure a top-four finish with a fifth straight Premier League win and Michael Owen back among the goals. Houllier had looked ahead to City's visit with contrasting views on the club's two returning heroes. Praise was plentiful for Fowler despite the pair's at times strained working relationship. The Frenchman hailed the home-grown player as 'a Liverpool son' in a warming testimony that, true to his schoolteacher background, still carried the caveat, 'I think Robbie made a mistake in wanting to leave. He should have been more patient.' When the conversation shifted to Nicolas Anelka, however, Houllier was less than forthcoming.

Sylvain Distin's first experience of Anfield a year earlier had come to pass in unusual circumstances after the stadium had been plunged into darkness before the hosts' eventual 3-0 win over Newcastle, an evening when Anelka had stolen top billing in all but goals. A year later, the pair would be heading back preparing to turn out the lights on the club's Champions League dreams.

'As a player, when you signed for City at the time, there was obviously the [Manchester] derby that you looked at and then the so-called "top four" that are the big games and the highlights of your season,' he says. 'Not that the other games don't count at all because, at the time, the goal was to stabilise and remain in the Premier League so every game counts. But as a player, you obviously look at those clubs and they're the clubs you want to play against and compete against. In that sense, yeah, that was possibly one of the big games in the season but there was no special setup.'

Anelka headed into the game with a goalscoring predicament that mirrored Owen's recent struggles. He had failed to find the net in eight games leading up to his highly anticipated Anfield return. 'I didn't feel anything special in Nicolas [beforehand],' says Distin. 'He's not that type of player who's just going to pick and choose the games he wants to play. He gave his maximum in every game so there was no special difference, just a good rhythm for us.'

As with their previous two meetings that season, Liverpool's command became evident in the first half when a foul by Shaun Wright-Phillips on Milan Baros allowed Steven Gerrard to strike a looping free kick which Peter Schmeichel had to tip around the post. Just before the interval, Dietmar Hamman tested Schmeichel from a similar distance after being teed up by both Danny Murphy and John Arne Riise but the advancing Dane, now 39 and in his final season of professional football, was able to deflect the ball out with his elbow. The hosts' pressure finally told shortly before the hour when El-Hadji Diouf hooked a cross into the penalty area that fell for Baros to volley home, leading to City's players lobbying referee Neale Barry over Hamman's challenge on Fowler in the build-up.

Diouf was also integral to City's late fightback when he was dispossessed deep in Liverpool's half by Ali Benarbia, who threaded a ball into the box for Anelka that was curtailed by a foul from Djimi Traore for remarkably the first penalty awarded in City's favour that season. He wrong-footed Jerzy Dudek to level up the clash with 16 minutes remaining. For all his continued ill feeling towards Houllier, Anelka's celebration was muted as his team-mates ran to congratulate him.

Then, in the third minute of stoppage time, Dudek's attempt to deploy a long-ball tactic swiftly backfired. Wright-Phillips won possession back from Murphy after he met Distin's headed clearance. The winger engaged in a spell of smart link-up play with Benarbia. Aided by a flick-on from Fowler, the pair combined to tee up Anelka for a half-volley that delivered City's first win in the red half of Merseyside since December 1981. 'It was probably written that he was going to do that,' says Emile Heskey. 'When you're coming up against someone like that that should've possibly been at the club and all of a sudden he's not, and you come up against him, it's kind of written.'

Anelka's decisive brace led to a muted lap of appreciation for Liverpool after a season where they had won the League Cup for a second time in three years. Houllier, particularly, struggled to hide his frustrations with the player returning to haunt his side when facing the media. A question from an ITV reporter about Anelka provoked a tetchy and almost muted response from the usually eloquent Frenchman. Beyond the cameras, he shut down similar requests from the written press to discuss the player that he had allowed to get away with a firm insistence of 'I won't answer that question'. The defeat had left Liverpool's Champions League qualification hopes hanging by a thread and still dampened the mood around Anfield several hours later when Keegan signed autographs for supporters outside. One asked whether his former club would still make the top four, prompting the response, 'In my day, you had to be champions to get in there. You had to be winners.'

Anelka's brace not only clinched a landmark victory for City, who finished the season in ninth, but arguably altered the course of Premier League history. Had Liverpool won, they would have leapfrogged Chelsea into fourth place with a three-point cushion heading into their final day showdown. The Londoners' failure to beat local rivals West Ham on that same afternoon meant they remained ahead of their closest challengers on goal difference alone and staring into the abyss. Senior figures at Stamford Bridge told players that their club risked going out of business without the financial trappings that a place in the Champions League brought. A 2-1 defeat of Liverpool, at the ground where the Reds had not won since 1986, not only removed the prospect of bankruptcy from the equation but practically obliterated it. That summer, Roman Abramovich completed the takeover which heralded a new era of success at Chelsea and changed the face of the English game.

Heskey, however, argues that Anelka was not the sole reason for Liverpool's failure to return to Europe's premier competition. 'You can't just pinpoint that one game to say that he kicked us out,' he says. 'There would have been games throughout the season where we could've possibly done better in and got more points from. But obviously having him come back and doing that wasn't good.'

Fowler and Anelka would again be the protagonists when Liverpool travelled to the Blues' new home at the City of Manchester Stadium. The venue which hosted the Commonwealth Games in 2002 symbolised the club moving back to its spiritual roots, located just under two miles from their first ground in Hyde Road, and was pioneered by majority shareholders John Wardle and David Makin, lifelong fans and business partners who founded the retail giant JD Sports. A tenancy deal of an initial £1m annually on a 200-year lease was struck with Manchester City Council for the stadium, which was increased to a capacity of 47,726 during its conversion for football, with the land on which Maine Road stood offered up as part of the deal.

Also heading to Eastlands was Steve McManaman. The winger had left Anfield under acrimonious circumstances in 1999 after joining Real Madrid under the Bosman ruling. Another free transfer brought him back to England after four successful years at the Bernabéu, where he had been frozen out by new manager Carlos Quieroz to the point of not being allocated a squad number for the forthcoming season.

McManaman's move to Manchester prompted Houllier to challenge misconceptions about the manner his one-time player had departed before their inaugural reunion on 28 December. 'It was not my fault Macca left,' he said. 'You never want your top players to leave the club. He went on a free under a new rule at the time and you have to live with that sometimes. I would have tried hard to sign him before he was able to leave, that's why I was fair to him. I wasn't going to prejudice the matter by not playing him; he played until the end of the season and I asked the fans to give him a great send-off in the final game against Wimbledon.'

The 31-year-old's reunion with former sparring partner Fowler had the potential to cause Liverpool myriad problems in attack, yet Heskey still pinpoints his erstwhile team-mate as the bigger danger man. 'Obviously you know what they're capable of and you do your best to cancel that out, but players like Robbie are another level,' he says. 'Everyone asks me who was the best finisher that I've seen and I always say Robbie. His finishing was second to none to be honest with you. You knew what he was capable of. But at times it is a little bit weird that you can know this person inside out that you're going to be playing against and you've got to try and stop them.'

Armed with an intimate knowledge of the former Liverpool marksman's capabilities, John Arne Riise still failed to contain Fowler's bustling presence and brought him down in the penalty area after 30 minutes. Anelka duly dispatched from the spot to provide a degree of justice to the game, with City denied a legitimate penalty in the opening stages for a handball by Igor Biscan with Fowler again causing problems by pressuring the versatile defender. The half-time deficit forced Houllier to later admit that any number of his players could have found themselves hooked at the interval. When they re-emerged, Liverpool turned the tables on their hosts with Vladimir Smicer sneaking in at the far post to meet a Danny Murphy corner before Dietmar Hamann struck an arching volley from outside the area which conjured up painful memories for City goalkeeper David Seaman, who had been beaten by the German during Keegan's final game as England manager. In the final seconds of the match Fowler provided Liverpool with a timely reminder of his own.

'I remember that quite well because I'd had the ball and was dribbling it along the wing,' says Heskey. 'I probably should have just knocked it down the line and ran but I carried on dribbling it, got it nicked off me on the halfway line and they went down and scored. I got a little bit of a telling off for that! But sometimes things are written that certain players are going to come back and bite you on the bum.'

From Heskey's dispossession, City worked the ball into Anelka for a shot which was blocked by Liverpool's defence but broke for substitute Trevor Sinclair to hit a miscued volley that evolved into an inch-perfect delivery for Fowler to convert from three yards out. 'When you've got two quality strikers like that, you just have to try and keep a clean sheet at the back,' says Distin. 'Obviously one goal is enough to win a game but if you concede, you want to make sure that you don't concede too many goals because something will always come out with those type of players. With the finishing qualities they've got, both of them, you don't need to dominate a game to win a game. They just need a couple of chances each and that's it, you can get back into the game.'

City's smash-and-grab equaliser failed to mask a run without a Premier League win stretching to 11 games, having taken up residence in the Champions League qualification places at the beginning of 2003/04, and left Keegan feeling a combination of pride and regret. 'Deep down, Gérard will be happy with a point because we murdered them in the first half,' he said. 'The last thing I asked the players at half-time was whether they could put in another 45 minutes the same. Unfortunately the answer was no. We had them rattled but we couldn't finish them off.' Houllier refused to dispute his contemporary's comments on his own 100th league outing in sole charge and admitted, 'If Manchester City had been more clinical, we would have lost.' Growing scrutiny surrounded the Liverpool manager's tenure ahead of City's return visit on 11 February 2004, with his side battling in vain to reach the final qualification spot for Europe's elite club competition. A four-game winless streak only served to add to the internal frustration growing among supporters.

Anelka's absence from the Anfield encounter through suspension gave the beleaguered Frenchman some genuine relief as three players formerly under his watch still returned to their former haunt. Taking his place in the homecoming trio was David James, who had joined from West Ham United a month earlier. Inside three minutes, James was picking the ball out of the net after City's loanee defender Daniel van Buyten escaped punishment for a push on Bruno Cheyrou, a player Houllier had previously hailed as the next Zinedine Zidane, as the ball ran through for Hamann to play a first-time pass for Michael Owen that saw the striker skip past Richard Dunne's challenge before ending a drought which stretched back to mid-October with a calm finish. But Liverpool's defence was driven to distraction early in the second half when Fowler's dummy run allowed McManaman to feign a pass to him and find Shaun Wright-

Phillips as the winger composed himself and fired a low effort across Dudek and into the far corner.

The parity lasted for all of 60 seconds as James rushed out to stop Owen but gifted Steven Gerrard for a simple follow-up in the process. Four months after being handed the captaincy, the midfielder had embraced his new responsibility by repeatedly dragging Liverpool out of the mire, a theme which would become recurring in his next 11 years with the club.

Gerrard later provided an inch-perfect delivery for Anthony Le Tallec but McManaman's goal-line heroics denied both the French forward's header and Owen's rebound attempt. Home and away fans traded chants, with The Kop responding to City taunts of 'Champions League, you're having a laugh' by repackaging the insult to reflect their precarious top-flight status. A slender lead still did little to satisfy an angst-ridden crowd as the final half-hour was played out against a backdrop of audible frustration.

'I think it's always that case when you're chasing a place in Europe, it can get edgy at times,' admits Heskey. 'We've got some of the best fans out there supporting us and they can be the 12th man. At times you need to get them on our side and really get them cheering us. But if it's edgy, they will be edgy as well and it just compounds it.'

Houllier was equally het up as he committed the cardinal sin of turning on the Anfield faithful after his side had moved into fourth place for the first time in the season. 'What are they moaning about?' he said. 'The whole team deserves credit – the fans must understand that football is a game where you have to work hard for victory and have to adapt to get results. The crowd were not happy, it's true, but you have to understand their psychology. The players were a bit edgy because they had not won in four matches.'

City's failure to win for a 14th consecutive league outing left them just three points away from the relegation zone and prompted Keegan to read his players the riot act. 'In the first 45 minutes we didn't compete enough, and I don't think the lads wanted it enough,' he said. 'I could look at everybody with the exception of one or two. In the second half I thought everyone raised it a little bit and some of them raised it a lot. We gave Liverpool a scare at 1-1 and threw away a goal at the other end almost immediately.'

A late-season rally allowed them to extend their margin for error to eight points by the time the 2003/04 season ended. Liverpool's quest for a Champions League return was also achieved with Houllier still firmly under the cosh.

Three days after the campaign had ended, the Liverpool boss sanctioned Heskey's departure to Birmingham City in an initial £3.75m deal which rose to £5m in line with their preserved Premier League status the following year. As he attempted to revive the club's fortunes, Manchester City duo Shaun Wright-Phillips and Joey Barton became viable signings in a combined £8m swoop. Houllier confirmed his pursuit of a 21-year-old Barton in a keynote speech at the SoccerEx convention in 2016, saying, 'It's true. I don't know why we couldn't sign him, it was something, but we were trying to sign him.' The boyhood Everton fan shared the same agent as Gerrard, who also hailed from the Huyton area, and was on the verge of entering the final year of his contract at the City of Manchester Stadium.

Barton later disclosed in his autobiography *No Nonsense* that he had verbally agreed to the move in a meeting with Houllier at the club's Melwood training ground. 'I wasn't aware of that at all but Joey and Shaun were two very important players for us,' says Distin. 'So no matter where they go, whether it was Liverpool or somewhere else, that's a dent in the club's ambition. I'm not sure at the time that the club's ambition was to break into the top four but whatever the ambition was, you don't want to lose your main asset.'

Houllier's pursuit of the pair was ended by his sacking on 24 May but Barton's hopes of a deal still going ahead were kept alive by his replacement Rafael Benitez, who as Valencia manager had broken Real Madrid and Barcelona's stranglehold on La Liga by winning the title twice in three seasons. Contrary to the player's later claims, it was not Xabi Alonso's £10.7m arrival from

Real Sociedad which put paid to the move but rather Benitez's reluctance to meet City's £3m valuation – news which emerged ahead of a return visit to Merseyside in the second game of 2004/05.

Michael Owen's departure for the Bernabéu had destroyed the Spaniard's hopes of building his new side around the striker but the Euro 2004 exploits of Milan Baros, who had won the tournament's Golden Boot, and club-record signing Djibril Cisse attempted to bridge the gap left by his exit alongside Gerrard, now assuming talisman status. Rough edges in the Liverpool captain's game still appeared in the closing stages of the first half as he tried to stop Wright-Phillips with a lunging tackle that his opposite number was able to ride out before clipping the ball into Anelka's path, only for Jamie Carragher to head the ball back towards Dudek. But the Polish goalkeeper spilled the ball back at Anelka's feet to open the scoring on the stroke of half-time.

Three minutes after the restart, Gerrard made amends for his earlier mistake by playing a defence-splitting pass for Baros to slip the ball past James in front of The Kop. Liverpool continued to test their former stopper before making a second breakthrough as Hamann played Baros through for another one-on-one with James, which Gerrard converted from the rebound.

City attempted to fight on with Wright-Phillips affirming Benitez's pre-match assertion that he would be one of the visitors' dangermen. Stephen Warnock, who had replaced Steve Finnan just two minutes after Gerrard struck, recalls the winger's unique style of play as he caused problems down Liverpool's right-hand side. 'Shaun was one of these players where you can try and kick and he just bounced up,' he says. 'He had this, I dunno, it's not a strange style of play but you'd hit him, he'd hit the deck and suddenly bounce back up into his stride. And you'd think, "How's he done that?" and, "How's it possible?" He was brilliant at running with the ball, either way, so you knew it was always going to be difficult. I'd grown up against Shaun, playing against him in the youth teams, so I knew what he was like and what type of character and player he was. They always possessed a danger, the forward players of City, like they do now. That's always been one of Manchester City's strengths: a very dangerous team to try and stop.'

Combating Liverpool's attack ended in humiliation when Richard Dunne's running battle with Baros left him walking the disciplinary tightrope before being sent off five minutes from time for pulling on Cisse's shirt. Benitez's start to his Anfield reign had produced a slice of history by recording the club's first win from a game where they had been trailing at the interval for over five years.

'It's a blow but no matter if it comes in the last second of the game or the first second, it's the points that you don't get,' says Distin. 'At the time you just feel like, "Oh God, we nearly got it," but really when you think about it, it doesn't change much. It's just three points, or one point, that you lost so you have to move on because there's a game the next weekend.'

An animated touchline demeanour drew complaints from Keegan, who claimed his vantage point had been obscured by the man he referred to as 'Mr Bennett'. 'When he improves his English, we'll have to have a word about it,' he said. Benitez took the criticism in good spirit, saying, 'I promise I will sit down more if we are winning.' Dunne appeared to be in less jovial mood when questioned about his late dismissal. 'It was a joke – the linesman just wanted to get himself noticed,' fumed the defender. 'It finished us off, but we sat back too much. We have to buck up our ideas.'

Those initial ideas had led Keegan to pursue a loan deal for another former Liverpool player in Sander Westerveld, with the goalkeeper falling out of favour at Real Sociedad. But Westerveld spent the season with RCD Mallorca rather than serving as David James's understudy. The Balearic Islands club held the key to Anelka's hopes and dreams, too, earlier in the month as he targeted a move away from the City of Manchester Stadium. Barcelona's prolonged negotiations for Samuel Eto'o had been complicated by Real Madrid's co-ownership of the Mallorca striker, giving the Blues striker hopes of becoming the latest in a long line of players to traverse El Clasico's divide. Monaco had also expressed an interest in luring Anelka back to his homeland with a loan offer which Keegan later described as 'a cheeky enquiry'.

Doubts over Anelka's future had become part and parcel of life at Eastlands, with the club's marketing department having the foresight to place him on the January page of their annual calendar due to a habit of speaking with media outlets in his homeland during transfer windows. One such interview soured his previous rapport with City fans when he told *France Football* magazine of his desire to move to a Champions League club while criticising his current employers' own lack of direction and ambition. 'To win titles you need players who have the capability of doing so,' he said. 'If we stagnate between eighth and 15th place it's impossible to progress.' A first outing since the controversial remarks on 11 December saw him booed by supporters in a 1-0 defeat to Tottenham Hotspur. Two days later, chairman John Wardle told the club's annual meeting that he would consider offers for Anelka in excess of £5m, the amount City still owed PSG from his original transfer. Barcelona again emerged as potential suitors with Henrik Larsson sidelined by injury.

Treatment table issues also brought Liverpool back into the equation as Benitez weighed up re-signing the player who had snubbed his predecessor Gérard Houllier after Cisse's double leg break ruled him out for the remainder of the season. Steven Gerrard backed his manager's idea by revealing how influential Anelka had been in their 2001/02 title surge. 'I remember a few years ago when we were going for the title, Everton came to Anfield and nearly turned us over. We were grateful to Nicolas Anelka that day,' he told the *Liverpool Echo*. 'He was great for us when he was here. He was on fire for us at that time. He is one of the best strikers in the world I have played with – and he proved it that day.'

The striker's candour led to him being confronted by an irate City fan during the club's fancy dress Christmas party at Manchester's Lucid nightclub on 19 December. The incident descended into a fracas as team-mates rushed to Anelka's aid on a night which became more notorious for Joey Barton stubbing a cigar in the eye of Jamie Tandy after catching the reserve-team player attempting to set fire to his shirt.

Liverpool's attention subsequently shifted to Fernando Morientes but an initial £3.5m offer amounted to just half of Real Madrid's valuation for the highly decorated Spain international. Wanderley Luxemburgo's recent appointment at the Bernabéu also placed the transfer in jeopardy. The delayed nature of Morientes's move to Merseyside brought Anelka back into focus, with *L'Équipe* claiming on 30 December that he had been approached with the offer of a three-year contract. The report drew an exasperated response from the City hierarchy as a club spokesman insisted, 'This is now becoming tiresome and we will not continue to respond to this crazy speculation. We have had no enquiry about Nicolas Anelka.'

Benitez still refused to discount a potential move when asked by the media ahead of the Reds' FA Cup third-round tie with Burnley on 7 January, which was postponed due to a waterlogged pitch, saying simply, 'We know all about Anelka and he's a good player.' An improbable prodigal return failed to materialise, with Morientes instead arriving on Merseyside for £6.3m. Half a month later, his former Real team-mate sealed a £7m switch to Turkish side Fenerbahce. Anelka would later return to England for spells with Bolton Wanderers and Chelsea, where he won a league and FA Cup double in 2009/10.

An enigmatic career took him from Paris to Mumbai and everywhere in between, winning virtually every major honour of club and international football along the way, but the perception remains one of a player whose outspokenness meant he never stuck around long enough to be truly appreciated. 'When you're at the top of the club or you take decisions for the club, you don't really take a decision depending on what you read in the newspapers. But for the fans, maybe that was a turning point, it's a possibility,' says Distin, his team-mate at the outset with PSG and later City. 'As a player, what you say is not necessarily written in the press and that's one of the bad things in England. You know how the press try to manipulate what the players say and take the first word or last word to make a headline which has nothing at all to do with what you said.

'Unfortunately, people read it and feel that that's it: you went to the press and spoke, and they forgot that speaking to press, as a player, is one of your obligations. You don't go to the press to make an interview – they come and ask for you. When they twist your words, at the time we didn't have social media or anything like that, you just had to live with the consequences. But it's a shame because it's part of why Nicolas has never been understood by people.'

Nothing about Anelka's final act in English football, over eight years later, could possibly be misconstrued. He made worldwide headlines in December 2013 after celebrating a goal for West Bromwich Albion by performing the 'quenelle', a hand gesture described as an inverted Nazi salute. Although he disputed that the action carried a political motive, it had gained prominence through the controversial French comedian Dieudonne M'Bala M'Bala, his friend and a self-proclaimed anti-Zionist. Anelka was hit with a five-game ban by the FA for the offence, a fortnight before his contract at The Hawthorns was terminated on 14 March 2014 on grounds of gross misconduct after announcing plans to leave the club 'with immediate effect' via social media.

Fool's Gold

CONTINENTAL AMBITIONS burned brightly for Liverpool and Manchester City as the 2004/05 season neared its conclusion. But while Rafael Benitez's side soared in the Champions League, Kevin Keegan decided that enough was finally enough.

He had already planned to retire at the end of the campaign but chose to accelerate that parting of ways after a home defeat to Bolton Wanderers on 7 March. Relentless demands of 35 years' active involvement in frontline football, both as a player and coach, had finally taken its toll with intermittent periods outside the game in that time amounting to less than 24 months.

Keegan's personal recommendation led to City appointing his assistant Stuart Pearce as interim manager. The former left-back had become part of the furniture in east Manchester after seeing out his playing career during the club's return to the Premier League in 2001/02.

For those who had come to know Pearce as a coach, like Sylvain Distin, the transition was relatively painless. 'I actually signed for City when he retired and he had always been around City so I knew him as a player before knowing him as a manager,' he says. 'That was just easy for me because I didn't have that feeling of a player/manager [relationship], more like player and friend to be honest with you. He's someone that I respect; I respect what he's done as a footballer and as a manager he had a good defensive mindset as well, which for me was great. But he was still open to work offensively, not just parking the bus and everybody defending. He wanted to be strong defensively but then create chances as well. He was learning the trade and I think that was a good time for him.'

Pearce's start to life in the hot seat should have produced at least one win from his opening two games but a late Charlton Athletic equaliser in the week leading up to Liverpool's visit denied them. Sandwiched in between two legs of a Champions League quarter-final encounter with Juventus, Benitez's side travelled to the City of Manchester Stadium with an eye on overtaking Everton into the Premier League's final qualification place for Europe's elite club competition. Pearce's first home outing on 9 April came on an afternoon when Robbie Fowler faced his old club on the striker's 30th birthday while Anfield's latest home-grown heroes shared their own personal milestones; Jamie Carragher made his 350th club appearance while captain Steven Gerrard started competitively for the 250th time. Yet it was the hosts who were celebrating when Atlético Madrid loanee Kiki Musampa met Lee Croft's delivery to stab the ball past Scott Carson and record a 90th-minute winner.

Benitez's split priorities between European success and the English top flight had led to a heavy rotation policy and seen three changes from the line-up which had edged out Juventus just four days earlier.

'He [Musampa] was one of those players who just played on the shoulder and likes to play it behind and things like that,' says Stephen Warnock. 'But the big thing for me, and it was probably the story of my Liverpool career, was that I never felt fit in a game playing for Liverpool. I always found that whenever I went into a game, I didn't really do myself that much justice because I felt off the pace. In between the two Juventus games, it was almost like he'd rested other players ready for the Juventus games and the other lads would get used in games and things like that. I never felt fully up to speed going into games. I remember breathing heavily in that game – that's one thing I do remember – it was quite a frantic game. But that was the way it was under Rafa.'

Caught up by the euphoria of his first victory, Pearce attempted to make an early dart down the tunnel at the final whistle without shaking Benitez's hand. His goalkeeping coach Tim Flowers, who had lifted the Premier League title at Anfield a decade earlier with Blackburn Rovers, was quick to drag his superior back by the arm and remind him of the touchline etiquette. Overcoming the visitors became a greater feat in light of Liverpool's coronation as European champions just two and a half months later.

A draw would have taken Liverpool into fourth, above Everton on goal difference, before their local rivals returned to action 24 hours later. The stoppage-time slump drew an irate response from Benitez about his team's lapse in concentration. 'We need to learn that, if you can't win a game, sometimes a draw is a good result,' he said. 'We were in the last minute, we had a throw-in, then we gave the ball away, they counter and we end up losing a goal. It is more important for us to finish fourth in the Premier League than it is to do well in the Champions League. If we play to the level we can, we can still get there but if we do not improve on the mental approach we had today, it will be difficult for us.'

The Spaniard also acknowledged that an alternating approach between domestic and European matters had led to the disparity between their two most recent results. 'Everybody knows that the Champions League has another repercussion,' he insisted. 'A lot of people are watching around the world and it makes the players feel different. In the Champions League, we have a different mentality.' Pearce deemed the win as 'poetic justice' for City's own slip-up against Charlton while also hailing the strength of their competitors. 'Liverpool are a big scalp,' he said. They are on a good run of form. I watched them in midweek, and they played Juventus off the park.'

Liverpool's 3-1 defeat at Arsenal on 7 May ended their hopes of qualifying for the Champions League on domestic merit, with a cardigan-clad David Moyes prematurely declaring, 'There's no denying Everton are the best team in the city this season.' The Toffees' manager was left eating his words little over a fortnight later as Benitez's side pulled off an improbable comeback against AC Milan, having trailed 3-0 at half-time, to win the Champions League Final on penalties.

City's season had ended in a more bizarre fashion than Moyes's wardrobe choice as they pursued a place in the UEFA Cup with a final-day showdown with fellow challengers Middlesbrough. Pearce took the unprecedented step of deploying goalkeeper David James as an auxiliary striker in efforts to create confusion within the visitors' defence. His presence at the opposite end of the pitch almost paid dividends when Franck Queudrue handled the ball for a penalty, which Robbie Fowler missed to produce a 1-1 draw and dash those European hopes. James's cameo appearance in attack was not even the most unusual decision at the City of Manchester Stadium that day, with the hosts' players wearing their upcoming navy away shirt instead of the traditional choice of a sky blue home strip.

Pearce's permanent appointment as manager, similarly, failed to stop City falling prey to the Premier League's hierarchal vultures as Shaun Wright-Phillips attracted interest from a host of clubs including Liverpool. Benitez revived predecessor Gérard Houllier's pursuit of the winger and was understood to be preparing a £15m offer to tempt him to Merseyside. Yet it was Chelsea, newly crowned champions, who won the summer race for Wright-Phillips with a £21.5m transfer. The fall-out from Keegan's resignation just months earlier saw Steve McManaman released after failing to feature at all in Pearce's team-mate's plans during the final weeks of 2004/05. His former England team-mate continued to evolve City's squad with Darius Vassell joining from Aston Villa for £2m alongside the free transfer of one-time Manchester United hero Andy Cole, who had recently left Fulham. Pearce's extensive rebuilding plans included a pursuit of Southampton striker Peter Crouch, but the timing of Wright-Phillips's move to Stamford Bridge saw those attempts arrive too late as Liverpool swooped in to sign him from the south coast club for £7m.

The Macclesfield-born player's move to Merseyside raised eyebrows due to his 6ft 7in frame being better suited to the City manager's approach of utilising a target man figure than the pattern play which had swept Benitez's side to the summit of

European football. An inability to find the target in his first 18 games from all competitions did little to disprove the suggestion of being a poor fit. His penultimate outing in the drought came at the City of Manchester Stadium on 26 November 2005 and marked the first matches played since George Best's death two days earlier. The late Manchester United star's name was met with warm applause by both sets of fans as it was read out ahead of a planned minute's silence. A vocal minority within Liverpool's 3,000-strong travelling support interrupted the period of reflection at its outset which led to a growing clamour of disagreement from their City counterparts in response. Amid the confusion, referee Alan Wiley chose to halt the period of reflection after just 15 seconds, which prompted widespread booing.

A cagey affair was settled on the hour when John Arne Riise struck a thunderous effort that extended Liverpool's unbeaten run to six games in all competitions while also handing Benitez a victory on his 50th league outing.

City legend Mike Summerbee was quick to condemn Anfield's travelling support for desecrating the memory of his lifelong friend Best, describing them as 'an embarrassment' and expressing his incredulity 'that some small-minded people would stoop so low'. When pressed further for his reaction to the unsavoury events, he declared, 'All the noise was from the Liverpool end. There's rivalry between the two Manchester clubs but if you go to Old Trafford and look at the shrine to George you will see lots of City shirts among the United shirts. Unfortunately, there is an unruly element among the Liverpool fans who weren't prepared to respect a man who deserved our respect.' The former winger also claimed that every other ground in the country had impeccably observed the silence that weekend, which belied the reality.

As with Sir Matt Busby's 1994 passing, the scenes before City and Liverpool's latest meeting were not an outlier. Leeds United fans also disrupted the planned tribute before their game at Millwall with a litany of chants that expressed an overriding hatred for their Old Trafford arch-rivals and led to it being cut short after 30 seconds. Both managers were forced to address the events which preceded kick-off in their post-match press conferences. 'It is a pity,' said Benitez. 'It was only a few people and most of them did applaud but it is a pity, you can't say anything else.' Pearce added, 'I have no idea which group of supporters it was but the vast majority paid tribute to a legend of the game who gave a lot of pleasure to a lot of people and that is the important thing. You have to look at the positives rather than dwell on the actions of a handful of people in a crowd of 47,000.'

Warnock, who was Liverpool's right-back in the game, takes issue with Summerbee's view that away fans had approached the planned tribute to Best with malice aforethought. 'I don't think either team or either fans would have done that out of spite or anything like that. It will have been a genuine mistake,' he says. 'I think both teams recognised the quality of George Best and what he brought, not only to Manchester United but the game in general. I think that will have been a misunderstanding. It will have been a little bit of heckling that they were sort of caught unaware of and it carried on for a little bit. But that's something I wouldn't have noticed on the pitch anyway or being involved in the game. I'd have been concentrated on doing the minute's silence and what have you and then getting ready for the game. There's other thoughts going through your mind at that time as well.'

Robbie Fowler's own thought process was about what lay immediately ahead. Injuries had limited him to just two substitute appearances in the first half of the season and discussions over an extension to his current Eastlands contract appeared ominous as it entered its final six months. His penultimate outing in a 3-1 win over Manchester United led to his final goal in City colours, which was celebrated with a five-fingered salute to signify Liverpool's number of European Cups. Less than a fortnight later, on 27 January 2006, Fowler unexpectedly rejoined the ranks at Anfield on a free transfer until the end of the campaign, with the option for the club to extend it beyond that. The striker's delight in securing a homecoming was noticeable for Benitez, who admitted, 'I'm not sure I've ever seen a player quite so happy to be joining a club before.' Fowler paid tribute to Pearce's willingness to allow him to leave, saying, 'No one wanted this move more than me and Stuart knew that. He helped me get here.' The City manager conceded that the decision to allow the 30-year-old to depart for his 'dream club' had been a mutually agreeable one for all parties. 'If I'd refused him this opportunity of fulfilling his ambition it would not have been good for him or City,' he said.

Fowler sat out the latest meeting between his current and former employers at Anfield a month later as part of a gentlemen's agreement struck in the deal which saw him move across the M62 completely gratis. Liverpool's midfield ensured that their returning hero's absence was not sorely felt as Steven Gerrard played a through ball for Harry Kewell to breeze into City's half before slotting past David James in the 40th minute. The visitors' failure to impose themselves on proceedings saw Joey Barton's indiscipline get the better of him. A high studs-first lunge on new Liverpool defender Daniel Agger saw him cautioned early in the first half before a follow-up on Sami Hyypiä's ankle shortly after the interval earned the second dismissal in his professional career. A game of limited chances was enlivened a short while after when winger Albert Riera, signed on loan from RCD Espanyol, sent a cross into the penalty area which Bradley Wright-Phillips turned back to the edge of the box for a masked Trevor Sinclair to strike a half-volley that appeared destined for the top left-hand corner but was beaten away by Pepe Reina.

The win moved Liverpool level on points with a second-placed United, but Benitez slammed his players for failing to take advantage of their other goalscoring opportunities by insisting, 'That was not good enough. I am not happy because we needed the second goal and we needed to finish the game [off], but we didn't play well enough to do it.' Pearce offered little defence for Barton's dismissal but admitted that the fiery midfielder might need 'to be a little cuter in his tackling'. The City manager also refused to sugar-coat the view on his team's overall display against their below-par hosts. 'We gave Liverpool too much respect,' he insisted. 'They haven't been free-scoring lately but once they get their noses in front, they are difficult to break down.'

Benitez's second season in charge saw an FA Cup Final win over West Ham United that supplemented a credible third-place Premier League finish while City's ongoing struggles saw them drop to 15th in the table.

Anfield hosted a third meeting between Liverpool and City later in the campaign as both clubs did battle in the FA Youth Cup Final. Watched on by academy graduates Steven Gerrard and Jamie Carragher, the Reds raced to a three-goal lead in the first leg, with Micah Richards's absence from the visitors' line-up proving costly after the defender had been called up to the senior ranks. When the defender returned for the corresponding game at the City of Manchester Stadium, Daniel Sturridge's goals in either half offered the young Blues hopes of a fightback but they ultimately faltered. Their Merseyside counterparts claimed the trophy for the first time since 1996, when Carragher and Michael Owen first caught the eye. Yet it was City's fledgling players who would enjoy a greater success in their club's first-team ranks, with Sturridge, Richards and Michael Johnson making the grade while only Jay Spearing became a semi-regular fixture in Liverpool's squad in the years which followed.

Richards's elevation coincided with several familiar faces finding their way to Eastlands before the start of the 2006/07 season with Pearce re-signing Paul Dickov, City's goalscoring hero in their 1999 play-off final win over Gillingham, as well as securing the services of veteran Liverpool midfielder Dietmar Hamann. The former Germany international joined just 24 hours after reneging on an agreement to join Bolton Wanderers when his Anfield contract expired on 11 July. City paid £400,000 compensation to the Trotters, whose manager Sam Allardyce described the agreement as 'the best transfer deal I have ever done in my life' after commanding a fee without Hamann kicking a ball for his would-be new employers. The 32-year-old later explained his reasoning for shunning a move to the Reebok Stadium, saying, 'I had the offer from Bolton for a few weeks and thought it was the right thing to do. But after going on holiday I felt it wasn't the right decision. It is something I have got to live with, and they allowed me to speak to other clubs. As soon as I heard Man City was interested, I made my mind up pretty quickly.'

Benitez also moved swiftly to sign players with Premier League and European experience in the form of Dickov's former Blackburn Rovers strike partner Craig Bellamy, Birmingham City winger Jermaine Pennant and Feyenoord captain Dirk Kuyt. The Dutchman's industry became a valuable commodity when his new club welcomed Manchester City on 25 November 2006 as he pounced on Barton's poor back-pass to Sylvain Distin with a sliding interception that teed up Gerrard for a 20-yard blast past Nicky Weaver for his first league goal in seven months.

Taunts from travelling supporters that his opposite number was 'just a shit Joey Barton' failed to lift the City midfielder's spirits as his already dismal afternoon in front of new England manager Steve McClaren was made worse. A trip by Steve Finnan on the edge of Liverpool's penalty area failed to convince referee Rob Styles to award a free kick. Pearce, who had ranted and raved at the fourth official over the incident before kissing him on the cheek by way of apology, was in no mood to offer another round of constructive criticism to Barton on his latest Anfield outing. 'You can't afford to give Gerrard the ball 25 yards out with a written invitation on it,' he said. 'All your hard work goes down the pan.'

Liverpool's home record at the time appeared near-identical to reigning champions Chelsea, still aiming for a hat-trick of titles, but abject away form left them languishing in mid-table as the New Year approached. Travel sickness merely scratched the surface of Anfield's problems as boardroom strife reached fever pitch, with chairman David Moores facing increasing pressure to bring his family's half-century association with the club to an overdue end. A previous £70m takeover attempt by Steve Morgan, a rival shareholder and founder of housebuilders Redrow, had been rejected in 2004 but the Reds' search for fresh investment continued and appeared to have found a viable suitor in the form of Dubai International Capital, the investment arm of the United Arab Emirates's ruling family. Strengthening their credentials was the fact that Sameer Al Ansari, the group's founder and CEO, was a Liverpool season ticket holder. Yet Moores's successors at the helm came from a different world to Dubai's astute investment as Tom Hicks and George Gillett sealed a £470m buyout.

Rick Parry, Liverpool's chief executive, justified the decision to sell to the Americans, whose collective sporting portfolio included the Texas Rangers baseball team as well as the Montreal Canadiens and Dallas Stars hockey clubs, by saying, 'You can only sell the family silver once.'

Hindsight proved that Moores had flogged his kin's greatest asset to a pair of snake oil salesmen, but the warning signs had first appeared when Hicks and Gillett first sat before the media on 6 February 2007. Anfield's most ill-advised joint press conference since the pairing of Roy Evans and Gérard Houllier together, a managerial double act that even Dr Frankenstein would have rejected, saw lies almost immediately tumble from the Americans' mouths. Hicks insisted that the club had been purchased with no debts saddled upon it and insisted that the buyout shared zero similarities with the financial ransacking that his compatriots the Glazer family had overseen at Manchester United since 2005. Gillett went further by promising that the pair would finally start construction on a proposed new stadium in Stanley Park. He claimed the saga, which had already dragged on for the previous seven years, would be ended in a 60-day period by claiming 'the shovel needs to be in the ground'.

As Hicks and Gillett's web of lies rapidly began to unravel, City were facing their own investment challenges. Chairman John Wardle had raised the prospect of a new ownership at the club's AGM in December of the previous year with SISU Capital, a London-based hedge fund operated by former Blues defender Ray Ranson, emerging as one of a number of viable suitors. Michael Ball had joined Stuart Pearce's side in the January transfer window on a short-term deal and remembers the hand-to-mouth existence he experienced after arriving from PSV Eindhoven. 'There was talks of numerous takeovers going to be happening, but we were all sort of in the dark,' he says. 'The club had a lot of transfer policies going on, a lot of players coming and going back then. The money was very, very tight and I think that was because of takeover talks. There were so many rumours about who was going to take over the club that the investment sort of basically stopped. I knew it was going to be difficult for me to get a contract if the club couldn't get taken over and it was just up to myself to prove to the manager that I could do a job for them.'

Ball made his tenth outing in City colours against familiar opposition as the former Everton left-back featured in a forgettable 0-0 draw with Liverpool on 14 April – the first time in 20 Premier League meetings between the sides that the game had finished scoreless. A late effort by DaMarcus Beasley which crashed against the crossbar constituted the hosts' best chance of scoring a goal at Eastlands since New Year's Day in a game where Benitez rested several of his senior players. But the Spaniard disputed suggestions that he had one eye on the upcoming Champions League semi-final against Chelsea. 'A very disappointing game,' he said. 'No clear chances, but I can assure you, our minds weren't on other things.' Pearce delegated post-match duties to his assistant Steve Wigley in order to pursue a scouting mission elsewhere.

Extending City's unbeaten run to a fifth consecutive game failed to save their manager, who had recently been appointed to oversee England's under-21 side, from the sack exactly a month later after steering them to a 14th-place finish in the table. 'Stuart knew what he wanted from every player,' says Ball. 'He obviously wanted to stay but everything was all unsure in that summer. When he asked us to go away, he gave us a training dossier of what to do in the summer and [said], "Get back for pre-season and hopefully I'll be here." It was disappointing to see him go but we knew the club in the summer got a sort of change of hands, was going fast-paced and it did sort of get took over.'

Potential successors were being touted even long before Pearce's eventual departure. Among the more notable was Gérard Houllier, who had rebuilt his reputation in the three years since leaving Liverpool by guiding Lyon to consecutive Ligue 1 titles. Houllier's link with the City of Manchester Stadium aligned with the emergence of a figure whose path almost crossed with his own in those final months at Anfield. On 21 June, a managerless City was taken over by Thaksin Shinawatra to the tune of £81.6m. The former Thai prime minister had previously attempted to buy a 30 per cent stake in the Reds before his country's questionable human rights record and plans to fund the bid through a state lottery led to the proposal being rejected in July 2004. He had spent the past few months exiled in London after a bloodless military coup brought his five-year premiership to an abrupt end. Arrest warrants were issued for Shinawatra and his wife by their homeland to stand trial on various corruption charges, while his personal and family assets totalling £800m were frozen.

Despite the political and financial turmoil, Shinawatra's takeover was ratified and led to boastful claims about how he could make City 'as popular as Manchester United and Liverpool in the next two years, especially in Asia'. Fans instantly dubbed their new benefactor 'Frank' due to his surname sounding like Frank Sinatra and believed the good times were set to roll when he followed predecessor John Wardle's lead in appointing another manager who had become a celebrated figure in the England hotseat. Sven-Göran Eriksson became the first overseas appointment in City's history just 12 months after walking away from the national side, following their 2006 World Cup knockout stage exit to Portugal. Yet the Swede's arrival remained clouded in uncertainty as he oversaw pre-season training while his tenure was still in the process of being rubber-stamped.

'He was there or thereabouts but his contract hadn't been agreed,' says Ball, who had previously been handed his sole international England call-up by Eriksson in 2001. 'There were issues over the takeover and money and stuff, so the players were still a bit unsure what was going to happen. Sven still took the training. He spoke to every player in a big team meeting. He goes, "Hopefully I'll be your manager if everything gets sorted out. But you're all very good players. If you're not happy here, come and knock on my door and I'll help you move on to another club but there will be investment here so it's all up to you to fight for your place if you want to be at this football club. But I will be bringing players in to bring competition to each and every one of you and to get this club up the league as high as possible." So we knew where we stood and it was up to each individual what they wanted to do.'

Benitez was also dealing with a confusing ownership in the wake of Liverpool's Champions League Final defeat to AC Milan. Hicks and Gillett had continued to make grandstanding media pledges of backing their manager, who wanted to see the colour of their money. 'We are in the same position as two years ago,' Benitez said the day after the Athens loss. 'The new owners say they will support us, but now is not the time to talk but [to] take decisions. It is not just about new faces; it is about the structure of the club.'

Unprecedented levels of spending in the summer saw Fernando Torres spearheading an influx of new arrivals that cost a combined £45m. To impartial observers, the American owners had been true to their word, but the reality was that over £22m was recouped. In the months ahead, it became ever clearer that Hicks and Gillett were gambling Anfield's future on bank loans. The absentee owners became increasingly distant, both with the club and each other, as the 2007/08 season dragged on. Hicks later admitted that the pair had sounded out former Germany manager Jürgen Klinsmann, now residing Stateside, as a viable replacement for Benitez.

Any hopes of a Premier League title assault wilted as Liverpool drew another blank at Manchester City on 30 December that left them ten points off the pace. Beforehand, Eriksson had confessed his affection for the visitors after striking up a friendship with Joe Fagan during his formative years in coaching which extended to an invitation to the fabled Boot Room when the Swede's Benfica side travelled to Anfield in the 1984 European Cup quarter-finals. Any sentiment for the club he had once admired was quickly forgotten with both clubs neck-and-neck in the table,

Joe Mercer and Bill Shankly chat in the Anfield tunnel in 1971 but the Liverpool manager could easily have found himself in the City hot seat

Tommy Smith receives his marching orders from Clive Thomas during a fiery 1-1 draw at Maine Road in February 1973

Rodney Marsh wheels away in celebration as City inflict Liverpool's first defeat under Bob Paisley

Ray Ranson challenges Kenny Dalglish in the controversial 1981 League Cup semi-final first leg at Maine Road

Joe Corrigan lies prostrate on the Anfield turf after being struck by a bottle during City's first win for 28 years on Boxing Day 1981

City are left to rue passing up on signing Ian Rush as he scores Liverpool's final goal of a 5-0 thrashing in April 1982

Clive Allen snatches at a shot as City are roundly beaten by Liverpool in March 1991

Keith Curle and John Barnes tangle in the first Premier League meeting between Liverpool and City at Anfield in December 1992

Emile Heskey lashes out at City defender Paul Ritchie during a 3-2 win for Liverpool in September 2000

Nicolas Anelka provides Gerard Houllier with a timely reminder of his qualities with a late brace to record City's first Anfield win since 1981

Revenge is sweet for Craig Bellamy as his goal tips the balance in Liverpool's League Cup semi-final with City

Sergio Agüero revels in squeezing a shot past Pepe Reina to salvage a 2-2 draw at the Etihad

Philippe Coutinho strikes a crucial third goal that gives Liverpool an upper hand on City in the Premier League title race

Breaking new ground as Liverpool and City's rivalry moves Stateside during the 2014/15 pre-season

Jürgen Klopp and Pep Guardiola take Liverpool and City's feuding to another level from the 2016/17 season

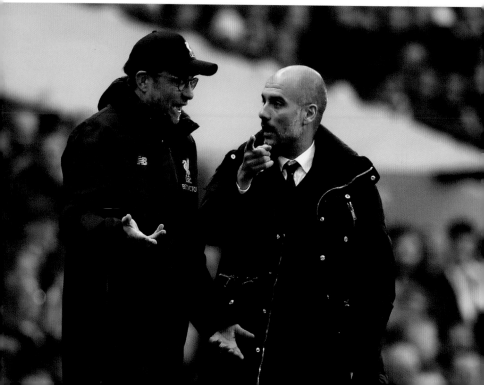

Ederson comes off worse in a brutal collision with Sadio Mané during City's eventual 5-0 thrashing of Liverpool

City's team bus comes under heavy fire from Liverpool fans before their Champions League quarter-final encounter at Anfield

Roberto Firmino's strike sparks scenes of delirium inside the Etihad as Liverpool progress to the Champions League semi-final

John Stones defies all logic to scoop the ball off the line as City's 2-1 win over Liverpool becomes a catalyst to reclaiming the title

Joe Gomez and Raheem Sterling come to blows near the end of Liverpool's 3-1 win in a clash which carried on to the international break

City's players form a guard of honour for Liverpool in their first outing as Premier League champions

with Liverpool holding on to fourth place by just two points. 'To get a result against Liverpool would be fantastic,' said Eriksson. 'We will try to win and, as I've always said, we'll know so much more about how strong we are after this weekend. I think it will be difficult to finish above Liverpool this season. But on Sunday evening I'll have a much better idea.'

City's unbeaten home record, with only a draw against Blackburn breaking a 100 per cent run from their opening ten games, was further helped by captain Richard Dunne subduing Torres as he went in search of a fourth goal in three games. The Republic of Ireland international's goal-line heroics in the 86th minute also prevented Dirk Kuyt scoring a follow-up after his initial header had been spilled by Joe Hart before denying Yossi Benayoun with a vital block in the closing stages.

Frustration would engulf both clubs by the time they met again at Anfield on 4 May in the season's penultimate league fixture. Liverpool had comfortably qualified for the Champions League with a nine-point advantage over fifth-placed Everton heading into their final two matches but the unrest over Hicks and Gillett's ownership had converted supporters from simple matchgoers into fully fledged activists with the creation of Spirit of Shankly, an umbrella organisation which represented fans' interests and became an initial focal point in opposition to the Americans. The group's acronym doubled as a plea from visiting supporters as Eriksson stood on the brink just 12 months into a three-year contract. Shinawatra had publicly expressed his dissatisfaction at results in the second half of a season where City had already produced their first league double over Manchester United, soon to be crowned domestic and European champions, since 1969/70. The manager had cancelled his pre-match press briefing in the run-up to the game with reports claiming that players were preparing to go on strike in solidarity while UEFA Cup qualification was still within reach.

'Sven took all the pressure,' says Ball. 'The players went out and hopefully did a job for him. Since I'd walked through the door, there was always things going on upstairs. We knew the owner came in a few times and had meetings about situations. [We were told] "Don't worry what you hear about the press. Everything's in hand, everything's fine, nothing's underhand. If money gets frozen, there's other money there to invest so keep doing what you're doing." That's what the press never knew about – that we got told that if even in the situations that money gets frozen that there's money there to invest so carry on, so that's what we did as professionals.

'Sven took all the questions and pressure. As players we just got on and did our job and just hoped that upstairs would get a bit quieter to make our jobs a little bit easier. Sven was the one who took it all. Even the last game of the season, we didn't really know if he was going to go or not. It was still all up in the air.'

Eriksson's penultimate outing became a farewell affair with Swedish flags and multiple banners declaring 'Save Our Sven' taking pride of place in the Anfield Road End's away section alongside chants of 'hey, Thaksin – leave our Sven alone!' set to the tune of Pink Floyd's 'Another Brick in the Wall'. Their manager had taken the unusual step of venturing out of the tunnel earlier than planned to realise a lifelong ambition of hearing The Kop sing 'You'll Never Walk Alone' in the flesh. City's players repaid Eriksson's unwavering faith by weathering the storm until the 58th minute, when an unforced error from Ball allowed Torres to equal a club record in scoring on his eighth consecutive home outing, matching Roger Hunt's feat set in the 1961/62 season.

'I remember that very well – my mates were all happy with that one!' he says. 'We thought we were holding our own a little bit. Liverpool had quite a few chances, but we were still in the game. Sven wanted to keep us tight and with our players going forward that they'll break the deadlock and we'll snatch three points and, if not, just come away with a draw which he was never really happy with but he'd take it. We were on course and doing everything right. Unfortunately for myself, I got the ball and saw a little gap to chip it into the striker and I've done it too short. Dirk Kuyt sort of got his head on to it and they counter-attacked. Torres got down the side of Dunny and put it in the net. It was my fault and I was apologetic after the game to everyone. After all the hard work that we'd done and just threw it away with one mistake that we got punished from it. Especially against Liverpool, it was a bitter pill to swallow.'

Ball's most recent Anfield visit with Everton in October 2000 had also ended in defeat as Nick Barmby haunted his former employers by heading the opening goal after Christian Ziege's cross deflected off Emile Heskey and had broken for him at the far post. Robbie Fowler's shove on Ball in the build-up earned him a place in modern Kop folklore before his part in a two-man wall led to further ridicule as it was cleared by Gary McAllister with a free kick from 44 yards which stole the spoils in the final second of the following April's five-goal thriller at Goodison Park. But the self-inflicted nature of his latest reversal was a more painful experience than those in a royal blue shirt.

'When you go to that place and you just want basically to put in the best performance of your life against them to show what you're all about,' he says. 'We were doing well and then to make that mistake that led up to the goal is just so frustrating and so disappointing. Coming home and half your mates are Reds as well, so they're all buzzing and that makes it even worse. As a kid going [there], I never really liked it but as a schoolboy, scoring there and scoring hat-tricks, it was always, very early in my life, a good place to go. I used to enjoy it. Coming away from Anfield and winning as an Everton player in 1999 – the last time Everton have won there – it's always a difficult place to go and when it goes against you, it's even worse.'

Things did not get much better for City in the death throes of Shinawatra's regime. Sasin Monvoisin, one of his appointed directors, had observed Liverpool's players warming down following their final home game of the season and inquired, 'Are they going to play another match now?' That appalling lack of footballing knowledge became further evident when Eriksson was forced to take his squad on an end-of-season tour of Asia that incorporated his paymaster's former Thai fiefdom, where he was definitely told that the sack was imminent. Mark Hughes's arrival as his replacement was proof of a clique beginning to form at the City of Manchester Stadium with Kia Joorabchian. The super-agent had previously brokered Javier Mascherano's £18.6m move to Liverpool from West Ham United in January 2007 and played a key role as a known associate of Shinawatra. The Blues still spent north of £30m at the start of the summer transfer window, which included the return of Shaun Wright-Phillips from Chelsea, but their owner's inability to negotiate an unfreezing of the vast financial resources in his homeland still left them facing an existential threat.

At the height of the crisis, ex-chairman John Wardle had lent his beloved club £2m several times over just to cover monthly staff wages. The likelihood of Shinawatra losing his grip on power by failing the Premier League's fit-and-proper-person test only added to the uncertainty, despite the flawed process waving through Hicks and Gillett's debt-ridden Liverpool takeover.

City's 2008/09 season began in similarly farcical circumstances as the return leg of their UEFA Cup qualifier with Faroe Islands side EB Streymur on 31 July had to be moved to Barnsley's Oakwell home after the Eastlands pitch had to be resurfaced due to damage caused by a Bon Jovi concert held over the summer. A month later Shinawatra was looking for an out, both from his personally cultivated City nightmare and the Thai authorities, having skipped bail for corruption charges after attending the Olympics opening ceremony in Beijing. His prayers for the former were finally answered when a £210m buyout was agreed with the Abu Dhabi United Group on 1 September.

The deal had been brokered by Amanda Staveley, a former model who once dated Prince Andrew and was now an eminent financier with strong connections to investors in the Middle East. Graeme Souness told Sky Sports in May 2020 that she had revealed to him during a chance meeting in a Dubai restaurant that City's new owners had previously attempted to stage a buyout of Liverpool but that 'Gillett and Hicks were so difficult to deal with, they just walked away in the end'. Links between Anfield and Staveley did exist at the time, but it was Dubai International

Capital who had lodged a series of failed attempts to win control in the previous two years rather than their Abu Dhabi peers. Personnel details of City's takeover remained sketchy, with Sulaiman Al Fahim credited as the unofficial public face after making several media appearances in its direct aftermath.

A precondition for the deal was that a marquee signing had to be sourced by the outgoing hierarchy in the limited time remaining before the transfer window closed. Heated conference calls between Pairoj Piempongsant, Shinawatra's right-hand man, and Paul Aldridge, the club's new chief operating officer, led to a £70m offer mistakenly being tabled for Barcelona forward Lionel Messi. Other ambitious names entered the equation as deadline day progressed, with talk of hijacking Manchester United's pursuit of Tottenham Hotspur striker Dimitar Berbatov with a £32m bid. The *Daily Telegraph* reported that Liverpool had also been sounded out over a £45m move for Fernando Torres. City left-back Michael Ball remembers how the dressing room cynicism borne from Shinawatra's shambolic 12-month ownership quickly eroded as the list of high-profile targets grew.

'At the time I think the majority of the players were thinking, "Oh here we go again,"' he says. 'Shinawatra came in and said he wanted to build developments of Manchester City all around the world, starting in America, China, Thailand, Australia and developing Manchester City as a brand. So when the new owners came in and took over, they were saying the same thing about investing in the team and we're going, "Well, we've heard all this before."

'We knew they had a lot of wealth behind them and more than what we had previously, but it was the same sort of sell to the players. Probably the majority of them were sick of hearing it and probably didn't believe what they were saying. As a player, you're hoping these are going to be the right owners and are going to kick-start the challenge for trophies and start challenging the best clubs in the world. That's what they're saying they want to do, but can they do it? Have they got the knowledge and know-how to actually do that? Shinawatra had the money but he made reckless decisions and that sort of cost us as a team and as a club. So it was a sort of "here we go again" from the players and all we had to do was sort of just concentrate to see who they brought to the club. Straight away there was talk of big players coming in and you're thinking, "These are serious."'

Robinho became the statement signing that the new City board had desired, joining from Real Madrid for a British transfer record of £32.5m as City beat off competition from Premier League rivals Chelsea. More stellar players were touted to join the Brazilian forward with Al Fahim later claiming that Torres and Liverpool team-mate Steven Gerrard remained high on the transfer wish list of the club's new ownership alongside United talisman Cristiano Ronaldo and Arsenal's Cesc Fábregas. Al Fahim was later pulled from active involvement over concerns that his continual interview boasts were undermining the aims of the Abu Dhabi operation, headed up by its country's future deputy prime minister Sheikh Mansour bin Zayed Al Nahyan. But Ball believes signs of City's renewed ambition were already becoming clear with the interest in Gerrard, a fellow Scouser, and several other high-profile names at the time, including AC Milan's Ballon d'Or winner Kaka.

'It's hard to prise top players from the top teams at the best of times, especially if you're not in the Champions League and fighting as title contenders,' he says. 'It's difficult to entice players unless they're sold the dream and sold what they're trying to do, and the players believe in it. They knew they had to overspend on transfers and wages to bring the players who did sign to the club but the ones who did, they got sold the dream and they got it. Gareth Barry had a few options to go to and he chose Man City, who weren't Champions League [at the time], but he helped them, grew with them and ended up winning the title with them so it worked out the best situation for Gareth and Man City. City knew that but they had the dream to go for the best. They were after Kaka, John Terry and Stevie so they were willing to go for it. They were willing to pay for it. Whether the players signed, that's out of their control.'

Barry had proved a particularly sore point for Benitez in the summer 2008 window. The spendthrift nature of Liverpool's hierarchy meant that the Spaniard would need to sacrifice Xabi Alonso to accommodate the Aston Villa midfielder's arrival, having already sourced Robbie Keane for £19m from Tottenham, a move which would be reversed just six months later for £3m less. Anfield's unimpressed support let their manager know in no uncertain terms their feelings on the subject during a pre-season friendly with Lazio when chants of 'you can stick your Gareth Barry up your arse' were repeatedly aired. Juventus and Arsenal emerged as forerunners for the Spain international, who enjoyed a starring role in his country's Euro 2008 triumph, but both clubs refused to meet his £18m asking price. City's newly accumulated wealth still drew a warning from Benitez that it would not automatically ensure success.

'I think that you cannot guarantee anything just spending money,' he said. 'Chelsea, for two years, they won the title spending big, big money. But after, it was United spending big money. If we talk about [just] money, maybe City will win the title this year. I think it's important to know that we have to do the right things as a club and it's not just a question of money. If you have more money, it's always easier but if you don't have too much money it's just to do your job as well as you can.'

As the credit crunch developed into a full-blown recession, Liverpool started to feel the pinch of Hicks and Gillett's financial misdeeds. Speculation abounded over several of the club's prized assets, including Torres, becoming collateral damage, with City widely tipped to move for the striker, a notion which Benitez shot down on the eve of the trip to Eastlands on 5 October by declaring him 'unbuyable'. He also cast doubt on the hosts' ability to develop into genuine title contenders, with his own team keeping pace with Chelsea at the Premier League's summit. 'I don't know when they can become genuine title contenders,' he said. 'They are a good team with good players and a good manager, so they can be top of the table, but there are other teams that have spent big money, like Aston Villa. But you must realise how hard the Premier League is to win. Every year you hear about possible challengers, from Aston Villa, Newcastle, West Ham. Now it is City. We shall see.'

When the teams stepped out on an unseasonably sun-soaked October afternoon at the City of Manchester Stadium, it was Hughes's side who struck first. Alonso helped on Wright-Phillips's cross as the ball ricocheted off him and reached Robinho. Another fortuitous bounce allowed Robinho to cut back to Stephen Ireland for a volley which flew into the South Stand's net. Shortly before half-time, City's lead was doubled when Albert Riera fouled Wright-Phillips on the edge of Liverpool's box. The winger had joined the visitors in an £8m move from RCD Espanyol but was swiftly reminded of the loan spell on his former stomping ground two seasons earlier with taunts of 'City reject' accompanying his infraction. From the set piece, Javier Garrido's curling effort beat Pepe Reina to put the Blues two goals clear at the interval. Liverpool's onslaught in the second half began early with a reducer arriving just ten minutes after the restart when Álvaro Arbeloa allowed Javier Mascherano's pass to run through for Gerrard. The right-back's foresight was rewarded with a pass into his path before sending the ball through the legs of Garrido into the far post for Torres to slide home.

Pablo Zabaleta would play a key role in turning the game's tide as his two-footed lunge took down Alonso at ankle-height and earned the Argentine an instant red card from referee Peter Walton. Six minutes later, Gerrard's corner picked out an unmarked Torres to get ahead of Joe Hart and head home for Liverpool's equaliser and 1,000th Premier League goal. Hughes responded to the setback by hooking his entire Brazilian front line of Robinho, Jo and Elano all within 15 minutes of each other. City's counter-attacking threat still remained as Gerrard drifted into a deep-lying role, practically partnering centre-back and fellow academy graduate Jamie Carragher. The Reds captain's quarterback position eventually led to a stoppage-time winner with a pass that released Yossi Benayoun down the hosts' right before a pull-back to Torres was deflected off Richard Dunne into the path of Kuyt to stab home in front of the travelling supporters.

Liverpool's best start in the league for 12 years had allowed them to remain hot on Chelsea's heels in the early stages of the title race while City slipped to 11th after a third defeat in four matches, prompting Hughes to admit that he would need to make fresh reinforcements in January to stand a fighting chance of Champions League qualification.

With the Abu Dhabi United Group's takeover now ratified, stories appeared linking several names but only one drew a public denial from the club. On 10 October, Spanish newspaper *Marca* claimed that City had approached Torres with a 'double your money' offer worth £200,000 weekly to join their ranks. The Madrid-based newspaper's report was strewn with inaccuracies, including the fact that the Euro 2008 winner's contract at Anfield was due to expire in 2010, despite only signing a new six-year deal in July. Eastlands officials still felt it necessary to issue a definitive statement through a club spokesman: 'At no time has any Manchester City official, or anybody representing the club, contacted Fernando Torres, his representatives or Liverpool Football Club.'

City did, however, have their eye on a one-time Anfield favourite in the form of Craig Bellamy and clinched his return to the north-west on a £14m deal in a January window that also saw Nigel de Jong, Wayne Bridge and Shay Given all move to east Manchester. The Wales international's latest appearance against his former club on 22 February 2009 came as Liverpool looked to overtake Manchester United in the battle for the Premier League title. Sir Alex Ferguson had got a rise out of Benitez with the Spaniard's infamous 'facts' press conference a month earlier which coincided with the Reds subsequently falling behind in the race before welcoming a side whose own poor form on the road had produced just one win in their previous 12 outings. Bellamy proved how misleading statistics can be as he drew first blood against his old club. Already coping with Gerrard's loss through a hamstring injury, Liverpool's Lucas Leiva was held off by Vincent Kompany in the penalty area before teeing up the striker for a swivelling effort which took a deflection off Arbeloa as it flew into the net. Twelve minutes from time, a floated Benayoun cross found Torres, who mishit but found an on-running Kuyt for a close-range finish to mirror the one he had scored in the corresponding fixture.

Liverpool's seven-point shortfall effectively killed off their title hopes, but Benitez refused to throw in the towel and pointed to their upcoming trip to Middlesbrough as a must-win fixture. A bizarre afternoon at the Riverside saw Martin Skrtel deployed in an unfamiliar right-back role as the visitors slumped to a 2-0 reversal. The Slovakian's positional switch barely constituted a surreal development at a time when the civil war between Tom Hicks, George Gillett and the club itself had been escalated to new levels. Hicks had publicly demanded the resignation of chief executive Rick Parry, insensitively branding his tenure 'a disaster' during a broadcast interview recorded in the week of the 20th anniversary of Hillsborough. Rumblings about Benitez's own future gained traction as he refused to sign a new long-term contract as his existing deal ticked into its final 18 months. A new five-year deal was eventually agreed in mid-March, by which point his side were trailing United by the same four-point margin that ultimately denied them the title.

Parry's position was later filled by Christian Purslow, the co-founder of private equity firm MidOcean Partners and an Anfield season ticket holder who previously advised Steve Morgan during his unsuccessful 2004 takeover. A year earlier, Hicks had approached City chief Alistair Mackintosh with the proposal of taking over from his opposite number. Just days after the Texan's power play, Thaksin Shinawatra jettisoned Mackintosh from Eastlands' corridors of power for questioning his wisdom in sacking Sven-Göran Eriksson. Purslow's appointment came at a time when Benitez's battle with the boardroom continued into the summer months as he revisited the pursuit of Gareth Barry. This time, however, Liverpool would not be running unopposed for his signature. Benitez tabled a £7m offer to Aston Villa, less than half the amount of the £15m bid which had been rejected by the Midlanders a year earlier, and returned with a fractionally improved yet still meagre figure of £8m. It was at this point that Villa officials informed him that Manchester City had already met their current £12m valuation for the player and were holding talks. Barry became the first signing in an army of new arrivals at Eastlands, the stand-out being Carlos Tevez's shock move from Old Trafford on a third-party ownership technicality.

City heralded the Argentine's capture by erecting posters of him throughout their home city in an outstretched arm pose in front of the slogan 'Welcome to Manchester'. It was a stunt which would have gained the late Peter Swales's approval and provoked an outraged response from Ferguson, who had been rendered powerless in the deal. Fury emanated from Merseyside, too, as Benitez triggered a war of words with Barry by insinuating on 9 July that the player's decision to spurn Liverpool's renewed overtures had been driven by financial incentives.

'In this market, money is not the main thing because everyone at this level earns big money. If it's just for money sometimes you make mistakes, like Barry,' he said. 'I won't say too much but that was clearly for the money, 100 per cent. It is not a bad thing to miss out on him.' Eight days later, the England international responded to Benitez's jibes, branding them 'a bit disrespectful', and set the record straight about his decision-making process, with events in the previous 12 months cited as a far greater bearing.

'The difference was that City made me feel wanted,' he revealed. 'Liverpool had a chance to buy me last season but failed to pay the money, and only found it this year when they knew someone else had reached an agreement. There was a feeling of being let down. Excuses were made about things going on behind the scenes and in the boardroom, but I came out of it looking like a bad person. It took a long time for me to get back into the squad at Villa afterwards. It was tough to deal with. That's why there's nothing better than a club making you feel wanted and getting a deal done in days. It's not about money, it's about the chance to be part of something big from the very beginning at a club who really want you.'

Barry later admitted, in January 2012, that hearing the derogatory chants aimed at him by Liverpool fans while watching the Lazio friendly on television had been among the contributing factors in his eventual decision to move to Eastlands. 'I was at home, but I could just hear it vaguely. That might have got into my head a little bit,' he said. 'Liverpool were still interested when I decided to join City. I thought about it really hard, but I felt City were on the up, whereas Liverpool were maybe finding it a bit tougher than City.'

Benitez's failed 12-month pursuit of the player resulted in him firing a warning to the Anfield hierarchy that losing out on another transfer target to City would send out a statement that their well-heeled rivals, who had finished tenth in the previous season, were in the box seat for the league's final Champions League qualification place over their own club, which was increasingly on the wane. The Reds manager counted the cost of chasing Barry by seeing Xabi Alonso join Real Madrid in a £30m switch on the back of a landmark campaign for the playmaker. Roma midfielder Alberto Aquilani arrived for £17.1m but injury problems and a deficient talent to the man he had been tasked with replacing rendered the move doomed at its outset. Efforts to fill the void of Álvaro Arbeloa's own departure to the Bernabéu saw Benitez go all-out for Portsmouth right-back Glen Johnson, beating Chelsea with a £17.5m deal that elevated the defender to a £100,000-per-week contract. Despite the high fee reported, Liverpool had paid a reduced figure owing to the south coast club's outstanding payments on Peter Crouch's £10m move to Fratton Park a year prior.

Injury ensured Johnson played no part in Liverpool's 22 November encounter with a City team that had a place among the Continental elite high on their list of priorities. Mark Hughes was fully aware that the hosts' track record gave them an advantage but remained confident of setting down their own marker. 'We're going to Anfield in a good frame of mind,' he said. 'Liverpool have the confidence of knowing they have the ability and history of getting into the top four. They are expected to be successful.

That expectation has been there for decades and they live with that on a daily basis. But if you can get a foothold on the game at Anfield, you can sense a bit of anxiety in the team that filters through to the crowd.' His side held firm until the 50th minute, when Martin Skrtel outwitted Emmanuel Adebayor to turn a Steven Gerrard corner home. Roles were reversed little more than ten minutes later as the Liverpool defender not only conceded the corner from which his City counterpart equalised but also failed to beat him at the set piece in front of The Kop.

Tevez's introduction on his centenary Premier League appearance offered the visitors a renewed attacking impetus and acted as a catalyst for them taking a shock lead when he released Shaun Wright-Phillips, who turned Sotirios Kyrgiakos before setting up Stephen Ireland to strike. Virtually from the kick-off, City's defence dropped off and allowed Yossi Benayoun to earn a point by pouncing on a deflected cross from David Ngog which had eluded everyone inside the six-yard box.

Hughes's frustration at surrendering two points in the space of 60 seconds was barely masked by a reflection on the strides taken in recent months. 'We felt we would have seen the game out quite comfortably had we defended the second goal properly,' he conceded. 'But we have come to Anfield, and we are disappointed with a draw. Previous City sides would have been delighted with that. Maybe that shows how far we have come.' His efforts were clearly not considered sufficient as evidenced by his sacking a month later. On 19 December, just two hours after overseeing a 4-3 win against Sunderland, Hughes officially became persona non grata at the City of Manchester Stadium.

Roberto Mancini's appointment in place of the Welshman drew widespread criticism. Confirmation of the former Inter Milan manager's arrival had broken almost simultaneously with the news of his predecessor's sacking. City's unctuous chief executive Garry Cook attempted to quell the fall-out by speculating days later that Mancini had previously been approached by Liverpool about the prospect of replacing Benitez. 'It is naïve to think that clubs are not looking at their options. Of course they are,' he said. 'Do we think that Liverpool just talked to Klinsmann? I am sure that they spoke to others and I have no doubt that Roberto Mancini was one of them.'

The claims drew a furious response behind the scenes at Anfield, where it was perceived as an attempt to use Tom Hicks and George Gillett's failing ownership as a smokescreen for City's decision to sack Hughes despite no other managers emerging as potential suitors at the time of their late 2007 interest in Klinsmann. Mancini himself also refuted the suggestion. 'This is false –Liverpool never contacted me,' he insisted. 'Rafa is a good manager, so no, absolutely they haven't contacted me.'

Compliments from across the M62 became Benitez's sole crutch in a bleak midwinter where Liverpool had already been eliminated from the Champions League at its group stage and risked missing out on the following season's competition by sitting in seventh by Christmas. The Spaniard's mistake of declaring 'I guarantee we will finish in the top four' in a pre-match press conference internalised the heat on him from sections of the Anfield stands as well as at boardroom level. Ongoing fears over several of the club's talismans being sold to the highest bidder by their unscrupulous owners led to dubious quotes being attributed to Mancini by *The Sun* on 31 December that raised the possibility of City staging a transfer raid. 'If they put Steven Gerrard, Javier Mascherano and Fernando Torres on the market, City will be interested,' he allegedly said. 'We at City will do everything possible to prevent Liverpool from finishing fourth.' Given *The Sun*'s track record on Merseyside, where it remains universally boycotted, the purported comments did not even register locally but Xabi Alonso's exit had allowed such idle tittle-tattle to gain credence elsewhere.

At the start of the new decade, the mood within Anfield had taken a turn for the worse. One official from that period goes as far as labelling it 'toxic'. Hicks's son, Tom Jnr, had resigned from the board in disgrace after an e-mail exchange over the lack of support being afforded to Benitez in the transfer market led to him telling a Liverpool supporter, 'Blow me, fuck face.' Mass protests against the remaining American hierarchy became a regular feature of Liverpool's matchday experience as Champions League qualification remained attainable. Away from the battleground of L4, Benitez's side faced a showdown with new top four rivals City on 21 February which brought their contrasting financial situations into sharp focus.

Dirk Kuyt's pre-match comments about Mancini's well-heeled team, which had just added Patrick Vieira and Adam Johnson to its ranks, added a fresh layer of acrimony to proceedings as the forward told Sunday newspaper journalists, 'I would always go for Liverpool before City's money. The history of Liverpool is much, much bigger. It is very difficult to buy the history of Liverpool. Every now and again you see a Manchester City or, a few years ago, Chelsea – clubs doing things like this. It happens. But it's not the same when a club just throws money at it.' Many of the 47,203 inside Eastlands felt like their own money and time had been wasted on a goalless draw devoid of spirit to the point that even a chorus of boos which greeted the final whistle was decidedly half-hearted.

A month later, Iceland's Eyjafjallajokull volcano erupted and brought European airspace to a literal standstill as a cloud of ash covered the continent. But events in Scandinavia took a backseat to the smouldering row between City and Liverpool on 22 April after Mancini opened himself up to the prospect of a move for Fernando Torres. Unlike the quotes that appeared in *The Sun* four months earlier, there was no room for ambiguity in the Italian's latest words. 'We are a top team and I think all the top teams are interested in Torres but sometimes it depends on the player because they want to play in the Champions League,' he said. 'If we don't get into the fourth position, I think it will be difficult.'

The City manager further expanded on his interest in the Liverpool striker, saying, 'For me, he is with Carlos [Tevez], [Wayne] Rooney, [Lionel] Messi, [Zlatan] Ibrahimovic, [Cristiano] Ronaldo as the best in Europe. Fernando is a fantastic striker; all the teams in Europe would like him.' Benitez gave his counterpart the short shrift when the comments were brought up ahead of Liverpool's Europa League semi-final meeting with Atlético Madrid. 'There are some things you cannot change in football,' he said. 'I was not happy about [what Mancini said] but when you talk to Fernando, I think he is happy and so hopefully everything will be okay … I try not to talk about players at other clubs because I want to focus on the games we have.'

Results could not save Benitez from his fate and his declaration of a top four 'guarantee' returned to haunt him as Liverpool finished seventh, two places and four points behind City. He left behind a club teetering on the verge of financial collapse after the Royal Bank of Scotland grew tired of the boardroom shenanigans and called in the £237m loan that had facilitated Hicks and Gillett's leveraged buyout. The previous search for investment was upgraded into a full sale with British Airways chairman Martin Broughton installed to oversee the process. Efforts to move on the Americans went hand in hand with appointing Benitez's successor. Former City manager Sven-Goran Eriksson, now in charge of the Ivory Coast, threw his hat into the ring by declaring, 'I have been a Liverpool fan all my life … I didn't feel it was right to mention it when I was in England.' His newly stated allegiances failed to curry favour as the job went to Roy Hodgson.

Guiding Fulham to the previous season's Europa League Final failed to mask the underwhelming nature of the 62-year-old's ascension to the Anfield hot seat. He was the same age that Joe Fagan had become Liverpool's oldest managerial appointment in 1983 but shared nothing else in common with the late Boot Room stalwart. His 35-year spell in coaching had been varied, with spells at both club and international level, but a brief stint with Inter Milan in the mid-1990s was the height of his football CV. A meek persona also appeared a poor fit for a club whose name still carried gravitas throughout world football, in spite of its recent pitfalls. Players who had previously run through brick walls for Benitez, like Fernando Torres, were now wondering whether their future should lie elsewhere.

City's interest in Torres had already established with Mancini's April remarks and the Italian reaffirmed his desire to bring the new World Cup winner to Eastlands on 26 July. 'Torres is one of the best strikers in Europe and is already playing in the Premier League for three years and knows it very well,' he said. 'But it depends on his situation – his price and whether he wants to come. There are two or three strikers that we could go for, but it is the same situation as it is with James Milner. First there is the price and then it depends if the players want to change team.'

Torres clearly possessed the appetite for a move away from Merseyside after being worn down by Hicks and Gillett's catalogue of false promises over the previous three years. City's signing of his international team-mate David Silva from Valencia in a summer where their transfer spending comfortably surpassed £100m made them a more enticing prospect than his debt-laden current employers. Hodgson's propensity to put his foot in it during what would be the shortest reign of any Reds manager, lasting just six months and one week, laid bare the uncertainty over Torres's immediate future by publicly disclosing that the striker had a 'beef' with the hierarchy before resignedly adding, 'If he has problems with the club for things in the past, it is difficult for me to dismiss that.' Although he chose to stick around in the short term, the 26-year-old often cut an isolated and at times disinterested figure on the pitch during his final appearances in a red shirt.

One such outing came just two games into the new Premier League season against Manchester City, before which several Liverpool players went to great lengths to emphasise superiority over their hosts. Dirk Kuyt pointed to his club's timeless ability to draw on an avid global following as a key factor, saying, 'It doesn't matter where you are in the world, everyone knows Liverpool. You can't say the same at the moment about Manchester City.' His new team-mate Christian Poulsen echoed the view that Eastlands revolution was a pale imitation to English football's old order. 'You can't compare their history with Liverpool or Manchester United,' he said. 'In Denmark, Liverpool is number one and I am sure it is the same in other places.' Higher up the Anfield food chain, the view of City was far less diplomatic. 'It makes you wonder why the Abu Dhabi owners bought Manchester City rather than wait to buy Liverpool,' an unnamed senior figure told the *Mail on Sunday.* 'If they had spent the £1bn on Liverpool, they would be sitting back now with the best team in the world. When you look at the two clubs, it's King Kong versus Mickey Mouse.'

That pointed analogy proved evocative when the teams met on 23 August 2010 as Sheikh Mansour received a hero's welcome when he stood in the City of Manchester Stadium's directors' box ahead of his first live game since becoming the club's owner two years earlier. His Liverpool counterparts, meanwhile, chose to remain thousands of miles away, going door-to-door to financial institutions in a desperate attempt to remortgage the club. Another conspicuous absence for the visitors was Javier Mascherano, who had been omitted from their 18-man squad with Barcelona's negotiations for him stalling. The want-away midfielder's loss was keenly felt as Lucas Leiva lost out in a duel with Yaya Touré, which culminated in Gareth Barry haunting his one-time admirers with a low effort that Pepe Reina failed to keep out. Another simple finish would leave Liverpool's besieged goalkeeper grasping at air early in the second half when, on 52 minutes, Micah Richards rose above Daniel Agger to convert James Milner's corner. Insult was added to injury less than a quarter of an hour on after Adam Johnson was upended by Martin Skrtel in the penalty area.

Players from both sides confronted each other about the decision; Steven Gerrard pointed the finger at Milner while Jamie Carragher took Johnson to task for reminding referee Phil Dowd that Skrtel was eligible for a second booking. From the spot, Carlos Tevez completed a win which gave rise to premature talk of City challenging for the Premier League title. Home fans responded by gleefully chanting Rafael Benitez's name to remind their north-west rivals of what had been lost in parting with the Spaniard. A 73-year record had also been surrendered as Liverpool suffered their heaviest defeat at the hands of the Blues since a 5-1 drubbing in March 1937. Hodgson attempted to defend Mascherano's omission by insisting he was 'not in the right frame of mind' for the game. Within five days of the Eastlands humbling, the Argentina international's brain fog had been cleared in the form of a £17.25m move to the Camp Nou. Less than two months on, his former team-mates were still trying to wrap their heads around how their manager had not only dragged Liverpool into an early relegation battle but was also talking up them finishing the season there.

Greater threats than Hodgson's middling mentality were posed to the Reds as the battle to rid itself of Hicks and Gillett reached its endgame. Desperation reeked from the Americans as they attempted to cling to what little power remained by sacking its Merseyside-based board members when two legitimate offers were under consideration. On 5 October, a delegation of club officials travelled to headquarters of law firm Slaughter and May in London in efforts to finalise a proposed takeover. Singaporean billionare Peter Lim appeared the forerunner with his offer edging out that of New England Sports Ventures (NESV), a sports investment firm who boasted the Boston Red Sox baseball team, cable TV channel New England Sports Network and NASCAR outfit Fenway Roush Racing in its portfolio.

But Lim's major error was that he was not personally in the UK to conclude negotiations, which were a strict condition of any sale. In separate rooms, his legal representatives and NESV jostled for position to become preferred bidders. The following morning, a club statement announced its sale to the consortium led by John W. Henry. Hicks and Gillett stalled the £300m deal by immediately filing a temporary restraining order which was granted by a Texas court. Nine days later, with the prospect of administration and an automatic nine-point deduction just hours away, the High Court lifted the restriction and cleared NESV to complete their takeover.

Henry was quick to warn that the group, which was rebranded Fenway Sports Group (FSG) in March 2011, would not be following Manchester City's approach to governance by opening a response to questions in a media briefing with the words, 'I don't have "Sheikh" in front of my name.' His first meeting with Liverpool's nouveau riche rivals on 11 April 2011 came in very different circumstances to the humiliation that his acquisition had suffered earlier in the season.

Kenny Dalglish had replaced Hodgson in the dugout, exactly 20 years after quitting the role, and presided over a changing of the guard. A fading Fernando Torres had been shipped off to Chelsea for £50m and paved the way for the signings of Luis Suarez and Andy Carroll. Expectations over Carroll's arrival from Newcastle United were heightened by becoming the most expensive British player at £35m and a two-month delay for his debut owing to a pre-existing injury. The ponytailed striker's start to life at Anfield suggested the wait had not been worthwhile after failing to score in his opening five appearances.

Roberto Mancini faced similar issues as City headed to Merseyside with designs of reclaiming third place in the Premier League and a first domestic double over their hosts since 1937. There was also the small matter of preparing for an FA Cup semi-final clash with Manchester United the following weekend. Dalglish empathised with his opposite number's plight, having faced scrutiny himself while managing Blackburn Rovers to the title in the mid-1990s. 'It's not his fault that Manchester City have wealthy owners and are prepared to spend money,' insisted the Scot. 'He will be judged on results and that is the only way you can be judged. There is no guarantee of instant success just because he has money at his disposal. There is nobody anywhere who has won a trophy without having had some money to spend. He might have more to spend than most people would expect, or most people would hope for, but along with that comes added pressure.' Omens for Wembley did not appear promising when Carroll dispossessed Carlos Tevez deep in his own half before Raul Meireles hoovered up the ball and drilled a shot which bobbled between Vincent Kompany's ankles and back into the marksman's path on the edge of the penalty area for a first-time strike into Joe Hart's bottom-right corner for his first Liverpool goal.

The innocuous 50-50 challenge which led to Carroll's opener, against the same opposition that he had closed his Newcastle account on Boxing Day of the previous year, carried repercussions for City as Tevez handed the captain's armband to Kompany and requested to be substituted with a hamstring injury which would rule him out of the clash with his former employers. Mancini's side were almost left counting the cost further when Adam Johnson was floored by a two-footed lunge by Fabio Aurelio that earned him a booking.

Aurelio was involved in Liverpool doubling their advantage when he broke into City's penalty area and fired a shot which Kompany thwarted with a sliding interception that fell for Dirk Kuyt on the opposite side to slot the ball past Hart into the same corner that Carroll had previously broke the deadlock. A minute later, Carroll struck again as he outmuscled Aleksandar Kolarov to meet Meireles's cross from the left to back-head the ball past Hart. The visitors' only meaningful effort came in the form of a powerful long-range effort by Yaya Touré which was punched clear by Pepe Reina. Mancini conceded after the game that his team 'only started to play after 20 minutes' and alluded to the 'mistake' of resting David Silva and Nigel de Jong in anticipation of the United clash.

City bounced back from their Anfield reversal by clinching a place in the FA Cup Final as Touré's strike proved enough to down Sir Alex Ferguson's side. A 35-year trophy drought was finally ended in the Wembley showpiece against Stoke City and complemented an achieved aim of sealing a Champions League place by finishing third.

Dalglish's best efforts to banish Liverpool's dismal first half of the campaign under Hodgson, where they had lurched between the relegation zones and mid-table, proved in vain as his side failed to qualify for European football for the first time in 12 seasons and ended 2010/11 in sixth. United's clinching of a 19th Premier League title saw them surpass Anfield's previous record haul. Painful as the feat was for Kopites, it paled in comparison to the previous three years of sheer hell that had completely altered the way many ardent supporters viewed their lifeblood. Now, at least, they could again enjoy what was happening on the pitch rather than pounding the pavements.

Boy on a Pedestal

IN THE afterlife of the club's turbulent first American ownership, Kenny Dalglish's homecoming had restored a semblance of normality to Liverpool. Fans heralded his move from the directors' box back to the touchline as an act which would take a sleeping giant back to the pinnacle of English football after a 21-year slumber.

Belief in a return to Anfield's pre-1990 hedonism grew with the emergence of Raheem Sterling. At the end of the previous year, Manchester City had been one of four Premier League clubs in the hunt for Sterling but a personal call from Dalglish, occupying a senior role in Liverpool's academy at the time, convinced the Queens Park Rangers prodigy that his destiny lay on Merseyside.

An initial £500,000 transfer was ratified on 27 February 2010, potentially rising to £2m through a series of performance-based targets. Liverpool sensed that they had mined a diamond when he was thrust into an under-18s game against Everton just days after arriving from west London and received an early and full-blooded introduction to a Merseyside derby courtesy of a hefty challenge. Watching on, Dalglish and academy director Frank McParland feared the clattering by Toffees left-back Luke Garbutt would take the wind out of the slight teenager. Instead, Sterling shook off the tackle with a smile and sought retribution on the upcoming left-back at his earliest opportunity in the game at Finch Farm, which the visitors won 4-3 with the winger contributing one of the goals.

When Sterling racked up five of the goals as Liverpool's under-18 side administered a 9-0 thrashing to Southend United in an FA Youth Cup tie on 14 February 2011, talk of another John Barnes in the making heightened. The parallels became inescapable; both were born in the Jamaican capital of Kingston and had moved to southern England as youngsters before showcasing their talents domestically. Unbeknownst to the pair, Sterling also would be forced to withstand the same racist taunts from the terraces that had previously been reserved for Barnes throughout the 1980s.

A much-anticipated senior bow also appeared to be in the offing as Dalglish included the prodigy in the club's travelling party for the opening leg of their Europa League last-16 tie with Sparta Prague, less than 48 hours after observing his Valentine's Day massacre at a sparsely populated Anfield. Sterling's call-up to the senior ranks may have come sooner but had to coincide with the half-term break of Rainhill High School, where many of the club's youngsters completed their education. Growing expectations around Sterling were harnessed by his omission from the matchday squad in the Czech Republic but would reach fever pitch a year later when Dalglish finally handed him a senior bow.

Before then, Liverpool's manager and new director of football Damien Comolli set about transforming the existing squad into one capable of vying for Champions League qualification with over £50m lavished on players, yet Craig Bellamy's surprise return on a free transfer from City proved the most impactful signing. The Wales international had spent the previous season away from the Etihad Stadium on loan with hometown club Cardiff City but his heart remained at Anfield. Bellamy left under a cloud in 2007 after setting about John Arne Riise with a golf club during a team bonding trip to the Algarve ahead of a Champions League knockout encounter with Barcelona, where the striker both scored the opener and assisted his stricken team-mate for a second goal. That fiery demenaour continued to burn when he joined City in 2009 and, was banished to his nation's capital over an alleged fall-out with Mancini. Now 32 and still with a year remaining on his current £90,000 per week deal, the Blues allowed him to fulfil a childhood ambition of playing under Dalglish while also taking a rare chance to redeem himself.

Bellamy's move came shortly after Liverpool had ascended to the Premier League's top spot for all of 24 hours, before his old club and Manchester United renewed hostilities in a season-long tussle. Tragically, his first clash with Mancini arrived on the day that it emerged Gary Speed had taken his own life. Dalglish's own experience with trauma following Hillsborough prompted him to stand down his distraught player after breaking news of the Wales manager's sudden passing just hours before the match. In his absence, City set about trying to extend an already commanding lead in the title race to seven points and succeeded just after the half-hour when Vincent Kompany broke free of Dirk Kuyt's shackles to shoulder a corner from David Silva into The Kop net. Barely a minute later, though, the visitors surrendered their lead in unfortunate fashion as Joleon Lescott tried to intercept a wayward shot from Charlie Adam but his outstretched foot diverted the ball away from Joe Hart's grasp and into the opposite corner of the goal. Hart continued to keep the score level with a series of impressive saves that thwarted Liverpool's blitzkrieg, something which became a regular pattern for goalkeepers visiting Anfield throughout the 2011/12 season.

But Mario Balotelli's introduction for Samir Nasri ensured City would only match the best start to a league season set by Liverpool's class of 1990/91 under Dalglish rather than beating it with a 100 per cent return from their opening 12 fixtures. The Italian striker pulled down Glen Johnson by his left arm before catching Skrtel with a flailing arm to earn a second booking. He headed down the tunnel but not before expressing his bewilderment to Mancini, who pointed to Johnson and Adam's remonstrations with referee Martin Atkinson as the reason for his compatriot's sending-off.

'I don't think it was a yellow card and I don't think the referee thought it was a yellow card,' he said post-match. 'My impression was the referee gave a free kick but didn't want to give a yellow. Then the Liverpool players went over saying, "Yellow card, yellow card." This is not correct. I'm disappointed with Mario because the first booking was a yellow card but not the second. Mario has to pay attention because there are many players who will try to provoke him.'

Dalglish hit back at the suggestions of his own players prejudicing the outcome. 'Balotelli got himself sent off,' he insisted. 'Sometimes you get yourself sent off. Sometimes if you look in the mirror, you get the answer. Sometimes he doesn't help himself and others and then maybe he doesn't get the leeway, but I don't think any of our boys influenced the referee in any way, shape or form.'

Influence was something Liverpool lacked as they meandered between fifth and seventh place in the league shortly before Luis Suarez was found guilty of racially abusing United defender Patrice Evra and hit with an eight-match suspension by the FA. The ban ruled the Uruguayan out of a triple-header with City, with the League Cup semi-final draw pitting the sides against each other. Hours before the first, a league meeting at the Etihad on 3 January 2012, Dalglish's side announced it would not be contesting the FA's punishment despite a staunch defence campaign fought by the club and its fans that Suarez's repeated use of the word 'negro' to Evra was actually a term of affection in the player's native South America.

Stewart Downing spurned Liverpool's best opening early in the first half when he started and finished a move which placed him in a one-on-one situation with Hart but a weak finish allowed his England team-mate to see off the effort. That profligacy proved costly on ten minutes when Sergio Agüero hit a swerving shot that slipped under Pepe Reina with the aid of a rain-lashed turf. Silva repeated his party piece from the Anfield encounter with a corner which found Touré for a header which struck the underside of the crossbar en route.

Recent history repeated itself as City were reduced to ten men, this time with Gareth Barry sent off for two cynical fouls on Jay Spearing and Daniel Agger. The midfielder sat out the remaining 17 minutes as Liverpool's humiliation was completed when Skrtel tripped Touré in the penalty area, causing Mancini to demand the Slovakian's dismissal by waving an imaginary card at fourth official Stuart Attwell, who rebuked the City manager for his act of gamesmanship. Milner sent Reina the wrong way from 12 yards to give the hosts a first win of the new calendar year. Mancini later apologised for the incident while Dalglish was deluged with questions about Liverpool's decision not to contest Suarez's suspension. His sharp responses would have appeared more in keeping eight days later when his side again travelled to the Etihad for the first leg of their latest League Cup encounter.

A returning Steven Gerrard imposed himself on proceedings with a distant drive that forced a sprawling early save from Hart at his left-hand post. From the ensuing series of corners, Kompany's stand-in Stefan Savić hacked down Agger with a challenge at chest height that forced Lee Mason to point to the penalty spot. One City fan attempted to distract Gerrard as he stepped up to face Hart by shining a green laser pen in his face which only added to his determination in squeezing the 13th-minute spot kick narrowly down Hart's right-hand side to give his side an upper hand in the tie.

In stoppage time, Johnson's flying challenge on Lescott led Mancini to condemn the full-back's hit as 'worse' than the one which had seen Kompany dismissed in an FA Cup third-round exit to Manchester United on the previous weekend. Speaking to TV reporters, Gerrard described the intervention as 'a clear winner of a tackle' and criticised what he believed to be the City manager's attempts to see his team-mate unfairly sent off. Midway through Mancini's huddle with radio broadcasters in the tunnel area, the Liverpool captain took him to task over the remarks.

'You say to the press,' said Gerrard.

'I say what I want,' retorted Mancini.

'Yeah, I know – you say to the press that Wayne Rooney tried to get Kompany sent off.'

'Yeah, yeah.'

'And you try to get Johnson sent off?'

'Yeah, yeah. I did. I did.'

Efforts by City's head of media Simon Heggie to steer the interview back on track prompted his manager to end the exchange with Gerrard by roaring almost unintelligibly, 'It wasn't the same tackle, this was worse!'

Mancini's excessive reaction reflected the growing pressure that had been instigated by Carlos Tevez fleeing to Argentina after refusing to emerge from the substitutes' bench in a Champions League group fixture at Bayern Munich. That unapproved return to his homeland was later compounded by Balotelli receiving a four-game ban for stamping on Tottenham Hotspur midfielder Scott Parker's head, leaving the Blues with Agüero and Edin Džeko as their only available strikers for the semi-final return leg. Dalglish, too, was feeling the heat in the dugout with just one win in their previous six Premier League matches ahead of the showdown with City signalling an abrupt end to his second Anfield honeymoon. Back-to-back cup ties with both Manchester clubs in the space of three days, with United travelling to Merseyside in the FA Cup's fourth round after their local rivals' visit, set up a season-defining week for the Liverpool manager.

Against City, Nigel de Jong's initial poor control of a square pass from Silva on the half-hour allowed the ball to run ahead of him and into the path of an advancing Gerrard, but the midfielder was able to recover and slide a curling 25-yard effort that put the visitors ahead on the night and level in the overall tie. That momentum lasted all of ten minutes, when Bellamy sent a cross into the penalty area which broke for Agger to strike; the defender's shot was blocked by Micah Richards's boot and deflected upward and on to his raised hands for a penalty. Gerrard stepped up to produce a carbon copy of his effort at the Etihad Stadium a week prior with another clinical spot kick down to Hart's right.

Early in the second half, City retook the lead in the match and racked up a priceless second away goal in the process as Džeko ghosted in at the far post to meet a low cross from Kolarov. But Bellamy's starring role against his old club ultimately settled the tie with 16 minutes remaining as he exchanged passes with Glen

Johnson before curling a shot past Hart to set up an emotive
League Cup Final meeting with Cardiff City on Liverpool's first
return to Wembley since 1996.

Mancini was in no mood to loiter at the scene of his side's
second League Cup semi-final defeat in three seasons and
attempted to make a swift exit by beginning his post-match
briefing before most reporters in attendance had made their way
down the stairs from the Main Stand's press box. Those who
managed to make it through the door just in time witnessed
the City manager raging against 'a sense of injustice' over the
penalty given against Richards, while his own players were denied
one when Charlie Adam had kicked Džeko from behind when
the game remained goalless. However, Bellamy's match-winning
heroics did not carry any added heartache for the man who had
set him adrift less than five months earlier. 'It doesn't make it
more difficult for me that Craig scored the winner. I am happy
for Craig,' he insisted. 'Of course I am disappointed we didn't
reach the final but I am happy for Craig. What difference does
it make if Bellamy scored or Gerrard scored?' Dalglish hailed the
veteran Welshman's display as 'unbelievable' and added the quip,
'If Manchester City have anyone else that they don't want they
know where we are.'

Those words would return to haunt the Liverpool boss in the
coming days after it emerged that an informal enquiry had been
made to Brian Marwood, City's director of football development,
shortly after the League Cup semi-final about a remarkable swap
bid for Carlos Tevez. Anfield officials were willing to take a £10m
hit on Andy Carroll just a year after he had arrived by offering
the striker in a swap deal for the exiled Argentine. Talks did
not progress beyond the initial telephone call to Marwood, who
rejected it out of hand. Mancini publicly insisted that he had
no knowledge of the incident aside from newspaper reportage.
Dalglish responded to questions about the headline-grabbing
proposal in a blunter fashion by challenging those responsible
for leaking news of the alleged approach to stand it up. 'We don't
need to get involved to justify what people have said. Ask them to

justify it, not us,' he snapped back. 'I am not talking about any specific incident but if you are going to do business in any way, shape or form in whatever life it's in, you don't disclose it until it's done, do you? As we've said before, and [Liverpool chairman] Tom Werner said, there's no point letting the facts interfere with a good story.'

Damned lies were far less damaging to Dalglish's latest Liverpool tenure than actual statistics. Reaching Wembley coincided with a reversal of his side's form from the first half of the season. Where they had won nine Premier League games and lost five prior to the second leg, the Reds finished the campaign with five wins and nine losses, with Wigan Athletic, West Bromwich Albion and Fulham all earning precious away wins at Anfield in that period. They were more fortuitous in the cup competitions, winning a first trophy in six years by taking the League Cup after defeating Cardiff City on penalties following a 2-2 draw. They also reached the FA Cup Final but were defeated by Chelsea. Despite avenging their London counterparts in a penultimate league fixture, the season ended on a particularly low note as a 1-0 defeat to Swansea City saw them finish eighth, with Everton claiming domestic superiority by virtue of sitting one position higher.

As Liverpool laboured at the Liberty Stadium, Manchester City were on the verge of making history. United had taken a seemingly unassailable eight-point lead in the title race with a month of the 2011/12 season remaining, only to see their local rivals obliterate it in five weeks, ably assisted by a returning Carlos Tevez. City had to either equal or better the Red Devils' result at Sunderland in their own finale with Queens Park Rangers to clinch a first championship in 44 years.

As stoppage time approached, the visitors held a shock 2-1 lead but, during four minutes of added time, Mancini's side struck twice, with Sergio Agüero's finish on 93 minutes and 23 seconds snatching the title away from Old Trafford on goal difference, helped largely by their 6-1 thrashing of Sir Alex Ferguson's side in October. City's joyous celebrations were in stark contrast to the dark mood on Merseyside when, after barely 12 months at the permanent helm, Liverpool's owners FSG sacked Dalglish and embarked on a lengthy search for his successor.

On 1 June, Brendan Rodgers was unveiled as the second-youngest managerial appointment in the club's history. The Northern Irishman's path to Merseyside had started as an academy director at Reading before he was invited to join Chelsea's youth setup under Jose Mourinho in 2004. Spells in senior management with Watford, Reading and latterly Swansea followed, and his time in Wales gained widespread acclaim for executing the 'tiki-taka' principles that had been the bedrock for both Barcelona and the Spanish national team in their recent period of unparalleled success. At 39, Rodgers was the same age that his predecessor Dalglish had been when he originally stood down from the Anfield hot seat. Still, his route to the top nearly encompassed a spell at Manchester City with Mancini courting him as a potential assistant manager, shortly before moving to the Liberty Stadium, which was hosting Premier League football within two years of his arrival. Rodgers's Anfield in-tray contained a reminder of that polite decline as the Premier League champions targeted Martin Skrtel and Daniel Agger in quick succession to provide back-up to Vincent Kompany and Joleon Lescott.

Mancini had identified Agger as a potential incoming some 18 months earlier, only for his poor injury record to lead to the signing of Stefan Savić instead. But with the Montenegrin's performances failing to inspire confidence, attention again shifted back to the Denmark international. City chief Brian Marwood contacted Liverpool's managing director Ian Ayre on 31 July to register his club's interest in Agger yet did not extend to a formal offer. More than a week later, the Reds rejected successive offers of £12m and £18m in the belief that the 26-year-old commanded a fee in excess of the £22m that the Blues had paid to lure Lescott away from Everton in 2009. Rodgers admitted that only 'a ridiculous offer' would force his hand on Agger.

The player himself appeared far from enamoured by the prospect of leaving Anfield, having returned for pre-season with the acronym of the club's anthem 'You'll Never Walk Alone' tattooed on his knuckles. 'I can't imagine playing for any other club in England but you never know, if the club think it's better to sell,' he admitted. 'I'd rather stay but that decision is not up to me at the moment,' he said. 'Liverpool can do a deal even though I have two years [left] on my contract, but I haven't changed my mind on the subject.'

Interest in Skrtel arrived at a time when talks over a new long-term deal had stalled, offering hope to City and his former club Zenit St Petersburg that he could be swayed into moving. In the week leading up to a clash with the reigning champions, the Slovakian penned a four-year contract that cushioned the blow of Liverpool's heaviest opening-day defeat in the top flight since 1937, a 3-0 reversal at West Bromwich Albion. The crushing nature of the result at The Hawthorns did little to shake Mancini's belief that his north-west rivals would be among City's biggest challengers for the Premier League. 'I think Liverpool will fight for the title this year,' he said. 'They have bought good players, they have a good manager, they change their style of play and I'm sure they will fight for the title.'

Rodgers's preparations for his domestic Anfield bow were captured for Fox Soccer's fly-on-the-wall series *Being: Liverpool*, marking the first time that camera crews had been handed unfettered access to the club's internal mechanisms.

Throughout filming, Raheem Sterling became a focal point after Rodgers had administered a dressing-down to him during Liverpool's pre-season tour of the United States for a perceived act of insubordination, warning that he would be 'on the first plane back' if it persisted. The winger's stock had risen exponentially since being handed a second-half debut by Dalglish during a 2-1 home loss to Wigan Athletic. An eager Anfield crowd had afforded Sterling a rare standing ovation before entering the fray and he offered glimpses of his obvious talent with a succession of surging runs that were heightened by supporters desperate to salvage something from the jaws of another embarrassing reversal. His every touch, no matter how far from goal, was greeted with palpable anticipation. Two further appearances from the bench that season did little to stifle the hype surrounding the teenager, who was handed his full first-team debut for City's visit on 26 August.

In the home dressing room, Steven Gerrard attempted to fire up his team-mates with a short and sharp rallying call. 'No one hiding out here,' he declared. 'Let's have belief. No risks, boys. Let's not overplay it. If it needs to go, it can go.' Rodgers took a more statesmanlike approach to his captain by insisting, 'Our league begins today. All I ask is two things: you go and play with passion, for the shirt, and you go and you play with energy. You have those two things, along with your talent, we will win the game. We must fight for our life and make sure here, at Anfield, we make this the most difficult place it can be this season.'

Liverpool suffered a setback in the opening minutes when midfielder Lucas Leiva picked up a thigh injury that would sideline him for the next three months and had to make way for Jonjo Shelvey. City's best chance after the Brazilian's departure came when Samir Nasri sent Carlos Tevez to the byeline, where he squeezed the ball past Pepe Reina and Martin Kelly but saw his effort hit the inside of the post before bouncing back out.

Skrtel later punished both slack defending and the visitors' failure to sign him with a well-timed run that eluded the watch of Aleksandar Kolarov and Pablo Zabaleta to power home Gerrard's corner on 34 minutes to put his side ahead at the interval, when Rodgers again singled out Sterling for constructive criticism after a series of take-ons that easily bypassed Kolo Touré. 'If you start dancing like that, you'll be dancing on the side with me,' he warned Liverpool's prodigy. 'You've been terrific. Don't start all that carry-on.'

Mancini waited until after the half-time break to enact City's first change, with Nasri making way for Jack Rodwell, a surprise £12m arrival from Everton in the close season, just before the hour to allow Yaya Touré to occupy a more offensive position upfield. Within four minutes, the tactic had paid off as Tevez shook off Sterling's warding threat to float a cross in from the right-hand side which Reina failed to collect and saw Kelly's leaden touch gift the ball to the Ivory Coast midfielder to pounce with a ruthless close-range finish.

Equilibrium proved short-lived as the circumstances which contributed to City's League Cup semi-final exit of the previous season resurfaced when Rodwell conceded a free kick in the 65th minute. A sliding challenge to block a long-range effort from Gerrard had struck the midfielder's knee and bounced up to his raised hand; a fate which befell Micah Richards at Anfield exactly seven months earlier. Luis Suarez's effort was swept in low and crept past Joe Hart. But another impactful substitution drew City level with ten minutes remaining as Skrtel attempted to outwit Edin Džeko by turning him and playing a weak back-pass which Tevez gleefully pounced on before rounding Reina and sending the ball into an empty Kop net.

Skrtel's misfortune stole the headlines yet Sterling's first full outing in English football hardly flew under the radar. Roy Hodgson's decision to include him in the England squad for their upcoming World Cup qualifier with Ukraine reflected the growing anticipation that surrounded the former Wembley resident. In a nod to future events, he had left the Anfield pitch wearing a City shirt after swapping his with Tevez.

Mancini's post-match assessment was spent pleading for his club's hierarchy to ensure they had the necessary additions to sustain a successful title defence. Liverpool had struck a blow to City's recruitment plans by poaching Dave Fallows and Barry Hunter, leading figures in their scouting department. The pair were placed on gardening leave and only allowed to move to Merseyside once the summer transfer window closed on 31 August. Julian Ward, Rob Newman and David Fernandez were all lined up to join their former colleagues in trading the Etihad Stadium for Anfield but the latter two reneged on agreements to stay with their current employers. Fallows, Hunter and Ward would all later be implicated in an alleged hacking of City's online player tracking database Scout 7 over an eight-month period until February 2013 by using Newman's login without permission.

Suspicions were aroused when the Reds had expressed a sudden interest in Real Zaragoza's midfield prospect Paolo Fernandes, who City later signed. Liverpool paid a £1m settlement fee which was made without admitting to any wrongdoing or taking liability for itself or its employees.

Fallows and Hunter's departures coincided with a shake-up of the Etihad's management operations as former Barcelona chiefs Ferran Soriano and Txiki Begiristain arrived as the club's new CEO and director of football respectively, within two months of each other. Invariably, talk of Pep Guardiola linking up with his former allies surfaced despite the Catalan coach recently embarking on a sabbatical after resigning from the Camp Nou. Mancini's efforts to strengthen his own position led to widespread newspaper reports on 15 November that suggested City were plotting a shock January move for Luis Suarez, with an underperforming Mario Balotelli expected to be sacrificed for his fellow maverick striker. The Uruguay international had recently signed a new four-year deal worth £120,000 per week and moreover was happy to remain with the club that had stood by him, for better and worse, through the previous season's racism row with Patrice Evra.

Rodgers shot down the suggestions that Liverpool would countenance any potential sale. 'There will be no bidding war, he's staying here,' he insisted. 'I don't know if City want him, you would have to ask Roberto Mancini that. But if we lose Luis then we have no strikers, so we can't afford to lose anyone.' The claims were met with a similar level of bemusement at the Etihad, where Mancini railed against his purported interest and reports of Guardiola's potential incoming. 'I don't know where these stories came from,' he said. 'For two weeks we talk about Monaco, Guardiola, now Suarez. We have a good team and we don't need to buy another player in January. We can't buy Suarez or another player because we have four strikers and Suarez plays for Liverpool.' Liverpool's chairman Tom Werner completed the collective hat-trick of denials by saying, 'We wouldn't even consider selling him – absolutely not. We made a long-term contract with him in the summer. Our intention is to strengthen but actions will speak louder than words.'

The £12m capture of Daniel Sturridge on 2 January 2013 attempted to send out a statement that Suarez was remaining at Anfield for the long haul and no longer toiling single-handed in attack. City's former striker returned to the north-west less than four years after he had left the Etihad disillusioned at a lack of playing time. The striker chose to run down his contract before joining Chelsea on a free transfer. His former club received an initial £3.5m when the move was brought before a tribunal the following year, by which point he had helped the Londoners to a Premier League and FA Cup double. That figure would eventually rise to £8.3m after he became an established England international, but injury problems had restricted the 23-year-old to just one start in seven league appearances at the end of his Stamford Bridge career.

A swift return to Sturridge's one-time stomping ground arrived just one month later as Rodgers sought a response from his players in the wake of their humiliating FA Cup fourth-round humiliation to League One outfit Oldham Athletic, led at the time by former Blues favourite Paul Dickov. Meanwhile City attempted to claw back a ten-point deficit in the title race and hunt down a Manchester United side enjoying one final flourish under Sir Alex Ferguson.

The champions broke the deadlock in fluid fashion when, on 23 minutes, Sergio Agüero turned away from Steven Gerrard to slip the ball into David Silva for a first-time pass which James Milner proceeded to pull across the six-yard box for Edin Džeko, who outsmarted Agger's sliding interception to slot home.

Sturridge's role as a returning villain in the eyes of City supporters was fulfilled on 29 minutes as he levelled in controversial circumstances after Agger clipped Džeko's heels in the build-up but saw play waved on by referee Anthony Taylor. Gerrard and Stewart Downing exchanged passes before setting up their new team-mate for a left-footed flyer that Joe Hart was unable to stop. A combination of Taylor's refusal to award a free kick and Liverpool neglecting to put the ball out of play, despite being under no obligations, saw Sturridge pelted with abuse as he refused to celebrate against the club where his professional career had started. Mancini raged at linesman Andrew Garrett for refusing to flag and was joined by City's assistant manager David Platt as well as Milner and Džeko himself, who was booked for dissent, in remonstrating with the official nearest the dugout. Chants of 'there's only one greedy bastard' later reverberated around Eastlands for Sturridge when he was substituted off in the game's final minute, having been booked earlier in the second half for going to ground far too readily after the slightest contact by Matija Nastasic in the penalty area.

Liverpool's inability to score against City in their previous three away league outings was officially consigned to the archives in the 74th minute as Gael Clichy cleared Jose Enrique's cross but only as far as Gerrard, who chested the ball down and launched a 30-yard rocket which beat Hart down to his right. The hosts' title defence built on sand was unravelling yet lived to fight another day thanks to an inspired moment from Agüero. As Gareth Barry dinked a ball down the Reds' left for the Argentine to chase, Pepe Reina suffered a rush of blood to the head and attempted to block him off just outside the penalty area. From an impossible angle, Agüero slipped the ball beyond the Spaniard and into an empty net to keep Mancini's side in with a feasible chance of repeating their previous season's heroics by hunting down United.

But Ferguson brought the curtain down on an unprecedented 27-year tenure at Old Trafford by silencing a club he glibly referred to as 'a noisy neighbour' and avenging the memorable swing of the pendulum on the final day of 2011/12 by coasting to the title with 11 points to spare. City's woes continued with an FA Cup Final defeat to a Wigan Athletic team just days from Premier League relegation.

Ferguson's departure triggered a summer of upheaval for English football, with a managerial merry-go-round that began with Everton's David Moyes becoming his anointed replacement. Ferguson had outlasted 15 City managers in over a quarter of a century at the helm and increased that count shortly before retiring when Mancini was sacked on 14 May, exactly a year since Agüero's title-winning moment.

In February, four days after denting City's reclamation bid, Jamie Carragher had announced his own retirement from football's highest level. A 16-year spell at the top had left him as Liverpool's second-highest appearance-maker and seen him win virtually every major honour available with the notable exception of the Premier League. Replacing the versatile defender's wealth of experience led Brendan Rodgers to move quickly to clinch a free transfer for City's out-of-contract stalwart Kolo Touré on 28 May.

Handling the problem of Luis Suarez proved far more difficult for the manager after his controversial marksman incurred another lengthy suspension, this time for ten matches, having bitten Chelsea defender Branislav Ivanovic. The Uruguayan later attempted to engineer a transfer to Arsenal, who lodged a bid of £40,000,001 bid in a lazy attempt to trigger the player's release clause. City moved on from Mancini with the appointment of a manager who was previously the object of both theirs and Liverpool's affections at different times. Manuel Pellegrini was first lined up for the Eastlands hot seat while at Villarreal in 2007 before Thaksin Shinawatra hired Sven-Göran Eriksson instead. He was also in the frame to succeed Rafael Benitez at Anfield in 2010, just weeks after his own tenure with Real Madrid had ended, and had flown to England to hold discussions with Kenny Dalglish but was overlooked for Roy Hodgson's brief tenure. Past links with Merseyside counted for little as the 59-year-old declared his belated arrival as 'the right moment with the right club'.

Pellegrini's Premier League entrance aligned with one of the players from his time at El Madrigal moving on as Rodgers brought Pepe Reina's eight-year spell at Anfield to an abrupt end. When the goalkeeper's hopes of a return to Barcelona failed to materialise, the Liverpool manager had already sanctioned a £9m signing of Sunderland shot-stopper Simon Mignolet as his direct replacement. Reina later joined Napoli on a season-long loan as the Belgian enjoyed instant acclaim with a late double save against Stoke City which helped his new club to a narrow win and to momentarily lead the Premier League table after 2013/14's opening fixture. Rodgers joked about his side being 'top of the league' before City mounted their own title bid 48 hours later in a similar fashion to the one that had culminated in glory just two seasons earlier. Likenesses to their opening gambit against Swansea City just two seasons prior were mirrored in another Monday night exhibition against Newcastle United with Sergio Agüero, Edin Džeko and David Silva again on the scoresheet alongside Yaya Touré in another 4-0 rout. A four-way fight for the title ensued with Arsenal and Chelsea joining the north-west pair in vying for top spot but it was Liverpool who sat in the driving seat at Christmas with City just one point behind in third ahead of their Boxing Day meeting.

Rodgers's side faced a daunting prospect on their latest visit to the Etihad Stadium, where the hosts had become the only club to maintain a 100 per cent record in the Premier League, but he remained bullish, insisting, 'We arrive there with no fear. We outplayed them last year, home and away. We had two draws and we should have won both games. But we will go there with every respect for them. I believe, with the squad they have, it is their title to lose.' Fearlessness was in equally plentiful stock across the M62 as Yaya Touré insisted that City would continue to play with freedom against their domestic challengers while also expressing admiration for them. 'I'm glad Liverpool are there,' he said. 'They have always been a big club, and maybe it is a surprise they haven't been up there for a few years. These clubs always return though, and that's what is happening at Liverpool. They have some good players – [Daniel] Sturridge, my brother Kolo, [Steven] Gerrard, [Luis] Suarez. People shouldn't be surprised to see them at the top. But I think this game will be watched by every fan of the Premier League around the world.'

Global audiences tuned in hoping to see Suarez extend his impressive league tally of 19 goals in 12 league outings since returning from the wilderness at Anfield. The Uruguayan was more provider than predator in east Manchester as he threaded a through ball for Raheem Sterling to round Joe Hart but the youngster was flagged offside before trickling the ball into an empty net. Five minutes later, Jordan Henderson's defence-splitting pass allowed Sterling to beat City's offside trap at a second attempt and sidestep England team-mate Hart once more before Philippe Coutinho followed up to his left.

City's fightback took hold in the 31st minute as Martin Skrtel failed to track his runner and allowed Vincent Kompany to power a downward header past Mignolet and Joe Allen's unsuccessful attempt to hook the ball clear on the goal line. In first-half added time, Liverpool's defence was further carved open by Samir Nasri and Jesús Navas before the latter teed up Álvaro Negredo for a shot on the edge of the area which Mignolet misjudged and brushed with a weak hand as it travelled towards his net. A search for an equaliser saw Suarez pick out Sterling with the goal at his mercy but the 19-year-old blazed over from close range as the Reds dropped down to fourth while City maintained their one-point push on new leaders Arsenal.

The top-of-the-table clash between the league's two highest-scoring teams had still managed to live up to its lofty expectations and led Kompany to describe it as 'the hardest game we have had at home so far' in a season where Pellegrini's players had already locked horns with Bayern Munich in the Champions League's group stage. Rodgers's own post-match thoughts were not dominated by the poor finishing or goalkeeping clanger which had seen his side leave Eastlands empty-handed as he took particular issue with the appointment of Bolton-based referee Lee Mason to oversee the game. 'I was surprised to see that the referee came from Greater Manchester,' he said. 'If it was City v Liverpool at Anfield I don't think we would get a referee from the Wirral. It was a horrendous performance from all the officials. Nothing went our way at all.' The FA hit the Ulsterman with an £8,000 fine and a warning about his future conduct. Liverpool's miserable festive period plunged fresh depths as they fell into fifth place three days after the trip to the Etihad with another 2-1 reversal on the road, this time at the hands of Chelsea.

Another 92 days would pass before the Anfield club again occupied the Premier League's top spot, by which time City had recruited Liverpool's highly respected former coach Rodolfo Borrell. Rafael Benitez had enlisted his compatriot in summer 2009 to help revamp the club's faltering academy structure after a 13-year spell with Barcelona during which he had nurtured the likes of Lionel Messi, Gerard Piqué and Cesc Fábregas. Borrell took charge of the Reds' under-18 and under-23 sides before being elevated to head of academy coaching. But a subsequent overhaul of the Reds' youth setup in November 2013 saw him heading up the departures from its Kirkby centre of excellence. The 41-year-old's appointment as City's new global technical director coincided with his new and former employers slugging it out at the business end of the title race. Pellegrini's side had clinched a first League Cup since 1976 but slipped to third place in the table and were four points off the top before a trip to Anfield on 13 April despite still possessing the fallback of two games in hand.

A tense afternoon began on a sour note as a minibus carrying members from the Eccles branch of the City Supporters' Club was ambushed while making its way to Anfield. A group of young men wearing tracksuits and baseball caps emerged from a side street close to the stadium and proceeded to pelt rocks at the vehicle. No injuries were reported but one of the windows smashed had been just inches away from where a teenager was sitting while the remaining 11 members of the travelling party, which included a 70-year-old woman, were left shaken by the ordeal. Hours later, Liverpool's players arrived to great fanfare as supporters welcomed their team coach by lining the route to the Shankly Gates with flags, banners and smoke bombs. Inside the dressing room, Rodgers continued a season-long tradition of delivering personal missives. He had personally spoken to the mothers of each Liverpool player to relay heartfelt messages which were read out before each game in the season; for City's visit, the manager revealed one written by Philippe Coutinho's mother.

Emotions continued to pour ahead of the final match played before the 25th anniversary of Hillsborough. City took out a

full-page advert in the matchday programme to pay tribute to
the fallen alongside a club delegation of Mike Summerbee, Tony
Book and Joe Corrigan handing over a floral tribute to Reds
counterparts Ian Rush and Kenny Dalglish. Before an impeccably
observed minute's silence, a banner bearing the legend 'YNWA
96' was held up in the visitors' section of the Anfield Road End.
Within six minutes of kick-off, Liverpool had made good on plans
to extend the chasm between the sides as Suarez turned away
from Martin Demichelis and shrugged off Gael Clichy's follow-
up challenge before finding Sterling with a pass that allowed
the winger to sneak in behind Kompany and then torment
the City captain by tying him in knots before slotting past Joe
Hart in front of The Kop. The lead was doubled 20 minutes
later as Martin Skrtel met Steven Gerrard's near-post corner to
replicate his headed effort against the same opposition in the
previous season.

Yaya Touré's groin injury midway through the first half added
to City's woes at the break but his side rallied to a fightback in
the second 45 courtesy of James Milner's introduction. The
industrious midfielder forced the opening on 57 minutes after
a neat one-two with Fernandinho allowed him to tee up David
Silva to fire past Mignolet. Five minutes later, Milner was also
the architect of City's equaliser as he combined with Samir Nasri
before Silva sent a low cross into the danger zone that was diverted
into the net by a combination of ricochets between Glen Johnson
and Mignolet. A winner-takes-all finish saw both sides throw
everything at a winner. A throw-in from Johnson deep in City's
half was back-headed by Clichy and then half-cleared by Kompany
into the path of Coutinho for a sweeping close-range finish.

Anfield erupted as the Brazilian ran towards the touchline
but Liverpool rode their luck towards a tenth consecutive Premier
League victory. In the second minute of stoppage time, Jordan
Henderson overran the ball and lunged in on Nasri to earn a
straight red card that would rule him out of all bar one of the
final four games. Skrtel succeeded where his team-mate failed
in escaping punishment from referee Mark Clattenburg after

handling the ball in the closing moments of the match. The euphoria which greeted the final whistle was embodied by Steven Gerrard, whose ten-year-old cousin Jon-Paul Gilhooley had been the youngest victim at Hillsborough, shedding tears as he was mobbed by team-mates. The Liverpool captain quickly regained his composure to deliver a stirring on-field team talk to his team-mates in the centre circle. 'Hey, this does not fucking slip now!' he shouted. 'Listen, listen! This is gone: we go to Norwich, exactly the same. We go again – come on!'

The conflicting mood after Liverpool and City's fierce contest continued away from the streets of L4 as rival fans clashed inside Lime Street station after the game. A mass brawl involving 30 people broke out at one of the station's entrances before spilling on to the concourse after a Liverpool fan headbutted a City supporter, causing blood to stream from his nose. Two men from Merseyside, identified as members of the Liverpool hooligan firm 'The Urchins', were handed three-and-a-half-year football banning orders for their part in the violence in addition to suspended prison sentences. Their counterparts, both from Cheadle, received 12-month community orders while one had to pay £250 compensation to the plain clothes police officer he had assaulted after being reprimanded.

* * *

History still weighed heavily on Liverpool as the Premier League title race neared a nervy finale, but Manchester City endured their own baggage problems. A 2-2 home draw with Sunderland on 16 April, the 120th anniversary of their modern inception, left them six points adrift of the current champions-elect with just over three weeks of the 2013/14 campaign remaining. The following weekend, Brendan Rodgers's side followed Steven Gerrard's words to the letter by holding on to record another 3-2 win against Norwich City. Manuel Pellegrini's title hopefuls returned to winning ways by seeing off West Bromwich Albion before a trip to Crystal Palace on the same afternoon that their challengers entertained Chelsea at Anfield.

Jose Mourinho's tactical masterplan caused unforced errors in the hosts' setup, typified by Gerrard's slip which gifted Demba Ba the opener. Fernando Torres heaped further misery on his old club in a late counter attack which set up Willian for a simple finish that allowed City to close the gap to three points while retaining the Londoners' outside chances.

Liverpool's own trip to Selhurst Park eight days later saw them race to a three-goal lead at the break, only for Rodgers's attempt to close down City's +9 goal difference with a kamikaze second-half display which fell away inside the final ten minutes to draw the game. Pellegrini decided against watching his rivals' downfall due to studying videos of Aston Villa ahead of his side's upcoming fixture but admitted that the result had provided a timely reminder of how unpredictable football can be. 'It's a good lesson for everyone,' he said. 'No one knows what will happen in football. It depends on a lot of things, not just what you can do. Liverpool were winning 3-0 but the score changed. It's not just a lesson for this moment. Football is always the same.'

The point gained allowed the Reds to cling on to top spot for another 48 hours but came with a growing acceptance that their best chance of winning the Premier League title had gone as City overtook them by winning their last game in hand against Villa to require only a point against West Ham on the final day for the championship.

Anfield's increasingly faint hopes were officially killed off by news from the Etihad Stadium that its hosts had raced to a 4-0 win while Rodgers's side had to produce a late fightback to overcome a Martin Skrtel own goal against Newcastle and seal second spot with 84 points. Pellegrini's players had spent a combined 15 days at the summit throughout a remarkable season which saw the title race's lead change 25 times in total, with Liverpool spending 59 days there, yet City had finished champions. For the Chilean, winning English football's top honour in his debut season was vindication of the gamble taken in appointing him as Roberto Mancini's replacement when fans were largely opposed to it. Some of those who sang disparagingly of the former Real Madrid manager outside Wembley before the previous year's FA Cup Final were now eulogising him in their home stadium. One of the homemade signs on display inside the Etihad during the celebrations gave thanks to the efforts of Palace, Chelsea's '2 buses' and Gerrard himself for helping deliver the title back to Manchester, before asking 'Suarez, u still crying?'

The striker's tears after Liverpool capitulated at Selhurst had provided an enduring image of his club's doomed end to the season. His 31 goals may have failed to deliver the title but earned him both the Premier League's Golden Boot and the respective Player of the Year awards from the PFA and FWA. Four days after the season had ended, on 15 May, Rodgers delivered an acceptance speech for Suarez at the FWA's annual awards ceremony in London. FA chairman Greg Dyke had preceded the Liverpool manager's appearance with an inaugural address which eulogised at length about his side's exploits during the campaign. Senior City officials in attendance at the Royal Lancaster Hotel were bemused that the former BBC director-general's address had failed to include any references to the fact that their own club had pipped their north-west peers by two points but not hugely surprised. Ahead of the final day of the Premier League season, Dyke had lamented the fact that Pellegrini's side were about to win the title as 'pretty depressing' due to having only two English players regularly finding their way into the club's starting line-up.

Widespread plaudits for Suarez were rescinded not long after his raft of personal accolades following a third biting incident in four years. Sinking his teeth into Italy defender Giorgio Chiellini during Uruguay's World Cup group campaign saw him incur the full weight of FIFA's disciplinary powers with a four-month ban from all football-related activities. His £65m move to Barcelona within weeks of the flashpoint led to Liverpool redistributing more than three-quarters of the fee to Southampton with the captures of Dejan Lovren, Adam Lallana and Rickie Lambert. Other additions to the post-Suarez ragtag included Lille striker Divock Origi and future Germany international Emre Can as Liverpool attempted to evolve beyond the 'Moneyball' strategy that FSG attempted to implement at the start of its ownership three years earlier.

The previous season's top two sides renewed hostilities with an early clash as part of the International Champions Cup on 30 July 2014. The meeting at Yankee Stadium saw Liverpool stepping behind new enemy lines. Twelve months earlier, the Blues' parent company City Football Group had entered into a partnership with the owners of the New York Yankees to create a new Major League Soccer (MLS) franchise in the form of New York City FC. The pact with the sworn enemies of the Boston Red Sox, operated by Anfield powerbrokers FSG, added a transatlantic layer to the re-established north-west rivalry.

A leisurely pre-season contest burst into life on 53 minutes when Jesús Navas beat Jack Robinson, powered down Liverpool's left side and sent in a cross which Steven Gerrard attempted to intercept but lost his footing and turned it towards goal, where Stevan Jovetic poked the ball home. Six minutes later, the Reds responded as Raheem Sterling picked out Daniel Sturridge, who went down under the weight of a challenge by Aleksander Kolarov before the ball broke to Jordan Henderson for a first-time hit to bring the game level.

City retook the lead in the 67th minute through Jovetic, who skipped past Kolo Touré and sent the ball to Navas on his right to tee up Kelechi Iheanacho for an effort which was blocked by Sebastian Coates but fell for Jovetic to double his tally. Five minutes from time, Sturridge's cross to Lucas Leiva was helped on by the Brazilian into the path of Sterling to fire a right-footed effort for the second equaliser. A penalty shoot-out saw City's first three takers – Kolarov, Yaya Touré and Navas – all denied by Simon Mignolet from the spot while Sturridge failed to convert against his former employers. Iheanacho's attempt to restore some credibility for the reigning champions was short-lived as Henderson stepped up to hand Liverpool a non-competitive victory over the team that had beaten them to the punch three months earlier in the title race. Liverpool's group position secured a place in the final, where they lost 3-1 to Manchester United.

Their second game had been a goalless draw against AC Milan on 2 August. Rodgers's praise for one-time City striker Mario Balotelli, lining up for the Serie A side, fuelled talk of a shock move to Merseyside. The following day, the Northern Irishman shot down the links, saying, 'I can categorically tell you Mario Balotelli will not be at Liverpool.'

Balotelli eventually undermined Rodgers's public claims by completing a £16m transfer on 25 August, the same day that his new club travelled to the Etihad Stadium to take on City. The 24-year-old sat out the first return to his old haunt, before which Manuel Pellegrini claimed that the pressure of leading from the front had caused Liverpool's late-season collapse in the 2013/14 title race. 'I was not surprised because I was absolutely convinced when I said the words "careful, it's not finished"', he said. 'They had to play four games more and the pressure when you are at the top of the table is increasing after every game. From my experience, when you are finishing the season, the pressure increases every week for every team. That's why I was absolutely sure they weren't going to win the five games they had to play. The most important thing for us was not to think about Liverpool but think about what we had to do and we had to win the five games, and we did.'

City fans greeted the emergence of both teams with a banner proclaiming 'We are the champions – Champions of England' and mercilessly ridiculed Gerrard in the opening stage of a first Premier League meeting with City since his *Schadenfreude* moment. Focus soon shifted to his new Liverpool team-mate Alberto Moreno when the left-back casually sliced Dejan Lovren's headed interception of a Jesús Navas cross into his path, allowing Jovetic to steal in and drill through the legs of Mignolet on 41 minutes. Ten minutes into the second half, the Montenegrin doubled his tally with an unchecked run to meet Samir Nasri's return pass. Those who had endured the end of Rafael Benitez's tenure knew the threat that Jovetic posed, having first performed a two-goal trick for Fiorentina at Anfield that eliminated his current visitors from the Champions League's group stage in December 2009.

Sergio Agüero put the game further out of reach within 23 seconds of coming on as a substitute by anticipating a through-ball from Navas to fire a low shot beyond Mignolet. Liverpool pulled back a consolation in the final ten minutes as Daniel Sturridge dispossessed Martin Demichelis before floating a cross in for Rickie Lambert, who saw his initial header saved by Joe Hart before a deflection off Pablo Zabaleta steered it over the line.

Pellegrini hailed the impact of City's first home win of the season against one of their previous title challengers as twofold and forecast that Liverpool would again be preparing to snatch their crown. 'For me these are games of six points – especially when you play at home,' he said. 'Liverpool is an important team and one that will be fighting for the title.' The Chilean's prediction rang hollow as Rodgers's transitional side crashed out of the Champions League group stages and failed to replicate their 2013/14 form in the league, where they veered between sixth and tenth in the table.

When their corresponding fixture with City rolled around on 1 March 2015, the cycle had been broken, with Liverpool arresting a dismal return of 21 points from their opening 16 matches to take 24 out of a possible 30 in their next ten matches while equalling a 30-year feat of five consecutive league clean sheets. A meeting with Pellegrini's side carried permutations for both sides with the hosts coming off the back of a humiliating Europa League exit to Besiktas on penalties while City had a chance to temporarily close their gap with Chelsea in the title race to two points.

Liverpool's energetic start to proceedings belied the 55-hour turnaround they had endured between leaving Turkey and stepping out against the champions as Raheem Sterling robbed Vincent Kompany of the ball before feeding Jordan Henderson for a long-range effort that flew past Hart on 11 minutes. City's strike-back saw Sergio Agüero weight a pass to Edin Džeko, who drew Simon Mignolet off his line and slotted home. But Rodgers's side snatched victory in the game's final quarter as Philippe Coutinho received a pass from Sterling on the left of the penalty area and stepped inside Samir Nasri before unleashing a powerful curling effort that galvanised his team's bid to secure a Champions League return. That proved as good as things got for the Brazilian and his team-mates as they slipped to an FA Cup semi-final defeat to Aston Villa and finished sixth. Steven Gerrard's final outings for his boyhood club both ended in losses. His Anfield farewell was upstaged by Crystal Palace while a final day bow at Stoke City saw Liverpool slump to a 6-1 humiliation in the Potteries.

Developments over the long-term futures of several first-team mainstays created a distraction from the often underwhelming on-field performances that bookended Liverpool's 2014/15 campaign. Gerrard's expiring contract forced supporters to face up to an imminent threat of soldiering on without their talisman. Clubs across the world watched with interest as the 34-year-old mulled over his next destination, with City firmly among them. Pellegrini admitted that advancing seniority would be no barrier if Gerrard were to become available at the end of the current campaign, with his former England team-mate Frank Lampard already spending a season-long loan by the champions from sister club New York City. The Huyton-born player later followed Lampard to the MLS by joining LA Galaxy on an 18-month deal.

Gerrard's future was still not as widely debated as the fate of Raheem Sterling, who was caught in a tug-of-war between the club and his representatives.

Contract talks with the England international had stalled and left him weighing up whether to accept improved terms of £100,000 per week to reaffirm his commitment to Merseyside. His dithering placed several of Europe's elite, including Real Madrid and Bayern Munich, on high alert. The winger later broke ranks to conduct an unauthorised television interview with BBC Sport on 1 April. Set against a backdrop of the city's iconic Liver Building, he confirmed the rejection of an improved contract at Liverpool but insisted, 'It's not about the money at all. It's never been about money. I talk about winning trophies throughout my career. That's all I talk about … I don't want to be perceived as a money-grabbing 20-year-old. I just want to be seen as a kid who loves to play football and to do the best for the team.'

Nine days later, Sterling finally faced the Anfield faithful again at the launch of Liverpool's home kit for the upcoming 2015/16 campaign. One man in the audience assembled in the Centenary Stand for the event heckled the want-away player as he answered questions about the new strip, shouting, 'Make sure we see you in it next season!' Fellow supporters cheered the sentiments as Sterling was left appearing sheepish.

Stories about the winger's extracurricular activities began to appear in the days that followed. Two days on from the kit launch incident, as Liverpool prepared to take on Newcastle United, Sterling was pictured in Sunday newspapers smoking a shisha pipe. Further depictions of his off-field behaviour went to press in the next 48 hours, with mobile video footage allegedly capturing him passed out after inhaling nitrous oxide, nicknamed 'hippy crack', from a balloon at his Southport home. Another photograph showed Sterling again partaking in shisha, this time alongside fellow academy graduate Jordon Ibe, at a London bar earlier in the season. The negative coverage had little bearing on the growing list of suitors willing to offer him an escape from the Anfield pressure-cooker, with Manchester City's interest becoming increasingly known.

On the eve of Liverpool's Wembley trip, Rodgers responded to the Etihad's pursuit of Sterling by reaffirming a personal view on English football's hierarchy. 'If you say that Manchester City is a bigger club than Liverpool, you're wrong,' he insisted. 'At this moment in time Manchester City are on a great project. They're a wonderful club, I've seen it for myself a few years ago when I spoke with them [about becoming assistant manager]. I've got big respect for what they're doing there. They're trying to build it the right way and hopefully they'll get young players through … but at this moment in time you can't compare as a club the size of the two. You've got Liverpool and Manchester United, the two biggest clubs in this country, and the rest of them are fighting to be there over the next 20 years.'

Despite the stand-off, Sterling was still crowned Young Player of the Year at Liverpool's end-of-season awards but faced further hostility with supporters present for the ceremony at the city's Echo Arena booing him when he appeared on stage to collect the award. Two days later, the club placed scheduled contract talks indefinitely on hold in the wake of an interview by his agent Aidy Ward in the *Evening Standard*, where he insisted that the 20-year-old would not be committing his future to Anfield – even if an offer of £900,000 per week was put on the table. 'I don't care about the PR of the club and the club's situation. I don't care. He is definitely not signing,' said Ward, before turning his ire on Sterling's former team-mate Jamie Carragher, now a leading television pundit with Sky Sports, over his public comments about the star. 'Carragher is a knob. Everybody knows it,' he said. 'Any of the criticism from current pundits or ex-Liverpool players – none of them things matter to me. It is not relevant.' Ward later denied the quotes attributed to him and was said to be 'taking legal advice about it'.

Three days after his representative's outburst, Sterling endured a barrage of abuse from Liverpool's travelling fans during the 6-1 loss to Stoke. The muted end to the club's season was followed by a team holiday to Dubai that doubled as Gerrard's farewell, with the outgoing captain leading the squad in a rendition of the chant that City fans penned for Kolo Touré and his brother Yaya set to the tune of 2Unlimited's 'No Limits'. Life at the Etihad would continue to dominate Anfield's summer, not least with James Milner agreeing a free transfer to the Reds on 4 June. City's attempts to lure Sterling in the opposite direction with an opening £25m bid were flatly rejected on 12 June. An improved offer of £35m rising to £40m arrived a week later but was similarly rebuffed. When Liverpool reported back for pre-season on 6 July, Sterling requested that the club omitted him from their upcoming tour of south east Asia and Australia during showdown talks with Rodgers.

Illness was cited as the reason for a two-day absence from training before the protracted saga was finally drawn to a close with confirmation that City's third bid, worth an initial £44m and potentially rising to £49m overall, had been accepted was announced on 12 July as the Reds jetted out to Bangkok. Sterling's declaration of 'I'm just glad it's all over and done with' in his first interview with his new club's in-house media after the deal was finalised reflected the sentiments of all parties. But the ill feeling which had festered over several months dragged on in the years that followed, with Sterling's every touch booed relentlessly whenever he faced them alongside the same 'one greedy bastard' chants that City fans had previously reserved for Daniel Sturridge.

Three months after his client's move to the Etihad, Ward claimed in an interview with the *Daily Mail* that Rodgers had undermined the bond of trust between the player and the club by airing the dirty linen of negotiations in public. 'In December I spoke to Liverpool and said "we'll sign a contract if there is a buy-out clause" – those clauses are now common practice. They said no to that,' he said. 'Then there was an underhandedness, there were sly remarks. In press conferences, Brendan told everyone Raheem would sign – why do that? I knew, Brendan knew, and Liverpool knew there was an issue. Right now, he probably should be a Liverpool player, but he's not and he's in a great place at City.'

Had Sterling toughed it out for just three months longer, he would have discovered a hugely different lay of the land at Anfield.

The Bottle

LIVERPOOL'S HEAVIEST top-flight defeat since 1963 left Brendan Rodgers standing on the brink. In the year since narrowly missing out on the Premier League title, the Northern Irishman had fallen into the same trap as Rafael Benitez by replacing a departed mercurial player with an Italian dud, all with a freshly signed long-term contract under his belt. Unlike the Champions League-winning coach, however, he could not mask the dismal campaign behind severe financial constraints.

Answers were demanded from the club's owners FSG in a robust end-of-season review. In 2012, the Americans had summoned Kenny Dalglish to their Boston headquarters for a similar purpose and decided to part company with Anfield's greatest living legend shortly afterwards. If Rodgers were about to suffer a similar fate, he was at least being spared the indignity of a long-haul journey with the appraisal taking place on Merseyside rather than Massachusetts. He survived the cross-examination by FSG's president Mike Gordon but only after cutting the cord with assistant manager Colin Pascoe, whose link with him dated back to their time together at Swansea City, and first team coach Mike Marsh.

Distrust reigned as supporters viewed Rodgers's decision to go along with the ditching of his trusted lieutenants as an act of desperation to save his own skin. A cat-and-mouse game between the beleaguered Liverpool manager and the club's transfer committee intensified in a summer where Roberto Firmino, an emerging Brazil international, arrived alongside the target-man figure of Aston Villa's Christian Benteke. That confusion led to similar results as back-to-back wins at the start of 2015/16 devolved into just one from their next nine games.

Following an anaemic 1-1 draw with Everton on 4 October 2015, Rodgers received the news he had dreaded for over four months. Barely a mile into his drive away from the club's Melwood training ground, Gordon called to officially bring an end to his three-year tenure. A day of humiliation was completed when he later flew out for a pre-arranged trip to Marbella with his future wife Charlotte and was photographed by a fellow passenger asleep and open-mouthed on the plane. Liverpool fans were left similarly gaping when the identity of his replacement became known in the days ahead.

Jürgen Klopp had witnessed the beginning of Rodgers's end first-hand when his Borussia Dortmund team where drubbed 4-0 in a pre-season friendly. Some 14 months on, FSG explored the possibility of him taking up a permanent residency on the Anfield touchline. Days before Rodgers's fate was sealed at Goodison Park, the German met with FSG chiefs Gordon, John Henry and Tom Werner at the offices of law firm Shearman & Sterling on New York's Lexington Avenue to discuss the prospect of him taking over the soon-to-be-vacant hot seat.

Managing in the Premier League strongly appealed to Klopp even before he had asked to be released from his Dortmund contract at the end of 2014/15. That feeling seemed to be mutual with Manchester City and Tottenham Hotspur making speculative enquiries during his time at the Westfalenstadion. Manchester United's eagerness to install the former striker as David Moyes's replacement came off as desperation when Ed Woodward, the club's executive vice-chairman, unflatteringly described Old Trafford as being 'like an adult version of Disneyland'. As a football romantic, Klopp later revealed to a friend that he had found the fetishisation 'unsexy'. Liverpool had also been rebuffed, minus a toe-curling sales pitch, in their initial attempts to sound him out through an intermediary when Dalglish was dismissed for delivering tangible silverware but not a Champions League place. At a second attempt, FSG had finally landed the box-office managerial appointment that both they and supporters had craved since wresting the club from Tom Hicks and George Gillett.

Where Rodgers had produced a 180-page dossier and used technical doublespeak to outline his blueprint for success, Klopp preferred to articulate his vision by speaking to fans in more simplified terms by vowing to turn 'doubters into believers' and pledged to deliver a first trophy within four years. His reputation for playing an anglicised style in the Bundesliga earned his teams the moniker of 'heavy metal football'. Liverpool's opening three games under their new manager were more akin to an acoustic warm-up act with a hat-trick of tepid stalemates before bringing the noise by winning six of their next seven matches with resounding displays, most notably in a 21 November meeting with Manchester City. Manuel Pellegrini's side had again formed part of the Premier League's chasing pack in the title race, now led by Leicester City, but failed to stifle the relentless counter-pressing hallmarks of Klopp's new charges.

Bacary Sagna became an early victim of Liverpool's new tactic on seven minutes when Philippe Coutinho snatched the ball from him and released Roberto Firmino, whose cutback was turned into Joe Hart's net by a flat-footed Eliaquim Mangala. The Brazilian duo combined again to double the visitors' advantage, this time with Firmino returning the favour for his compatriot by breaking through a gap between Mangala and Martin Demichelis, making his first league start in over a month, before squaring the ball for Coutinho to slot home. The Blues were further undone by a clever spell of interplay that saw Emre Can send Coutinho racing clear with a clever back-heel before the playmaker drew Hart from his line and laid the ball off to Firmino for a rolled finish.

A glimmer of hope appeared shortly before the half-time break when Aleksandar Kolarov's header from a poor Martin Skrtel clearance allowed a returning Sergio Agüero to shake off a challenge from Lucas Leiva and hit a curling 25-yard shot with his right foot. Skrtel later made amends for his role in City's reducer by converting Adam Lallana's corner with a powerful effort to complete Liverpool's biggest away win over City since December 1989. Raheem Sterling's first outing against his former club failed to even tell the tale of his brief Anfield career as flashes of promise were non-existent.

A largely anonymous display was rounded off by the winger's failure to connect with a loose ball in front of an open goal five minutes from time and was gleefully celebrated by travelling fans, who broke out into chants of 'Sterling, what's the score?' Pellegrini reflected on the performance as 'a complete disaster' after his side surrendered a seven-year unbeaten home record to Liverpool and conceded three first-half goals at the Etihad for the first time since losing to Arsenal 12 years earlier. Klopp, meanwhile, attempted to temper lofty early expectations of his tenure by refusing to offer guarantees that the Reds would qualify for the next season's Champions League while also alluding to the reasons behind his appointment in place of Rodgers a month prior. 'It wasn't because of the weather and it wasn't a problem with Brendan Rodgers, because he is a brilliant manager,' he said. 'But they had to change something.' His words seemed to resonate within the Etihad's corridors of power just three months later, as both teams advanced on a meeting in the League Cup Final.

City's attempts to undergo a 'Barcelonafication' process began in the mid-1970s, when Peter Swales sought inspiration from the Catalan club's hierarchal structure by appointing multiple vice-presidents to oversee the running of Maine Road's various footballing departments. Ideology and reality rarely aligned under the club's late chairman, but the Abu Dhabi ownership's efforts fared significantly better when it was announced on 3 February 2016 that Bayern Munich manager Pep Guardiola would succeed Pellegrini, whose contract expired at the end of the season. The announcement marked the end of a process which had been four years in the making, with two of Guardiola's strongest allies from his time as Barcelona manager enlisted as part of the process. Txiki Begiristain had played alongside the midfielder in Johan Cruyff's 'Dream Team' that delivered the club's first European

Cup in 1992 before a seven-year spell as the club's director of football, the final two of which were spent working alongside his former team-mate. He had been a lone voice in the boardroom backing the unproven Guardiola to take charge rather than pursue Jose Mourinho, who had also applied for the vacant position.

Rubber-stamping Begiristain's bid to see Guardiola promoted from the club's 'B' team at the Camp Nou hot seat was Ferran Sorriano, now City's CEO. The pair's arrivals within a month of each other in 2012 laid the groundwork for negotiations which were initially curtailed that year, with their former colleague still enjoying a sabbatical before taking the reins at the Allianz Arena. The Catalan's meticulous attention to detail meant that even the minutiae of his new surroundings had carried a degree of familiarity. City's new state-of-the-art training complex at the Etihad Campus, opened in 2014, was modelled on AC Milan's pioneering Milanello base but the structural proximity of the facility to the Etihad Stadium, adjoined by a footbridge above Alan Turing Way, bears striking similarities with the footprint that existed around Barça's iconic home during Guardiola's time at the helm. Previously, the 45-year-old had appeared as a fanciful name atop Liverpool's managerial wish list in their 2012 pursuit of Kenny Dalglish's replacement.

Some 25 days after Guardiola's coronation was announced, Pellegrini led City out at Wembley for his side's first of two meetings with Liverpool in the space of four days. The Chilean's previous appearance at England's national stadium had ended in glory with the Blues clinching the League Cup en route to overhauling their north-west rivals in the Premier League title race. Memories of Klopp's own last outing beneath the arch was less favourable after Borussia Dortmund were sucker-punched by Arjen Robben's last-minute goal for Bayern Munich in the 2013 Champions League Final. A brutal early clash of heads between Mamadou Sakho and Emre Can suggested his latest visit would follow a similar path of disappointment. Kolo Touré replaced the struggling French defender, who raged against his manager's sound judgement with a touchline tantrum.

Little separated the sides in a disjointed opening 45 minutes before the restart delivered a swift opener through Fernandinho, who slipped a shot under a diving Simon Mignolet after receiving an overlapping pass from Sergio Agüero. Eight minutes from time, however, Liverpool equalised with their first shot on target as Sterling gifted his former club a previously unlikely lifeline. The winger's failed clearance allowed Daniel Sturridge to drill the ball across City's penalty area for Adam Lallana to hit the far post before the rebound broke for Philippe Coutinho to take the clash into extra time and eventually a penalty shoot-out. From 12 yards, Can handed Klopp's side hopes of taking the trophy by converting his spot kick, while City counterpart Fernandinho missed but Willy Caballero's heroics denied Lucas Leiva, Lallana and Coutinho, handing City their second League Cup triumph in three seasons. Pellegrini had discounted the Argentine goalkeeper being stood down from the Wembley occasion after featuring in City's route to the final itself, saying, 'I'd rather lose a final than my word.' Klopp carefully chose his own words when expressing his downcast mood and sought approval from Matt McCann, Liverpool's head of press, to upgrade a personal feeling from 'rubbish' to 'shit'.

Revenge came three days later, on a cold night at Anfield, when City's quest to haul back Leicester's ten-point lead in the Premier League title race was derailed. Lallana's low effort slithered past Joe Hart in the 34th minute before James Milner recorded a first goal against his former employers with a stabbed finish shortly before the interval.

More illuminating for the home crowd was a running battle between Raheem Sterling and Jon Flanagan. The Liverpool full-back had last featured for his boyhood club in the Premier League during their unsuccessful 2013/14 title challenge. A knee injury sidelined him for the next 12 months and hopes of a regular return to the starting berth failed to materialise. Yet Flanagan's first league appearance of the season became the stuff of nightmares for his former team-mate on a maiden return to Anfield. Sterling was withdrawn at half-time after being comfortably second-best.

In their record signing's absence, City's humiliation continued as Lallana danced through their defence before teeing up Roberto Firmino on 57 minutes to finalise a comfortable home win from close range. Klopp's developing lexicon of English produced an oft-quoted moment when he was interviewed by BT Sport about the league double over his side's Wembley tormentors. 'It was for sure our best home game,' he said. 'The best word that I can say to describe this is "boom!"'

The German's exclamation reflected the considerable strides that Liverpool were making under him as they cast aside Manchester United and his former club Borussia Dortmund in an unexpected route to the Europa League Final. But Sevilla's second-half fightback to a 3-1 victory in Basel served as a learning curve for Klopp that many of the players he had inherited lacked the mental fortitude to withstand the onslaughts that he hoped they would inflict.

Pellegrini's end to his time at City yielded a Champions League semi-final appearance against eventual winners Real Madrid while also guaranteeing a place in the next season's competition by finishing fourth, ahead of United on goal difference. But both Manchester clubs and the rest of the Premier League's chasing pack could only marvel at a distance as Leicester recorded the most unlikely title triumph with a ten-point margin. Bookmakers had priced Claudio Ranieri's side as 5,000/1 outsiders at the beginning of 2015/16. The Foxes' fairytale coincided with a year of sheer unpredictability in which the UK later voted to leave the European Union.

More intense than the Leave versus Remain argument was the dynamic between Klopp and Pep Guardiola, which had been reignited following the latter's arrival at the Etihad Stadium. The genesis of the pair's duelling had started in the Bundesliga three years prior, with Guardiola's bow as Bayern Munich manager derailed by Klopp's Borussia Dortmund side in the 2013 German Super Cup. Payback arrived for the ex-Barcelona coach at the end of that season as the Bavarians clinched a domestic double courtesy of a 19-point lead in the league and an extra-time win over their nearest challengers in the German cup final. A repeat meeting in the Super Cup yielded the same result as the previous season before Bayern again exuded their Bundesliga superiority but their defence of the German cup ended in a semi-final penalty shootout to Klopp's side to leave the managers on four wins apiece. Similarities existed between the principles of Guardiola's 'tiki-taka' and Klopp's *gegenpressing* models yet their contrasting executions put them in direct opposition. City's new manager set down a marker by making Ilkay Gündoğan his first signing for a modest £20m.

Gündoğan spent three years working under Klopp at Dortmund, where he won a league and cup double in 2011/12, but the midfielder opted against a reunion with his former manager when Liverpool and City fought it out for his affections in the transfer market. 'I had a great four years with Jürgen and I love him as a person and a manager but I felt it was time for something else,' he explained to *Fantasy PL* in February 2020. 'I wanted to leave Dortmund in Dortmund and didn't want to think about the time that I had with him when I was joining a new club. That was a bit of the reason why I didn't want to join Liverpool.'

Klopp's efforts to overhaul the Reds' squad saw a former City prospect heading to Merseyside in the form of Loris Karius, signed for £4.7m from the Liverpool manager's old club Mainz. The goalkeeper arrived with a promising reputation after his being voted as the second-best player in his chosen position by 235 fellow Bundesliga players polled by *Kicker*, their country's leading football magazine, behind Bayern stopper Manuel Neuer. Joining the Germany under-21 international at Anfield were several Premier League mainstays with Southampton striker Sadio Mané and Newcastle United midfielder Georginio Wijnaldum acquired for a combined £55m.

Those astute additions helped Liverpool keep pace with Chelsea in the Premier League title race before a first encounter against City on New Year's Eve. Guardiola personally checked in on the Blues' upcoming opponents as they racked up a third straight league win by overcoming an early setback against Stoke

City on 27 December and relished the contest between the league's second- and third-placed teams. 'This is not a final but like a final – an important game for both teams,' he said. 'I like a lot the way they play, for the spectators, because in three or four seconds they are attacking. When he [Klopp] speaks about his football being heavy metal, I understand completely, it is so aggressive.' His opposite number was similarly enthused about the game handpicked to see out the calendar year. 'I know people are excited when they think about it,' said Klopp. 'There's nothing to do except prepare the party for afterwards while everyone watches the television. The good news is we are involved. It's not City versus someone else, it's Liverpool against Manchester City. We're some kind of a challenger. We don't care about being favourite, it feels like we're challenging in each game and now we have to make the people happy again.'

An increased capacity of 53,120, made possible by the Main Stand's recent redevelopment, rang in 2017 in largely high spirits after Adam Lallana floated a cross in from the left side and Wijnaldum rose above Aleksandar Kolarov to power beyond Claudio Bravo in the eighth minute. City's latest Merseyside excursion became as frustrating as their previous one when their first shot on target arrived on 54 minutes as Sergio Agüero fired tamely at Simon Mignolet. Raheem Sterling was again upstaged by an unheralded full-back, this time in the form of ex-City utility man James Milner.

The visitors' failure to bridge a ten-point gap to leaders Chelsea in the table led to Guardiola venting his frustrations to Txiki Begiristain, his former Barcelona team-mate and now City's director of football, in the bowels of Anfield. He agitatedly paced around the makeshift dressing room while punching his fist into the palm of his hand over an hour after the defeat. Klopp shared Guardiola's feelings of rage just weeks into the new calendar year as his own side's title bid fell away with a series of draws and dismal exits from both the League Cup and FA Cup.

His Liverpool side won just three of their next 14 games in all competitions as City overtook them in the battle to be the

Premier League's best of the rest, with Chelsea's coronation fast approaching. The table's second and third teams met again at the Etihad Stadium on 19 March. As their players traded challenges throughout the first half, Klopp and Guardiola engaged in a heated exchange which ended with the latter racing over to the opposite technical area to offer a flamboyant high five to his counterpart while continuing to debate. Early in the second half, Roberto Firmino beat the offside trap but was met with a high-footed challenge from Gael Clichy. Widespread protests from City's players to referee Michael Oliver in the aftermath of the decision saw the club later hit with a misconduct charge and fined £35,000.

Milner recorded a second goal in three outings against his old club with a penalty which wrong-footed Willy Caballero. Klopp superstitiously turned away until the outcome became clear by the euphoric reaction from Liverpool fans behind the South Stand's goal. City's response arrived on 69 minutes when Kevin De Bruyne played a clever pass which saw Agüero race clear of Ragnar Klavan and stroke a first-time shot past Mignolet to preserve the current order of business, with one point still separating them.

The gap had doubled by the end of a season which saw Guardiola enduring the rare feat of finishing empty-handed for a first time in his elite-level managerial career. His work at close quarters would finally be shown to wider audiences as City allowed a third major broadcaster to peek behind the curtain with Amazon documenting the club's 2017/18 season for its *All or Nothing* series. Over £250m was spent on six new additions that the Catalan believed would elevate his underperforming side to the standards to which he had become accustomed at Barcelona and Bayern Munich. Klopp, too, strengthened significantly with former Chelsea misfit Mohamed Salah and Arsenal's Alex Oxlade-Chamberlain leading a spree that approached almost £85m.

A clash between the sides at the Etihad on 9 September, just four games into the new campaign, became billed as a potential showdown between two of the Premier League's early-season title contenders after taking seven points apiece before the international break.

Sergio Agüero broke the deadlock midway through the first half after Kevin De Bruyne sent a simple pass through the heart of Liverpool's defence for a matching comfortable finish that extended the Argentine's 100 per cent record against the visitors at Eastlands to six consecutive outings. Eight minutes before half-time, Sadio Mané's attempts to chase a ball over the top from Joël Matip forced Ederson to rush 25 yards off his line and into a high-footed challenge. The forward's boot clashed with his opponent's face and floored him. Referee Jon Moss immediately dismissed Mané while the Brazilian goalkeeper was stretchered off to undergo tests and receive eight stitches for the wound inflicted.

A close contest devolved into a one-sided exhibition from that point on, with City doubling their lead during the sixth minute of injury time. De Bruyne was again the architect, performing a Cruyff turn to tie Trent Alexander-Arnold in knots before sending a cross which Gabriel Jesús glanced past Simon Mignolet with ease. The hosts' opening scorers combined after the interval as De Bruyne found Agüero with a weighted pass which placed him in a one-on-one with Mignolet. Instead of rounding Liverpool's hapless goalkeeper, however, the striker selflessly rolled the ball to Jesús on his left to dink the ball into an empty net. One-way traffic continued to travel at a rush hour pace in the final quarter courtesy of substitute Leroy Sané. The winger exchanged passes with Benjamin Mendy before rolling a smart near-post finish past Mignolet which was trumped by a sumptuous 25-yard strike.

Klopp felt Mané's first-half dismissal was 'very unlucky' and insisted that it had altered the course of the match. 'It had a big influence on the game. It was not a foul but it was a red card and you have to accept it. That changed the game and we know it,' he said. 'There was not one second he looks on the goalie. He just wanted to get the ball as soon as possible. Hopefully the goalie is not seriously injured.' Asked whether he would appeal against the Senegal international's automatic three-game suspension, Klopp replied, 'It would be a waste of time, like the game today.'

Anfield officials lobbied for the ban to be overturned but it was upheld by the FA, prompting the German to reaffirm his post-match view on 12 September by admitting, 'I didn't expect anything different.' Hours after the match, Mané had posted an apologetic message on his Instagram account to Ederson following the unfortunate coming together.

A clash in the transfer market followed the incident as Liverpool and City both vied for the affections of Virgil van Dijk. Klopp's pursuit of the Southampton centre-back had been boosted by his commonality with Jordan Henderson with the pair represented by the same agency. Anfield officials had previously made efforts to sign Van Dijk in the summer before the south coast club's threat to report them to the Premier League over an alleged tapping-up forced them to withdraw an initial interest in a public climbdown.

City saw their rivals' wrist-slapping as an invitation to revisit the possibility of signing the Netherlands international. He had previously appeared on the Blues' radar during his final year with Celtic in 2014/15. A personal recommendation from manager Ronny Deila was met with requests for him to select Van Dijk's best European appearance for the SPFL champions. When the Norwegian coach admitted that the towering defender had not fared well in Continental outings and been sent off against Inter Milan, the Blues' initial interest cooled. Scouts from the Etihad later observed him for the Saints' goalless draw with Liverpool in November 2016, where he was named man of the match. But chairman Khaldoon Al Mubarak baulked at the £75m valuation of the player when discussing the asking price with CEO Ferran Soriano alongside director of football Txiki Begiristain in front of Amazon's cameras.

'Txiki, a central defender, come on, what are you doing?' said Al Mubarak.

'I told him about the price tag,' insisted Soriano.

'You can't be serious.'

Frosty relations between the Reds and Southampton quickly thawed to pave the way for the towering defender to seal an eight-figure switch to Merseyside on 1 January. Klopp's joy was offset by Philippe Coutinho's move to Barcelona following a 14-month courtship. Apparent injuries had seen him fail to feature for his current employers during the previous summer's transfer window, when three successive offers were rejected. His absence from the FA Cup third-round win over Everton, where Van Dijk scored a late winning goal on his debut, also coincided with the market reopening. Less than 24 hours on, a £142m deal was finally agreed with the Spanish giants. Liverpool's first outing devoid of their diminutive playmaker on 14 January saw City travel to Anfield with designs of extending a 22-game unbeaten run that had propelled them to the Premier League's summit. In the away dressing room, Guardiola's assistant Mikel Arteta attempted to fire up his players by declaring, 'We went to Stamford Bridge, we went at Old Trafford – we won every fucking duel, boys,' he said. 'That's why you win on this ground as well.'

A hamstring problem ruled Van Dijk out of a showdown with the runaway leaders as Liverpool raced into an early lead after Roberto Firmino escaped Fabian Delph's clutches to release Alex Oxlade-Chamberlain. The £35m midfielder shook off Fernandinho to sweep a right-footed effort across Ederson and into The Kop goal. City suffered their own injury issues as Delph limped out on 31 minutes, risking the visitors being exposed down their right. But the clash remained on a knife-edge as they pulled level in the 40th minute when Kyle Walker's cross-field pass found Leroy Sané, who chested the ball down to take it past Joe Gomez before beating Joël Matip for pace and squeezing a shot beyond Loris Karius.

Shortly before the hour, Oxlade-Chamberlain returned his first-half compliment to Firmino by setting him up for a clipped finish after outmuscling John Stones. Two minutes later, Mohamed Salah pounced on a Nicolas Otamendi error deep in his own half to tee up Sadio Mané for a left-footed finish. Salah's place on the scoresheet also emerged from a defensive blunder as Ederson rushed off his line to launch a clearance which barely

FINE MARGINS

reached the centre-circle as Liverpool's leading scorer floated a 40-yard lob into an empty net.

In the final nine minutes, City mounted a previously implausible fightback; first through substitute Bernardo Silva bundling the ball past Karius after it had ricocheted in the penalty area. Ilkay Gündoğan restored further respectability to the scoreline by prodding home after chesting down Sergio Agüero's cross into the six-yard box. The loss of City's unbeaten record and potentially a place in Premier League history left Guardiola's players downcast as he attempted to motivate his beaten troops in the dressing room. Facing the media, he declared 'football is unpredictable' before admitting that Anfield's fervour had been an underlying factor in the defeat. 'We were involved in the environment from Anfield for many, many reasons,' he said. 'You have to try and be stable, especially as good lessons for the knockout games in the Champions League. We can concede a goal but you cannot lose – we lost that a little bit. But we were still fighting … It was our first defeat. You need to live [through] that kind of situation to realise what we have done so far and are expecting for the future.'

His reference to Europe's premier club competition proved prophetic barely two months later; on 16 March, City were handed a quarter-final meeting with Liverpool. Txiki Begiristain, the club's director of football, sat uncomfortably in the auditorium of UEFA's Nyon headquarters as the headline tie was drawn, something which did not go unnoticed by Klopp when giving his reaction. 'They didn't want us – we all know about that,' he said. 'We are not the team they love to play constantly let me say it like this. I saw Begiristain's face after the draw and it didn't look like his Christmas and Easter had come in the one day. It's hard work, that's good.' Fewer than 4,000 miles away, Guardiola's side were already concentrating on Anfield and attempting to rewrite recent history.

During a mid-season training camp in Abu Dhabi, City's squad attempted to rework a Liverpool supporter chant inspired by The Archies' 1969 hit 'Sugar, Sugar', which name-checked

322

the club's previous 'fab four' front line of Salah, Mané, Firmino and the recently departed Philippe Coutinho. Aboard their flight to the Gulf state, players chanted. 'We've got Razza, ta-da-ta-da-ta-da,' they sang. 'Oh Sane Sane, ta-da-ta-da-ta-da, and Kun Agüeeeeerooo, but we sold Edin Džeko.' The ditty was also given an airing during the trip, with Kyle Walker acting as grand conductor. The jovial mood would soon become a distant memory for their manager. As City edged nearer to capturing the Premier League title with a 3-1 win at Everton on 31 March, Guardiola began to grow anxious. Fears over a swift return to Merseyside left the Catalan pacing nervously around Goodison Park's away dressing room. The upcoming Champions League quarter-final clash with Liverpool led him to confide reservations about facing Mohamed Salah, Sadio Mané and Roberto Firmino to his assistants Carles Planchart and Domenec Torrent.

'The forwards for Liverpool are good,' he admitted.

'Sorry?' asked Planchart.

'Those three up front,' reaffirmed Guardiola.

'Yes, Pep but it's only them.'

'They scare me. They're dangerous.'

'I mean it.'

'I have the feeling that Salah will play as the striker.'

'Salah will play as number nine and Firmino will move towards the wing.'

'Our wing-backs can't cover their wing-backs.'

'I notice that when they don't have space they suffer a lot, like today against Crystal Palace,' said Planchart, referencing Liverpool's win at Selhurst Park just hours prior. 'But we are a team that risks a lot.'

'I watched our game yesterday, when we went there and we lost … They played on another level,' conceded Torrent. 'If you want to beat them, you have to work for it. If we're at our best, we are better than Liverpool.'

Guardiola's misgivings about his latest Anfield visit had been heightened by an image becoming widely circulated on social media in the days leading up to the game that implored home supporters to descend on the stadium in their droves to greet the arrival of both teams. The incendiary call to arms downgraded City's European history to 'one time semi-finalists' against its five-time champions and warned, 'There will be thousands of Scouse voices ready to scare 'em back to Mancland with their tails between their legs before the match even starts. We're going to show them exactly what money can't buy.'

The vitriolic wording of the anonymous digital flyer, coupled with the previous ambushing of their own supporters outside the stadium in 2014, forced City officials to express their concerns to Greater Manchester Police. Their counterparts, in turn, sought to limit the impact of any planned gathering in the congested area at the foot of Anfield Road, near to the designated meeting point of the King Harry pub, by diverting both team coach routes to the opposing side of the stadium where the traffic flow could be managed more effectively. Separately, Liverpool issued a statement pleading that any supporters wishing to converge outside 'do so in a friendly, respectful and considerate manner'.

A powderkeg backdrop dominated conversations on both sides of the M62 in the immediate build-up to the game. Jürgen Klopp took a measured view to the potential pre-match high jinks: 'For us it's wonderful,' he said. 'It shows the passion and as long as it happens in a legal way I'm completely fine with it. I like it but I'm not the guy who organised it or whatever. For the team it is actually for, it's brilliant.' City winger Leroy Sané attempted to downplay the impact any potential hostility would have on his team-mates by insisting, 'It's a really good stadium ... but I don't think we'll bother too much about the noise.' His indifference was echoed by Kevin De Bruyne when asked by assembled media inside Anfield on the eve of the game. 'I expect nothing less. It's the way it goes,' said the Belgian. 'I like to play in big stadiums, big crowds. In the end it's what it's all about. There's a lot of passion on the field: you need to try and manage it.'

De Bruyne's calmness, however, was not universal within the Etihad Stadium as Guardiola made an impassioned pre-match plea for safety and sensibility: 'We come here to play a football

game. Hopefully everything, everybody, our fans, Liverpool fans
– can be correct and polite. It is just a game. People cannot forget
that there is a good rivalry. Liverpool fans will put pressure on
their players in good terms … It's a nice place to play football.'

Attention on the pitch was also dominated by a fear factor,
with City's unassailable march towards a third Premier League
crown in seven seasons considered a red flag for their hosts. Andy
Robertson, Liverpool's left-back, begged to differ: 'I don't think
we can be afraid. They won't be afraid of us and we won't be
afraid of them. Yes, they've been the best team in this league this
season undoubtedly – they're going to win the league. But it's two
games, a one-off in the Champions League, and we've got every
right to be in the quarter-finals as they do. There's no seeding in
it so it'll be a big occasion, but we'll look forward to it. We won't
fear it but we'll obviously be cautious of their strengths.'

Adding to Liverpool's relish was the continuing absence of
Sergio Agüero, who had been absent for the previous five weeks
with a knee injury and subsequently not travelled to Merseyside
for the last-eight encounter. At the Etihad Campus, Guardiola
attempted to downplay his previous foreboding about Liverpool's
front line during a pre-match tactical briefing. Using video
analysis to pinpoint the movements of Roberto Firmino and Sadio
Mané, he told City's players bluntly, 'That is Liverpool – no more
than that, okay?'

The image promoting the coach welcome had become so
heavily shared by prominent Liverpool-supporting accounts
on social media that it spiralled into a cultural phenomenon.
Overwhelming numbers of people flocked from all corners of
the country to converge outside the stadium and be a part of the
event, despite a sizeable number not being in possession of tickets
for the game, while local youngsters mounted lampposts seeking
a focal vantage point. Liverpool's team bus passed through with
a typically vibrant welcome as flags, scarves and pyrotechnics all
combined to paint the terraced streets red. When City's coach
made its approach to the stadium, events began to turn ugly.
The vehicle had not even reached the Arkles pub, situated on

the corner of Anfield Road, before missiles, including bottles, cans, flare canisters and cigarette lighters, rained down on it. Red smoke bombs were deliberately thrown into the road as the bus followed a police escort to the stadium in attempts to obscure its vision. One of the more dramatic images captured from the incident showed a bottle of Kopparberg cider hurtling towards the windows where the leaders' players were sitting.

Inside the bus, any emotions of fear among City's technical staff had morphed into blind rage. As objects flew at their vehicle from all angles, one pointed the finger of blame firmly at the home side, saying, 'They knew this was gonna happen. They should've fucked 'em off.' Every ping that hit the vehicle's shell was heard within. Such was the frequency that objects were thrown, a member of the visitors' backroom was advised to move away from his seat at the front of the coach out of fears for his personal safety. One of his colleagues actively welcomed home supporters beginning to fling raw eggs in their direction instead of the more hardened objects. Some of his colleagues appeared far less thankful.

'Fucking scumbags! I hope the world has seen this because they're the fucking shittest city in England.'

'UEFA should fine them.'

'Yeah, they'll get done for this.'

At the end of the four-minute ordeal, City's on-board crew estimated that no fewer than four windows and the vehicle's glass roof had been smashed in the process and would not be fit for completing the trip back to the Etihad Campus. The bombardment provided chilling echoes of the missile assault on City's team coach after their Boxing Day win in 1981 and, more starkly, memories of the tear gas attack on Manchester United upon their arrival just five years later. On that occasion, Red Devils manager Ron Atkinson frantically cast aside anyone in his path including opposite number Kenny Dalglish and his own player John Sivebaek, a Denmark international making his United debut in the subsequent 1-1 draw, en route into the stadium. As most of his team-mates scrambled on to the turf in a desperate

THE BOTTLE

search for fresh air, captain Bryan Robson helped treat the 22 victims, many of them children, caught up in the incident in the away dressing room.

By the time United next travelled to Anfield, ten months later, they had enlisted Bob Paisley, Liverpool's most successful manager, as their personal chaperone in a bid to prevent a repeat of the ugly scenes. Atkinson, a Liverpool native from the Old Swan area, would later describe clashes between United and his hometown club during that period as being 'like the Vietnam War'.

Once ensconced in the safety of the Main Stand's underground car park, Guardiola showed symptoms of an experience closer to being led blindly through the Ho Chi Minh Trail rather than the back streets of Anfield. He had experienced fierce receptions in his playing days, most notably at Barcelona, where far-right ultra supporters' group the 'Boixos Nois' routinely produced welcoming committees for Real Madrid's visits in El Clasico, but the incident still left him incandescent. As he disembarked the vandalised bus, the City manager addressed the nearest steward with a sarcastic thumbs-up gesture and the words 'thank you for protecting us, thank you very much. I appreciate what you have done. Thank you for the fans,' before appearing to mutter 'shame' as he headed towards the dressing rooms.

Liverpool's public response to the attack was swift and unequivocal. A club statement condemned its supporters' misbehaviour 'in the strongest possible terms' while apologising 'unreservedly to Pep Guardiola, his players, staff and officials caught up in the incident'. Anfield officials also pledged to 'cooperate fully with the authorities to identify those responsible', while adding, 'The priority now is to establish the facts and offer Manchester City whatever support is necessary.' Merseyside Police, which reported that two of its officers had suffered minor injuries from the projectiles, echoed the club's intention to robustly identify the perpetrators. Five months later, the force confirmed that it had been unable to make any arrests due to their footage being 'either clouded by smoke from flares thrown during the disorder, or didn't show the faces of the culprits'.

327

'The moment that happened, and especially because of the way it was so poorly organised for us to get into the stadium for a big match, things changed between City and Liverpool,' Vincent Kompany later reflected in his book *Treble Triumph*. 'The rivalry increased, and they became our number one team to beat ... None of us were sitting on that coach saying that we were scared. We just thought and said to each other, "All right, let's sort it out on the pitch."'

City's intentions of avenging their pre-match bruising unravelled before the game had even begun when Guardiola handed Ilkay Gündoğan a starting berth ahead of Raheem Sterling. Dominating the midfield battle appeared at the heart of the Catalan's thinking, only for it to catastrophically backfire in the opening stages. Sane gifted possession deep in Liverpool's half to Sadio Mané, who sprayed the ball out wide to Robertson. The left-back's threaded pass allowed Mohamed Salah to break downfield before eluding the looming presence of Kyle Walker with a pass into Roberto Firmino; the Brazilian got the better of Nicolas Otamendi but could not find a way past his compatriot as Ederson parried the ensuing effort, which Salah seized upon following a botched attempt by Walker to clear the ball and swept home his 38th goal of the season.

Eight minutes later, James Milner dispossessed Gündoğan and fed the ball into Alex Oxlade-Chamberlain to unleash a powerful 25-yard strike which beat Ederson, prompting a frustrated Guardiola to throw his arms out to the side in his technical area. From another Liverpool counter-attack, Salah blasted the ball into Kompany's body before it rebounded back for the Egyptian to float a cross into the far post for Mané to convert. Within little more than half an hour and typified by their captain's pained expression at the restart, City's hopes of conquering the pinnacle of European football had been decimated. Guardiola belatedly saw the error of his ways as Gündoğan was replaced by Sterling early in the second half, which coincided with the visitors' renewed bid to regain a foothold in the tie. Their best move came when De Bruyne laid on a ball for David Silva, who found Sane down Liverpool's right-hand side. He drew Loris Karius off his line before a deflection allowed Gabriel Jesús to turn into an empty net. But an offside ruling against Sane denied City a priceless away goal.

Liverpool's elation at the final whistle was offset by doubts over Salah's involvement in the return fixture after picking up a groin injury and the realisation that captain Jordan Henderson would sit out the clash at the Etihad after picking up a booking for catching former team-mate Sterling in the closing stages. For the first time in the season, Guardiola's domestic dominators had failed to register a shot on target but Klopp refused to make premature forecasts on the tie or discount his side suffering another humbling at the Etihad: 'We've conceded there already five [in September] – how could I say that's not possible? I don't think it makes it more likely we are through. I don't feel it. We have to work. You have to celebrate the party when the party starts, not four weeks before and I cannot ignore that we have to play in between another game ... No one in the dressing room was dancing around.'

Guardiola, conversely, acknowledged that the odds were stacked against City in his post-match assessment but invariably found himself drawn to the attack on their team coach. 'Normally when the police know that is going to happen, they try to avoid it happening. I didn't expect that from the Liverpool side, from the people,' he said. 'We come here to play football and I don't understand this kind of situation. Okay, nothing happened [apart from] the bus is destroyed. But I didn't expect that a club as prestigious as Liverpool would do these kind of things. Of course it is not Liverpool, it is the people – but it was not only one, only two, only three. Hopefully it doesn't happen again.'

Before leaving Merseyside, City revisited the scene. The visitors' replacement coach parked up close to the Arkles after their eagle-eyed medical staff spotted the aftermath of a hit-and-run incident. Guardiola and his players watched on as their colleagues rushed to the aid of the injured woman and treated her until the emergency services arrived, an act which Klopp later hailed as 'an outstanding thing to do' while adding, 'It leaves us in an even worse situation.'

When Guardiola dissected the defeat with City's players the following day, he turned the lights off in the Etihad Campus's lecture theatre to avoid seeing their dejected expressions. 'When I saw the game, I don't believe it but I can accept it,' he told the squad. 'We conceded five shots on target, three goals. In the game we lost 4-3 [in January], we conceded 14. After 15 minutes of the game – 15 minutes – they didn't shoot once on target. They didn't do absolutely anything, and we were 1-0 down. I know it's tough but you recovered good so you didn't know you were not there. That is my feeling, guys – the team was there. We cannot deny that we lost 3-0, okay. We cannot deny that. Sometimes we make a fault, we are not aggressive enough. It was so easy for Salah. It was so easy for the other ones that we have to improve and improve. We have to be aggressive all the time.

'Maybe you believe it's to convince you but when it's shit, I'm going to tell you it's shit and I'm going to show you,' continued Guardiola. 'For 27 minutes to 45, it was a disaster. But I understand; I was a football player and when that happens, it feels like a knockout. Being stable is sometimes so complicated. I completely understand but we have to try.'

Three days later, both clubs headed into their respective local derby encounters with contrasting priorities. Liverpool exercised caution in a 231st meeting against Everton. Klopp made five changes from the line-up that comprehensively put City to the sword, with Salah rested completely and Firmino dropped to the substitutes' bench. In defence, Nathaniel Clyne made his first appearance of the season alongside centre-back Ragnar Klavan, whose last taste of senior action had come over four months prior. The Liverpool manager's best-laid plans still did not run to schedule as Alberto Moreno suffered a thigh injury during the warm-up at Goodison and was replaced by Rafael Camacho, a 17-year-old winger.

The end result was a dour goalless draw that held the rare distinction of being the first all-Merseyside affair since 1992 to not see a single yellow card issued. City, meanwhile, attempted to clinch the Premier League title in emphatic fashion with United's visit to the Etihad for a 176th derby clash. Feuding between the city's two sides had been stoked ahead of the game by Guardiola being asked about comments made by super-agent Mino Raiola that labelled him both 'a coward' and 'a dog'. His response was to reveal that City had been offered the chance to sign Red Devils players Paul Pogba and Henrikh Mkhitaryan, two of Raiola's clients, in the previous January transfer window.

On the pitch, the champions-elect reaped the early benefits of Agüero's return from injury by dominating the first half with a two-goal cushion courtesy of a Kompany header which was followed up five minutes later by Gündoğan, who prodded beyond David de Gea. But United managed to overturn their early setback by scoring three goals in 16 minutes, two of them coming from Pogba, to put the title celebrations on ice.

Avoiding the psychological scars of the derby defeat from seeping into the consciousness of City's players when their focus shifted back to the Champions League and Liverpool's visit preoccupied Guardiola. He knew that they would need to pull off the greatest comeback since Barcelona's decimation of PSG the previous season to stand a chance of reaching the semi-finals. After the first leg, Guardiola had warned detractors not to bet against his former employers reaching the quarter-final 'because they will be back and prove you wrong'.

In 2017, led by Guardiola's former team-mate Luis Enrique, Barça defied the odds to cancel PSG's 4-0 advantage with a 6-5 aggregate win. Guardiola also had first-hand experience of seeing comprehensive reversals overturned in Europe's premier club competition. He had been a ballboy at the Camp Nou when his boyhood club overcame a 3-0 deficit against Gothenburg to reach the 1986 European Cup Final after a penalty shoot-out. If City could emulate 'La Remontada' at the Etihad, he believed, it would accelerate their ambitions of one day winning the competition.

'To win titles we need to start with nights like this so the people understand it,' said Guardiola ahead of the game. 'Maybe not tomorrow, but with what this club has done in the last ten years in terms of creating a lot of facilities. Of course with a lot of investment, but there are a lot of people working here with the desire that sooner or later that is going to happen. Hopefully we can do it; if it doesn't happen this season then hopefully in the next one.'

In the close confines of City's training ground, he called on City's players to produce 'a perfect game' in both defence and attack. He audibly winced in frustration as they watched back one of their spurned second half chances in the Anfield tie before attempting to rouse the troops at the end of the meeting by relaying his opposite number's remarks from earlier in the day. 'Jürgen Klopp said today two things,' concluded Guardiola. 'Maybe I cannot convince you, but maybe he can. He said, "Tomorrow we're going to play the best team in Europe for the past ten months."'

City's already slim hopes of progressing were further compounded by UEFA's decision to appoint Antonio Mateu Lahoz to oversee the Liverpool showdown. A week earlier, Guardiola had criticised the Spanish referee after he booked Agüero for simulation when he was felled by goalkeeper Danijel Subasic in the penalty area during the previous season's breathless last-16 first leg encounter with Monaco. Lahoz later awarded the visitors a spot kick in the game at the Etihad and had done similar for Napoli in October's group stage meeting with City, where the Italian side were given two of their own.

In spite of the omens auguring well for his side, Klopp and his players remained guarded against the prospect of their hosts repeating the first-half onslaught that United had suffered only days earlier.

The Liverpool manager had particular cause for concern of facing what he described as a 'thunderstorm', having seen his side already surrender a comfortable advantage at the midway stage of a Champions League clash earlier in the season when they were held to a group-stage draw by Sevilla, having led 3-0 at the interval. 'We can go through all scenarios, they score early, we score early, all that stuff, but it is not to plan like this,' said Klopp. 'I can tell the boys, "Score early!" but I am not sure that really helps. We have to think about football, what we have to do, where we have to do it. This is half-time. It was the same at half-time in Anfield; the game is not over. We were in the lead, nothing else. Being in the lead is not winning. We are still in the lead but we didn't win so far. We need a little bit more from this game.'

When Liverpool stepped out before a sea of blue-and-white flags at the Etihad the following night, Klopp's prophecy rang true. City dictated the tempo of the game with 200 passes strung together in the first half-hour alone to the visitors' 58. For once, the German found his side on the receiving end of *gegenpressing* as Guardiola's charges swarmed them and reaped an instant reward in the opening stages. Sterling immediately shackled Virgil van Dijk as he attempted to play the ball out from Loris Karius's short throw. The Dutchman's appeal for a free kick after being dislodged by the winger fell on deaf ears as Bernardo Silva intercepted the touchline clearance and sent it into Fernandinho's path; the Brazilian released Sterling down Liverpool's right and squared to an unmarked Jesús to side-foot past Karius for a second time in six days, this time without the fear of an offside flag being raised.

Efforts to reverse the trend saw Mané reopen a raw wound from September's Premier League game as he slid into Otamendi, who attempted to clear the danger after Ederson had adventurously attempted to play the ball from outside his penalty area. Still reeling from the high-footed challenge which had ended his own involvement just seven months earlier, the Brazilian proceeded to push his Liverpool counterpart while Otamendi continued to writhe in agony on the turf, leading Lahoz to issue yellow cards to both players.

City's ascendancy continued with a host of a chances. De Bruyne lofted a cross-field ball into Bernardo's path, deep in Liverpool's penalty area. The playmaker produced multiple step-overs in attempts to deceive Robertson before angling a shot which was diverted wide by Firmino. Two minutes later, another deflection denied a driving effort from the Portugal international as Dejan Lovren's head sent the ball crashing against the post.

Just when the tide seemed to be turning in their favour, Guardiola's side were dealt another crushing blow as Sane played a clever pass to De Bruyne, whose perfectly weighted ball into the Liverpool box was punched clear by Karius but straight into the path of James Milner, who sent it back goalwards and allowed Sane to slot the ball through Oxlade-Chamberlain's legs for what City believed was a definitive lifeline. Again, however, the offside flag intervened despite Milner's touch legitimising the goal. In the final moments of the opening 45 minutes, Firmino, Salah and Oxlade-Chamberlain all combined before the latter rounded Ederson at his near post but skewed the sign-off.

The half-time interval drew widespread boos from the home crowd and outrage from Guardiola, who marched on to the pitch to join City's players in taking Lahoz to task over Sane's disallowed goal. 'It was a penalty! It was a goal and a penalty!' he told the official before walking away shouting 'shut up!' while making a hushing gesture. The City boss reaffirmed his views as his compatriot left the pitch, which saw Guardiola immediately ordered to see out the remainder of the game from the stands.

In the away dressing room, Lovren implored his Liverpool team-mates to 'wake up' and stop sitting deep as they had done in the opening 45 minutes. His full-throated rallying cry was given the seal of approval from Klopp, who acknowledged that his side needed to push up more and stop City having too much of the ball. A tactical tweak saw Salah occupying the central role in attack while Firmino switched out to the flank. Within a quarter of an hour, they reaped the rewards of a transformative interval as Georginio Wijnaldum, occupying the holding midfield role in lieu of a suspended Henderson, found Oxlade-Chamberlain deep in his own half to release Salah, who played in Mané on the overlap. The Senegal international surged into City's penalty area, where he was challenged by both Fernandinho and Ederson in quick succession before the ball broke for Salah, who took it past the goalkeeper and squeezed a deft left-footed chip from the byeline into the net. As the Egyptian stood before the euphoric away supporters housed behind the South Stand's goal with his arms outstretched, a plume of blue smoke surrounded him from a flare thrown on to the pitch. Just as they had done against United on the previous weekend, City found themselves succumbing to pressure at the start of the second half.

An already uphill task had now swelled into a mountain to climb without Guardiola's touchline guidance to call upon. Any previous momentum in their pursuit of a four-goal remit had ebbed away. It fully evaporated 13 minutes from time, when Otamendi's misplaced pass gifted possession to Firmino to again bear down on goal and roll a shot past an advancing Ederson. The 5-1 aggregate victory saw Liverpool reach their first Champions League semi-final in over a decade. Sitting in the luxury confines of the Colin Bell Stand's executive seats, Guardiola could only watch on dejected as his previously stellar record in the competition disintegrated. This was his sixth latter-stage exit in the tournament since winning it with Barcelona in 2011 and his teams had shipped no fewer than five goals in all bar one of those encounters.

Understandably, the contentious officiating which had underpinned the tie was at the heart of his post-match thoughts. He argued that Salah's opener in the game at Anfield should have been flagged up for offside and claimed that Sterling had been denied a legitimate penalty after a challenge by Robertson in full view of the fourth official. In addressing Lahoz's conduct, there was also no holding back. 'Mateu Lahoz is a special guy, he likes to be different, he likes to be special,' Guardiola pointedly remarked. 'He's a referee who likes to feel different, he's special. When everybody sees things, he is going to see the opposite. It's too much to send off because I didn't say any wrong word.'

The City boss remained magnanimous in defeat as he congratulated Liverpool, saying, 'I hope they can defend English football in the semi-finals. They are a top team and a top manager. They deserve to be in the semi-final.'

Klopp's eighth win over Guardiola did little to diminish a personal view that his side had just scalped the current powerhouse of European football. 'I really think they are the best team in the world at the moment, but I knew we could beat them,' he said. 'But that doesn't make us the better team. It's football, it's the cool thing in the game, that it's still possible.'

Jubilant away supporters left the Etihad that night with plenty to shout about. As they made their way down the South Stand's staircases, passers-by outside could hear the rhythmic banging and chanting of 'Allez Allez Allez', a terrace anthem which was fast providing the soundtrack to Anfield's season. A select few in the family enclosure learned about running the gauntlet the hard way with one away fan embroiled in a brawl with home supporters mid-game after celebrating Salah's second-half equaliser. The fallout from the double-header continued in the days that followed as UEFA opening disciplinary proceedings against both clubs.

Liverpool faced four charges for the supporter disorder in the first leg that led to the damage caused to City's team coach and were subsequently fined £17,500. Anfield officials were also ordered to pay an additional £5,270 for the use of pyrotechnics, crowd disturbances and damage caused by travelling supporters inside the Etihad during the return leg. Guardiola was found guilty on two counts of improper conduct in that follow-up fixture after being sent to the stands by Lahoz and proceeding to communicate with his backroom staff during the game, which is forbidden by European football's governing body. The City manager was hit with a two-match touchline suspension with half of the sanction deferred for a probationary period of one season.

Salah's 44-goal haul in 2017/18 earned him the season's PFA Player of the Year award ahead of fellow favourite De Bruyne and City team-mates David Silva and Leroy Sané. He became the second African player to win the award in the space of three years, but Guardiola affirmed his view that De Bruyne was a more deserving winner in the hours leading up to the unveiling ceremony. 'If he doesn't win, then congrats to the guy that wins, but in my opinion, there is no player better than him in terms of continuity, every three days [playing] competitions,' he said after City's 5-0 win over Swansea. 'Maybe the numbers say someone is better than him but this season there has been no one better than him. That's my opinion but players can have another one. But in the end, in the summertime, we will be at home being champions.'

Klopp countered the City manager's view when delivering a video message to Salah after he became the fifth Liverpool player to simultaneously claim both the PFA and FWA's top accolades. 'In a season when Manchester City have been outstandingly good and played outstandingly well, football from another planet, you have won the two major awards,' he said. 'The one voted for by your fellow professionals and now the one voted for by the football writers. You are world-class, Mo, truly world-class.'

City's lack of individual recognition was adequately compensated just five days after their European exit as Manchester United's inability to overcome relegation candidates West Bromwich Albion handed the Premier League title to their local rivals. In the leafy Cheshire suburb of Hale, Francis Lee's utopian vision for City finally came to life. Led by Kompany, some of the best-paid players from the happiest club in the land descended on the Railway pub to celebrate and sing until they were hoarse.

Having dispatched City in the last-eight, Liverpool went on to reach the Champions League Final against reigning holders Real Madrid. Oxlade-Chamberlain's season had ended in the semifinal first leg against AS Roma, following a challenge by ex-City defender Aleksandar Kolarov. The quest for a sixth European Cup, similarly, fell away when Salah was forced off during the early stages of the final at Kiev's Olympiyskiy Stadium with a shoulder injury inflicted by a collision with Real captain Sergio Ramos. Karius also suffered at the hands of the Spanish giants' captain as a collision early in the second half led to the goalkeeper receiving a concussion, later confirmed further assessment at Massachusetts General Hospital.

Rest did not come easily for Klopp after losing a third showpiece in as many years. At 6am the following day, he and his backroom staff were partying with Andreas Frege, better known as 'Campino' from the German punk rock band Die Toten Hosen in the Liverpool manager's Formby home. Footage of the group singing an impromptu chant about bringing the European Cup back to Anfield went viral on social media. Unbeknown to everyone apart from Klopp's inner circle, his plans were already afoot.

High Tension Line

EVENTS IN the previous season had elevated Manchester City and Liverpool's rivalry to an exponentially higher plane. The cult of personality that accompanied both Jürgen Klopp and Pep Guardiola took their current battle far outside the confines of its traditional north-west setting. Theirs was now a meeting of two broad churches being played out on the world stage.

Klopp discovered first-hand how the sharply evolving nature of his contest with Guardiola had stretched when the two clubs took part in the International Champions Cup at New York's MetLife Stadium on 25 July 2018. A patchy playing surface had been caused by a stage being laid over it to accommodate a Taylor Swift concert at the stadium three days before the match took place. Poor conditions aside, the Premier League duo produced a close-run contest which began with Leroy Sané bursting ahead of Virgil van Dijk to fire a tight-angled opener in the 56th minute. Klopp's side struck back seven minutes later as Rafael Camacho floated a cross in for Mohamed Salah to power past Joe Hart despite being offside. In the second minute of stoppage time, Tosin Adarabioyo's needless clattering of Dominic Solanke conceded a late penalty from which Sadio Mané netted to steal the spoils. Neither team took a great deal away from the game itself, but the Liverpool manager was treated to a strand of Big Apple hostility, four years after the Reds' previous trouble-free visit.

An underlying proxy war had existed between the clubs due to their vested interests with Major League Baseball's most vitriolic rivalry – the Boston Red Sox and New York Yankees

– but previously never rose to the surface. Klopp's accidental interruption of Pep Guardiola's post-match press conference saw it finally manifest with local reporters angrily heckling the Liverpool manager for encroaching on his opposite number's space. The German apologised profusely to his City counterpart, who beckoned him over to the top table before offering a handshake and addressing the room, 'Jürgen Klopp, please,' before exiting stage-right.

Equally bemused, Klopp attempted to open his own media briefing with a joke: 'That's how we finish press conferences. Maybe Jose Mourinho will come and finish *my* press conference.' Few inside the room appeared willing to humour him for unintentionally disrupting the Catalan in full flow. Poor organisation had led to the awkward moment, yet it also exposed the growing dichotomy between the clubs ahead of the 2018/19 season. A tribal battle between City and Liverpool was now incorporating more than just their two clubs. It was also Guardiola and Klopp; 'tiki-taka' and *gegenpressing*; the Yankees and the Red Sox.

Fewer than 48 hours after a chastening Champions League Final loss to Real Madrid, Klopp had set about planning for the new campaign with the £43.7m capture of Monaco midfielder Fabinho in a summer where Liverpool's spending would surpass £175.2m. To challenge City's growing dominance, on the biggest stages of both domestic and European football, they had to think as big as the reigning league champions in more than the market. Klopp put his fondness for the *Rocky* film series to articulate the challenge that lay ahead of his side before preparing to lay siege to City's crown. 'We are still Rocky Balboa and not Ivan Drago,' he said. 'We have to do more, to fight more, to do all these things. That must be our attitude.'

Liverpool's start to the season was more befitting of a bona fide heavyweight than a plucky underdog. An emphatic opening-day win over former City manager Manuel Pellegrini's West Ham United only fuelled a growing belief that Anfield's 29-year wait to become English champions was almost certainly going to end.

That momentum saw Klopp's side take an early lead in the title race with a flawless six-game run before a stalemate with Chelsea saw them overtaken at the top by City on goal difference.

A first meeting between the top two on 7 October became a genuine six-pointer with both teams on 19 points and memories of their recent Continental showdown, on and off the pitch, still fresh in the mind. City's attempts to prevent a repeat of the damage inflicted on their team coach in its previous Anfield visit led to a series of extensive security measures. The vehicle used for travelling to Merseyside had been specially adapted to include 15 high-definition cameras that could identify any potential assailants should any objects again be thrown in its direction. Validating their precautionary measures was the circulation of another anonymous flyer on social media imploring fans to converge at the foot of Anfield Road to welcome both team vehicles ahead of the game. The 1894 Group, a collective of fans who organise pre-match displays at the Etihad Stadium, argued that travelling supporters should take it upon themselves to ensure their team's safe passage into the stadium on account of Merseyside Police's failure to both prevent the previous season's attack and reprimand those responsible.

It was front and centre of Guardiola's pre-match thoughts also. 'The police knew it before it happened. Now they know it, I don't know what's going to happen,' he said. 'I think the best way to protect the bus is down to the Liverpool fans who are there. The best way is that we should not need the police. Why should the police need to be there? For what? We arrive there both sides, to play a Premier League game. Why should our fans have to protect our bus? Are you kidding me? I would like the police to go home at 4.30pm with their families, drinking a beer and loving the show, that is what they should do. But that depends on the Liverpool people, not on Manchester City.'

Guardiola and his players eventually arrived at Anfield unscathed but events of the previous seven months did not fly under the radar with the home supporters. One of the more noticeable banners displayed on The Kop ahead of kick-off depicted an upright bottle of Kopparberg cider, the most prominent object which had flown through the air towards City's team coach, surrounded by the title of Oasis's 2002 single 'Stop Crying Your Heart Out'.

Guardiola's rare attempt at ultra-conservatism reduced the visitors to their lowest possession statistics in the league – 51 per cent – since he took charge two years earlier. A hat-trick of defeats against Klopp's side in all competitions had clearly left the Catalan eager to appear more street-smart on his latest visit to Anfield Road. The tactic had a desired effect in limiting Liverpool's attacking outlet, with the front three of Salah, Mané and Roberto Firmino cutting forlorn figures. City's overall performance, similarly, did little to inspire confidence that they would be producing a smash-and-grab victory on the ground where they had not won for over 16 years. But a clumsy trip from Virgil van Dijk on Leroy Sané in the penalty area, five minutes from time, handed them an unlikely chance. With designated spot-kick taker Sergio Agüero substituted earlier after another ineffectual display in front of goal, the onus fell to Riyad Mahrez to convert. The Algerian's track record of five penalty misses from his previous eight attempts failed to inspire confidence that City's new club-record signing would break the habit. His skied attempt into the Anfield Road End handed Liverpool a late reprieve in a game which neither side deserved to win.

Their hosts dropped into third with the stalemate but resumed a neck-and-neck battle with Guardiola's side the following weekend. The lead changed hands just three times over the next nine weeks before City suffered a hat-trick of defeats in their next four games. A seven-point advantage could have potentially become season-ending if Klopp's charges were able to extend it to double figures in their 3 January meeting at the Etihad Stadium. But the mood within Anfield remained one of cautious optimism, with fans resisting the temptation to jinx their latest domestic push. Xherdan Shaqiri also refused to describe the upcoming meeting with Guardiola's side as a potential title decider. 'For us, we don't go there to take Man City out of the race,' he said.

'We go there for a Premier League game. We go there to make a good performance first of all and try to win games. That's the only goal that we have. There are no other things in our minds at the moment.'

Guardiola talked up his side's chances and pointed to the previous season's comprehensive five-goal thrashing in the league as grounds for optimism. 'Everyone is talking if we lose, but we can win,' he insisted. 'Last year, we beat them 5-0 here. It's Liverpool, the best team in England's history. We can beat them. I know today nobody trusts us, but it is what it is.'

Eastlands's high-stakes encounter began with a seminal moment as Salah and Firmino combined to set Mané away for a shot which cannoned back off the post before the ball looped towards an open goal after John Stones hit an attempted clearance straight into the City goalkeeper. Home fans held their breath and half-expected the worst before Stones rushed back to perform a 180-degree turn which scooped it off the line and out of Salah's attempted follow-up. Technology showed that just one-tenth of the ball, equating to 11.77mm, had not crossed the line before the defender's logic-defying interception. Liverpool's official Twitter account encapsulated the views of the watching world with its reaction of 'HOW DID THAT NOT GO IN?!'

The hosts' narrow escape provoked an opener five minutes before half-time as Sergio Agüero gave Dejan Lovren the slip to meet Bernardo Silva's near-post ball to drill past Alisson.

Klopp wildly gesticulated as his team toiled following the interval before a diving header by Firmino, meeting Robertson's cross to the far post, levelled up the clash to preserve the seven-point gulf. But Leroy Sané's sweeping finish eight minutes later shifted momentum back in City's favour as they inflicted Liverpool's first domestic defeat of the season, after 21 matches, and cut the points gap down to almost half. A fraught closing stages saw Guardiola's frustrations boil over as he confronted fourth official Martin Atkinson when referee Anthony Taylor allowed play to resume for Firmino's foul on Fernandinho which led to Salah almost levelling from the ensuing chance. The outburst led to the City manager later receiving a warning from the FA about his future conduct.

Fuelled by a renewed belief that they could recapture the title, home fans gleefully chanted 'Campeones! Campeones!' at the final whistle. Stones's remarkable first-half intervention had galvanised both his side's ailing team and their supporters. In the bowels of the Etihad, he triumphantly shouted 'Hadouken!' while watching back replays of his goal-line heroics.

On Merseyside, the perceived injustice behind the no-goal led to half-baked accusations of impropriety. An online petition was set up demanding a 'review of 100 per cent accurate goal line technology' in the game at the Etihad, with a subheading, 'It's not fair. We want justice.' Liverpool fans' podcast *The Anfield Wrap* also theorised that City had prepared their stadium's playing surface with the sole intentions of deliberately frustrating Klopp's side. 'It looked like a pitch that had been prepared for one thing – to stop fast passing,' claimed host Neil Atkinson. 'This is a Pep Guardiola pitch that's been set up to stop fast passing and I think that tells the story of how Manchester City approached the game about as much as anything else.' Those claims were shot down by Guardiola within a matter of days, when he previewed City's League Cup semi-final first leg at home to Burton Albion.

'I am not the groundskeeper. If Liverpool want to play quick, we want to play quicker,' he insisted. 'Never we manipulated it, always we try to put water [on the pitch] but it's not necessary here with the weather, it rains a lot. We want to cut the field all the time, all my career, ten years as a manager. The better conditions for both teams, I never put in some trick about this. Always when you do this, karma or something punishes you. You have to do the best for the opponents, for the game, respect the game and the rules. I never speak with the groundsmen ... how many issues do I have in my head to think about the pitch? I trust the groundsmen. I never made a phone call to say, "Do this to damage our opponents."'

With minimal room for error, Guardiola took to publicly warning his players that one defeat in their remaining 15 fixtures would practically kill off City's title hopes. Those worst fears appeared to be confirmed on 29 January as Rafael Benitez did his former employers a favour with Newcastle rallying to a 2-1 victory. The following night, a giddy Anfield greeted their team's visit of Leicester City believing that the early-year gulf would be restored. But a combination of heavy snowfall and poor finishing saw the Reds fail to take full advantage of the reigning champions' slip-up. Guardiola chose not to watch City's rivals losing further ground in the title race. Instead, he spent the evening watching *Jersey Boys* with his family at the Palace Theatre in Manchester's Oxford Road.

Kyle Walker, however, could not resist poking fun at his rivals' expense on Twitter. The City right-back posted a picture of Leicester's scorer, his England team-mate Harry Maguire, shooting the breeze with his girlfriend Fern Hawkins in Moscow's Otkritie Arena following the previous year's World Cup penalty shoot-out win against Colombia with the caption, 'So basically they thought they were gonna go 7 points ahead.' Guardiola insisted he was 'not concerned' by the post but Klopp took issue with the defender's since deleted tweet. 'I'm not sure what that says about us, it says a bit more about the other person,' he said. 'I never celebrated another team dropping points or losing a game … For supporters it's a bit different. For people involved I don't understand it. But how can I criticise if I don't understand it?'

A lack of comprehension became a common theme in Liverpool's upcoming form. Ex-City boss Manuel Pellegrini hoped to 'give a hand' to his old employers when his West Ham side took on Klopp's charges. The Chilean fulfilled his end of the bargain as Klopp's charges were held to a 1-1 draw at the London Stadium on 4 February. James Milner, Pellegrini's former player at the Etihad, appeared perplexed by questions about whether the Reds' recent form had become cause for alarm. 'Concerned being top of the league in February? No, I'm happy!' Two days later, the versatile midfielder was no longer sitting pretty at the summit. City's upcoming League Cup Final appearance saw their trip to Everton brought forward, with the ensuing 2-0 victory propelling them above Liverpool for the first time since 15 December. A stalemate with Everton, their fourth in six previous games, further eroded the previous advantage as City took a one-point swing in the title race. Klopp shrugged off the power shift, saying, 'I'm completely fine with chasing. Who wants to be top of the table at the beginning of March? It is nice but there are lots of games to play.'

Only City's prior engagement in the latter stages of the FA Cup afforded Liverpool fleeting moments to reclaim pole position. By 24 April, some Kopites had resorted to the sacrilege of cheering on Manchester United in the vain hope that their one-time adversary could somehow throw a roadblock in the way of City's juggernaut. Just 24 hours after Guardiola's side won at Old Trafford, Liverpool clinched their first FA Youth Cup since 2007 in defeating City's under-18 side on penalties. The hosts had led until four minutes from time, when Bobby Duncan unleashed a 25-yard strike that slipped through Louis Moulden's hands. The teenager had previously been part of the ranks at Eastlands but grew frustrated with a lack of opportunities. He was left in limbo for the best part of a year after rejecting a new contract offer from the Blues, who retained his registration, in August 2017. A compensation fee in the region of £200,000 was later agreed to allow Duncan to join Liverpool, following in his cousin Steven Gerrard's footsteps. Within months of the final, the relationship with his boyhood club soured when his agent Saif Rubie publicly accused several senior figures, including sporting director Michael Edwards, of 'mentally bullying' the promising forward, who subsequently joined Fiorentina.

Ahead of a potentially defining weekend, Klopp likened the intensifying battle to the plot of the 1980s movie *Highlander*, because 'only one of us will be there at the end'. A comprehensive 5-0 win over Huddersfield Town allowed his side to assume the driving seat for just under 48 hours before City took on Burnley. Sergio Agüero's bundled 64th minute effort was hooked off the line by Matthew Lowton but not before technology awarded the visitors an opener which ultimately settled the scrappy encounter. The champions' official Twitter account posted an image captioned 'Fine Margins', accompanied by a magnifying glass emoji, showing the difference between the 11mm of Stones's clearance against Liverpool and the 29.5mm the ball had travelled over the line at Turf Moor.

Consolation for the former leaders arrived that evening as Virgil van Dijk was named the PFA Player of the Year. The Dutchman saw off competition from City trio Raheem Sterling, Bernardo Silva and Sergio Agüero as well as Liverpool team-mate Sadio Mané to win the award, voted for by his fellow professionals. Sterling won the organisation's Young Player accolade and scooped the FWA's top honour with 62 per cent of the vote, beating Van Dijk by over 100 nominations, to become his club's first winner since Tony Book in 1969.

Van Dijk's PFA win threatened to be the season's only tangible success at Anfield as their secondary position in the title race was exacerbated by Barcelona racing into a three-goal lead at the midway point of their Champions League semi-final. Before the return leg, Liverpool faced a reunion with Rafael Benitez at St James' Park on the same weekend that City would entertain Leicester, now managed by ex-Reds boss Brendan Rodgers. But Guardiola was quick to warn against any prospect of an old pal's act. 'Brendan and Rafa were in Liverpool, but they'll want to win,' he said. 'I cannot imagine them [Newcastle] not wanting to win the game. I don't have doubts.' The Catalan's words proved accurate as the Magpies contested a five-goal thriller that was settled by Divock Origi's late finish. At the Etihad, on 6 May, a thunderbolt from outgoing captain Vincent Kompany was enough to seal City's 13th consecutive win to make the title all but certain.

Foregone conclusions were not being readily accepted on Merseyside as Guardiola's former club saw their previously comfortable advantage decimated inside 72 minutes as Liverpool booked their place in the Champions League Final with a 4-3 aggregate win over the Catalans. In the build-up to the game, the City boss had paid tribute to both teams by declaring them as his toughest challenges as a manager. 'In my career as a manager, I played against incredible sides,' he said. 'But there are two that were "Wow!" One is Barcelona managed by Luis Enrique, with Neymar, Messi and Suarez. The other is this Liverpool. They're the best two sides I've faced as a manager. That's why being there, with it in our hands, fighting against them until the end, being seven points behind, is so good. It's the toughest league I've ever played as a manager, for the quality from the rivals. No doubts. That's why being there is incredible. But, of course, only one will take the prize and the other one will be at home sad.'

Fuelled by the momentum of their recent European exploits, Liverpool headed into their final Premier League fixture against Wolverhampton Wanderers daring to believe in the improbable as City travelled to Brighton and Hove Albion. Sadio Mané put the hosts ahead before cheers going up around Anfield informed them that their challengers were trailing at the Amex Stadium. For 83 seconds, the famous old stadium dared to dream that a near three-decade drought was about to come to an end before Agüero struck a swift equaliser. Soon afterwards, with the score on the south coast unchanged, pockets of Wolves supporters mischievously attempted to lull their home counterparts into a false sense of security by hinting that Brighton had gone ahead again with cheers. Once the ruse was foiled, news of every City goal drew wildly euphoric celebrations from the Black Country outfit's fans as their hosts ran out 2-0 winners with Mané scoring again.

Andy Robertson reflected on the domestic shortfall by vowing that Liverpool would return emboldened by their close-run title race. 'We will go into next season as strong as ever. Man City know, hopefully, we are here to stay,' he said. 'We know they are definitely here to stay; they are incredible. Then all the teams have to catch us as there was quite a gap between second and third. They all need to come up to us and if they do it will be an incredible title race next season.'

Klopp congratulated his victorious opponents after 'an incredible season' and warned that his team would need to again raise the stakes to stand a chance of overhauling the back-to-back champions. 'As long as City are around with the quality they have, the financial power and all that stuff, it's not like any other team will pass them easily,' he said. 'That's clear. So we need to be very, very close to perfection to win the Premier League. But we have made unbelievably big steps and I really expect there's more to come.'

The goodwill would last barely 48 hours after video footage of City's flight back from Brighton showed players and staff members gloating in their rivals' misfortune by singing a crude cover version of the 'Allez, Allez, Allez' chant which referred to Liverpool fans 'crying in the stands ... and battered in the streets' in their 2018 Champions League Final defeat to Real Madrid.

The tasteless lyrics drew a raft of criticism including from the family of Sean Cox, who had suffered life-altering injuries a year earlier after being set upon by Italian hooligans outside Anfield shortly before the semi-final with AS Roma. His brother Martin deplored the glorification of football-related violence. 'City should be singing about their club and the euphoria of winning the league,' he told *The Guardian*. 'It is hard to understand why you would bring up a song about Liverpool and people being hurt when you should be singing about Manchester City. Obviously there is banter between football fans but people being battered on the streets is not banter. This is tarnishing their achievement.'

City attempted to defend the on-board performance by disputing allegations that it contained underhand reference to both Mr Cox and the Hillsborough tragedy. 'The song in question, which has been a regular chant during the 2018/19 season, refers to the 2018 UEFA Champions League Final in Kiev,' said a club spokesperson. 'Any suggestion that the lyrics relate to Sean Cox or the Hillsborough tragedy is entirely without foundation.'

Guardiola maintained the party line about the song's ambiguity but offered up a public apology for the fall-out that it had caused in his press conference before the FA Cup Final. 'It was not what people say,' he insisted. 'Do you think for one second someone could imagine we would give offence about Hillsborough or the guy who was hurt against Rome? It's incredible to think anyone could believe that. Those were tragedies for the Liverpool people. We were happy for ourselves, but if someone was offended for another issue, I'm sorry. I apologise. It was never our intention. We celebrated because we win the Premier League against an incredible contender.'

City's comprehensive 6-0 Wembley win over Watford clinched an unprecedented domestic treble but the widespread acclaim that Liverpool continued to receive following their Champions League run still hit a nerve for followers of Guardiola's all-conquering team. Towards the end of the one-sided affair, an irate supporter found his way into the Wembley press box and attempted to confront the working media: 'We've done the domestic fucking treble!' he bellowed. 'No one's ever done it before. But you'll all have Mo Salah on the back of the fucking papers tomorrow!' Antipathy towards Liverpool had grown so much that a survey by the *Manchester Evening News* revealed 80 per cent of fans surveyed expressed a stronger dislike for their Merseyside rivals than Manchester United.

Sterling admitted in the days leading up to the FA Cup Final that his former club were now the side that City supporters relished facing the most. 'Every time we play Liverpool now, that's when the stadium is at its loudest, the fans are roaring,' he told the *Daily Mirror*. 'The game against Liverpool at home, I don't want to sound arrogant, but we did say as a group that if we win that game then we can still have a chance of winning this title race. It was a must-win game for us. We knew how high the stakes were and you realise this is getting serious now, it's crunch time now and I'm just grateful that we were able to get over the line.'

At a fourth attempt, Liverpool finally ended their own quest for silverware under Jürgen Klopp by seeing off Tottenham in the Champions League Final. Searing temperatures of 29°C combined with a three-week break between the English season's end and the showpiece at Madrid's Wanda Metropolitano contributed to a languid contest which was settled by goals in each half from Salah and Origi.

Shortly after his crowning moment in the Anfield hot seat, Klopp revealed that he had already begun making plans for the new campaign. 'A second ago I had Pep Guardiola on the phone and we promised each other that we will kick each other's butts again next season,' he told reporters. 'We will go for everything and see what we get. Getting 97 points in the Premier League and winning the Champions League is an unbelievable long way to go and we did it. That's incredible. Now we've won something, we will carry on.'

Stop the Clocks

THOUSANDS OF miles away from the 750,000-strong crowds that celebrated Liverpool's sixth Champions League triumph, Barcelona were still smarting from their semi-final exit. Inquisitions into how Ernesto Valverde's side had surrendered a three-goal lead so wilfully continued long into the summer. Pep Guardiola took time out while holidaying in Catalonia to try to shed some light on his former club's capitulation in a wide-ranging interview with local newspaper *ARA*.

'The motto "This is Anfield" is no marketing spin. There's something about it that you will find in no other stadium in the world,' he said. 'They score a goal and over the next five minutes you feel that you'll receive another four. You feel small and the rival players seem to be all over. We've all gone through what happened to Barça. They were laughing at me when we were losing 3-0 after the first 15–20 minutes of the quarter-final. It's a bugger of a ground.'

Asked about the Reds' failure to overhaul Manchester City in the previous season's Premier League title race, Guardiola admitted that the shortfall would only make the new European champions more determined. 'Winning the Premier League is really tough, and I speak from experience; this is the first time in 11 years that a team has won two consecutive league titles, which Barça did many times,' he said. 'In contrast, Liverpool hasn't won the league for 30 years and we've all seen what a team Liverpool were this year. I am certain Liverpool are extremely eager to win the Premier League.'

Jürgen Klopp's pledge from Madrid descended into verbal sparring before the clubs' first meeting of the 2019/20 campaign in the Community Shield after the reigning Premier League champions had already spent almost £70m in capturing highly rated Atlético Madrid midfielder Rodri and luring full-back Angelino back from PSV Eindhoven. Three days after taking part in English football's traditional curtain-raiser, they would add Juventus's João Cancelo for another £60m but failed in a pursuit of Harry Maguire, earmarked as a replacement for the departed Vincent Kompany, as he joined Manchester United in an £80m deal, with Guardiola later claiming that the Blues 'could not afford' the outlay on the England centre-back. Comparatively, Klopp had made only incremental changes to his squad in the form of youngsters Harvey Elliott and Sepp van den Berg. The Liverpool manager responded to questions about his lack of spending by insisting that his own club could not justify an annual spree like several of their European peers.

'I can't say anything about what other teams are doing. I don't know how they do it,' he said. 'We have to pay bills. Sorry. Everybody has to pay bills; we have to pay bills. We invested money in this team. Now it looks like we are not. But we are not in this fantasia land where you just get whatever you want. You cannot do it constantly. It looks like there are four clubs in the world who can do it constantly. Madrid, Barcelona, City and PSG. Whatever they need, they do. You cannot compare that. That is the situation.'

Although insistent that his comments were not intended as a criticism of the quartet, Klopp's view still irked Guardiola when he looked ahead to the Wembley showdown. 'Of course it bothers me because it's not true,' he said. 'It's Liverpool – "You'll Never Walk Alone" – so it's not a small team; it's Liverpool. Two seasons ago, when we spent a lot … But we cannot spend £200m every season like, for example, Liverpool spent more than £100m last season but cannot do it this season. Today, the clubs cannot spend a lot of money every season. I don't know what happened at Barcelona because I'm not there. If they think they can do it, it's because they can do it. That's why Financial Fair Play, when something is wrong and the clubs are not correct, they are punished. That is the reality. Other managers can say what they say but I can only say that is not true.'

Fiduciary gripes aside, the City manager remained effusive in his praise for the German coach. 'He is a class manager, a top manager. It is an incredible challenge for me when I face his teams,' added Guardiola. 'The way he plays, his behaviour, his smile, hugging; I think it's so good for football. His message is always in a positive way, sometimes with some exceptions, but most of the time it's good.'

Klopp had triumphed over Guardiola when they faced off in the German Super Cup, in 2013 and 2014, but placed little emphasis on what might happen in the English equivalent. 'I won it twice but nobody mentions it,' he said. 'The Super Cup – you win it, nobody cares; you lose it and some care.' That mutual respect did not extend to the club's respective fan bases as violence broke out less than an hour before their latest on-field meeting. Liverpool and City supporters punched and kicked each other on the London Underground after a train had pulled into Great Portland Street station. A glass bottle was thrown during the brawl, which lasted several minutes, as the fighting took place between the train's exit doors and adjoining platform. Seven men were later arrested on suspicion of violent disorder for their part in the skirmishes.

A forgettable pre-season campaign had seen Liverpool concede the opening goal in their previous five fixtures, winning just one of those outings against star-studded opponents including Napoli, Sevilla, Lyon and Klopp's old club Dortmund. That pattern repeated itself at Wembley as City swarmed their goal in the opening stages. Raheem Sterling comfortably dispossessed England team-mate Joe Gomez and threaded the ball for Leroy Sané to take on Alisson Becker but he fired into the side-netting. Liverpool's attempted response came in the form of Divock Origi and Roberto Firmino combining to tee up Mohamed Salah but the Egyptian's shot went the wrong side of the post. On 11 minutes,

Kyle Walker's floated pass was headed into David Silva's path by Kevin De Bruyne before the Spaniard hooked it into Sterling's path to skim the ball through Alisson's legs. Helped by Rodri's masterful debut outing, City's grip on the game appeared near-total as the teams headed in for half-time. Guardiola's animated touchline demeanour led to him becoming the first manager to be issued a yellow card under the new guidelines after taking issue with Gomez's challenge on Silva.

Liverpool ramped up the pressure after the interval with Virgil van Dijk rattling the crossbar from Trent Alexander-Arnold's corner. Memories of John Stones's timely intervention at the Etihad Stadium just seven months earlier came flooding back as the ball bounced halfway across the goal line but was not adjudged to have fully crossed it in the eyes of the Goal Decision System.

Joël Matip's introduction two minutes later proved a catalyst as Klopp's side continued to pile on the pressure and they belatedly made a breakthrough in the 77th minute when Walker headed a free kick from Jordan Henderson into Van Dijk's path at the byeline. The PFA Player of the Year sent the ball back in for Matip to get the better of Nicolas Otamendi and power a downward header past Bravo to level. Tensions continued to simmer on the sidelines as Klopp and Guardiola traded opinions before Henderson attempted to confront the City manager following his 80th-minute substitution.

In the thick of the action, Van Dijk's distinction of not being dribbled past in over 65 competitive matches was finally broken by Gabriel Jesús, who had replaced an injured Sane just moments earlier. Otamendi's defensive frailties again showed as he allowed Salah to bear down on goal and test Bravo with a shot which rebounded back for the Egyptian to head the ball into an empty net. Only Walker's supreme athleticism kept it out with an acrobatic overhead clearance in front of an end of disbelieving Liverpool supporters. With the game still even at the final whistle, Klopp playfully rubbed Guardiola's head when the two managers shook hands as the showdown went into penalties. Bravo denied Georginio Wijnaldum to give City an upper hand which Alisson almost cancelled out as he got a hand to Oleksandr Zinchenko's powerful effort but could not keep it out. Jesús clinched the Shield with the final spot kick to seal a 5-4 win for City.

Liverpool's players watched on as their opponents clambered up Wembley's 107 steps to claim the first silverware of the season before Klopp admitted that his side's fightback from an initially sluggish start offered hopes for the nine months ahead. 'With the amount of chances we created, it is a very good sign,' he said. 'The best thing is that they showed they were really hungry. The character was incredibly good. The boys did what they have to do.' Reflecting on the strength of Guardiola's triumphant squad, he added, 'I said before the game, if you want to be prepared for Man City you have to make a pre-season game against Man City; no team plays like them.'

His opposite number refused to discount the prospect of another two-horse race in the Premier League. 'I don't think there will be two contenders to win the Premier League. United have signed Maguire. There will be many contenders this time,' insisted Guardiola. 'Liverpool are the champions of Europe that's why I give a lot of credit for our victory today. They are a top-class team. The difference was one penalty. It's good to face them to see how well prepared we have to be to try and win the titles.'

The City manager was already contending with an injury headache due to Sane's withdrawal with what later emerged as season-ending knee ligament damage. Liverpool suffered their own setback on the Premier League's opening night as Alisson sustained a calf injury while taking a goal kick in the first half against Norwich City. Former West Ham United goalkeeper Adrián was thrust into the spotlight mere days after arriving as Simon Mignolet's replacement in reserve. In total, the Brazil international would miss 11 matches in all competitions, including the Reds' win over Chelsea in the UEFA Super Cup.

Alisson's absence did not detract from Klopp's players taking a commanding lead in the title race. At the Etihad, City's hopes of keeping pace with the early leaders against Tottenham Hotspur were dealt a blow by VAR, which had denied them in the previous season's Champions League quarter-final against the Londoners, as Jesús's last-gasp winner was ruled out at the same end that Sterling's would-be clincher had been chalked off. Technology may have conspired against them in the final stages, but the hosts had mustered 30 shots at goal compared to the Spurs tally of three in the 2-2 draw.

An early two-point gap between the Premier League's main challengers led to a series of attempts by small sections of the English media to stoke their already fierce rivalry. The first appeared in the *Daily Express*, which claimed on 11 September that James Milner's every touch had been booed by City fans when he appeared for their Legends team in Vincent Kompany's testimonial – despite the Liverpool midfielder not playing any actual part in the game. The tabloid newspaper subsequently doubled down on its false reporting by claiming that 'unconfirmed claims on social media' of Milner receiving abuse upon his return to the Etihad had formed the basis of its online article. A ruling by the Independent Press Standards Organisation in April 2020 later forced the *Express* to admit that the story had been written in advance of the charity game and published in error.

The lead more than doubled on 14 September as City slumped to a 3-2 loss against Norwich. Peter Moore, Liverpool's CEO, greeted the result by posting a picture of a canary on his personal Twitter account, before later deleting it. At Carrow Road, Guardiola was left facing questions on whether his reigning champions were capable of again overhauling Klopp's runaway charges as they had done in the closing stages of the previous seasons. 'Five points [behind Liverpool] is five points but we are in September,' he pointed out. 'What are we supposed to do, say, "It's September and congratulations to Liverpool, you are champions"? Not for one second am I going to doubt my players. We'll recover, train and come back. We've dropped five points.'

A month later, he was forced to revisit that prediction after the gulf had stretched to eight points with Liverpool maintaining their 100 per cent start to the season before City suffered an unexpected home loss to Wolverhampton Wanderers, their first such result since 1984. 'The distance is big, I know that,' conceded Guardiola. 'For many circumstances, they [Liverpool] didn't drop points. It is better not to think one team is eight points ahead. It is only October … It is better to think about what is next.'

Later that month, summer signing Rodri admitted that he had been taken aback by the frightening nature of Klopp's charges as he acclimatised to life in the English top flight. 'I touched down to find one of the best teams I've seen in recent years,' he told *The Guardian*. 'Liverpool get seen as a counter-attacking team, but they dominate, score from set plays, the attacking mechanisms are well-worked, they have variety. Klopp's teams are tough, physical. They go at you like animals. They're like a knife: one comes at you, then another.'

Only Manchester United's ability to hold Liverpool to a draw allowed City to bridge the gap to six points ahead of their 10 November showdown at Anfield. Beforehand, Guardiola took aim at Sadio Mané after the striker had helped his team to a late win at Aston Villa on the same afternoon that his own side had seen off Southampton. 'It has happened many times, what Liverpool have done in the last few years,' he told BBC Sport. 'It's because [Mané] is a special talent. Sometimes he's diving, sometimes he has this talent to score incredible goals in the last minute.'

Klopp sought to downplay the growing furore by insisting he had not heard Guardiola make direct reference to the Senegal international while suggesting that his opposite number was fixated on the Anfield club. 'When I came into the interview after the game [at Villa Park] I really had no clue what the other Premier League results were … Then someone told me City won in the 86th minute and all this happened. I don't understand these types of things. My brain is not big enough to think about another team as well. I have enough to do to think about us.'

Three days on from the initial fall-out, the Catalan attempted to backtrack by claiming his remarks were related to a late penalty that Mané had won the previous week against Leicester City rather than events of the previous weekend. 'In the 94th minute against Leicester, it was a penalty and it was "wow" – that was the intention for my comment,' he explained. 'Far away from my intention to say Sadio is this type of player because I admire him a lot.'

Mané himself saw no issue with Guardiola's remarks or a need to change his playing style. 'I think it's a bit clever from him to get the attention of the referee,' he told reporters after Liverpool's Champions League group stage win over KRC Genk. 'But I will just play my football like I'm always doing. I don't pay attention to what he's saying because it's part of football. It doesn't make anything [different] for me. Even though I saw him commenting about it, what he said, for me, I think it's positive.'

Guardiola's preamble for his side's trip to Merseyside was a nightmarish one, with Ederson limping out at half-time of their 1-1 draw with Atalanta in the Champions League with a muscle complaint while his replacement Claudio Bravo was sent off after the interval, forcing right-back Kyle Walker to deputise in goal for the remaining nine minutes. As focus gravitated towards Anfield, the City manager rejected claims that they would be unfancied against the league leaders. 'I've never gone into a game feeling like an outsider or an underdog, thinking I am not going to win,' he said. 'I am not going to take the bus to Liverpool thinking I am going to lose the game. That has never happened in my career.' Whether intentional or accidental, Guardiola's reference to the team coach had revealed an underlying concern within the Etihad Stadium's corridors of power. Fears that their players would face a similarly hostile ordeal to the one which had overshadowed their Champions League quarter-final first-leg visit two seasons earlier had resurfaced.

Justifying their reservations once more was another digital flyer on social media in the days leading up to the game which invited home supporters to line the route to welcome both teams. The unidentified individual had again implored 'bring your pyro, pints, flags and banners – let's make it like a European night!' Klopp attempted to defuse the prospect of powder-keg atmosphere by offering a retrospective *mea culpa* to his counterparts for what he described as a 'senseless' attack. 'If somebody at Man City is concerned still – I don't know if they are – then it's our fault,' he said. 'We all didn't throw the bottle or whatever it was, but it was one of us. So that's why we are responsible for that and all of us have to make sure something like this will never happen again. I don't think it was Man City-specific. I wish I could say that it never happens again, but unfortunately I can't. What I can say is that we do everything that [ensures] it will never happen again.'

Heightened fears of another pre-match attack failed to materialise as City's coach drove past home supporters gathered outside the King Harry pub on Anfield Road without incident. Offensive hand gestures and customary chants of 'oh Manchester is full of shit' were the sum of the ire that the visitors were subjected to amid clouds of billowing red smoke from flares being set off. Inside the stadium, speculation that Guardiola's declarations on the absences of Ederson, Rodri and David Silva had been a psychological ploy gained traction when all three players' shirts were laid out in the away dressing room in preparations for the game. Only Rodri featured in the top-of-the-table clash with the Spain international sitting at the heart of a three-man midfield bank.

Controversy still reared its head in the opening minutes of the clash as Bernardo Silva's attempted lay-off to Sergio Agüero was intercepted by Dejan Lovren and rebounded off Trent Alexander-Arnold's arm, leading the Argentine to appeal for a handball decision which was not given. From the breakaway, Andy Robertson sent Mané surging down City's right before his cross was cleared by Ilkay Gündoğan as far as Fabinho, who unleashed a 25-yard drive which flew past Bravo. Alexander-Arnold played a key role in what Klopp would later describe as a 'perfect football moment' when his cross-field ball to Robertson saw his fellow full-back float the ball into the far side where a bounce took it away from Fernandinho's sliding challenge and allowed Mohamed Salah to head across Bravo's goal into the corner.

Soon after half-time, Guardiola was left eating his recent words when Henderson beat Gündoğan before sending a cross from the byeline that found Mané at the far post for another header which was helped on by Bravo into The Kop's net. City's attempts to mount a fightback were hampered by controversy when Sterling's shot struck Alexander-Arnold's arm and left Guardiola apoplectic on the touchline at his side being denied another legitimate penalty claim. He held up two fingers to fourth official Mike Dean alongside anguished cries of 'twice!' before directing them into the autumnal sky. A belated consolation arrived in the 78th minute when Kevin De Bruyne recovered possession in Liverpool's six-yard box and laid the ball off to Angelino, whose cross was deflected into Silva's path for a sweeping first-time finish which reduced the deficit but not the gap to their hosts, which had expanded to nine points with the 3-1 victory.

Anfield had already held little fondness for Guardiola, having failed to win in five previous visits as a manager, but the nature of this latest outing heaped further misery on his personal statistics. The 25 points that City had accrued constituted his worst return as a coach from the opening 12 top-flight games while the 13 goals conceded set a new club record as their worst return since the 16 shipped in the 2009/10 season. Guardiola's frustrations told at the final whistle when he shook hands with referee Michael Oliver and his assistants while saying, 'Thank you so much. Thank you so much!' in a move which had echoes of his immediate response to the 2018 coach shellacking. However, the City manager denied post-match that there was any sarcasm in his words as his side fell further off the pace in the battle for domestic supremacy.

Guardiola refused to discuss any of the contentious decisions his side suffered and warned his players to do similar. 'I don't have regret; if I'm not happy I tell the players,' he said. 'But at the end I said "heads up guys", I tell them don't use social media to say your thoughts about what happened today in some departments, talk about football and how good it was for both sides. Maybe one day we'll have a chance to win.' City's deafening silence to the defeat still failed to prevent obituaries being pre-written, with Stuart Brennan admitting in the *Manchester Evening News* that the incisiveness of Liverpool's performance against the reigning champions 'felt like a sea change' despite two thirds of the season still remaining.

The following day, Klopp and Guardiola attended UEFA's annual Elite Club Coaches Forum in Nyon, where the Liverpool manager downplayed any suggestions of a fall-out between the pair. 'Of course we spoke,' he told assembled television camera crews. 'Why shouldn't we speak?' He then proceeded to add a degree of humour to proceedings by whispering, 'Pep Guardiola is coming!' and jokingly running out of sight before his counterpart arrived in shot, completely oblivious to the act. Jokes were in short supply when their respective players joined up with England on the same afternoon. Raheem Sterling and Joe Gomez had come to blows during the Anfield clash, with the City winger telling his opponent, 'Don't fuck with me, Joe. Don't fuck with me.' Gomez responded, shouting, 'Come on!' as he was dragged away by team-mates before the pair later embraced at the final whistle to seemingly draw a line under any of their in-game acrimony.

But that ill feeling permeated when both players reported for duty at St George's Park. Gomez was among the first players to arrive at the Three Lions' training base and greeted several of his international team-mates in the canteen area. When he attempted to shake hands with Sterling, the winger rejected his offer and asked, 'So you think you are the big man?' which was initially laughed off by Gomez. Several onlookers described how the 24-year-old then 'lost it' as he attempted to grab the Liverpool defender, who instinctively stepped back when the attempted confrontation became apparent. Several players tried to lead Sterling away from the scene, but England responded by initially sending him home in disgrace. Only the intervention of Jordan Henderson prevented his former team-mate's banishment becoming absolute with Gareth Southgate.

Henderson had been a late arrival to the England camp on account of his suspension for their game with Montenegro but was made aware of the fracas by several players who were present. The Liverpool captain subsequently acted as peacemaker between the pair while also imploring Southgate to reconsider the original punishment. Sterling later apologised to Gomez and his fellow squad members but was still stood down by Southgate for the Euro 2020 qualifying match, which would be the country's 1,000th international fixture. When the pair appeared at open training the following day, keen-eyed photographers captured a distinguishable scratch which ran from below Gomez's right eye and down to his beard. Despite the injury, both he and Sterling appeared in good spirits as they trained together. The one-time Reds player had also taken to Instagram to explain that they had 'figured things out and moved on' in hopes of marking an end to the surprising row.

Fall-out from the incident still dragged on, with Tottenham Hotspur and England defender Danny Rose suggesting that the ongoing animosity from Liverpool supporters towards Sterling may have been a contributing factor. 'It's probably the first time I have sat back and actually realised and took note of how much the Liverpool fans dislike him,' he told BBC Radio 5 Live. 'I take that for granted whenever I'm watching Raheem. I think he just gets on with it and maybe it had a part to play in whatever happened.'

When Gomez warmed up as a substitute during his country's cruising 7-0 win over Montenegro, loud boos echoed around Wembley and continued when he replaced Mason Mount in the 70th minute. Sterling and Southgate publicly rallied round the versatile centre-back, who was said to have been left distraught by the experience, which took place in the presence of his fiancée and infant son. Gomez later admitted that the incident and subsequent backlash he endured at the hands of England fans that night led him to become 'a bit more stand-offish'.

Klopp and Guardiola took a rare break from their own on-field duelling to appear at the FWA's Northern Managers Awards held in Manchester's Radisson Blu Edwardian Hotel, previously home to the Free Trade Hall that had hosted an early Sex Pistols concert and more prominently the site of the Peterloo Massacre. In his acceptance speech, the Liverpool manager revealed his thought process when watching Kompany's thunderbolt against Leicester at the end of the previous season. 'A second ago, I told Pep what I did when Kompany scored his screamer against Leicester. It was … I can't tell you,' he said. 'But the next day we play against Barcelona, so the day was full of training and preparing for that game. So I get home and my missus told me, "Come on we watch the game," and I was like, "oh, I'm not sure." But I watched it and I was on my sofa and both hands were in my left pocket and right pocket and if somebody would have measured my heart rate … really the whole season was completely fine. I thought, "Anyway they win" – as they did all the time. But in this game, second by second by second, I started hoping. And then when I saw Leicester getting tired – I was really angry with them. And then Kompany, like he didn't all season, scores from outside the box. The first goal like this from Vincent Kompany, right? A good moment.'

Guardiola's follow-up was equally well-received as he opened by admitting, 'What Jürgen doesn't know is what he felt about the Vincent Kompany goal, I felt every week when he is scoring in the last minutes every time. Every time I'm there [thinking], "this time, this time it's going to happen." But it never happens.' He continued to pay tribute to the challenge posed by his counterpart in the previous 12 months. 'We won a lot of leagues … but I think last season was the most, most difficult one for the contender, the quality they have. Always it's difficult, always I learn to play against Jürgen teams,' he said, before admitting, 'But I would like to win my trophy' while nodding towards Liverpool's Champions League trophy at stage right. 'I'm pretty sure he [Klopp] would like to win mine,' while pointing to City's Premier League title positioned on the opposite side. 'Maybe we can swap?'

Already finishing off on a solid joke, the Catalan proceeded to bring the house down by adding, 'Manchester City is a rich, rich club so we pay [for] that later! Because when you win a lot in the league you live 11 months of the year happy.'

City's fortunes in the top flight were anything but enjoyable as they lost further ground on Liverpool with a 2-2 draw with Newcastle United before a midweek trip to Burnley on 3 December saw them encounter far from ideal preparations due to an electrical issue at Turf Moor which plunged the away dressing room into darkness. A portable studio light was later provided by Amazon Prime, which was covering the game as part of its first live broadcast, while Guardiola's players performed a rendition of Oasis's 'Wonderwall' before rallying to a 4-1 win over their hosts that maintained an eight-point gap. The City manager reacted to the increasing talk of his players being discounted from the title race with typical sarcasm. 'The title is over. From what I read, nobody gives us a chance – it's done,' he said. 'I don't believe it, but it is not about whether I believe it, or I don't believe it. It is about the next game. Our team is stable and that's what we want. For the distance we have against Liverpool it would be crazy to think about the title, honestly.'

Former City midfielder turned media pundit Trevor Sinclair celebrated his old club temporarily closing the gulf by posting 'bin dippers we're coming for you' on Twitter. Liverpool fans reacted angrily to the slur against their city, which mocked people in poverty, on social media which drew a defence from the ex-footballer, a Manchester native, of, 'So sensitive. Calm down, you're still eight points ahead,' accompanied by a poo emoji. The following day, Sinclair apologised during his guest appearance on talkSport and vowed to donate his fee to The Whitechapel Centre, a leading homeless charity in Liverpool.

Hours later, the Reds trounced Everton 5-2 to spell the end of Marco Silva's time at Goodison Park. City suffered their own derby humiliation on the following weekend in a 2-1 home reversal to Manchester United that left Guardiola attempting to accentuate the positives of falling 14 points behind Liverpool, who had won at Bournemouth. 'We have to try to continue, there are many things to play for,' he said. 'It's difficult because the opponents are on an incredible run winning 15 games out of 16. It is not time to think about that. We have to think about what we have to do and think about the next game. Doesn't matter if six, eight or 14 points we have to continue. We are a fantastic team.'

As Christmas approached, only Liverpool's involvement in the FIFA Club World Cup allowed City to reduce the gap to 11 points with Leicester now occupying second place. The European champions returned from Qatar with a long-awaited global title to match after overcoming Flamengo, their nemesis in the 1981 tournament. Even in absentia, Guardiola could not escape questions about the Anfield club. 'When a team has 16 victories from 17, it's unrealistic to think we are going to chase them. It's unrealistic right now,' he said. 'We have to try to win our games, secure Champions League [qualification] for next season and then you never know, no? If they [Liverpool] drop a couple of games, and we win and win … I don't know. When one team lose one game in the last 53, 54, I'm not optimistic they are going to lose four or five in ten or eleven games because they are incredibly strong. So we must relax and play like this and we'll see in the end what happens. Hopefully Leicester can make a good performance against Liverpool but we've to think about our incredibly tough game against Wolves.'

Guardiola's complaints about a congested fixture schedule over the festive period struck a chord with Klopp, who described his opponents playing two games in a space of less than 48 hours as 'a crime'. The Liverpool manager also acknowledged that the fallen champions had helped bring the best out of his own team when looking ahead to their Boxing Day trip to Leicester. 'I think City moved the bar massively – massively. The kind of consistency that they showed in the last three years is incredible and difficult to do,' he said. 'They became champions two years ago and I think last year we helped a lot. They helped us with trying to catch up with them and whatever. But they did it in an incredible way to be honest and that's just changed [that] you're not allowed to lose games. That's how it is. It's difficult obviously but winning the Premier League should be difficult. It's such a strong league with all the teams you see now.'

Liverpool's credentials were further solidified by a 4-0 win at the King Power Stadium a day before City suffered another defeat, this time to Wolves, after which Guardiola reaffirmed that the current 13-point margin was too great to overcome. 'It's unrealistic to think about catching Liverpool,' he said. 'It has been a big gap for a long time. It is not realistic to think about the title race. I have been asked the question for a long time and it is the same answer.'

Off the pitch, Liverpool continued to snap at City's heels by becoming the seventh-richest club in world football according to Deloitte's Football Money League, with increased revenue streams placing them to within just £5.2m of their north-west rivals in the place above. As focus shifted back to competitive action and the FA Cup's fourth round, Guardiola continued to face questions about the possibility of his side's title rivals shattering the 100-point record they had set two seasons earlier. 'Yeah it can happen. Records are there to be broken,' he admitted. 'We broke it when someone said we couldn't and sooner or later it will be broken again. History speaks clearly about that. It is not easy to beat Liverpool, they have found a way to win games.'

The subject arose again following City's comprehensive 4-0 home win over Fulham. 'Liverpool obviously will be champions of the Premier League but they would be champions in Spain, champions in Italy, champions in Germany,' said Guardiola. 'They would be champions everywhere after 23 games, 22 victories and one draw. In the recent past, when Chelsea won the league, the next season they didn't qualify for the Champions League, Leicester the same and Chelsea again the same. When we won the league, we repeated [it in] the league. In Spain, with the points we have, we would be one or two points behind the leader; in Germany we would be there, one or two points behind the leader and in Italy as well. But Liverpool are just fantastic, phenomenal, overwhelming – so we have to accept it and learn from that.'

City's ailing title defence ceded further ground with a 2-0 defeat to Tottenham Hotspur, now led by Guardiola's eternal nemesis Jose Mourinho, which saw Liverpool move 22 points clear at the summit. The Catalan remained effusive in his praise for Klopp's side, describing them as 'unstoppable', but equally took issue with comments by Richard Scudamore, the Premier League's former chief executive, in the summer of 2018 that wished 'someone would get a little bit closer to City' following their title win by 18 points. 'Two seasons ago there was the owner of the Premier League who said that could not happen again, it's not good for the Premier League for City to win the title in that way with 100 points. Now it's Liverpool, you have to be concerned if you are the owner of the Premier League.'

Fresh evidence of Liverpool's growing dominance presented itself in the week following City's reversal in the capital as Klopp was named the Premier League's Manager of the Month for January. The German had won the personal accolade in five of the season's opening six months to move ahead of Guardiola's seven awards. An already difficult few days was made worse by news that UEFA had hit City with a two-season ban from the Champions League for alleged Financial Fair Play breaches between 2012 and 2016. The charge threatened to further intensify their rivalry with Liverpool as the Premier League confirmed that it was also looking into possible infractions of its own set of rules during that same period with a retrospective points deduction threatening to see the 2013/14 league title, that they won by just two points, awarded to Liverpool, that season's runners-up.

Steven Gerrard, whose costly slip against Chelsea late in the campaign saw momentum shift back in City's favour, admitted that he was 'really, really interested' in any potential outcome, adding, 'For obvious reasons.'

Klopp, however, was more sympathetic to the plight of Guardiola's side after Liverpool moved 25 points clear of their closest challengers with a 1-0 win over Norwich City. 'The only thing I can say, I'm a football coach so I can speak about football, and what Pep and Man City did since I'm in England is exceptional,' he said. 'About all the rest I have no idea. What happened, who did what and stuff like this … I really feel for them, to be honest, for Pep and the players, but that will not help.'

Liverpool equalled City's 18-game winning streak courtesy of a 3-2 victory over West Ham United but their bid to surpass Guardiola's class of 2017/18 fell short as they suffered a first league defeat in 42 matches with a 3-0 reversal at Watford. The following day, City's 2-0 defeat at the hands of Manchester United nudged Liverpool to within just six points of the title. As focus gravitated towards when, rather than if, Liverpool would be crowned champions for a first time since 1990, the prospect of City's involvement in those long-awaited celebrations grew ever stronger. Guardiola's side were due to entertain their Merseyside rivals on 5 April, by which point the runaway leaders could have clinched the six points required to be mathematically out of reach. The likelihood of the Blues' players forming a guard of honour for the team that had so emphatically replaced them at the Premier League's summit became a genuine possibility. No one, however, foresaw the world grinding to a literal halt following the outbreak of COVID-19.

Mikel Arteta's return to the Etihad Stadium just three months after he had left to become Arsenal manager was postponed after he tested positive for the coronavirus just a fortnight following his side's Europa League exit to Olympiacos, whose owner Evangelos Marinakis also confirmed he had contracted the virus. Before the cancelled reunion with his former assistant, Guardiola was asked about the prospect of games being played behind closed doors to contain the virus's spread. 'You have to ask whether it is worth playing football without the spectators,' he said. 'It doesn't make any sense to play professional football without the people, because they are the ones we do it for, but obviously we are going to follow the instructions we are given. I would prefer not to play games without people watching, but clearly health is the most important thing, not the competition. I do think playing games behind closed doors is going to happen here, but just one or two games, maybe. No longer than that.'

Klopp was similarly unsure about the impact of playing games without fans present, saying, 'Some things are more important than football, we realise that in this moment. I don't know enough about how much it would help with the football games. The problem with football games is if you are not at the stadium you are in closed rooms watching, maybe together. I'm not sure what is better in this case.'

The Liverpool manager's words arrived on the eve of a Champions League last-16 defeat to Atlético Madrid which became the final elite-level game played in front of a full crowd. More than 3,000 away supporters poured in from the Spanish capital, which had become the country's epicentre for the virus, in a move which was later widely condemned for causing a spike in COVID-19 cases in Liverpool. Analysts directly attributed 41 of the area's first 481 recorded deaths to the game itself due to the government allowing the tie to go ahead in full on the same day that the World Health Organisation had upgraded the virus to a pandemic. Further findings placed Merseyside among the country's worst-affected region for coronavirus-related fatalities with only London producing a higher death toll.

In light of Arteta's positive diagnosis and that of Chelsea midfielder Callum Hudson-Odoi, the Premier League called an immediate three-week halt to its upcoming schedule on 13 March, with a provisional return date of 3 April, the same weekend that City and Liverpool had originally been due to do battle at the Etihad. As the pandemic rapidly spread throughout the UK and the wider world, those plans were hit by numerous delays and revisions. In line with the new lockdown measures, players were instructed to remain at home for the foreseeable future with individualised fitness plans created during their imposed absence from training grounds.

Such was the indiscriminate nature of the virus that City and Liverpool were each profoundly impacted by it in a variety of ways during the weeks which followed. Construction on the Reds' new training facility in Kirkby, due to open in the summer of 2020, was immediately halted and left them facing up to an additional 12-month stay at their long-standing Melwood base, while the timeline for a planned rebuilding of the Anfield Road End was also extended a year, to the start of the 2023/24 season. Premier League rules over mid-season kit manufacturing changes meant the club's new deal with Nike also had to be pushed back from its original 1 June start date to the beginning of August due to New Balance being the designated supplier for 2019/20. The pandemic carried far-reaching ramifications, too, for City's appeal against their Champions League ban with a potential two-month wait between the case being heard and a final decision handed down by the Court of Arbitration for Sport.

More pressing, though, became the direct impact on those closest to both clubs. Benjamin Mendy was forced to self-isolate after it emerged on 12 March that a member of the City left-back's family had been hospitalised with symptoms of a respiratory illness. Tests on Mendy and his relatives later confirmed that neither had contracted COVID-19. But the Etihad Stadium was plunged into mourning on 6 April when it was announced that the virus had claimed the life of Dolors Sala Carrio, Pep Guardiola's 82-year-old mother. Just two days later, Kenny Dalglish tested positive for COVID-19 during a hospital visit to treat an infection which required treatment by intravenous antibiotics. The Liverpool legend, who had been asymptomatic of the virus, was later discharged and continued to self-isolate at home.

Football became secondary in the face of an unprecedented health crisis as the UK showed a belated appreciation for its underfunded National Health Service, with Klopp admitting he was moved to tears by a video of healthcare staff singing 'You'll Never Walk Alone' on a hospital ward and paid tribute to their tireless endeavour, saying, 'I couldn't admire them more and appreciate them more.' Guardiola personally helped the efforts in his native Catalonia by donating €1m to the Barcelona Medical College for use in purchasing protective equipment. City's manager later hailed the efforts in his current surroundings. 'There are many, many people in the NHS who put their own lives at risk to save ours,' he told the club's YouTube channel. 'It's incredible what they have done, and we have to follow them.'

Yet even in hiatus, the game again found itself being scapegoated by the government on 2 April, when health secretary Matt Hancock demonised footballers for not 'playing their part' by taking voluntary pay cuts. Barely 24 hours later, it was proven that they were playing a far more active role than his public deflection tactic suggested. Liverpool captain Jordan Henderson had already reached out to his counterparts across the Premier League to create Players Together, a support fund which would help frontline NHS workers with their efforts in tackling the pandemic. Wage contributions led to an initial donation of over £4m being pledged to the cause. A combined 25 players from Liverpool and City joined their top-flight peers in openly backing the initiative.

As the coronavirus continued to rage through the country, both clubs went beyond the call of duty. Anfield officials pledged £40,000 to Fans Supporting Foodbanks, a food collection initiative set up by Spirit of Shankly and Everton supporters' group The Blue Union, to supplement the loss of donations to the charitable cause in the club's final four games of the Premier League season. Ian Byrne, the Walton MP and co-founder of the initiative, also revealed that Henderson had informed him Liverpool's players had 'committed to covering all of the shortfalls' that the charity would incur. City, meanwhile, offered full use of their Etihad Campus to the NHS which led to an initial three-month partnership that helped with the training of over 350 nursing staff as well as providing a much-needed safe space for essential workers between 7.30am and 10pm daily. The club extended its duty of care to the wider community by making a joint £100,000 donation with Manchester United to The Trussell Trust, which oversees the UK's national network of foodbanks.

Liverpool's players resumed training at Melwood on 7 May, initially in small groups that observed social distancing protocols over a one-hour period. City's squad commenced their preparations on 22 May, four days after undergoing new tests for COVID-19. Their rescheduled meeting with Arsenal became the designated fanfare fixture for the league's return on 17 June, with Liverpool's Merseyside derby clash against Everton taking place four days later on 21 June.

With the resumption of games drawing ever nearer, Ilkay Gündoğan reflected on how City's previous fixtures had led to their challenge falling away. 'We were left behind in the title race this season in the Premier League. We couldn't show an effect like the last two seasons [when] we are champions,' he told Turkish newspaper *Fanatik*. 'Whether we play good football or play good matches, there are points we have simply lost. Liverpool came to this level without losing many points, so we lost a lot of points, so the difference increased.'

But plans to resume games under the banner of 'Project Restart' were conflated by fears by the authorities that Liverpool fans would descend on stadiums to celebrate their first league crown since 1990 – including from Joe Anderson, their own city's elected mayor. Mark Roberts, the UK's national football police chief, drew up a list of six matches earmarked for potential relocation to neutral venues that included City's clash with Klopp's side on 2 July. The controversial plans threatened to see the runaway Premier League leaders potentially completing the season without playing any of their remaining four home games at Anfield. Merseyside Police allayed those concerns by reaffirming they had 'no problem' with the Reds and Everton completing their remaining fixtures in their traditional setting. Manchester City Council's safety advisory group also raised no objections to the Etihad meeting going ahead as planned. A goalless draw at Goodison Park and a 4-0 romp over Crystal Palace set Liverpool up for a potential title clincher against City, who recorded back-to-back victories against Arsenal and Burnley. Only the reigning champions' failure to overcome Chelsea on 25 June would bring forward their long-awaited coronation.

Guardiola hinted at resting several of his key players for the Stamford Bridge encounter in preparation for their FA Cup quarter-final with Newcastle United at the weekend, which drew a disbelieving response from Klopp. 'He should play poker, probably', said the German after seeing his team put Palace to the sword. The Liverpool manager was also keeping his cards close to his chest by refusing to disclose whether he would be keeping a keen eye on events in west London. 'I don't even know if I'll watch it,' he told Sky Sports. 'The last one I watched until 3-0 and then I thought "come on, that's now really a waste of time!".'

Mere hours before City locked horns with Chelsea, a plan was formulated for Klopp and his squad to hole up at Formby Hall. Since football's return, the four-star golf resort situated 14 miles north of Anfield served as the club's pre-match base and carried an added symbolism as the venue where Klopp previously ordered Liverpool's players to cut loose for their Christmas party on the same day as a humiliating 3-0 loss at Watford in December 2015.

In the capital, City trailed at half-time to a strike from Christian Pulisic, previously drafted into Borussia Dortmund's senior ranks by Klopp during his final season with the Bundesliga club. Kevin De Bruyne redressed the balance within ten minutes of the restart through an exquisite free kick but Fernandinho's handled goal-line clearance from Tammy Abraham killed off any hopes of the visitors salvaging victory. The fatalism which had routinely conspired against Liverpool in their numerous attempts to end a 30-year hoodoo was finally reversed as the Brazilian departed with a red card as compatriot Willian converted from the penalty spot. Assembled on a terrace overlooking Formby Hall's golf course, Klopp's players watched events unfolding at the other end of the country on a projector screen with contrasting emotions. Joe Gomez could not bring himself to view the game's remaining seconds in full while Virgil van Dijk and Alex Oxlade-Chamberlain prepared to record the historic moment on their mobile phones. Klopp spoke with his family in a FaceTime call which continued until Stuart Atwell signalled the end to Liverpool's three decades of hurt.

Guardiola graciously offered 'big congratulations' to City's successors at the summit when reflecting on the manner of his side's defeat at Stamford Bridge and consequently the end of their 803-day reign as champions of England. 'They have played an incredible season,' he said. 'We are not consistent like the previous seasons – I think we arrive after four trophies in one season thinking: "We have time, we have time", but Liverpool won the Champions League and it gave them an incredible confidence. The fact that they had gone 30 years without winning the Premier League gave them incredible focus and they played every game like it was the last game. In the beginning we didn't play in that way and when they took that advantage of course the pressure on us was bigger.'

Bedlam ensued across Merseyside and continued long into the night. Van Dijk's reaction interview with BT Sport was gatecrashed by a squad rendition of 'Campeones!' – the chant which had rung in their ears following their previous season's defeat at the Etihad. Elsewhere inside Formby Hall, Klopp broke down in tears as he spoke to Sky Sports in the presence of club legends Kenny Dalglish, Graeme Souness and Phil Thompson. Overwhelmed by the emotion of the occasion, he admitted: 'This is a big moment, I have no real words... I never thought I would feel like this!' Players and coaching staff drank and danced continuously in a function room basked in red lighting with even Klopp twisting and shuffling to Nightcrawlers' 1995 club classic 'Push The Feeling On'. Within half an hour of the final whistle, an estimated 2,000 supporters had flouted social distancing regulations and descended on the streets outside Anfield to herald the once-in-a-generation moment. Thousands more continued the festivities at the Pier Head just 24 hours later amid ugly scenes. Fireworks were deliberately launched in the direction of the Royal Liver Building, leading to a small fire on the balcony of the Grade I listed building, and on-duty police officers faced a hail of missiles as they attempted to prevent the widespread disorder on the city's waterfront, which Liverpool condemned as 'wholly unacceptable'.

In the days that followed, Guardiola confirmed City's players would form a guard of honour for the new champions. 'Of course we are going to do it,' he said. 'Always we receive Liverpool when they come to our house in an incredible way. They cannot complain and, of course, we are going to do it because they deserve it.' Immediately ahead of the latest meeting between the Premier League's top two sides, Klopp admitted that the gesture was 'nice' but added: 'I don't need it, to be honest. We go there to play, and win, a football game. We don't celebrate a thing that happened a week before.' He also shot down the notion that

Liverpool would be protecting their new accolade in the months ahead. 'We will not defend the title next season,' he vowed. 'We will attack it.' Just 15 points from their final seven games would see Liverpool set a new league record by surpassing the 100-point haul by City's class of 2017/18 and led to claims of a potential shift in superiority. 'I don't think we have to make a statement,' insisted Klopp. 'What will change if we beat City tomorrow night, and what will change if City beat us? People will say a few things, but that's really not important.'

The passing of the baton clearly mattered to at least one home supporter outside the Etihad who temporarily halted Liverpool's arrival by standing in the middle of the road and administering two-fingered gestures with both hands before being ushered away by onlookers. When the moment of truth finally arrived in the stadium's cavernous surroundings, City's players stood on ceremony and applauded Jordan Henderson as he led the visitors out. A muted opening stage was given a literal rocket as a series of fireworks were set off near the ground to deafening sound. On the pitch, Mohamed Salah produced Liverpool's clearest opening when his low effort cannoned back off the post. Minutes later, Raheem Sterling and Joe Gomez resumed their feuding from the Anfield meeting as the defender pulled down his England teammate in the penalty area. Kevin De Bruyne broke the deadlock by wrongfooting Alisson by tucking his spot kick into the bottom left-hand corner. City proceeded to carve open Liverpool's defence at will as Sterling scored in his own right when Phil Foden teed him up to record a first league goal against his former employers after 11 hours and 17 minutes. Shortly before half-time, Foden added a third himself from a well-worked move by picking up a threaded pass from De Bruyne and firing the ball past Alisson. Fears of a hangover from Liverpool's title triumph had become a swift and embarrassing reality.

Klopp's response at the interval was to withdraw Gomez in favour of Alex Oxlade-Chamberlain, with Fabinho dropping into the vacant centre-back role. Further humiliation was spared by the Brazilian's defensive partner Virgil van Dijk, whose goal-line clearance denied Foden a chance to double his personal tally. City further extended their superiority over the champions with a moment of tragicomedy as Oxlade-Chamberlain's attempt to cut out a wayward effort by Sterling turned the ball into his own net. Riyad Mahrez appeared to have added a fifth in the final minute of stoppage time when he squeezed a shot past Alisson at his near right-hand post, only for VAR to overrule it for an accidental handball by Foden in the build-up. Liverpool's first outing as Premier League holders ended in both an abject defeat and historical ignominy as a fifth consecutive away outing in all competitions finished scoreless for a first time since April 1992. Exactly seven days since he had gushed on live television, Klopp was in combative mood when fielding questions about his side's second-heaviest defeat – once again at the Etihad – post-match, although he still acknowledged the quality of City's performance. Guardiola returned the compliment by hailing his vanquished opponents as 'the best team I have ever faced in my life' and refuted suggestions that the Anfield club's post-title excesses had a key bearing on the outcome. 'I think they drank a lot of beers in the last week,' he said. 'But they arrived here with no beers in their blood to play and compete against us and that's why I give a lot of credit for what they have done.'

As the world continued to adjust to the 'new normal', Manchester City and Liverpool's age-old rivalry had successfully passed the first of many tests in this truly uncharted territory.

Acknowledgements

UNDER NORMAL circumstances, producing any book tends to be something of an arduous process. But finishing one in the grip of a global pandemic is an entirely different prospect.

Even my best-laid plans for *Fine Margins* went out the window once the full extent of COVID-19 became evident to both football and the wider world, midway through March 2020. Fortunately, there has been no shortage of people who have been on hand to help deliver this book despite such trying times.

Thanks firstly and foremost must go to everyone at Pitch Publishing, especially Paul and Jane Camillin, for putting their total faith in this project from the very beginning and providing feedback at regular intervals. Duncan Olner also deserves huge credit for producing such a striking front cover design that perfectly encapsulates the rivalry between the clubs.

I am incredibly grateful for the support from within the football media industry, not least the combined encyclopaedic knowledge of Gary James, John Keith, Gavin Buckland and Carl Clemente, which was an invaluable resource when piecing together the rich tapestry of Liverpool and Manchester City's historic rivalry. Several of my press box colleagues were equally instrumental in helping set up some of the interviews, including Richard Tanner, Simon Hart, Neil Jones, Paul Joyce, Simon Hughes, Tim Rich and Jeff Pickett. Additional thanks go to Fred Eyre, Tom Rennie from Sirius XM and Ashley Houghton at Wigan Athletic. Fellow journalists with first-hand experience as published authors have made immeasurable contributions to this one too; Colin Millar's personal experience was integral throughout while Sanj Shetty planted the original seeds for writing this book in late 2019.

Ultimately, though, this rivalry would be nothing without the numerous players and coaches who contributed to it over the previous half-century and I am eternally indebted to some of those that generously gave up both their time and memories to offer first-hand accounts, in alphabetical order: Michael Ball, Ian Bishop, Ian Callaghan, Sylvain Distin, Gary Gillespie, Emile Heskey, Brian Horton, Alan Kennedy, Chris Kirkland, Rodney Marsh, Andy Morrison, the late Glyn Pardoe, Paul Power, Joe Royle, Mike Sheron, Kit Symons, Stephen Warnock, Sander Westerveld and Jim Whitley.

Last but by no means least, the biggest thanks must go to Manchester City and Liverpool themselves for creating one of the most fascinating rivalries that elite-level football has known. It has been a genuine privilege covering both clubs as a journalist over the previous decade, when so much has happened between them both on and off the pitch, and I cannot wait to see what their years ahead together will have in store.

Bibliography

Books

Bellamy, C., *GoodFella* (Sport Media, 2012)

Dohren, D., *Ghost on the Wall: The Authorised Biography of Roy Evans* (Mainstream Digital, 2011)

Fagan, A. & Platt, M., *Joe Fagan: Reluctant Champion – The Authorised Biography* (Aurum Press, 2011)

Herbert, I., *Quiet Genius: Bob Paisley, British Football's Greatest Manager* (Bloomsbury Sport, 2018)

Hooton, P., *The Boot Room Boys: The Unseen Story of Anfield's Conquering Heroes* (Virgin Books, 2018)

Honigstein, R., *Bring the Noise: The Jürgen Klopp Story* (PublicAffairs, 2018)

Horton, S., *Ending the Seven-Year Itch: The Story of Liverpool's 1972-73 First Division Championship and UEFA Cup Triumph* (Vertical Editions, 2012)

Hughes, S. & Twentyman, J., *Secret Diary of a Liverpool Scout* (Sport Media, 2009)

James, G., *Football with a Smile: The Authorised Biography of Joe Mercer* (Polar, 1994)

James, G., *Manchester: The City Years* (James Ward, 2012)

Kompany, V. & Cheeseman, I., *Treble Triumph: My Inside Story of Manchester City's Greatest-ever Season* (Simon & Schuster, 2019)

Lake, P., *I'm Not Really Here: A Life in Two Halves* (Arrow, 2012)

Moran, P. & Baldursson, A., *Mr Liverpool: Ronnie Moran – The Official Life Story* (Sport Media, 2017)

Morrison, A., *The Good, the Mad and the Ugly: The Andy Morrison Story* (Fort Publishing, 2011)

Reade, B., *An Epic Swindle: 44 Months with a Pair of Cowboys* (Quercus, 2011)

Rich, T., *Caught Beneath the Landslide: Manchester City in the 1990s* (deCoubertin, 2018)

Royle, J., *Joe Royle: The Autobiography* (BBC Books, 2005)

Shankly, B. & Roberts, J., *Shankly: My Story* (Sport Media, 2009)

Tossell, D., *Big Mal: The High Life and Hard Times of Malcolm Allison* (Mainstream, 2009)

White, D. & Lake, J., *Shades of Blue: The Hidden Torment of a Football Star* (Michael O'Mara, 2017)

Wilson, S., *A View From The Terraces – Part 1* (lulu.com, 2015)

Magazines and Periodicals
Liverpool Echo
Manchester Evening News
FourFourTwo
The Blizzard
Daily Telegraph
Daily Mirror
The Times
The Independent
The Guardian

Online resources
British Newspaper Archive
lfchistory.net
bluemoon-mcfc.co.uk
clickliverpool.com
bbc.co.uk/football
citytillidie.com
playupliverpool.com

Filmography
All or Nothing: Manchester City (Amazon Prime, 2018)
Being: Liverpool (Fox Soccer, 2012)
City! A Club in Crisis (Granada, 1981)
Granada Soccer Night (ITV, 1995)
Kick Off (Granada, 1989)
Match of the 70s (BBC, 1995)